RECESSION

THE REAL REASONS
ECONOMIES SHRINK
AND WHAT
TO DO ABOUT IT

RECE$SION

TYLER GOODSPEED

BASIC
VENTURE

New York

Basic Venture

Hachette Book Group

1290 Avenue of the Americas, New York, NY 10104

www.basicbooks.com

Printed in the United States of America

First Edition: March 2026

Published by Basic Venture, an imprint of Hachette Book Group, Inc. The Basic Venture name and logo is a registered trademark of the Hachette Book Group.

The Hachette Speakers Bureau provides a wide range of authors for speaking events. To find out more, go to www.hachettespeakersbureau.com or email HachetteSpeakers@hbgusa.com.

Basic Venture books may be purchased in bulk for business, educational, or promotional use. For more information, please contact your local bookseller or the Hachette Book Group Special Markets Department at special.markets@hbgusa.com.

The publisher is not responsible for websites (or their content) that are not owned by the publisher.

Print book interior design by Amy Quinn.

Library of Congress Control Number: 2025944840

ISBNs: 9781541704947 (hardcover), 9781541704961 (ebook)

LSC-C

10 9 8 7 6 5 4 3 2 1

For Mom and Dad
For teaching me that it is not about whether you
fall but whether you bounce back.

CONTENTS

INTRODUCTION

THE ANNA KARENINA PRINCIPLE

> All happy families are alike; each unhappy
> family is unhappy in its own way.
>
> —LEO TOLSTOY, 1877

Tuesday, August 25, 1857, was a temperate late-summer day in New York City—warm, with a gentle westerly breeze and mostly clear skies.[1] Though approaching the peak of the Atlantic hurricane season, it had also been a dry and sunny month.[2] Yet despite the pleasant, seventy-four-degree weather, Charles Stetson, president of the Cincinnati-based Ohio Life and Trust Company, was solemn.

Over the weekend, Stetson had been hastily summoned to New York by a series of urgent telegrams from the bank's cashier, Edwin Ludlow. From the plush location of the luxurious Hotel Astor in Longacre (now Times) Square, Ludlow informed Stetson that Ohio Life was on the brink of running out of money. Previously unaware of the severity of the New York office's liquidity constraints, Stetson's biggest fear as he set off from Cincinnati had been that Ludlow was stricken by severe illness. It was only at the hotel that he first learned of the firm's "serious difficulty."[3]

Ohio Life was something of an oddity. Rather as Voltaire remarked that the Holy Roman Empire was neither holy nor Roman nor an empire, the company never sold an insurance policy, let alone a life one, and conducted much of its business out of New York, not Ohio.[4] The Cincinnati home office mostly invested in real estate mortgages and railroad securities, which they funded in part by borrowing from their New York agency, which in turn borrowed in wholesale New York

1

City money markets. In essence, the New York office was Ohio Life's portal into New York's deep capital markets.

According to one contemporary banker, the company "had enjoyed the highest credit," its home business "managed in the most careful manner" and "distinguished for its conservatism." Another banker, the abolitionist Quaker James Sloan Gibbons, noted that "the institution had stood high in the public esteem."[5]

Yet unbeknownst to both, with three-fifths of its assets tied up in longer-term, illiquid loans funded overwhelmingly by short-term debt that lenders could redeem on demand and without notice, by 1857, Ohio Life faced a classic maturity mismatch problem.[6] When short-term *call money* lenders called in their loans, Ohio Life would have to liquidate longer-term mortgages and railroad securities to honor their liabilities. As money markets tightened and investor appetite for railroad bonds declined over the summer of 1857, the New York office thus struggled to continue financing the mounting liquidity requirements of the home office.

In a desperate bid to bolster their permanent capital base, Ludlow attempted to prop up Ohio Life's share price using misappropriated funds.[7] But when one of Ohio Life's trustees suddenly sold all his shares in the spring of 1857—either as retribution for the bank enforcing a default claim against his son-in-law or as an act of self-preservation after allegedly advising Ludlow to engage in the stock-buying scheme in the first place—the bank's continued operation rapidly became untenable.[8]

With railroad bond prices continuing to decline and short-term creditors increasingly calling in their loans, on Friday, August 21, Ludlow fired off three telegraphs—two to Stetson and one to the bank's highly respected doctor-turned-assistant cashier, Samuel Perkins Bishop, insisting they come at once to New York.[9] Stetson duly boarded an early Saturday-morning train from Cincinnati.

Despite a desperate but ultimately unsuccessful scramble to secure additional funding, shortly after noon on Monday, Stetson reluctantly concluded Ohio Life would have to suspend payment on its liabilities. Depositors would henceforth be unable to withdraw their deposits, while short-term money lenders attempting to call in their loans would be denied repayment. At one o'clock, he telegraphed a shocked Bishop that suspension had already taken place in New York, and that he saw "no other course than for you to close your doors." After a frantic attempt to obtain loans from Ohioan banks in Cincinnati and Covington, the following morning, the Cincinnati office reluctantly suspended payment.[10]

As one contemporary banker—future US treasury secretary under Presidents Lincoln, Johnson, and Arthur, Hugh McCulloch—put it, the failure of Ohio Life "was a bolt from a cloudless sky."[11] Another described it as a "cannon shot."[12] While press reports quickly revealed that the failure of Ohio Life was the consequence of isolated negligence and even fraud, the failure triggered justifiable alarm within the banking community.[13]

As Gibbons put it, if the entire capital of $2 million of a respected bank like Ohio Life "could be dissipated . . . without discovery," then "why might not similar transactions be concealed in other institutions?" To put it bluntly, Gibbons wondered how "with all the usual hypothecation of securities, and transfers, and extensive bank loans, of which the records of the Company must have given *some* evidence," the dissipation of so many millions did not excite "suspicion in the minds of the trustees," many of whom served as trustees of other institutions of similar esteem to Ohio Life.[14] If it could happen at as respected a house as Ohio Life, could it not happen at other financial institutions?

Within a week of Ohio Life's suspension, other banks thus began to prudentially and proactively curtail lending. Indeed, even as bank depositors—who nervously withdrew deposits in the two weeks following Ohio Life's failure—began to redeposit funds in the first two weeks of September, the banks themselves continued to contract lending.[15]

Then, tragedy struck. The SS *Central America*, a steamship bound for New York City from California laden with the 2024 equivalent of $1 billion in gold from the California gold rush, was caught in a rising storm off the Carolinas that shortly developed into a hurricane.[16] Despite valiant efforts by passengers and crew to save the fated vessel, on the evening of September 12, waves consumed the waterlogged ship, her gold, and the lives of the 425 passengers and crew remaining on board.

News of the tragedy reached New York City on September 18.[17] Though the gold, if not the ship, was fully insured and the mostly London-based underwriters acted with unprecedented haste to provide assurances that they would pay out without delay upon receipt of the bills of lading, the loss of the *Central America* intensified anxiety in the city.[18] Alarmed by the loss of gold, New York banks doubled down on their efforts to curtail lending and bolster their gold reserves.[19]

Under state law, every New York banknote had to be backed by state government bonds. To maintain their gold reserves, when a noteholder presented a note for redemption in gold, the bank would thus have to return the redeemed note to the state comptroller, who then sold the bond backing the note, with the issuing bank receiving gold for the proceeds of the sale.[20] This depressed bond prices precisely as increasingly nervous noteholders redeemed their banknotes for gold.

Moreover, as banks attempted to reduce their risk exposure by curtailing credit to securities brokers, the brokers increasingly had to liquidate their investments, further depressing bond prices.[21]

The situation was even worse for New York City banks specifically.[22] New York banking regulations required every bank located outside of New York City to assign a bank within the city as their agent, with the agent obliged to redeem the peripheral bank's notes for gold. By regulation, the city banks could not then return those notes to the peripheral banks without notice. While the peripheral banks also had to redeem the notes of their city agent, they could do so with drafts on other city banks, which meant little relief of the drainage of gold from New York City banks.[23]

Underlying this scramble for gold was the thorny issue that bank charters in many states, most notably New York and Pennsylvania, explicitly prohibited banks from suspending redemption of their notes, the penalty for which could include liquidation and forfeiture of their banking charter.[24] And simply refusing to redeem could constitute de facto insolvency.[25]

Indeed, in a letter to the British banking behemoth Baring Brothers, one prominent Philadelphia businessman, Charles Henry Fisher, even enclosed copies of the 1850 Pennsylvania law and 1846 New York constitution with a letter to his London headquarters. Fisher could not help but to observe that while it might have been rational for the banking system as a whole to expand credit under the circumstances, for the individual bank, it seemed entirely rational to contract credit. As bank loans ultimately had to be financed by bank liabilities, no bank wanted to be first to test the laws on the books by issuing notes that they could not ultimately redeem.[26] Moreover, as banks restricted lending, merchants and businesses increasingly had to make withdrawals to fund their own operations, exacerbating pressure on the banks.[27] By October, loans effectively could not be had at any rate.[28]

Though market participants looked forward to gold shipments from England and California shortly relieving pressures in credit markets, by October 16, it was clear those shipments were indefinitely delayed. In desperation, on October 13, New York City banks resolved to send a committee to Albany to ask the governor for an emergency legislative session.[29] The governor demurred, and in any event, there was nothing the legislature could do; the state constitution explicitly forbade the legislature from passing any law whatsoever that would sanction the suspension of payments.[30]

Yet as the demand for deposits by New York merchants reached stampede levels, all but one, the Chemical Bank, were forced to suspend payments. When the

Bank of New York refused to redeem two one-hundred-dollar notes, the noteholder promptly applied to a judge of the state supreme court for an injunction. But faced with a spiraling situation, within a week, the court cut the Gordian knot, ruling that a bank's suspension of payments during a period of general suspension was not proof of insolvency.[31]

Nonetheless, with businesses previously reliant on credit to finance operating expenses and capital outlays now unable to access it, by early October, there were reports of large spikes in unemployment. "Hundreds of mechanics, 'shop girls,' sewing women and day laborers" abruptly found themselves without work and unable to find it. In New York City alone, hundreds of men previously employed making improvements to Central Park were discharged on October 7.[32] Two days later, more than two thousand young women in the scarf- and clock-making trades were reported to be out of work, with nearly every establishment "of numerical importance" having reduced head counts by a third to a half, and some by more.[33] For many piece-rate workers, the issue was not so much the threat of outright layoff but rather that there were simply no new jobs upon completion of existing contracts.[34]

In search of an explanation for their present adversity, contemporaries were quick to blame their own extravagance. As one *New York Times* writer asked on the eve of the October suspension, "Have we been living too fast?"—concluding that "a good many of us must plead guilty to the charge."[35] Another lamented the origins of the current "revulsion" in a "lack of integrity on the part of the managers of certain great money corporations on both sides of the Atlantic," while also noting opinions on "the extravagance of the women, the gambling propensities of the men . . . and too many Railroads."[36]

With credit scarce and unemployment surging, by the autumn of 1857, the US economy was in recession, though by recessionary standards, the 1857–58 recession was a relatively mild affair. While bank lending fell 15 percent and the stock market plunged by nearly a third, economic output contracted by just over 2 percent per person and wages by 1 percent. Within a year, the US economy was rebounding at a healthy annual pace of just over 3 percent, and within two years, 5 percent.

In the decades since, historians have variously attributed the 1857 recession to the collapse of a railroad "mania," a western land "boom" gone bust, inflation following the California gold rush, plummeting European demand for American grains following the Crimean War, tariff reductions, and even the March 1857 *Dred Scott* decision, which allegedly depressed westward migration and land values by creating ambiguity as to the status of new territories as slave or free states.[37] Not to mention a grasshopper plage of providential proportions that rav-aged farms across twelve thousand square miles of Western and Midwestern grain states, consuming "every green thing cultivated by man."[38]

Yet more than any single factor, it was the chance confluence of multiple shocks to western land values and railroad securities, the failure of Ohio Life, the demise of the *Central America*, and a legally constrained New York banking system that generated the unfortunate economic calamity of October 1857. As we will observe frequently throughout this book, the economic crisis that erupted in the autumn of 1857 followed a rather random, even improbable, interaction of overlapping and interacting developments.

Financial journalists commonly refer to the rule of thumb that a recession is two consecutive quarters of negative economic growth. Yet such simple rules are inadequate for the task of identifying, let alone explaining, episodes of economic contraction, not least since they are of no use whatsoever for earlier years, such as 1857, for which the requisite GDP data is unavailable at quarterly frequency.

A more striking feature of recessions like the 1.5-year 1857–58 recession is not simply their duration, but rather the abrupt violence with which they typically interrupt periods of positive economic growth.[39] The eminent British economist

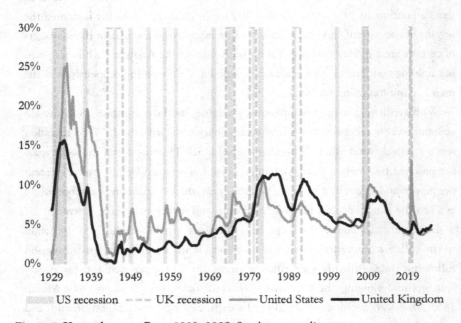

Figure 1: Unemployment Rate, 1929–2025. See data appendix.

John Maynard Keynes observed that "the substitution of a downward for an upward tendency often takes place suddenly and violently, whereas there is, as a rule, no such sharp turning-point when an upward is substituted for a downward tendency."[40] A *regime shift*, in modern economic parlance.

To Keynes's point, armed only with a plot of the unemployment rate (Figure 1), one could with highly respectable success identify historical economic recessions simply by noting the irregularly occurring moments of sudden, rapid increases in unemployment. These moments are then visibly succeeded by periods of more gradual declines.[41] Up like a rocket, down like a feather. Thus, rather as the late Supreme Court justice Potter Stewart described the task of defining pornography, while it may be impossible to ever satisfactorily define *recession*, one knows it when one sees it. Economic expansions do not "slip" or "tip" or "dip" into recession; as former Federal Reserve chairman Ben Bernanke once quipped, "They get murdered."[42]

As the unofficial-official arbiter of US recession dates, the wholly private National Bureau of Economic Research (NBER) defines a recession as "a significant decline in economic activity that is spread across the economy and lasts more than a few months."[43] The NBER's recession dating committee thus flexibly considers a combination of depth, diffusion, and duration, such that an economic decline of considerable depth and breadth across multiple sectors of the economy could constitute a recession even if, as was the case with the two-month-long 2020 pandemic recession, the duration of that contraction was brief. Throughout this book, I employ the qualitative NBER definition of a recession. I thereby employ or extend existing recession chronologies on both sides of the Atlantic back to 1854 on a quarterly basis and back to 1700 at annual frequency.[44]

Though the unemployment fluctuations in Figure 1 appear irregular and random, such apparent irregularity has not stopped economists and financial observers from purporting a regular, cyclical pattern to economic fluctuations. When the 1857 US recession spread to the United Kingdom, the eminent British banker and former member of Parliament Samuel Jones-Loyd, Lord Overstone, reissued a pamphlet he had published exactly twenty years prior when recession previously gripped both sides of the Atlantic. "We find," Lord Overstone wrote, that the state of trade is "subject to various conditions which are periodically returning: it revolves apparently in an established cycle" of "excitement" and excess followed by "convulsion" and "stagnation."[45] Overstone could certainly be forgiven for his confidence—this was the third major recessionary "convulsion" in thirty years, each one a decade apart: 1837, 1847, and 1857.

Echoing Overstone almost 150 years later in his acclaimed 1978 tome, *Manias, Panics, and Crashes*, MIT economist Charles Kindleberger similarly described the apparent "biologic regularity in the pattern" of observed cycles of mania, panic, and crash.[46] Even 200 years before Overstone's 1837 publication, his countryman, the eminent physician and empiricist Sir William Petty, had observed that a cycle of "Dearths and Plenties" seemed to revolve over a period of seven or so years.[47] More recently, when recessionary fears gripped Wall Street in the summer of 2019, David Rubenstein, billionaire cofounder and co–executive chairman of the Carlyle Group—one of the largest private equity firms in the world—noted on *CBS This Morning* that "normally, since World War II, we've had recessions every seven years on average. We haven't had one now for ten years. So we're due for a recession."[48]

But are economic contractions the inevitable, regular result of systematic or otherwise cumulative errors in the preceding economic expansion? Were Overstone's "cycle of trade," Petty's phases of "Dearths and Plenties," and Kindleberger's "biologic regularity" of manias, panics, and crashes genuine patterns of economic fluctuations?

Despite the august provenance of the view that recessions are regularly recurring, cyclical "busts" invariably following misbegotten and unsustainable "booms," it is also, I contend, wrong. Though we tend to think of economic recession as the result of preceding economic expansion, of inevitable retrenchment and cleansing following periods of misguided excess, in this book, we will find that the depth, duration, and diffusion of recessions bear no resemblance whatsoever to the height, age, and constitution of the expansionary periods that precede them.

Nor do they perform some cleansing, rejuvenating function, the economic equivalent of the sound forest-management practice of conducting the occasional controlled burn. Recessions are not periods of painful but necessary reallocation and reorganization. Several years out from a recession, economies typically look remarkably like how they would have looked had they continued uninterrupted along long-run trends from which recessions constitute temporary yet costly deviations. "Gales of creative destruction," as the eminent Harvard economist Joseph Schumpeter described them, recessions are not.

In his classic 1877 novel, *Anna Karenina*, Russian author Leo Tolstoy opened with the observation that "all happy families are alike; each unhappy family is unhappy in its own way." Similarly, while ongoing economic expansions are broadly similar—gradual yet inexorable recovery from an earlier contraction leading to positive economic growth over the long term—every recession represents an economic expansion that failed in its own way.

Fundamentally, recessions are, and have always been, about shocks—costly interruptions of positive economic growth. One can discern as much in Figure 1; the sudden spikes in the unemployment rate are irregular and intermittent, and surge from variable initial levels that reflect gradual recovery from prior spikes rather than unsustainable, low-unemployment "booms."

The idiosyncratic nature of recessions, however, rebels against evolved human logic. We are pattern-seeking mammals; patterns are how we relate observed stimuli to subsequent negative experiences—the ingestion of colorful mushrooms followed by illness, excess exposure to sunlight followed by sunburn. So too with the negative experience, even trauma, of economic recession do we thus seek to relate that trauma causally to some precipitate action or actions that we might endeavor to correct in the future lest we incur the same trauma again. Even economists who know and have written of the irregular, intermittent, and episodic nature of recessions therefore nonetheless find themselves slipping into the language of booms and busts.[49]

Moreover, the medium through which we retain, reexamine, and recapitulate these patterns is that of story. There is a reason that parables and fables remain among the most enduring and recognized of narratives. From the parables of Jesus to Aesop's fables, they convey moral lessons by which we might live better and freer from harm, and from guilt. Parables can provide us with a certain sense of comfort, even control over bad events; if we can identify past actions that appeared to precede trauma, and avoid repetition of those trauma-inducing actions, then it grants us at least some degree of agency over the future. As gloomy as it may be to be told that manias, panics, and crashes are a loop we are doomed to repeat, not only does the parable render our economic future legible and predictable, it also gives us hope for error correction. If fluctuations in economic activity are self-generating, if the bust is a direct consequence of the prior boom, then perhaps there is error in the latter that we might endeavor to correct to prevent or at least mitigate the former.

Even more profoundly, narratives of boom and bust encode these apparently moral lessons with the five essential elements of a successful, resonant story. They have characters—antagonists and villains like Edwin Ludlow, and protagonists and heroes, with former Federal Reserve and Treasury Department officials Ben Bernanke, Tim Geithner, and Hank Paulson even likening themselves to firefighters for their role during the financial crisis of 2008–09.[50] Stories of boom and bust have setting—often Wall Street, or the city of London—plot, and resolution;

after all, every recession has ultimately ended in renewed and redeemed economic expansion.

In his 2017 presidential address to the American Economic Association, Nobel laureate Robert Shiller documented the viral nature of stories during the Great Depression, even noting that sermons on the Sunday following the great stock market crash moralized the event, attributing it to "excesses, moral and spiritual." Though few before the 1930s described the decade preceding the Great Depression as the "Roaring Twenties," the boom-and-bust narrative of the 1920s—a decade that included the eponymously fraudulent scheme of one Charles Ponzi—framed the subsequent economic downturn as "a sort of day-of-judgement." As in October 1857, "the macro storyline in the Great Depression gradually morphed into a national *revulsion* against the excesses and pathological confidence of the Roaring Twenties" (emphasis added).[51]

Thus do we perennially observe that the typical response to a recessionary bust is to blame the preceding boom for its purported sins. From the Right, observers condemn alleged gluttony; from the Left, alleged greed. We cannot look at an economic recession without seeking some lesson, some warning, from the preceding expansion. Moral-laden stories about recessions help us to avoid not only suffering, but also guilt.

Yet our search for patterns can often lead us to connect data and events that appear related but are, in fact, unrelated. It is a common effect of our cognitive wiring known as *apophenia*. In contrast to an epiphany—the sudden realization of a genuine pattern in observed data—apophanies are when we identify causality between events that are merely synchronous or coincidental, or patterns that are merely correlated. Staring up at the moon and matching the sight of lunar maria to the image of a man's face in our memory is an apophany. Widespread panic in 1910 that the imminent return of Halley's Comet would bring disaster, as previous visitations had been shortly followed by plague and the Great Fire of London, was another.

Examining the long history of recessions in the United States and United Kingdom and marshaling more than five hundred primary sources, more than three hundred unique datasets spanning four centuries, and cutting-edge empirical analysis, in this book I answer fundamental questions while challenging widely held but ultimately apophanous conventional wisdom about recessions. Do recessions follow predictable patterns, with economic expansions inevitably sowing the seeds of their own demise? Or are apparent relationships between economic expansions and subsequent contractions instead merely apophanies rather than epiphanies? Do recessions end on their own, or do they require external intervention? If not the consequence of regular and periodic undulations in economic activity, nor busts following booms, then what does cause recessions?

If recessions are fundamentally about shocks, then some of these shocks we might describe as Acts of God, the most common example of which would be adverse environmental shocks, such as the 1879 UK harvest failure and consequent fuel "famine," or more recently the 2020 pandemic recession. As we have just seen, the 1857–58 recession likewise included a tragic share of destructive Acts of God, from grasshoppers to hurricanes.

Yet we will also see that many recessionary shocks could more accurately be described as Acts of Man, of which Ludlow's potentially fraudulent actions were just one example. Energy price shocks precipitating recessions in 1900, 1902, 1926, and 1927 were also of distinctly anthropological rather than divine provenance, each coinciding with industrial action in the then-essential coal industry. The recession resulting from the 1926 UK coal strike even rivaled the 2020 pandemic recession in speed and depth.

Indeed, man-made coal strikes and management lockouts were frequent contributors to US and UK recessions from the late nineteenth century through the mid-1970s, with the consequent energy shortages frequently described as "coal famines." Although such episodes of contraction were often deep, they were also typically brief. More recently, at the time of the 1990 Iraqi invasion of Kuwait and consequent oil price spike, UK energy supply was further disrupted by the recent explosion of the North Sea oil rig Piper Alpha, then the single-largest producer of oil in the world and accounting for 10 percent of UK crude production.[52] Authorities later determined that the disaster, which claimed the lives of 167 rig workers, resulted from human error.[53]

Yet other shocks, for want of a better label, we might describe as Acts of Church: the individuals, institutions, and laws officially governing economic activity. Examples of such ecclesiastical acts include the six-month recession from February through July 1980, when the United States federal government imposed credit controls and Federal Reserve chairman Paul Volcker hiked short-term interest rates to nearly 20 percent, bringing thirty-year home mortgage rates north of 16 percent.[54] With high interest rates crushing housing demand, Mississippi homebuilders mailed Volcker a block of two-by-four-inch wood with the words "Help! Help! We Need You Please Lower Interest Rates" inscribed in black marker.[55]

We will also find that governments are ultimately responsible for the single-most destructive force that can be inflicted on economies—namely, war. War and war-related disruptions have been serial killers of economic expansions on both sides of the Atlantic over the past four centuries, with war-induced recessions consistently ranking among the longest and deepest recessions in US and UK history. These include the recessions of 1944–47, 1919–21, and 1762–65 in the United Kingdom, and the Revolutionary War–era recessions of 1776–78 and 1785–87 in the United States, both of which rivaled the Great Depression in depth and duration. Oil price spikes precipitating the recessions of 1973–75, 1979–80, and 1990 were likewise of distinctly sovereign rather than divine provenance, with all three occurring in the context of wartime geopolitical shocks.

To be clear, in this book, I do not advance a uni-causal or "single shock" theory of recessions. Quite the contrary: Absent a single shock of the magnitude of, for example, the 2020 pandemic or the 1926 UK strike, recessions are generally characterized by a confluence of overlapping and often interacting factors, as well as propagation mechanisms that can protract elevated unemployment well after the initial impulses have dissipated. Indeed, we have already seen such interactions of adverse shocks in the unfortunate sequence of events that culminated in the 1857–58 recession. The 1980 recession similarly coincided not only with a credit supply shock, but also a severe energy supply shock in the aftermath of the Iranian Revolution.

Even during the recent 2008–09 recession, declining US home prices and the upward reset of adjustable-rate mortgages did not occur in isolation. Rather, the housing shock that both impaired US household balance sheets and triggered a "dislocation in the market" for wholesale bank funding impacted during one of the worst energy and food price shocks in postwar history. In fact, the historical record for the inflation-adjusted price of oil was not during the 1973–74 Arab oil embargo or in the aftermath of the 1979 Iranian Revolution but rather in June 2008. In the postwar period, the global price of energy was never higher than in the second and third quarters of 2008, *before* the collapse of Lehman Brothers.

Part of the challenge to dating recessions is that were it not for the intercession of a large shock or clusters of shocks—such as the terrorist attacks of September 11, 2001, which occurred during the relatively mild 2001 US recession—what might otherwise have been a random slowdown in economic expansion can in retrospect spuriously appear to have marked the inception of economic contraction.[56] Conversely, because an initial impulse—for example, an adverse harvest shock—may take time to propagate through such mechanisms as bank failures, the economic historian is at risk of overlooking underlying shocks whose initial impulse may predate the onset of outright economic contraction by several months. For example, a major factor in the susceptibility of the US economy to recession was that its historically fragmented and under-diversified banking system perennially amplified shocks, with bank failures often following other adverse shocks in agriculture or industry.

If recessions were fundamentally functions of manias, panics, and crashes, then unless we believe that people are systematically more or less rational over time and across countries, then we should expect recessions to be roughly evenly distributed over time and across countries. Yet recessions have become substantially less frequent over the past four centuries. In the United States, the two longest economic expansions since 1700 have both occurred in the past thirty years, and four of the five longest since 1960. Since 1945, the average US expansion has lasted 64 months, compared to just 26 months before World War II. The UK expansion that ended in March 2008 was tied for the second longest on record; the longest ended with the Arab oil embargo of 1973. Were it not for a novel coronavirus, nor is it a foregone conclusion that after 128 consecutive months of expansion the US and UK economies were by early 2020 "overdue" a recession on account of the advanced age of their recoveries.

Contemporaries of the 1857 recession lamented the speed with which news of bank failures spread contagiously via the novel technology of the telegraph, suggesting that episodes of financial panic would become more frequent as technology advanced.[57] Similar concerns emerged 166 years later following the 2023 failures of Silvergate Bank, Silicon Valley Bank, Signature Bank, and First Republic Bank, with depositor fears spreading rapidly through social media. Yet not only did the latter crisis avert recession, but banking crises more generally have also become substantially less, not more, frequent over time in both the United States and United Kingdom.

Even leaving aside the equanimity of more recent cohorts relative to their allegedly more excitable predecessors, are Americans really so much more prone to mania and panic than their British counterparts, who since 1945 have enjoyed an average economic expansion of 212 months? In any given year since 1945, there was a 15 percent chance that the US economy entered a recession, and a nearly one-in-three chance that it was in recession at some point during the year. In contrast, the United Kingdom experienced just a 6 percent probability of entering a recession in any given year and a nearly one-in-five chance that it was in recession at some point during the year. At eighty-nine months, even the average *pre*war UK expansion endured longer than the average *post*war US expansion. A case in point is the unbroken 16-year UK economic expansion from 1862 to 1879.

Meanwhile, no American expansion has lived longer than 10.5 years. In just the last 200 years alone, the United Kingdom avoided recession in 2001, 1970, 1960–61, 1957–58, 1953–54, 1948–49, 1936–38, 1923–24, 1913–14, 1887–88, 1869–70, 1865–67, and 1829, US recessions each. What makes the differential recessionary experience so striking is that the two economies are arguably more or most similar to each other than to any other economies and have long been deeply integrated economically, financially, culturally, and politically. Their differential recessionary experiences thus prompts the question: Why do recessions so often halt at the border?

At the end of the day, recessions are painful, traumatic events. Insofar as we apophanously perceive the height of any alleged excess to precede and predict the depth of the subsequent recessionary penance, our pattern-seeking minds thus command that we seek and tell moral lessons about our prior expansionary sins. Yet recessions are also the exception. On average, "happy" economic expansions live far longer than their unhappy recessionary counterparts, and the average speed of expansions ultimately matters more for long-term economic prosperity. The United Kingdom has had fewer recessions than the United States, but is also at least 30 percent poorer, indicating that over the long run the United States' greater susceptibility to recession is more than offset by its higher-trend growth rate.

And yet recessions keep happening. Why? Are they inevitable or avoidable? Why is the United States more susceptible to recessions compared to other major advanced economies like the United Kingdom's? Why are some long lasting, others short and severe? In the chapters to come, we will examine the factors that generate recession and, equally importantly, those that do not. Encouragingly, we will find that the evidence is unambiguous that we are gradually, over time, getting better at absorbing the kinds of shocks—in particular Acts of God—that historically tended to murder economic expansions.

Moreover, recognizing that recession is not the predictable consequence of fatal flaws in the preceding expansion, that booms do not sow the seeds of their eventual busts, should caution us against apophanous thinking about recessions, against the instinctual impulse to ascribe sin and illness to expansions that in fact die innocent and healthy. The key to better understanding recessions is not to focus on the happiness of the preceding expansion, but rather to understand the sources of their unique unhappiness.

1

EPIPHANIES OR APOPHANIES

The medium of seven years, or rather of so many
years as makes up the Cycle, within which
Dearths and Plenties make their revolution,
doth give the ordinary Rent of the Land.

—Sir William Petty, 1662

It is easy to see how Nouriel Roubini acquired the nickname "Dr. Doom." Stony-faced, with brow furrowed, never cracking a smile, the Harvard-educated economist can enumerate myriad risks looming before the US and global economies with remarkable alacrity and somber conviction. Typically clad in a black suit, with a black tie if any, and with the slightly crumpled look of the longtime university professor he is, he impresses the urgency of the impending confluence of calamities without the polished glibness of his more optimistic competitors in the market for economic prognostications.

According to media reports, he also lives like someone who expects that tomorrow might bring something not far short of apocalypse. According to a 2022 interview, the then-sixty-four-year-old noted that he had no kids and, "citing various threats," declared that "I don't want to have kids."[1] Instead, the grim Dr. Doom prefers to party hard; a rational choice if one expects the world to end. Scooping up a prime East Village penthouse for $5.5 million in 2010, Roubini frequently hosted lavish, often raucous parties. "The recession has been great for me," Roubini acknowledged.[2]

Of course, the main reason Roubini garnered his gloomy sobriquet was that from 2005, he issued loud warnings of a pending recession, and from 2006 warned of a looming housing bust; seemingly one of few economic commentators to do so. But upon closer inspection, was Dr. Doom really prescient? Since the end of World War II, the unconditional probability that the US economy enters recession in any given year is approximately 15 percent, implying about a one-in-six chance. So if an economic observer, like Dr. Doom, predicted in 2005 a recession that subsequently commenced in 2008, then he automatically had a better-than-even chance of being correct before January 2009.

However, journalists unconvinced by Dr. Doom's prophetic acclaim would later question whether Roubini was prescient even on the housing call. At least as early as March 2005, though Roubini was predicting recession, the recession he foresaw was one triggered by foreign central banks diversifying away from US dollars.[3] In February 2006, he was still warning that with the United States consistently spending more than its income, foreign investors would dump US Treasuries for equities.[4] Later in the year, as US housing prices began to decline sharply and inventories soared, Roubini shifted his focus, warning in August that the economy would "fall into a recession early in 2007 as a result of the combination of high energy prices, higher interest rates and a housing collapse."[5]

Yet a year later, with no recession having yet commenced, Dr. Doom was back to emphasizing unsustainable budget and current account deficits. Drawing an explicit parallel to the circumstances preceding the 1987 stock market crash, he now added a sharp criticism of rookie Fed chairman Ben Bernanke's inexperience and communications missteps. He again mentioned housing, but real estate was far down a long list of recession risk factors.[6]

As every economic expansion has ultimately ended in recession, a prediction of recession is eventually, inevitably going to prove "prescient," albeit perhaps premature. The question is over what time horizon. Unfortunately, the market for economic prophecies is highly asymmetrical, tending to punish those who predict continued expansion when a recessionary crisis ensues by far more than those who continually predict recessionary crisis when continued expansion ensues.

The poster child for that warning was famed Yale University economics professor Irving Fisher, a titan in the history of economic thought so much that, in 1924, *The Wall Street Journal* described John Maynard Keynes as "England's Irving Fisher."[7] By one measure, he was the most cited economist in English-language journals from 1886 to 1924, and at least in the top five.[8] In 2005, Nobel laureate and fellow Yale economist James Tobin remarked that "much of standard neoclassical theory today is Fisherian in origin, style, spirit and substance."[9]

A Yale man through and through—he earned both his BA and PhD from Yale, becoming the first recipient of a doctorate in economics from the university—Fisher was also a man with eclectic, even eccentric interests and passions.[10] Of their vegetarian host, who eschewed alcohol and tobacco, one dinner guest at Fisher's impressive home—a wedding gift from his wealthy industrialist father-in-law, Rowland Hazard—recalled that "while I ate right through my succession of delicious courses, he dined on a vegetable and a raw egg." Fisher's experimental research on nutrition, for which he used Yale student athletes as subjects, earned him sufficient recognition as an authority on the subject that cereal-maker Grape-Nuts included an endorsement from Fisher in a 1907 advertisement.[11]

But it was in the market for economic projections that Fisher gained both fame and infamy. By the early 1920s, economic forecasting was a burgeoning field, inspired by the commercial success of pioneers such as Roger Babson—founder of Babson College—and the Harvard Economic Service (HES). Utilizing his work on price indices, Fisher started a business selling indices of wholesale commodity prices and his economic views to newspapers. By 1929, Fisher's Business Page appeared in dozens of newspapers across the country, and his predictions were featured in *The New York Times* and *The Wall Street Journal*.[12] Keen to expand, in the summer of 1929, Fisher instructed his staff to "go ahead full steam," spending in excess of $30,000 (approximately $3 million in 2024 dollars) on office expansion and new equipment.[13]

But in early September, equity markets began to falter. Commenting to *The New York Times*, Fisher maintained that "stock prices are not too high and Wall Street will not experience anything in the nature of a crash." He noted that the ability to diversify through investment trusts had substantially lowered risks for equity investors. With "the margin of safety between high-grade bonds and common stocks . . . rapidly being equalized in actuality and in the popular mind," Fisher was convinced that the continual erosion of the equity premium justified higher stock prices.[14]

More importantly, though, Fisher noted that "we are living in an age of increasing prosperity and consequent increasing earning power . . . due in large measure to mass production and inventions such as the world never before has witnessed." "The rapidity," he continued, "with which worth-while inventions are brought out is the result of the tremendous research laboratories of our great industrial concerns," while "application of these inventions to industry means greatly enhanced earning power."[15]

Just over a month later, Fisher reiterated his arguments in an address to members of the Purchasing Agents Association at their monthly dinner meeting. In particular, he again emphasized the value of increased diversification through the rise of investment trusts, which not only allowed investors to "diversify their holdings among many kinds of common and preferred stocks and bonds, foreign and domestic," but also operated "to shift risks from those who lack investment knowledge to those who possess it." In a line that would haunt him for the rest of his life, Fisher suggested that stock prices had thus reached "what looks like a permanently high plateau."[16]

On the eve of what would subsequently be known as "Black Thursday," in evening remarks to the District of Columbia Bankers Association Fisher tripled down on the proposition that the economy was fundamentally sound. While acknowledging that it was impossible to "shake the market entirely free" from a "lunatic fringe of reckless speculation," he considered the "public speculative mania" to be the "least important of a dozen causes" for the rise in equity prices over the preceding three years. He then rattled off the increased economies of scale attributable to more corporate mergers under Presidents Coolidge and Hoover, wartime inflation and the depreciation of the dollar (which raised the dollar value of US firms' overseas revenues), increased diversification through investment trusts, a capital gains tax that disincentivized selling appreciated securities, and increased wariness of bonds due to inflation risk as legitimate economic justifications for the rise in equity prices in recent years.[17]

The next morning, the Dow Jones plunged 11 percent upon opening, which would have marked its biggest drop on record had not the heads of five leading New York banks—J. P. Morgan and Company, Chase National Bank, National City Bank (the future Citibank), the Guaranty Trust Company, and the Bankers Trust Company—met at J. P. Morgan's offices at 23 Wall Street to coordinate $20–$30 million in stock purchases.[18] As John Pierpont Morgan himself had similarly done in 1907, they managed to staunch the bleeding that day, with the Dow actually recouping some of its losses. But the following Monday—"Black Monday"—the Dow plunged 13 percent, followed Tuesday by a further 12 percent. While markets rebounded on Wednesday and Thursday, by the second week in November the Dow had dropped nearly 50 percent since September 3.[19]

Nonetheless, as stocks continued to recover throughout the rest of November and into January, Fisher remained optimistic.[20] In remarks to three hundred attendees of a Chamber of Commerce luncheon in Bridgeport, Connecticut, on December 2, he noted that as the flow of future earnings from equity in US companies had not been destroyed but merely transferred to other investors at discount, "no permanent ill effects of the market crash will be experienced." He added that President Hoover was "pursuing the right course in his campaign against reduced employment and productivity," and suggested that investors could either "proceed with courage and confidence in the great promise of the industrial and business future or to succumb to the false fear which the break in stocks might set up in business and industry."[21] Yet despite Fisher's optimism, over the next three years, the Dow would drop a further 83 percent; GDP would drop 21 percent, and unemployment would peak at 25 percent. His reputation would never recover from his failure at economic prognostication.

In a historic irony, Fisher's September 5 comments were reported in direct response to remarks the same day by famed market commentator and forecaster Roger Babson. In a speech that day before the National Business Conference, Babson warned:

> I repeat what I said at this time last year and the year before, that sooner or later a crash is coming which will take in the leading stocks and cause a decline of from 60 to 80 points in the Dow-Jones Barometer. Fair weather cannot always continue. The economic cycle is in progress today as it was in the past . . . Sooner or later a crash is coming and it may be terrific. Wise are those investors who now get out of debt and reef their sails. This does not mean selling all you have, but it does mean paying up your loans and avoiding margin speculation. . . .
>
> Sooner or later the stock market boom will collapse like the Florida [real estate] boom. Some day the time is coming when the market will begin to slide off, sellers will exceed buyers, and paper profits will begin to disappear. Then there will immediately be a stampede to save what paper profits then exist.

"Sooner or later." "May be terrific." "Some day." Like Dr. Doom, Babson had issued the same grim warning exactly a year before, and the year before that. Moreover, an 80-point decline in the Dow Jones Industrial Average—which peaked at 381 on September 3, 1929, would have marked a decline of 21 percent. As it happened, from its September 1929 peak to the summer of 1932 trough, the Dow Jones plunged 89 percent; Babson's possible "terrific" crash was off by a factor of more than four. The Dow would not reattain its precrash level until November 1954.[22] But at least Babson got the sign right.

Furthermore, rather like Roubini's evolving prediction of the cause of the forever pending crisis, when Babson issued his dire warning at the very same National

Business Conference twelve months prior, the cause of his concern was radically different. Then, he again warned that a depression was coming, but declared the cause of that looming depression would be the defeat of Republican presidential nominee Herbert Hoover in the upcoming 1928 general election. Speaking of Democratic nominee Governor Al Smith, Babson told the conference that "if Smith should be elected, with a Democratic Congress, we are almost certain to have a resulting business depression in 1929."[23]

Curiously, on one item, Babson and Fisher, both teetotalers, did agree.[24] Reflecting on how the United States had managed to escape financial panic in the aftermath of the Great War, Babson credited Prohibition, which came into effect more than a year after the war's end. According to Babson, following the Eighteenth Amendment banning alcohol, money that had previously been spent on the manufacture and sale of booze was instead diverted to other, more productive uses.[25] Evidently, Fisher concurred, crediting Prohibition for the economy's strength in his remarks to the District of Columbia Bankers Association on the eve of Black Thursday.[26] In any event, Babson would be lauded by history for his purportedly prescient anticipation of the pending crash. Like Dr. Doom and, for that matter, the oracles of Delphi, he had been sufficiently vague and adaptable in his predictions of economic calamity.

In the extreme, one might consider two types of forecasters. One who, similarly to Dr. Doom, predicts recession every year. The other predicts no recession every year. The former would, on average, be wrong approximately 85 percent of the time since 1945, while the latter would be wrong just 15 percent of the time. Moreover, consistently investing on the advice of the latter would generate substantially higher long-run returns than consistently investing on the advice of the former. Yet our loss aversion often leads us to discount so-called perma-bulls far more than perma-bears, and sometimes to even attach a premium to perma-bears.

However, the contrast between the vague, accidentally "correct" warnings of Babson and Dr. Doom and the intellectually precise but erroneous optimism of Professor Fisher raises a more fundamental question—are recessions even predictable at all? Are they regularly and periodically recurring? If not fully forecastable, are there at least some indicators or rules that offer clues to the likelihood of pending economic contraction? Recession chasing certainly has a long and venerable history, but how accurate are recession meteorologists?

Fisher was not alone in being precisely wrong while Babson was oracularly right. Yale-man Fisher's Harvard competitors, the Harvard Economic Service,

were similarly mistaken. Founded in 1922 by Harvard economics professor Warren Persons—himself inspired by Fisher and Babson—by 1924, the service already
boasted a staff of 43, 2,400 subscribers paying one hundred dollars per year, and
partnerships in the United Kingdom, France, Italy, Germany, and Austria.[27]

Strengthening the service's Austrian connections was future Nobel laureate Friedrich Hayek, who visited the United States during the 1923–24 academic year at
the invitation of New York University professor and US Treasury alum Jeremiah
Jenks.[28] The two had met a year earlier in Vienna when Jenks—having advised the
Weimar government following the German hyperinflation—suggested he might
employ Hayek as a research assistant. Struggling to cover the transatlantic fare,
to save money, Hayek declined sending a cable to NYU announcing his pending
arrival. He consequently arrived unannounced and with just twenty-five dollars,
only to find that Jenks was on holiday. After seeking work for two weeks and down
to his last cents, Hayek accepted a post as a dishwasher at a restaurant on Sixth
Avenue, only to receive word the morning he was due to start work that Jenks had
returned.[29]

Incidentally, among the HES's detractors was none other than Hayek's future UK
rival, John Maynard Keynes. Keynes was concerned that the service seemed to liken
economic fluctuations "to a natural phenomenon such as the tides" and worried they
might have "a vested interest in the due recurrence of the boom and slump."[30]

In any event, just five days before Black Thursday, the HES assured subscribers
there were no indications of recession, and if there were, the Federal Reserve would
"check the movement." Like Yale's Fisher, in the ensuing months, they doubled
down, noting in early November that the recent decline in interest rates was "evidence of the soundness of the present business situation."[31] Unfortunately, as future
Fed chairman Ben Bernanke would later demonstrate, the decline in *observed* interest rates after 1929 was in fact a symptom of the severe deterioration in credit conditions. As credit defaults mounted and the value of collateral dropped, lenders
increasingly withdrew credit from all but the highest-quality borrowers.[32]

The HES's persistent predictions of imminent recovery eventually elicited rid-
icule, with one Harvard graduate even lamenting in the *Alumni Bulletin* that the
prestige of the Harvard name had lent intellectual gravitas to disgraced forecasts.[33]
Two days later, university president Abbott Lowell issued a press release stating
unequivocally that the university had nothing to do with the HES.[34] With sub-
scriptions plunging, in the autumn of 1931 the service announced they would cease
publication of the *Weekly Letter*, though their more scholarly *Review of Economics*

and Statistics would continue and is today one of the top ten academic economics journals.[35]

In defense of Fisher and the HES, analysis published six decades later in the *American Economic Review* concluded that the Great Depression was fundamentally unforecastable. Fisher's "continued optimism," the authors concluded, "is consistent with our conclusion based on time-series methods that the Depression was not forecastable." In other words, both Fisher and the HES were "justified in holding what *ex post* was an incorrect view."[36]

Ultimately, while a detectable contraction in the US money supply began in 1928, the magnitude of that contraction was insufficient to cause a depression.[37] Rather, there were a series of subsequent policy shocks—mistakes by the Federal Reserve, corporate tax hikes, the imposition of high tariffs, and a tax on bank checks—as well as successive region-specific banking crises and commodity price declines that could have been neither foreseen nor forecasted by any econometric model.[38] Not to mention a severe locust infestation in the Midwest and Plains in 1931.

Yet Fisher was just one in a long history of economic forecasters who tried and failed to empirically divine natural patterns in the undulations of business activity. As early as 1662, English economist, philosopher, and surveyor Sir William Petty identified what appeared to be a regular cycle of surplus and deficit. "The *medium* of seven years," Petty observed, "or rather of so many years as makes up the Cycle, within which Dearths and Plenties make their revolution, doth give the ordinary Rent of the Land."[39]

Petty was no doubt a brilliant empiricist. He was described by the seventeenth-century English diarist Samuel Pepys as "the most rational man in England," though by Karl Marx as a "frivolous, grasping, unprincipled adventurer," and his biography was certainly anything but dull. Born to a family of humble clothiers, he had sporadic education before running away at thirteen to become a cabin boy on a merchant ship. After breaking his leg within a year, he was marooned on the coast of Normandy, where Jesuit priests discovered the boy and, impressed by his intellect, took him under instruction in Caen.[40] Returning to England with knowledge of Greek, Latin, French, and mathematics, Petty enlisted in the Royal Navy for three years before seeking refuge in the Netherlands and eventually France during the English Civil War, becoming personal secretary to the eminent philosopher and empiricist Thomas Hobbes.[41]

In 1646, the now twenty-three-year-old Petty decided to study medicine at Oxford, where he gained some notoriety for the treatment of Anne Greene, a young woman convicted and hanged for the crime of infanticide after she attempted to conceal the remains of her seventeen-week-old miscarried fetus.[42] Presumed dead after half an hour in the noose, during which time her friends and family tugged at her legs to expedite deliverance from suffering, Greene's body was conveyed to a private house for later dissection by Oxford physicians.[43]

Remarkably, when they opened her coffin the next morning, those present detected faint breathing. Thinking it an act of mercy, one man stamped on her chest with great force. Yet shortly thereafter, at nine o'clock, Petty and an Oxford colleague arrived and immediately observed that Greene still presented a faint pulse and muffled breathing, whereupon they applied a succession of treatments to resuscitate her.[44] Not only did Greene recover but also, believing her miraculous survival to be the hand of God, authorities pardoned her.[45]

Ever intrepid, two years later, Petty took leave from Oxford to serve as a physician in Oliver Cromwell's army during Cromwell's conquest of Ireland. After the war, with experience in nautical charting, Petty lobbied for—and received—the monumental job of surveying the confiscated lands of Irish who did not back the Commonwealth.[46] Employing former soldiers and remote cartographers, remarkably, he finished the survey in just thirteen months.[47]

Whether supremely "rational" or "grasping," Petty was, like his mentor Thomas Hobbes, an empiricist. Physician and anatomist, cartographer, nautical navigator, surveyor, and statistician—in all these pursuits, the challenge presented to the student is to identify multiple features; measure the sizes, shapes, and distributions of those features; detect and quantify patterns, relationships, and interactions between observed features; and, finally, form predictions based on those observed patterns. As a cognitive process of pattern recognition, feature analysis involves breaking down observed stimuli into key constituent features and then dissecting them— indeed, "pattern dissection" is a critical stage of feature analysis. The empirical physician Petty even explicitly likened analyzing the economy of Ireland to dissecting the human anatomy.[48]

Pattern dissection can serve a species well as it seeks to process incoming stimuli by detecting features and patterns and matching them to features and patterns stored in memory. Yet our search for patterns can lead us not only to observe genuine features and patterns we have already encountered, but also to apophanously miss features we have not encountered before, to prejudicially look for features or patterns we have previously observed, or even to detect patterns where in fact there are none.[49]

In the absence or even violation of a familiar pattern—such as an individual amazingly surviving execution by hanging—we often resort to the closest approximation to one. For example, if we generally observe that unanticipated events or unfamiliar designs arise because someone or something intentionally acted to cause or design it, then we might reasonably conclude that a young woman surviving what a physician would ordinarily consider a fatal ordeal could only be divine intervention.

Petty observed what appeared to him to be a regular, seven-year cycle of "Dearths and Plenties." Almost exactly two hundred years later, another physician turned economist, Frenchman Clément Juglar, would posit something similar. Juglar explicitly likened economic crises to disease, writing that "crises, like illnesses, appear to be one of the conditions for the existence of societies where commerce and industry dominate. We can predict them, soften them, protect ourselves from them up to a certain point, facilitate the resumption of business."[50]

More than that, to Juglar, the crisis appeared to constitute an essential stage of healing. He surmised that "every six or seven years, a general liquidation seems necessary to allow trade to take off again"; the "natural evolution restores equilibrium and prepares a firm ground" upon which recovery may proceed.[51] Call it the economic equivalent of therapeutic phlebotomy. Indeed, the very use of the term *crisis* emerged in the fourteenth and fifteenth centuries in medical contexts, referring to a "sudden change (for better or worse) in the condition of a patient occurring during the course of an illness; . . . a decisive turning point between recovery and continued illness or death."[52]

Like the anatomist Petty, Juglar could not help but to use words like *maladies* and *remède* to describe the cause and treatment of crises of a commercial rather than medical nature.[53] While he recognized that adverse events, such as war, revolution, and famine, may at times trigger crises, he did not view them as the underlying cause. Rather, "over a period of five to six years at least," Juglar concluded, the proximity, cause, and ultimate origin of commercial malaise lay not in "unrest and revolutions," but rather in "the deviations of speculation and the congestion of factories."[54] According to Juglar, one could thus observe regular, periodic fluctuations in economic conditions, with "crises" recurring every 5–10 years; 8.7 years on average.[55]

Joseph Schumpeter would later describe Juglar as "among the greatest economists of all times," noting that while he lacked formal training in economics, "his was the type of genius that walks only the way chalked out by himself and never follows any other." "Many people," Schumpeter added, "do this in a subject like economics. But then they mostly produce freaks. The genius comes in where a man produces, entirely on his own, truth that will stand." While the likes of Lord Overstone had discovered nearby islands, it was Juglar who "discovered the continent."[56]

Yet in the history of economic thought, Juglar was certainly not alone in contending that there was a predictable, periodic frequency to episodes of economic contraction, nor was his the final word. His hypothesized frequency of five to ten years was of course preceded by two hundred years by Petty's observation of a seven-year cycle. But in 1923, British statistician and businessman Joseph Kitchin suggested a shorter cycle of just three to five years.[57] Whereas Juglar's longer cycle is typically associated with cyclical fluctuations in the volume of investment in fixed capital (structures, equipment, and intellectual property), Kitchin's shorter, three-to-five-year cycle is commonly associated with cyclical fluctuations in the level of business inventories.

Just two years after Kitchin published his findings on what he described as "minor" cycles of 3.5 years—as distinct from "major" cycles of 7–11 years—Soviet economist Nikolai Kondratiev identified what he described as "long waves."[58] Kondratiev hypothesized that these long waves of 45–60 years' duration were driven primarily by the cyclical nature of technological innovation and adoption. At a cyclical trough, businesses have accumulated a backlog of new inventions and liquid capital, which precipitates a cyclical upswing as they begin to implement those new technologies and invest in long-term capital projects.[59] Yet as large-scale innovation and changes in production techniques generate social upheaval and eventually saturate profitable investment opportunities, profits decline, culminating in crisis and eventually recession.[60]

In a massive 1939 volume, Schumpeter would nest Kitchin cycles within Juglar cycles within Kondratiev waves. Schumpeter viewed forty-month Kitchin inventory cycles as fluctuating contemporaneously with longer-run Juglar fixed investment cycles, which in turn fluctuated contemporaneously with even longer-run fluctuations in innovation clusters.[61] Thus, each Kondratiev "should contain an integral number of Juglars and each Juglar an integral number of Kitchins," each overlayed on the other.[62]

Five years after Kondratiev published his evidence on long waves, Russian-born American economist and future Nobel laureate Simon Kuznets identified what he would call "secondary secular movements," or "long swings."[63] In Kuznets's analysis, such long swings in economic growth were driven by regular undulations in population growth and the corresponding effect on population-sensitive capital formation, particularly residential and railroad construction. However, why those demographic-driven long swings in population-sensitive capital formation should regularly involve outright negative growth Kuznets left vague.

Curiously, even as he wrote of periodic long swings, Kuznets—a native Russian speaker—was familiar with the recent work of the Soviet economist Eugen Slutsky on the potential randomness of economic fluctuations. Indeed, in September 1929—just as the 1929 stock market meltdown began—Kuznets even favorably discussed Slutsky's remarkable findings in an article for the *Journal of the American Statistical Association*.[64]

In a 1927 article published by Moscow's Institute of Conjuncture—of which Kondratiev served as director—institute scholar Slutsky had demonstrated that the summation of random and mutually independent series or "chance causes" could generate what appear to be periodic, oscillating cycles.[65] Specifically, Slutsky took random ten-digit lottery numbers to generate a long list of randomized numbers between zero and nine. He then sequentially added each rolling ten-number block of digits, essentially creating a moving sum.[66] Remarkably, when he plotted the randomly generated moving sum against an index of British business cycles from 1855 to 1877, the completely random summation mapped closely onto the undulations of the index, as seen in Figure 2.

While Slutsky did not go so far as to imply that the appearance of regular economic cycles was actually generated by random events, the exercise did suggest that

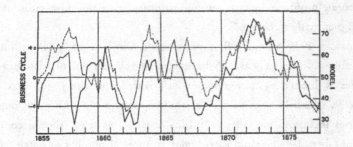

Figure 2: Index of UK Business Cycles, 1855–77, Versus Moving Sum of Lottery Numbers. The solid line reports the index of business cycles, scaled on the left-hand axis. The dashed line reports the results of Slutsky's moving sum, scaled on the right-hand axis. (Eugen Slutsky, "The Summation of Random Causes as the Source of Cyclic Processes," *Econometrica* 5, no. 2 [1937]: 110.)

the data generating process behind seemingly cyclical undulations could be quite different from the independent, regularly recurring causes to which various wave theorists attributed economic fluctuations.[67] Ironically, then, even as some of the great Western economic theorists of the interwar period labored to demonstrate that economic fluctuations were the inevitable consequence of flaws and contradictions in economic expansions themselves, a Soviet economist discovered that fluctuations could be completely random and unrelated to the process of economic growth.

Kitchin and Juglar cycles, Kuznets swings, and Kondratiev waves are examples of a subset of apophenia known as *clustering illusions*, in which even a scrupulous observer tends to erroneously infer that small clusters of outcomes in small samples, though actually randomly distributed, appear nonrandom. For instance, during World War II, Londoners observed that certain areas were hit by German V-2 rockets with considerably greater frequency than others; indeed, some areas were hit multiple times, while others not at all. Though observers therefore rationally concluded that the Wehrmacht were deliberately targeting some neighborhoods over others, statistical analysis found that the strikes in fact followed a random distribution.[68]

Similarly, while recessions may appear to cluster around three-to-five-, five-to-ten-, fifteen-to-twenty-, and/or forty-five-to-sixty-year intervals, we are mistaking for regularity what is simply a random distribution with chance clusters. A less formal way to put it is by analogy to the Texas sharpshooter fallacy—a Texan fires multiple rounds at the side of a barn, then paints a target centered on the densest cluster of shots before claiming to be a sharpshooter.

More formally, if recessions were phenomena recurring at regular periodicities, per Kitchin, Juglar, Kuznets, and Kondratiev, then the occurrence of a recession three to five, five to ten, fifteen to twenty, or forty-five to sixty years in the past should predict a higher probability of recession today. However, over the entire period since 1700, in both the United States and United Kingdom, the occurrence of a recession three to five, five to ten, fifteen to twenty, or forty-five to sixty years ago statistically has no effect on the probability of recession today. Annual lags at the frequency of Kitchin, Juglar, Kuznets, and Kondratiev cycles explain essentially none of the variation in the incidence of recession across years. In any given year, the occurrence of a recession three to five, five to ten, or fifteen to twenty years ago has precisely zero effect on the probability of recession today, while, if anything, a recession forty-five to sixty years ago is associated with a slightly lower probability of recession—exactly the opposite of Kondratiev's thesis.

This result would not have come as a surprise to the godfather of the study of economic fluctuations in the United States, the bespectacled, three-piece-suited Wesley Clair Mitchell. Contra Juglar et al., as early as 1913, Mitchell noted that while economies experienced "seasons of business prosperity, crisis, depression, and revival," their revolution through those seasons was recurrent but not periodic.[69] Recognizing that "cycles" vary "widely in duration, in intensity . . . and in the sequence of their phases," Mitchell thus embarked on what would become a more than three-decade-long effort to measure how hundreds of economic variables evolved over the course of each recurrent sequence of expansion, contraction, and revival.[70]

With the aid of his former student—future chairman of President Nixon's Council of Economic Advisers (CEA) and the Federal Reserve, Arthur Burns—Mitchell finally completed his long-anticipated tome in 1946. In the nearly six-hundred-page *Measuring Business Cycles*, Burns and Mitchell observed that while each cycle differed in duration and intensity, they shared the common characteristic of "expansions occurring at about the same time in many economic activities, followed by similarly general recessions, contractions, and revivals which merge into the expansion phase of the next cycle." It was this clustering of the transition from expansion to contraction across many different industries and locations at specific points in time that they identified as a defining feature of business cycles. Indeed, "if there were no bunching of cyclical turns" of output and employment across many sectors of the economy, "there would be no business cycles," just uncorrelated sector-specific downturns.[71]

For Burns and Mitchell, a key challenge was therefore to meticulously analyze the relationships between many different economic indicators to ascertain how they moved together from expansion to contraction and then in turn to renewed expansion. In particular, which industries or economic indicators tended to "lead" changes in overall economic activity, and which tended to "lag"?[72] It was this line of inquiry that led Burns and Mitchell to their observation that some economic indicators "lead with considerable regularity the turning dates that we accept for business cycles; some coincide with them on the average, others commonly or always lag behind."[73]

The NBER's work on leading indicators gained official currency between 1956 and 1960 when former Mitchell PhD student and then-chairman of President Eisenhower's CEA, Raymond Saulnier, successfully lobbied the Census Bureau to produce a monthly publication of economic indicators.[74] The publication, *Business*

Cycle Developments, included some eighty indicators that researchers, many affiliated with the NBER, determined were important gauges of national economic conditions. These included more than fifty that they classified as leading future changes in overall economic growth, "roughly coincident" with growth, or lagging changes in growth.[75] Examples include average weekly hours of manufacturing workers (leading), industrial production (coincident), and commercial and industrial bank lending (lagging). Since 1995, the private, nonprofit business organization the Conference Board took over curating the business cycle indicators and continues to publish them monthly.[76]

Yet despite its venerable provenance and longevity, the forecasting record of the business cycle indicators is unimpressive.[77] In discussing a 1973 conference paper on how to improve the performance of the composite index of leading indicators by filtering out noise in the index components, future CEA Chairman and Fed chair Alan Greenspan noted that the author had "done an impressive job in extracting about as much information as I think one can get from what I consider a very weak data base." "In fact," Greenspan continued, "his paper almost succeeded in shaking my belief in the ultimate unusability of a composite leading indicator."[78]

Nonetheless, advances in macroeconomic modeling during the 1980s suggested to several prominent scholars that there was value in summarizing the state of aggregate economic activity.[79] The basic insight in these more contemporary dynamic factor models is that co-movements in many macroeconomic variables may share a common element that can be captured by a single, underlying, or "latent," but otherwise unobserved factor.[80] Combining this insight with the observation—stretching back at least to Keynes and Mitchell—that macroeconomic variables can shift nonlinearly as an economy transitions from an expansionary regime to a contractionary one, economists were able to use a basket of macroeconomic indicators to accurately predict the peaks and troughs in the official NBER recession chronology.[81]

As shown in Figure 3, the results of this line of research perform remarkably well matching the official NBER recession chronology, with essentially no false positives or negatives. But as simple visual inspection reveals, while this approach may be useful for telling us whether we *are* or *were* in a recession, there is no economically meaningful lead time by which one might anticipate that we *will be* in a recession, especially considering the lags with which the data inputs become available.

More problematically, these models are generally trained on just six to eight postwar US recessions. While the availability of macroeconomic data at quarterly or monthly frequency may give the reassuring impression of a robust sample size,

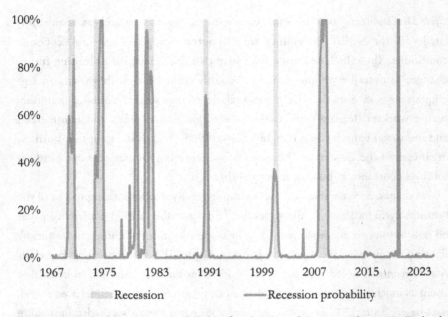

Figure 3: Smoothed Recession Probability for the United States, 1967–2025. (Federal Reserve Bank of St. Louis, "Smoothed Recession Probability (%) [RECPRS@USECON]," Haver Analytics; National Bureau of Economic Research, "NBER Based Recession Indicators for the United States from the Period Following the Peak through the Trough (USREC)," Federal Reserve Bank of St. Louis.)

there are thus still only six to eight outcomes of interest. Indeed, with many independent variables and just a few, rare recessionary outcomes in the sample, the risk is that the dynamic factor model approach is more an exercise in fitting a curve to observed recessions, rather than predicting them ex ante.[82] Even where models with relatively few variables can accurately map onto official recession chronologies, the lags with which economic data are released and revised mean that the model is not forecasting recession but rather indicating ex post facto that the economy was in recession at that time.[83]

Yet while some forecasters risk overfitting parameters to match the official US recession chronology, at first glance, others appear to perennially discount the predictive power of a recession indicator that both appears remarkably accurate and has been known for decades.[84] Since at least the 1980s, economists and financial market participants have recognized that prior to every US recession since 1955, the spread between long- and short-term Treasury yields turned negative as yields on shorter-term securities rose above those with longer maturities.[85]

Ordinarily, investors expect that yields on longer-term securities will exceed yields on shorter-term securities of the same default risk as compensation for the risks associated with holding securities over time. This generates a positive slope to a plot of yields as a function of bond duration. If, however, investors expect either that the average of future short-term yields will be higher than current short-term yields, or else that future inflation will be substantially lower than near-term inflation, then it is possible that yields on longer-term securities will be lower than shorter-term securities of the same default risk, a phenomenon known as a *yield curve inversion*. Such a phenomenon may arise when investors anticipate that the central bank will have to lower rates in response to weakening economic conditions, or else that weakening economic conditions will lower future inflation.

Common measures of the spread between longer- and shorter-term yields of the same default risk include the difference in yield between the ten-year Treasury bond and shorter-duration securities ranging from thirty-day Treasury bills to two-year Treasury bonds.[86] Both to take an intermediate spread and to maximize

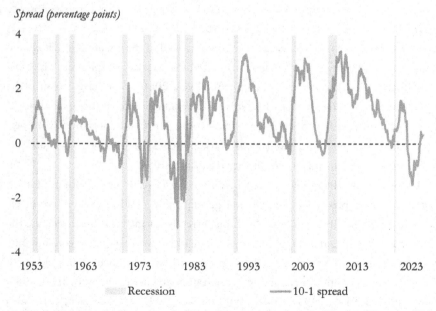

Spread (percentage points)

Figure 4: Yield Curve Spread in the United States, 1953–2025. (National Bureau of Economic Research, "NBER Based Recession Indicators for the United States from the Period Following the Peak through the Trough (USREC)," Federal Reserve Bank of St. Louis; Board of Governors of the Federal Reserve System, "Selected Interest Rates (H.15): Federal Funds (Effective) Rate (% P.A.) [FFED@USECON]," Haver Analytics.)

the length of time for which one has reliable yield curve data for both the United States and United Kingdom, I examine changes in the spreads between ten- and one-year sovereign bond yields.

Between 1954 and 2020, recession followed inversions of the US ten-to-one-year spread within two years on nine occasions, with an average lead time of thirteen months and a median of eleven months, ranging from six (2020 recession) to twenty-four months (2008 recession). During that time, the yield curve generated just three false positives. The curve inverted in December 1965 and remained inverted for fifteen consecutive months, but a recession did not materialize until January 1970, more than four years later. The recession beginning in January 1970 also succeeded by twenty-five months a second, discrete inversion in December 1967. Similarly, the curve inverted in July 2022 and remained continuously inverted for the next twenty-eight months, with no recession.

However, it is also likely that were it not for the exogenous shock of a novel coronavirus, the yield curve inversion in the summer of 2019 would have constituted a fourth false positive. Investors in August 2019 could not have anticipated widespread pandemic-related lockdowns in March and April of 2020, in the absence of which it is unlikely the objectively strong US economy of February 2020 was otherwise on the cusp of recession. Similarly, as noted in the introduction, it is even conceivable that were it not for the horrific terrorist attacks of September 11, 2001, the US yield curve inversion in the millennial year 2000 would have constituted a fifth recession positive. Nonetheless, it is still a reputable record; the unconditional probability of recession in any twenty-four-month period is approximately 30 percent, whereas even with as many as five false positives, the recession "hit rate" for yield curve inversions was still over 55 percent since 1954.

Unfortunately, though yield curve inversions have a respectable "hit rate" for US recessions, their predictive power is not generalizable.[87] While yield curve inversions in 1988–90, 2006–07, and 2019 did correctly (or fortuitously) anticipate the 1990–91, 2008–09, and 2020 UK recessions within two years, UK economic history is abundant in false positives for yield curve inversions. Since 1970, yield curve inversions in the United Kingdom generated discrete false positives in 1970, 1985, 1986, 1987, 1991–92, 1997–2001, 2005–06, and 2022–23. The yield curve also flashed false negatives ahead of the 1973 recession, and in 1979 only inverted after recession had already begun.

Moreover, not only does the predictive power of the yield curve weaken when we look across countries, it also loses its oracular sagacity when looking within

Spread (percentage points)

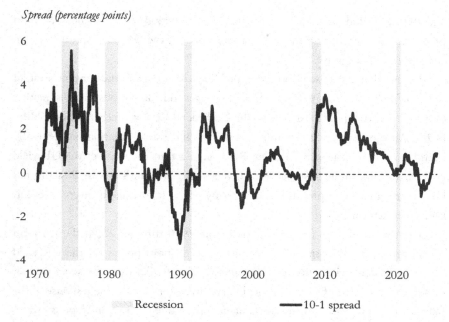

Recession   ———10-1 spread

Figure 5: Yield Curve Spread in the United Kingdom, 1970–2025. ("Monthly Government Liability Curve (Nominal): Archive Data," Bank of England; Stephen Broadberry et al., "Dating Business Cycles in the United Kingdom, 1700–2010," *Economic History Review,* January 27, 2023, ehr.13238. Note: One-year yields are missing for October and November 1972, so I substitute 1.5-year yields.)

the United States over time. Data extending back to 1862 reveals that while the downward-sloping yield curves of recent decades have been labeled "perverse," in the decades following the Civil War, at least, falling yield curves were nearly as common as upward-sloping curves.[88] When the yield curve inverted in late 1988, one Fed economist noted that when the gold standard credibly anchored trend inflation, the expected inflation rate incorporated into bond yields would generally remain stable and close to zero. The yield curve would thus "pivot around a relatively stable long-term yield."[89] In the context of a flat yield curve, inversions were therefore unremarkable, if not commonplace.

More recently, a former member of the Bank of England Monetary Policy Committee echoed the same point. Speaking in 2018, Gertjan Vlieghe observed that the yield curve had been flat during the gold standard era and argued that "since Bank of England independence, the fundamentals of inflation and inflation risk have become more similar to the gold standard era than to the 20th century average, and in particular are very different from the 1970s and 1980s." Unlike the 1970s and 1980s, "periods with stable inflation . . . were periods of low or negative term premium." In fact, during the gold standard period, the UK term spread was, on average, slightly negative.[90]

The abundance of false positives in the UK yield curve and the concentration of signal value in the post-1955 United States suggest one of two possibilities, neither of which is particularly flattering for the US Federal Reserve. Either the credibility of the Bank of England's commitment to low and stable inflation has generally been higher than that of the Federal Reserve, and thus the slope of the UK yield curve flatter and more susceptible to inversion, or else the Bank of England has been more effective in promptly recalibrating policy following an inversion event. Or a combination of both.

Over the entire fifty-four-year period from 1970 through 2024, the US term spread averaged 105 basis points, compared to 87 basis points for the UK yield curve, consistent with a flatter UK curve.[91] Meanwhile, over the same period, within three months of a discrete yield curve inversion, the average response of the federal funds rate was a 118-basis point *increase*, while the typical response was a 50-basis point increase.

In contrast, within three months of a discrete UK yield curve inversion, the average response of the Bank of England's policy rate was just a 6-basis point increase, while the typical response was no change. Prior to 2022 (when the Bank of England was battling high inflation resulting from pandemic disruptions and the Russian invasion of Ukraine), the average response of bank rate to a yield curve invasion was in fact an 8-basis point *decrease*. Meanwhile, the median response of bank rate to a UK yield curve inversion was again precisely 0.0 basis points.

That is, in the wake of an inversion event, the typical response of the Bank of England was to refrain from monetary policy tightening. Thus, the correlation between US yield curve inversions and subsequent recessions would seem to be less a market prediction of recession than a correlation between market perception of slowing economic activity and the Fed's imperception or delayed perception of the same, and thus tendency to err on the side of tightness at precisely the wrong moment.

The lags with which official economic data becomes available to economic policy-makers is one rationale for an increasingly popular and remarkably accurate recession indicator known as the *Sahm rule*. Developed by former Federal Reserve economist Claudia Sahm, the rule states that when "the three-month average national unemployment rate rises by at least 0.50 percentage points relative to its low in the previous

Change (percentage points)

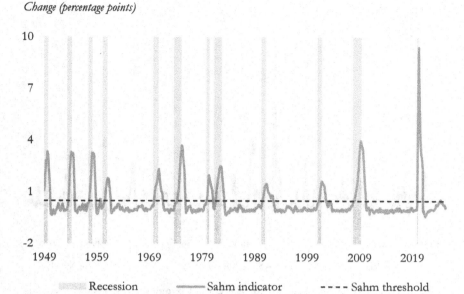

Figure 6: Sahm Recession Indicator for the United States, 1949–2025. For consistency with the UK series, which only includes current rather than vintage estimates of the unemployment rate, I use the current-time US unemployment rate data rather than the real-time. See data appendix.

12 months," a recession has likely begun and the federal government should initiate direct transfer payments to households to preempt a decline in consumer spending.[92]

The appeal of the Sahm rule is not just its simplicity and timeliness—the Bureau of Labor Statistics releases unemployment rate data for the previous month on the first Friday of every month—but also its apparent reliability. Since 1948, the Sahm rule has correctly indicated every US recession, with no false positives prior to 2024 (see Figure 6). I say *indicated* because the "rule" is just that—an indication that recession has already begun, rather than a prediction that a recession will occur in the future. However, in 2024, the Sahm rule flashed a false negative; the Sahm threshold was marginally breached in the summer of 2024, but the US economy was not in recession.

As with the yield curve, the United Kingdom again constitutes a historical foil. As shown in Figure 7, UK economic history is strewn with more than a dozen false positives for the Sahm indicator, including, most recently, 2023, 2011, 2006, and 1985. Perhaps more importantly, there were plenty of false negatives as well. During the 2008–09 global financial crisis, the UK economy did not breach the

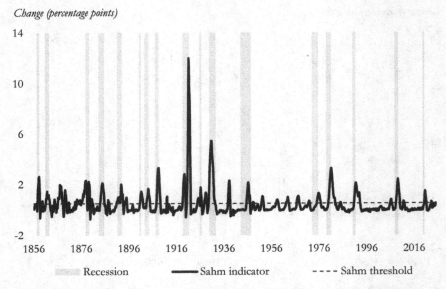

Change (percentage points)

Figure 7: Sahm Recession Indicator for the United Kingdom, 1855–2025. See data appendix.

Sahm threshold until September 2008—more than five months into a recession that was already underway. Similarly during the 1990–91 recession, the UK economy did not breach the Sahm threshold until January 1991—more than six months into that recession. During the severe 1979–81 UK recession, the Sahm indicator was more than eight months late. The indicator was also perennially late to the game during nineteenth-century UK recessions. During the UK recession of 1855, it is possible that the Sahm threshold was not breached at all.

Curiously, the United Kingdom generally has much lower "hit rates" for several common recessionary premonitions. Recent research reveals that while yield curve inversions, large central bank rate increases, and inflation spikes have each preceded more than 70 percent of US recessions, the same premonitions have preceded fewer than half of UK recessions.[93] So what might look like reliable indicators when applied to one country may just be randomly lucky—or Texas sharpshooter–style clustering illusions—or else reflective of the historically greater sensitivity of the US economy to common adverse shocks.

––––––––––

The historical evidence leads one to conclude that recessions are fundamentally unforecastable. They are certainly not periodic, as Petty, Juglar, Kitchin, Kuznets,

Kondratiev, and many others maintained. Nor are they reductive to indices or pseudo-indices, as Yale's Fisher and perhaps more recently the dynamic factor model literature suggests. Even seemingly reliable indicators like yield curve inversions or the Sahm rule are unreliable across time and space.

In one sense, the unpredictability of recessions should not be surprising. If one knew the stock market was going to fall tomorrow, one would rationally sell today. If one knew there was going to be a bank run tomorrow, one would rationally withdraw one's deposits today. Similarly, if consumers knew that they were going to lose income and employment tomorrow, they would rationally be inclined to spend less and save more today; if businesses knew demand was going to fall tomorrow, they would invest less, save more, and draw down inventories today. If recessions were "knowable," then they would occur today rather than tomorrow.

A prediction that an economic expansion will end in recession will always, ultimately, be correct, for the simple reason that there has never been an immortal economic expansion. But that does not mean that a prediction of recession one, two, or, in the case of Dr. Doom, three years prior to its eventual occurrence is evidence of prescience. As the saying goes, even a broken clock tells the correct time twice daily.

The fundamental unpredictability of recessions poses a challenge for those who posit that recessions are endogenously generated, cyclical phenomena proceeding through identifiable, sequential phases. It also poses a challenge for those who consider recessions the inevitable consequence of flaws in the preceding expansion, the accumulation of which should render recession more likely as the expansion proceeds.

In his classic 1913 tome on business cycles, Mitchell concluded that while the processes of economic expansion "work cumulatively for a time to enhance prosperity, they also cause a slow accumulation of stresses within the balanced system of business—stresses which ultimately undermine the conditions upon which prosperity rests."[94] But whether an expansion's prognosis deteriorates with age is thus a question we will examine further in the next chapter.

2

PETER PAN VERSUS DORIAN GRAY

Prosperity breeds a crisis.

—WESLEY CLAIR MITCHELL, 1913

On Thursday, August 15, 2019, fear gripped Wall Street. A day earlier, the Dow Jones Industrial Average had plunged eight hundred points after bond markets flashed a warning signal about the risk of a recession. Briefly on Wednesday, the yield on ten-year US Treasuries dipped below that on two-years, a classic—though, as we learned in the preceding chapter, unreliable—harbinger of recession. More than three years before, the legendary investor Jim Rogers told Bloomberg that there was a 100 percent probability that the US economy would enter recession within a year.[1] "It's been seven years, eight years since we had the last recession in the U.S.," Rogers noted, "and normally, historically we have them every four to seven years for whatever reason—at least we always have." As it turned out, the economic expansion then underway rolled on for just one month shy of another four years.

Roger's expectation that, after a lengthy expansion, the US economy was "due" a recession is a sentiment of venerable provenance. Most of the great economic theorists of the pre–World War II period—Friedrich Hayek, Lionel Robbins, Dennis Robertson, Ralph Hawtrey, Knut Wicksell, Gustav Cassel, and Alvin Hansen, each economic legends in their own right—postulated that as an economic expansion proceeded, "maladjustments" or "mal-investments" would tend to cumulate, rendering the expansion more vulnerable to the weight of imbalances and fragilities.

Hence the notion of a business *cycle*—successive, distinct phases of economic expansion and contraction as excesses during times of expansion generate untenable

investments, the resolution of which is the function of subsequent economic contractions. Charles Kindleberger or Lord Overstone might attribute such imbalances and malinvestments to "mania" or "overtrading," but the general principle is
analogous—misbegotten and therefore unsustainable investments accumulate over
the course of an economic expansion, eventually climaxing in crisis and terminat-
ing in remedial recession.

Such imbalances could include both *horizontal maladjustments*, or misallocations across sectors of the economy, as well as *vertical maladjustments*, or misallocations of investment and productive capacity between the production of consumer
goods versus plant and equipment or other intermediate inputs. For example, overinvestment in housing supply relative to housing demand might constitute a horizontal maladjustment, while excess accumulation of inventory or physical plant and
equipment would constitute maladjustments of the vertical variety.

Vertical maladjustment was the basis of various interwar overinvestment theories of economic contractions. At the core of such theories was the notion that as
credit conditions purportedly eased over the course of an economic expansion, the
demand for investment would outstrip the supply of household savings to finance
that investment.[2] Businesses would thus be investing in new capacity for greater
production tomorrow at the expense of current output to meet undiminished consumer demand today. Invariably, this unsustainable disequilibrium would require
the misguided investments to be scaled back or liquidated.

A particularly prominent proponent of such an over- or malinvestments theory
of economic contractions during the 1930s was the Austrian economist Friedrich
Hayek. A veteran of the Austro-Hungarian Army in the First World War, Hayek
arrived at the London School of Economics (LSE) in February 1931 at the invitation of Lionel Robbins, then the youngest professor of economics in the United
Kingdom. At the time, Robbins was battling John Maynard Keynes on the UK's
depression-era Economic Advisory Council. With three of the other four committee members all educated at the University of Cambridge, Robbins was keen
to enhance the LSE's standing as an intellectual counterweight to Keynes's Cambridge, which had dominated economic theory in the United Kingdom since Alfred
Marshall's long tenure from 1865 to 1908. As an Austrian, Hayek had a particular
appeal to Robbins, who sought to present the LSE as a more international and less
parochial alternative to Cambridge.[3]

One LSE student would later remark that Hayek "looked to me at least 50,"
though much later discovered he was only in his mid-thirties, perhaps due in part to

"his old-fashioned way of dressing, in a thick tweed suit with a waistcoat and high cut jacket." She gave him the nickname "Mr. Fluctooations," because he used the word frequently in his lectures on business cycles, and "pronounced it in that way."[4]

The crux of Hayek's theory, like those of many other prewar business cycle theorists, was that there was an inherent tendency in a credit-based economy for the interest rate at which banks lend to lag upward movements in the "natural" rate of interest that would equilibrate the supply household savings with the demand for business investment.[5] With the prevailing market rate of interest consequently "too low," firms would have an incentive to invest in longer-term investment projects, while a sufficient supply of savings to fund those investments would not be forthcoming.

Inevitably, Hayek postulated, as more and more resources were diverted to longer-term projects, the final output of which would only come on line in the distant future, there would be a decreased supply of goods for current consumption. Yet with consumer demand remaining undiminished, upward pressure on consumer prices would ensue, forcing a bidding war for labor and capital between producers of consumer goods today and longer-term investment projects whose completion would yield a greater volume of consumer goods only in the distant future.

This tension would ultimately result in the abandonment and liquidation of the long-term projects, as investments to produce more consumer goods in the distant future would be unable to compete with producers producing for unsatiated consumer demand today. Creditors and investors in misbegotten long-term projects would thus incur losses and unemployment would rise as shorter-term projects would be unable to immediately and seamlessly absorb workers released from abandoned long-term projects. Investment losses and mounting unemployment would thereby generate recession.

When he presented his theory at Cambridge to Keynes's colleagues, the Cambridge economists met Hayek with skepticism. "The general tendency," the devout Keynesian economist Joan Robinson later recalled, "seemed to be to show that the slump was caused by inflation," which prompted her colleague, Richard (later Lord) Kahn, to inquire: "Is it your view that if I went out tomorrow and bought a new overcoat, that would increase unemployment?" "Yes," Hayek answered, "but it would take a very long mathematical argument to explain why," his basic logic being that any increase in demand for final consumption goods today would merely hasten the abandonment and liquidation of unsustainable, longer-term investment projects.[6]

But Hayek was certainly not alone. His widely respected contemporary, Harvard economist Gottfried Haberler, wrote that "during the course of an expansion which has started from the depth of a depression, the economic system becomes the more vulnerable the nearer full employment is approached."[7] Wesley Clair Mitchell, Columbia professor and early pioneer of business cycle research at the National Bureau of Economic Research, argued that prosperity itself "breeds a crisis."[8]

More recently, economists at Stanford University and the University of Chicago have posited a "forest fire" theory of expansion duration and recession that similarly emphasizes the cumulative role of bad business decisions during economic expansions in generating and amplifying subsequent contractions.[9] In their model, firms face search costs as they look to acquire inputs into production. During periods of high demand and thus high profit potential, firms accept relatively low-productivity matches (no pun intended)—for example, they accept lower-productivity or otherwise lower-quality employees simply to meet current demand.

Consequently, the longer firms have operated without a decline in demand, the more they will have acquired low-productivity inputs (labor contracts, procurement contracts, credit lines), and thus the greater the volume of separations when a negative shock hits. In other words, long expansions generate more "dry tinder" in the form of low-quality matches (again, no pun intended), resulting in a larger fire when a spark eventually ignites it.[10] Left unstated but implicit is the argument that perhaps, like sound forest management, economies may require the occasional controlled burn.

In the cyclical "manic," "malinvestments," or "forest fire" view of recessions, the longer we have gone without a recession, the more we should anticipate that one is imminent. After all, that which cannot go on forever—such as an unsustainable, irrational mania—usually will not go on forever. "We're overdue a recession" is a line that often crops up late in an economic expansion, as it did in August 2019 and March 2016 with David Rubenstein and Jim Rogers.

In Oscar Wilde's famous novel *The Picture of Dorian Gray*, as the seemingly eternally youthful Gray pursues an ever-more debauched, hedonistic, and even violent lifestyle, a painting of him, locked away out of sight in an attic, manifests the blemishes and disfigurements of each misdeed. Increasingly consumed by anguish, Gray eventually concludes that the only way to liberate himself from his past, to kill the one enduring legacy of his wrongdoing, with all its "hideous warnings," is to destroy the horrid portrait once and for all. And so, with the very instrument of one of his crimes, Gray plunges a blade into his own image, releasing a cry of such agony that terrified servants rush to the attic, whereupon they find "a splendid portrait" of Gray, restored to his "exquisite youth and beauty," and beneath it the deceased body of a "withered, wrinkled, and loathsome" old man, identifiable as Gray only by his rings.

In the view of Hayek, Mitchell, and numerous other prewar economists, as well as contemporary commentators and proponents of endogenous, or "self-generating," business cycles, economic expansions are rather like the picture of Dorian Gray. To all outward appearances, the expansion, emblematized by Dorian Gray the man, remains youthful and vigorous. Yet, unseen, the blemishes, disfigurements, and haggardness of a debauched and aging enterprise accrue relentlessly, until the intolerable hideousness can only be cleansed by slaying it with the very instrument of its own indulgences and transgressions—ruthless market discipline—whereupon the youth and beauty of the original picture can be restored.

In stark contrast to Dorian Gray, J. M. Barrie's adored Peter Pan, while mischievous, spends his days innocently flying, embarking on exciting adventures, battling pirates, and never growing old.[11] Although Peter Pan never ages, he is mortal, and if he were to befall some accident or lose a battle with Captain Hook, he would die. The Peter Pan view of economic expansions is thus utterly at odds with the notion that recessions are fundamentally the inevitable consequence of systemic and systematic errors that accumulate during the preceding expansion and consequently render the economic host increasingly fragile over time.

Are economic expansions more akin to Peter Pan than Dorian Gray? To pose the question more concretely, are expansions more likely to end the longer they have been underway? Speaking at the annual meeting of the American Economic Association in Atlanta on January 4, 2019, just as a partial government shutdown and recent stock market slide had reignited fears of a recession, former Federal Reserve chairman Janet Yellen remarked that "I don't think expansions just die of old age." Colorfully reflecting the sudden violence with which adverse shocks can bring an end to economic expansions, her fellow former Fed chair Ben Bernanke replied, "I like to say they get murdered," drawing laughs from the economist crowd.[12]

In this chapter, I find that economic expansions are *not* the victims of their own cumulative deformity and that this pattern is true not only of more recent decades since the Great Depression and Second World War but, in contrast to prior studies, true also of the nearly 250 years prior. While prewar economic expansions in the United States were on average short, with a relatively high probability of ending in recession in any given year, the probability of that happening was generally constant regardless of the age of the expansion. The pattern is even more pronounced in the United Kingdom, where economic expansions both before and after World War II were on average longer and even more strongly age-independent than those in the United States. Expansions simply do not sow the seeds of their own destruction.

One way to formally test whether recessions are indeed the consequence of imbalances and fragilities that accumulate as an economic expansion ages is to estimate the probability of a recession based on how long the preceding expansion has been underway. If there are errors and imbalances that accumulate over time, then we should expect the probability of recession to increase the longer an expansion has endured.

In Figure 8, I plot the probability that a postwar economic expansion ends in the next quarter as a function of the expansion's age. The shorter curve for the United States ends at 42 quarters, as no US expansion has lasted longer than the 10.5-year expansion from 2009 through 2019. This compares to 104 quarters (26 years) for the longest UK expansion on record, the lengthy postwar recovery that endured from 1947 to 1973.

Though the US line is modestly upward-sloping, indicating that an older US expansion may appear to be somewhat more likely to die than a younger one,

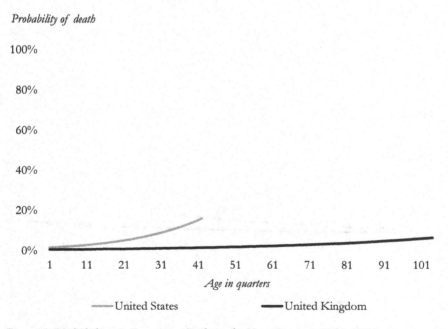

Figure 8: Probability an Expansion Ends in the Next Quarter, 1945–2025.

statistically, the effect of an additional quarter of age on the prognosis of older US economic expansions is zero—that is, an additional quarter may slightly raise the average probability of death, but given the wide variation in age at time of death for the thirteen US expansions since 1945, statistically, one cannot rule out that the apparent effect is simply due to random chance and the true effect is zero. If anything, the apparent positive effect of age on the probability of death declines rather than rises as an expansion ages.

Since 1980, the effect of an additional quarter of economic expansion on the probability of recession is not only zero but also is statistically no different for a one-quarter-old versus a forty-two-quarter-old expansion, indicating that the probability of a recession is not a function of the age of the expansion at all. This reaffirms extensive earlier work on business cycle duration by Francis Diebold and Glenn Rudebusch.[13]

Figure 8 also illustrates that economic expansions in the United Kingdom since 1945 are even less age dependent than US expansions.[14] For the entire period, the effect of an additional quarter of economic expansion on the probability of recession in the United Kingdom is not only zero, but also is statistically no different in the one-hundredth quarter of an expansion than in the first.

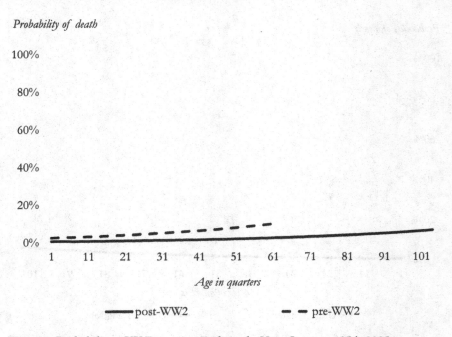

Figure 9: Probability a UK Expansion Ends in the Next Quarter, 1854–2025.

Furthermore, Figure 9 illustrates that this age independence of economic expansions in the United Kingdom is not a new phenomenon. Not only is the curve for the *pre*war UK economy flatter than that for the *post*war US economy—indicating greater age independence of UK expansions—but also the effect of an additional quarter on the life expectancy of an older pre-1939 UK expansion was statistically zero. In fact, the oldest *pre*war UK expansion lived to be older than the oldest *post*war US expansion—the sixty-two-quarter UK expansion from 1862 to 1878 lasted five years longer than the record forty-two-quarter US expansion that endured from 2009 through 2019.

In contrast, the same does not appear to be the case for the prewar US economy, as shown in Figure 10. Here, we see that the probability that a pre-1939 US expansion ended in recession was highly dependent on the age of the expansion. Indeed, at seventeen quarters (just over four years) old, the oldest pre-1939 US expansion had a statistically significant twenty-four-times-greater probability of ending in recession in the next quarter than an expansion that was only a year old.

However, scholars have questioned the accuracy of the NBER's official business cycle chronology for the period before 1927. For technical reasons, the official NBER chronology may tend to underestimate the length of pre-1927 expansions

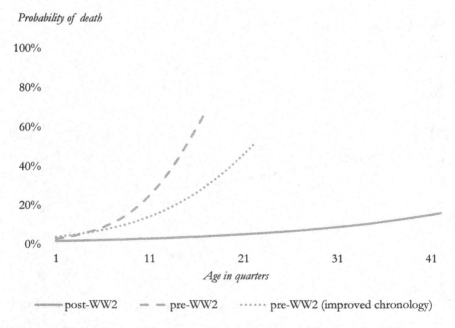

Probability of death

Figure 10: Probability a US Expansion Ends in the Next Quarter, 1854–2025.

while overestimating the length of pre-1927 recessions.[15] The NBER chronology thus implausibly implies that before World War I, the US economy was in recession nearly every other year.[16] To address this potential deficiency in the official NBER chronology, I therefore substitute an improved US recession chronology for the period from 1887 through 1940, which indicates that the longest economic expansion in the United States before World War II was a 5.5-year expansion from 1887 to 1893.[17]

As we can see in Figure 10, while the average probability of recession in any given year was still higher prewar than postwar and rising with age, using the improved chronology, the probability of recession in the pre-1939 period is substantially less a function of expansion age than using the older NBER chronology. Indeed, applying the enhanced chronology to 1887 through 1940—just over half of the nine decades between 1854 and 1940—more than halves the effect of expansion age on the probability of death, which implies that the apparent age dependance of prewar US expansions is simply an artifact of flawed measurement.

Going back even further in time using annual recession chronologies from 1700 through 1854, the same general pattern holds. Figure 11 plots the probability that a US (or colonial American) or UK expansion ends in recession in the next year as

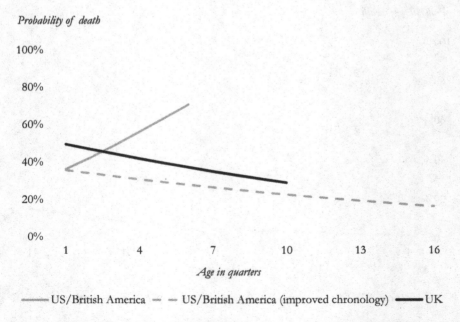

Figure 11: Probability a UK or US Expansion Ends in the Next Year, 1700–1854.

a function of the age of the expansion in years. While the probability of recession rises with expansion age for the United States and British America, the effect is not statistically significant.

Moreover, using an improved annual US recession chronology that avoids the false recession positives in the NBER-based chronology, though the slopes for both the United States / British America and the United Kingdom are statistically no different from zero, they actually slope downward.[18] This implies that, insofar as the probability of a US or UK expansion before 1855 ended in recession did depend on the age of the expansion, it was that expansions were in fact *less* likely to die the older they got. As we will find in Chapter 7, this can be entirely explained by a strong correlation during the eighteenth century between war and recession; an old eighteenth-century expansion was less likely to die for the simple reason that if it had already lived to a relatively advanced age, then it was likely to coincide with a period of peace.

In stark contrast to the seminal work of Diebold and Rudebusch, I thus find that the observation that economic expansions do not die of old age applies to the pre–World War II economies of both the United Kingdom and United States; it is not unique to the period since 1945. The same results hold if we use the end of the Great Depression in 1933 as the dividing line. Moreover, UK economic expansions are even more age independent than their US counterparts, with the probability of recession both lower across all ages and rising more slowly with age or, from a statistical perspective, rising not at all. That greater age independence of UK expansions likewise long predates the Great Depression and World War II.

Another way to test the Hayek et al. thesis that recessions are the result of the cumulative buildup of misallocations and malinvestments during an economic expansion is to determine whether the duration, rather than just the probability, of a recession is in any way related to the length of the preceding expansion. If indeed an economy becomes more distorted the longer it has been expanding, then one might reasonably expect that the volume of malinvestment and scale of misallocation requiring liquidation and reallocation when bust follows long boom must necessitate a correspondingly protracted recession.

Yet long recessions do not follow long expansions. Over the entire period since 1854, the effect of an additional quarter of economic expansion in the United Kingdom on the length of the subsequent recession was precisely zero. The result holds for both the period before World War II and since. Meanwhile for the United States, while the length of US expansions does explain variation in the duration of the subsequent recession, it is in the wrong direction to that predicted by those who think recessions are the inevitable consequence of cumulative distortions. Over the entire period since 1854, and particularly since the Great Depression, shorter US recessions actually follow longer expansions, a result that is statistically significant.

As the life expectancies of US and UK expansions have risen over time, the life expectancy of US recessions has become shorter, while the life expectancy of UK recessions has remained roughly the same or even risen. Before 1939, the average recession in the United States lasted twenty-one months, while the average UK recession lasted seventeen months. Since the war, US recessions have averaged just eleven months, while the average UK recession has lasted twenty-three months—longer the average *pre*war US recession. So while the United Kingdom has experienced fewer recessions since the Second World War, on average, those five postwar UK recessions lasted longer than their more frequent US counterparts.

But if older expansions are no more likely to die than younger expansions, are older recessions more likely to die on account of their advanced age? Figure 12 plots the probability that a recession ends in the next quarter as a function of the recession's age in quarters since World War II. The shorter curve for the United States ends at six quarters, corresponding to the length of the longest recession in

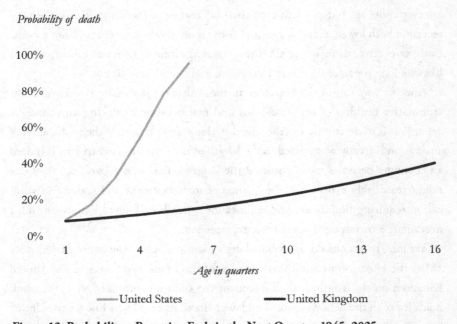

Figure 12: Probability a Recession Ends in the Next Quarter, 1945–2025.

the post-Depression United States—namely, the Great Recession from 2008 into 2009. This compares to sixteen quarters for the longest UK recession on record—the long, war-related recession that persisted from 1943 into 1947.

In contrast to postwar economic expansions, recessions in the United States have been highly age dependent since 1945. Each additional quarter of recession raises the probability of recession death, with the effect of recession age on the probability of death being highly statistically significant. At the 2008–09 recession's age of just six quarters, there was effectively a 100 percent probability that it would end in the next quarter, which indeed it did.

The same, however, cannot be said of recessions in the United Kingdom since the end of the war. Like UK expansions, postwar UK recessions appear at first to be largely age independent. As shown in Figure 13, though the probability that a postwar UK recession dies appears to moderately rise with the age of the recession, statistically, the effect of age is nil; the age of a UK recession has no effect on the probability that it ends in the next quarter with the start of an economic recovery. An additional quarter may raise the average probability of death, but given the wide variation in age at time of death for the six UK recessions since the start of World War II, one cannot rule out that the apparent effect is simply due to random chance.

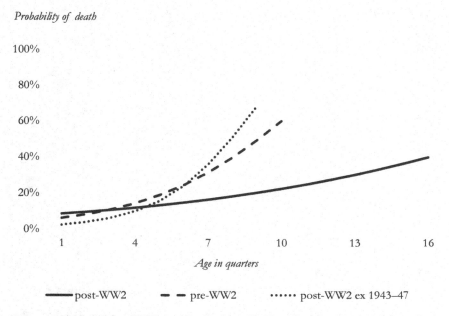

Figure 13: Probability a UK Recession Ends in the Next Quarter, 1854–2025.

However, this result is entirely driven by that extremely protracted, four-year wartime recession from 1943 to 1947. Excluding that historically unprecedented recession, we can with statistical confidence conclude that postwar UK recessions, like postwar US recessions, are highly age dependent.

Moreover, the age dependence of UK recessions is not a modern phenomenon, as also shown in Figure 13. Prior to the war, the probability that a UK recession ended in economic recovery was strongly and statistically significantly dependent upon the age of the recession. Furthermore, excluding the anomalously long 1943–47 wartime recession, the life expectancies of pre- and postwar UK recessions are remarkably similar—that is, UK recessions since World War II have generally aged no faster than earlier UK recessions.

Conversely, at first glance, the strong age dependence of post-1945 US recessions appears to be a relatively modern phenomenon, as seen in Figure 14. While the probability that a prewar US recession ended did rise with the age of the recession, the effect was modest and only weakly statistically significant. Similar results hold using the improved recession chronology in lieu of the official NBER chronology. However, this apparent age independence of prewar US recessions is entirely driven by the extremely protracted recession the United States suffered during the locust

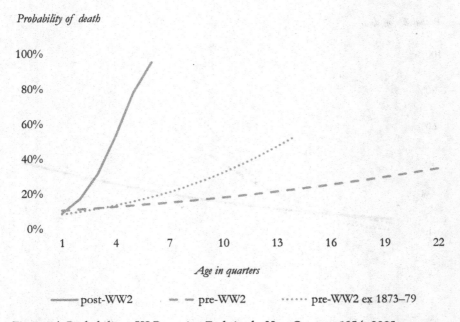

Figure 14: Probability a US Recession Ends in the Next Quarter, 1854–2025.

Probability of death

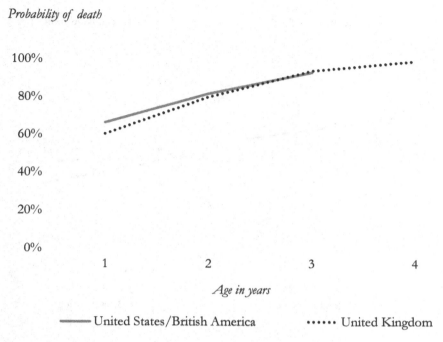

Age in years

———United States/British America   •••••• United Kingdom

Figure 15: Probability a Recession Ends in the Next Year, 1700–1938.

plagues of the 1870s, which we will examine in the next chapter. Excluding that record-long recession, not only were prewar US recessions age dependent, but also the positive effect of recession age on the probability of death was large and statistically significant using both recession chronologies.

Moreover, taking an even longer-run perspective using annual data and the improved annual US recession chronology, in Figure 15, we see that from 1700 until 1939, US and colonial American recessions were unambiguously age dependent. Indeed, over the entire 240-year period through the start of World War II, even including the long recession of the 1870s, the effect of recession age on the probability of death was positive and statistically greater than zero. Once again, these results hold for both economies if one instead uses the end of the Great Depression as the dividing line. Thus, like UK recessions, US recessions have always died of old age (or, perhaps more accurately given the shorter life expectancy of recessions relative to expansions, in childhood or adolescence).

An alternative test of whether expansions collapse under the weight of cumulative imbalances and misallocations is to examine whether longer expansions give rise to deeper—rather than just longer—recessions. In Figure 16, I therefore plot

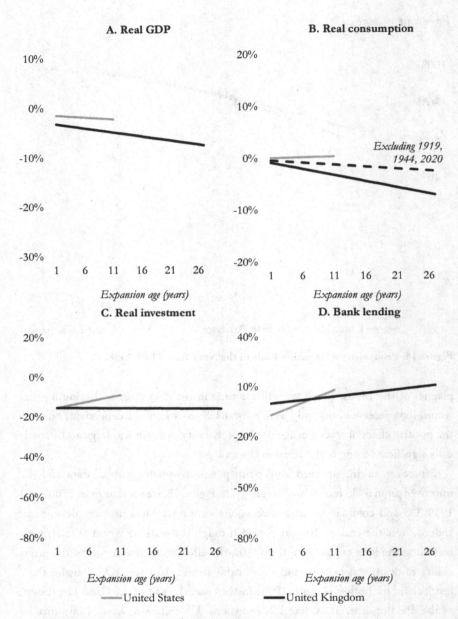

Figure 16: Effect of Expansion Length on Recession Depth, 1700–2020.

the estimated effect of the duration of an economic expansion on the peak-to-trough decline in real GDP, real consumption, real investment, and bank lending during the subsequent recession. The horizontal axes are scaled to reflect the maximum observed expansion age for each country, while the vertical axes are scaled to reflect the minimum and maximum observed declines from expansion peak to recession trough for each variable.

Figure 16 reveals that an additional year of economic expansion in the United States has no effect on the depth of the subsequent contraction in real GDP, real consumption, or real investment. In fact, an additional year of economic expansion in the United States is associated with a statistically significant *smaller* subsequent contraction in bank lending. Longer US expansions are simply not associated with deeper recessions.

For three of the four macroeconomic variables reported in Figure 16, we can also see that the length of a UK economic expansion is likewise entirely unrelated to the depth of the subsequent contraction. For real GDP, real investment, and bank lending, deeper UK recessions do not follow longer UK expansions. As in the United States, if anything, longer UK economic expansions are followed by shallower subsequent contractions in bank lending.

While an additional year of economic expansion in the United Kingdom is associated with a bigger decline in real consumption during the subsequent recession, we can see that this is entirely an artifact of the three largest contractions in consumer spending in UK history, when strict war-related rationing in 1919 and 1944 and pandemic lockdowns in 2020 severely curtailed consumer spending. But the enactment of such policies was entirely unrelated to the length of the preceding expansion; the length of the expansions ending in 1943 or 2019 in the United Kingdom did not cause wartime rationing in 1944 or pandemic lockdowns in 2020. Excluding these historically unique recessions beginning in 1919, 1944, and 2020, longer UK expansions are simply not followed by deeper contractions in consumer spending. Deeper busts do not follow longer booms.

––––––––––

To be sure, every economic expansion in both the United States and United Kingdom since 1700 has eventually ended in recession; as noted in the previous chapter, we have never observed an immortal expansion. So the cumulative probability that an expansion ends in recession eventually converges to 100 percent, albeit less quickly in the post–World War II than in the prewar period.[19] It is just that the incremental probability of death does not depend on the age of the expansion and, by implication, on how long potential misallocations and imbalances have purportedly been accumulating. Rather, earlier expansions converged on recession faster not because recession risk rose with the age of the expansion but rather because the probability of recession in any random year was simply higher. Recessions, in contrast, do die of old age, and always have.

Once again, there is something vaguely comforting, and certainly moralizing, in the Dorian Gray model of economic expansions. A cycle of debauchery, followed by absolution, followed by rebirth is at least predictable, and grants us hope for error correction and the economic equivalent of salvation. If fluctuations in economic activity are self-generating, if the bust is a direct consequence of the ill-conceived boom, then perhaps there is error in the latter that we might endeavor to correct. Indeed, it appeals to our very human longing for repentance and redemption. But like Peter Pan—and unlike Dorian Gray—economic expansions are innocent and do not sow the seeds of their own destruction.

3

THE PENITENT EXPANSION

It is not speed that kills, it is the sudden stop.

—BANKERS' ADAGE

The rise and fall of Alexander Fordyce was as spectacular as it was improbable. The youngest son of the former provost of Aberdeen and sibling of three distinguished Aberdonians—a philosophy professor, physician, and doctor of divinity—Fordyce was just four years old when his father died and responsibility for his education fell to his uncle, a notable historian and professor of classics.[1] Yet rather than follow his relatives into the academy, the young Fordyce decided to try his hand in the Aberdeen hosiery trade as an apprentice stocking manufacturer, before abandoning both hosiery and Aberdeen to venture south to London.[2]

In London, he found a job in Exchange Alley for a banker by the name of Boldero, operating out of a pub on Lombard Street called the Vine.[3] Demonstrating keen aptitude for arithmetic, by the age of thirty, Fordyce sufficiently impressed bankers Samuel Roffey, Henry Neale, William James, and Richard Down that they invited him to become a full partner.[4] It certainly did not hurt that the quantitatively inclined Fordyce was also "a handsome, dashing man, possessed of considerable energy of character, with a great flow of natural eloquence, and much suavity of manner."[5]

A keen investor, Fordyce regularly speculated on the London stock exchange. At considerable risk, his biggest bets paid off handsomely, particularly in 1763 and 1766, when he exploited early intelligence to go long on East India Company stock, netting approximately £200 million in 2024 pounds sterling equivalent.[6]

Purchasing a grand estate and villa in southwest London, the nouveau riche Fordyce hosted extravagant parties and banquets. He even built and personally funded an ornate, nearby church.[7]

Unsatisfied by material success, in 1768, Fordyce dropped a staggering £14,000 (£35 million in 2024 pounds sterling) on an unsuccessful campaign for a seat in Parliament.[8] Determined to succeed the next time, he financed the construction of a hospital and established multiple charities in his target borough, unabashedly declaring his aspiration to die a peer.[9] To that end, he even successfully courted the daughter of the Earl of Balcarras in his native Scotland and acquired several Scottish estates.[10]

But in early 1771, the wheels began to come off. As the threat of war between Britain, Spain, and France loomed, stock prices tumbled, with Fordyce losing more than the 2024 equivalent of £250 million.[11] To recover his losses, he began speculating with funds from the partnership. Alarmed, his partners confronted him and threatened to expose his questionable conduct, but Fordyce called their bluff, threatening to exit the partnership and "leave them to manage a business to which they were altogether unequal." He even produced a large pile of banknotes, which he had borrowed only hours before, as evidence of the financial resources at his disposal. They backed down.[12]

For months, Fordyce had been shorting East India Company stock—the very security on which he had first made his fortune going long—and ultimately shorted some £1 or £1.5 million (as much as £3–£4 billion in 2024 pounds sterling) worth of stock.[13] Amid reports the company was experiencing military setbacks and cash flow challenges, it was not an unreasonable directional bet. But as the stock mostly moved sidewise during the first half of 1772, the size of his levered position proved untenable.[14] On Monday, June 8, 1772, facing a margin call of 10 percent and nominal losses of £300,000, Fordyce disappeared, absconding to France and leaving his partners on the hook for £243,000.[15]

While remaining partners Neale, James, and Down initially insisted they would be able to meet creditor claims, as the extent of their liability became clearer, a commission of bankruptcy was issued against them, and, facing large withdrawals, they stopped payment on their liabilities on Wednesday, June 10.[16] With the stoppage of as prominent a banking house as theirs, and with Fordyce's name the counterparty on some £4 million worth of bills of exchange, the development sparked alarm in Exchange Alley.[17] Neale, James, Fordyce, and Down were known to have "had most extensive dealings" in the city, raising the distinct possibility that their suspension of payment could force others to suspend as well.[18] By the following Wednesday, at least ten London banking houses had stopped payment.

As bad as the situation was in London, it would soon be worse in Scotland. In remarkable time, a rider brought news of the collapse of Neale, James, Fordyce and Down to Edinburgh late Friday afternoon.[19] With the balance sheets of Scottish banks having expanded in the preceding years as they endeavored to meet the credit demands of the rapidly developing Scottish economy, the news was met with consternation. Unable to fund an expanding credit portfolio out of domestic bank deposits alone, Scottish bankers had increasingly turned to London for short-term funding. Unfortunately, not only had many relied upon Neale, James, Fordyce and Down for at least some of their short-term funding, but also a general freeze of interbank lending in London meant that many Scottish banks could no longer obtain funding.[20]

When markets reopened Monday, it was carnage. By the end of the day, the bank of Fordyce, Malcolm & Co.—to whom Alexander Fordyce owed approximately £64,000 and whose eponymous partner was a relative of the disgraced financier— had stopped payment, followed the next day by Arbuthnot and Guthrie.[21] But it was the following Monday, June 22 that would become known as "Black Monday."[22] The failure of Fordyce, Malcolm & Co. and their London correspondent, Fordyce, Grant & Co., was accompanied by the failure of the London arm of a second Scottish bank, Charles Fergusson and Company. Alexander Fordyce being a Scotsman and with the volume of Scottish bills being familiar to many London creditors, fears mounted that other Scottish banks could be adversely impacted by Fordyce's abscondence. Moreover, reports that the Bank of England had refused to discount Scottish bills drawn on very respectable London banking houses raised concerns that even otherwise sound London banks holding Scottish bills would be unable to fund themselves.[23]

According to one contemporary account, "Words cannot describe the general consternation of the metropolis on the 22d. An universal bankruptcy was expected, and the stoppage of every banker looked for."[24] Historian and politician Horace Walpole wrote at the time that it was even feared "there would be a run on the Bank of England itself as soon as the Dutch should learn the news."[25] In Scotland, meanwhile, of the eighteen private banking houses in Edinburgh, all but four stopped payment; by the time the crisis was over, sixteen Scottish banks would fail.[26] The eminent Scottish economist and philosopher David Hume noted with alarm to Adam Smith that the Carron ironworks company, Scotland's largest industrial enterprise, "is reeling, which is one of the greatest Calamities of the whole; as they gave Employment to near 10.000 people."[27]

With the sudden stop in credit, it was not just the Carron Company that struggled. Contemporary reports on the situation in Scotland observed that all construction and agricultural improvements, including the new town between Edinburgh and Leith, ground to a halt. Linen manufacturing plunged, while construction of the Forth and Clyde and Monkland Canals—the former crossing the entire width of the country from Edinburgh to Glasgow—stopped as the companies behind the enterprises struggled to obtain capital.[28]

Contemporaries were swift to ascribe the economic suffering to preceding excess and to call for penance. One writer to the June 1772 issue of *The London Magazine* suggested that "times of general distress are fit for general reformation and repentance." They even likened the economic calamity to the destruction of Lisbon seventeen years prior, when a catastrophic earthquake and subsequent tsunami and conflagration devastated the Portuguese capital, killing sixty thousand. Striking on the holy All Saints' Day and destroying nearly every church in the heavily Roman Catholic city, many viewed the disaster as divine punishment of one of the wealthiest cities in the world for "having advanced in luxury beyond the rules of prudence." The writer thus praised Portuguese merchants for availing themselves of the lesson and living more frugally, and suggested English and Scottish businessmen and financiers do the same.[29]

Adam Smith, whose pupil and patron, the twenty-six-year-old Duke of Buccleuch, was forced to sell the dukedom's fifty-six-room manor to cover his unlimited liability in a failed Scottish bank, had a more measured but still admonishing view. Referencing the period preceding the 1772 crisis, Smith noted that "many vast and extensive projects . . . were undertaken, and for several years carried on, without any other fund to support them" besides that which was raised at considerable expense from London. The "chimerical" and "bold" projectors, he suggested, "no doubt, had in their golden dreams the most distinct vision of this great profit." Unfortunately, "upon their awakening . . . either at the end of their projects, or when they were no longer able to carry them on, they very seldom, I believe, had the good fortune to find it."[30]

As the twentieth-century economic historian Henry Hamilton suggested in distinctly moral terms, "There had been a good deal of speculative activity in 1770–71 and this contained within itself the seeds of collapse . . . the boom was bound to burst."[31] Charles Kindleberger described the period leading up to the 1772 crisis as a broad-based boom, consisting of overinvestment in Britain in canals, houses, turnpikes, and other public works, all funded by excess credit.[32]

Yet while some investments may have been somewhat premature, far from misbegotten "golden dreams," in hindsight, they proved prescient. Work eventually resumed on the Forth and Clyde and Monkland Canals, which were completed in 1790 and 1794, respectively, and were commercially successful for more than a century. Smith, who died in 1790, was thus unable to see those large, capital-intensive investments come to fruition. New Town, Edinburgh, was completed in stages by the early nineteenth century, by which time the Carron Company had become the largest ironworks in Europe.[33] By 1800, Scottish linen production had nearly doubled from its precrisis level.[34] For the UK economy as a whole, despite a second recession in 1774 resulting from an adverse harvest shock, by 1775, real GDP had surpassed its 1771, precrisis level.[35]

As for Alexander Fordyce, after his abscondence to France, a commission of bankruptcy was issued against him, requiring that he surrender to bankruptcy commissioners on July 25, 1772, later extended by forty-nine days. On September 12, the disgraced financier thus duly appeared at London Guildhall, passing through a large crowd with considerable difficulty to answer his creditors.[36] As Fordyce was by then deficient some £100,000 for his liabilities, his assignees began the process of liquidating his assets.[37] Following a much-satirized sale of its contents, the grand estate was sold at auction to a London merchant for £20,000.[38] But in 1774, Fordyce's bankruptcy commissioners released him from the severer penalties that eighteenth-century bankrupts typically incurred. Moreover, like the Scottish economy, Fordyce himself appears to have recovered financially and lived his remaining years in relative comfort. He even again unsuccessfully contested the same Parliamentary seat of Colchester in 1780.[39]

The failure of Neale, James, Fordyce and Down is an example of what economic historian Hugh Rockoff has called "marquee failures"—high-profile failures of financial institutions with hitherto "outstanding reputations for prudence and financial acumen."[40] Indeed, contemporaries described the firm as "a house of the first eminence" with "most extensive dealings."[41] The failure of such a widely known, respected bank which "everybody trusted" could thus so undermine confidence in the entire banking system as to turn what otherwise might have been a period of tightening financial conditions into a complete seizure of credit markets.[42] And when the flow of credit stopped, there was no substitute—firms could not simply substitute retained earnings for short-term working capital. The shock may have been specific to the banking sector, but with high linkages to the rest of the economy and limited ability for firms to substitute away from credit toward alternative sources of funding, a sector-specific shock quickly had economy-wide repercussions.

As the old Wall Street saying aptly goes, it is not speed that kills, it is the sudden stop. There was no irrationally manic, unsustainable investment in British infrastructure in the lead-up to a June 1772 Judgment Day. The investment projects whose grand ambitions allegedly exceeded prudence were ultimately not only completed but were also profitable. The canals, new towns, ironworks. Even Fordyce's short of East India stock in retrospect proved discerning—over the next year and a half, East India shares plunged 40 percent, even as other UK securities declined by just 4–8 percent.[43]

What doomed Fordyce, his associates, and much of the Scottish banking system was not bad assets but unreliable liabilities; they were undone by a gradual, and then abrupt, unwillingness of their creditors to lend any further. In this chapter, we will find that while recessions swiftly spawn similarly moral-laden stories of unsustainably rapid boom and inevitable bust, with the benefit of retrospection, one can observe that recessions are not the consequence of the preceding expansion exceeding sustainable speed limits. Rather, they are the consequence of unanticipated stops.

A Scottish canal boom may have been the falsely accused and condemned suspect in the calamity of 1772, but almost a century later, it was an alleged US railroad boom, with the immediate handle of ruin, like Fordyce, an erstwhile financial rock star. Jay Cooke was a vaunted financial operative of reputable, albeit modest, origins. Descended from English Puritans who migrated to the colonies in the seventeenth century, he was born in Sandusky, Ohio, in the late summer of 1821. His father, Eleutheros Cooke, a lawyer and aspiring politician who was convinced he was cheated out of election to the Ohio legislature because voters misspelled his long and vowel-heavy name, decided to give his third child the short, simple name of Jay, after the first chief justice of the US Supreme Court.[44] No middle name.

The young Jay displayed a keenness, bordering on impatience, for business, selling small trinkets from a front window of his uncle's store from the age of nine or ten. By fourteen, considering himself "a full-fledged merchant," Cooke was hired and promoted to head clerk of a local dry goods, grocery, and hardware store within a year. After a brief but profitable stint in St. Louis, Missouri, Jay eventually moved east to Philadelphia, landing a position at a local bank, E. W. Clark and Company.[45]

It was a grueling job requiring long hours, close attention to arithmetic detail, and spotting counterfeit notes, for which the bank paid seventeen-year-old Jay a salary of $300.[46] But while Clark's commissions were modest, the rising volume of brokerage services meant they were soon grossing some $50,000 per day.[47] To his older brother Pitt—whom Eleutheros named in admiration of the younger UK prime minister—an eighteen-year-old Jay would write that "this business is always good and those who follow it always in time become rich."[48] By 1858, having amassed a fortune of some $250,000 ($150 million in 2024 dollars), the thirty-seven-year-old Jay Cooke announced his retirement.[49]

Yet retirement was short-lived. Just a couple of months before President Lincoln's first inauguration, Cooke started his own firm, Jay Cooke & Co. The decision was not so much with an eye for great profit but rather because both his nephew and own son had reached an age at which Jay thought it wise to expose the boys to the banking trade. But it was an opportune moment. With the outbreak of war, the state of Pennsylvania called for ten thousand men to serve as a reserve military force to guard the border, funded by a bond issue of $3 million. With the state already carrying a large debt and struggling to meet interest payments, default was openly discussed, prompting Pennsylvania bankers to insist that unless the bonds were sold below par—eighty cents or even seventy-five cents on the dollar—the issue would unquestionably fail.[50]

But Cooke held a contrarian view, convinced that he could sell the bonds at par on the back of a wave of patriotic zeal. When the state's skeptical banks persuaded the Pennsylvania legislature to amend the authorization bill to allow the bonds to be sold below par, Cooke noticed that the sloppily drafted amendment did not achieve its objective. Flagging the issue for the state attorney general and assuring him that they could sell the bonds at par, within days, Cooke's firm received a letter from the governor inviting them to underwrite the sale alongside the prominent Philadelphia firm of Drexel and Company.[51]

With Drexel, Cooke sold the entire $3 million issue in three weeks, placing advertisements of the names and amounts of all bond subscribers, and sending a message directly to Confederate president Jefferson Davis announcing that the North's millions stood ready "to suppress treason and rebellion."[52] In what would become a unique selling point, he even personally purchased $10,000 of the bonds; as a rule, Cooke only underwrote securities he owned himself.[53] Several months later, when federal censors failed to suppress news of the Union's defeat at the Battle of Bull Run, Cooke again took a contrarian view. As Philadelphia's financial community reeled in shock, Cooke used the defeat as a rallying cry to raise bond pledges of $1.75 million.[54]

His effectiveness eventually attracted the attention of the Lincoln administration, who were struggling to move a $50 million bond issue. Though Treasury secretary Salmon Portland Chase viewed Cooke as a potential rival, at Lincoln's prodding, he tapped Cooke, who in 1863 succeeded in selling $511 million in federal government bonds. So essential to the Union war effort did Cooke perceive himself to be that already in 1862, he personally lobbied President Lincoln to fire General George McClellan, a presumptuous liberty that thereafter left his relationship with the president distant. Nonetheless, he was veritably indispensable to the Union; all told, he sold over a quarter of the Union's wartime debt issuance.[55]

By now, Cooke was not just wealthy but spectacularly so. His primary residence, just north of Philadelphia, sprawled over two hundred acres, complete with a deer park, aquarium, pools, stables, faux Roman ruins, and a family mausoleum. The mansion itself was a gigantic, marble-walled edifice of seventy-five thousand square feet, fifty-three rooms, and a five-story tower, all lit by gas outlets and boasting a private telegraph line. He even donated $50,000 for the construction of a nearby Episcopal church.[56] "Like Moses and Washington and Lincoln and Grant," he declared, "I have been—I firmly believe—God's chosen instrument."[57]

Having heard tales of Lewis and Clark's expedition "almost firsthand" during his stint in St. Louis, Cooke was increasingly interested in the Northwest and Great Lakes regions, where he regularly hosted clergy on his own private island, "Cooke castle." In the summer of 1867, he visited Lake Superior, Wisconsin, and Minnesota, touring St. Louis Bay in a canoe paddled by Indigenous Americans. According to local legend, he even did so sporting a top hat, waistcoat, cloth shoes, and gold watch.[58]

The vast expanse from the Great Lakes to the Pacific boasted grain from the Dakotas and Great Plains, beef from Montana, timber in the forests of the Pacific Northwest, and a Great Lakes port on the eastern terminus and ideal natural harbor with access to the Pacific, Puget Sound, on the western. Settlers, he was convinced, would flock to the region. Cooke even eyed the unique geology of the area around Yellowstone Lake—recently detailed by the Cook–Folsom–Peterson Expedition—for its tourism potential. Indeed, he was a prominent advocate for designating Yellowstone a permanent public nature preserve, which Cooke-backed President Grant signed into law in 1872.[59]

Linking all this natural potential together was the bold venture of the Northern Pacific Railway. Promising to connect the Great Lakes in the east to the Pacific Ocean in the west, it was an audacious vision advocated as early as 1835, though only achieving a congressional charter in July 1864.[60] Moreover, unlike its more famous transcontinental predecessors, the Union Pacific and Central Pacific Railroads, Northern Pacific endeavored to complete the project without any direct federal government support.

Union and Central Pacific had enjoyed not only extensive federal land grants—which they could use as collateral for issuing private bonds, with the government retaining only a subordinate lien—but also received a loan for each mile of track. Depending on terrain, the US government granted Union and Central Pacific the 2024 equivalent of $50–$150 million in thirty-year government bonds, bearing 6 percent interest, for each mile of track.[61] The companies could then sell the bonds for cash, though would eventually have to repay the principal and interest upon maturity. In effect, it was a federally subsidized loan.

In contrast, raising funds exclusively through private capital markets proved more difficult than Northern Pacific's leadership and early investors expected, and it was almost six years before they even broke ground. But Cooke saw promise and, having pioneered innovations for successful large-scale securities issues during the war, was confident he could sell as much as $100 million in Northern Pacific bonds.[62] Passed over for Treasury secretary by President Grant, Cooke saw in the project his next calling to serve as God's "chosen instrument."

After commissioning his own reconnaissance party to inspect the proposed route—offending Northern Pacific board members and resulting in a costly eight-month delay—by mid-December 1869, Cooke made his decision.[63] On January 1, 1870, the railroad and the most prolific bond salesman in the United States inked a deal. Written on parchment, with sheets bound by ribbons of red, white, and blue silk, the agreement assigned Cooke & Co. as the sole fiscal agent for Northern Pacific, responsible for selling a staggering $100 million ($370 billion in 2024 dollars) in thirty-year bonds, which Cooke would acquire from Northern Pacific for eighty-eight cents on the dollar.[64] Moreover, not only were Jay Cooke & Co. to loan the railroad $500,000 (with the possibility of more) for construction and equipment, they were also to receive $200 in Northern Pacific stock as incentive compensation for each $1,000 in bonds sold.[65] Cooke and Northern Pacific's fates were heretofore inextricably linked.

Within thirty days, Cooke raised $5.6 million, and on February 15, the company broke ground for the first time.[66] That summer welcomed the formal opening of the Superior and Mississippi's line from St. Paul to Duluth. By the summer of 1872, track had reached Fargo, North Dakota; a year later, Bismarck.[67]

But challenges were already mounting. The hazards of surveying and building across such raw terrain proved more arduous and costly than Cooke had foreseen. Moreover, as the Northern Pacific encroached upon Indigenous hunting grounds, surveyors occasionally came under attack from Lakota Sioux led by the legendary Sitting Bull.[68] Sitting Bull's forces never numbered more than a thousand, and fewer than a dozen surveyors and their accompanying federal soldiers were killed in skirmishes while surveying the Yellowstone Valley, but lurid press coverage from embedded reporters and the flamboyant Lieutenant Colonel George Armstrong Custer adversely impacted bond sales, particularly in 1872.[69]

Cooke & Co. were further hit by a major setback when President Grant's Treasury secretary, George Boutwell—the man who pipped Cooke for the coveted cabinet position—decided he wanted to limit Treasury's reliance on Cooke and thus insisted on a consortium of US and European banks for a large US government bond issue. Boutwell authorized Cooke & Co. to sell just 8 percent of the issue.[70]

As Northern Pacific burned through cash during construction, they increasingly relied on overdrafts from Cooke & Co. to cover expenses, including payroll. Not only did Cooke now hold millions of dollars in Northern Pacific bonds, his equity in the company was also rising with each bond sale, and by August 1872, he had advanced $1.5 million in overdrafts.[71] The following month, Cooke's partner, Harris Fahnestock, warned him that "under no consideration must you allow your pride or interest in the company to place us in a position of even possible complications with its troubles."[72]

But worse was to come. That month, *The New York Sun* broke news of fraud by executives of the Union Pacific Railroad—Northern Pacific's older transcontinental rival—casting a reputational pall over all railroad investment projects.[73] When Congress authorized Union Pacific as the first transcontinental railroad in 1862, from Council Bluffs, Iowa, to San Francisco Bay, it did not permit them to sell their shares at less than par value and for anything other than cash.[74] But despite public subsidies, private investors were still unwilling to invest in shares of such a hazardous enterprise. Moreover, during the war, the federal government's insatiable borrowing requirements competed with private investment for American savings.

With the market appetite for Union Pacific stock just thirty cents on the dollar, by 1864, investors had subscribed to a mere $2,180,000 in Union Pacific stock, of which only $218,000 had been paid up.[75]

So to actually construct the railroad, in 1864, Union Pacific executives purchased a small, inactive corporation with limited liability called the Pennsylvania Fiscal Agency, which they renamed Credit Mobilier of America, and appointed themselves directors.[76] Credit Mobilier would invoice Union Pacific for construction contracts at inflated costs, which Union Pacific would then pay by cashable check. Credit Mobilier would in turn purchase Union Pacific stock and bonds—bonds secured by federal land grants—at par, which they could then sell in the open market below par.[77]

Thus, though neither Union Pacific nor Credit Mobilier had cash, aside from that they received from sales of mortgage-backed bonds or the loaned government bonds, they could fulfill the requirements of the act of incorporation that the company only sell shares at par and in cash.[78] The directors would then offset the losses from Credit Mobilier selling shares below par by inflating construction costs. By this setup, even if the railroad never became an operational, profit-making enterprise, the directors would at least have made money from construction.

Thus, having spent $100,000 grading twenty-three miles of line west of Omaha, Union Pacific vice president Thomas Durant informed one of the most eminent engineers in the country, Peter Dey, that they must abandon the route for a nine-mile detour that would garner an additional $144,000 in federal and mortgaged bond sales and more than one hundred thousand acres of additional federal land grants. Though Dey estimated that the line from Omaha through the Platte Valley could be constructed for $30,000 per mile, Durant instead opted for a contract with a local front man who offered to construct the stretch of rail for $50,000–$60,000 per mile, and insisted that Dey revise his proposal to $60,000.[79] Believing the cost "would so cripple the road that it would be impossible to ever build," in December 1864, Dey resigned "the best position in my profession this country has offered to any man."[80]

Contrary to later claims, no public funds were expended on the construction of the railroad, nor was the federal government defrauded—federal bonds were only lent after construction was certified, and only for the specific number of miles of track explicitly stipulated in the act.[81] But compounding the perception of corruption was that as they began to generate cash from bond and land sales, the company sought to buy goodwill among members of Congress through extensive bribes, particularly as the exigencies and public largesse of wartime yielded to peacetime austerity.[82]

Though Cooke and his brother initially observed the fallout from the scandal with detached amusement, by early 1873, they realized they were collateral damage. With elected representatives accused of accepting bribes, the new Congress held a series of highly publicized public hearings. Any hope Cooke had entertained of procuring a Union Pacific–style public bond loan for Northern Pacific was now decisively off the table; "To mention a railroad at Washington was enough to make bold men afraid."[83]

It certainly did not help that the scandal shortly followed another. In the summer of 1870, a strange man arrived in St. Paul, Minnesota. Registering at a local hotel as "G. Gordon, Scotland," the gentleman's "manner was unostentatious, but his distinguished bearing and evident superior birth and breeding soon drew attention to him as some one not of the ordinary."[84] When letters arrived from abroad bearing armorial crests and residents spotted an earl's signet on the stranger's horses' harness, the St. Paul rumor mill began to turn.[85]

Adding to the mystery was that just over two years earlier in a headline-grabbing tragedy, George Hamilton-Gordon, 6th Earl of Aberdeen, had gone missing, swept overboard during a violent storm en route from Boston to Melbourne.[86] Though the present gentleman, whose monogram also bore the name *G. H. Gordon*, refused to confirm whether he was a lord, he conveyed to officers of the Northern Pacific his interest in acquiring fifty or sixty thousand acres of land along the route of the Northern Pacific, where he might hope to resettle tenants from his overcrowded Scottish estates.[87] When the stranger deposited $20,000 or $40,000—accounts vary—in cash at the local Westfall Bank, it confirmed locals' suspicions.[88]

Northern Pacific promptly arranged a two-month excursion to assist the gentleman in surveying and selecting land. The party included six teams and a carriage, twelve men to pitch tents and arrange the camp, a French chef, waiters, and silk-glove service.[89] The company spared no expense, with China, fine silverware and linens, and champagne served at each meal. The company even organized a buffalo hunt and flew the banner of Clan Gordon.[90] The two-month expedition cost $15,000, with the party returning "half frozen" in November.[91] Though Lord Gordon Gordon found some seventeen thousand acres of suitable land along the Northern Pacific route, when he left Minnesota in January 1872, he did so without actually executing the transaction or acquiring title to the selected tracts.[92]

Instead, he traveled to New York City, settling into the luxurious Metropolitan Hotel, then managed by the son of infamous Tammany Hall boss William Tweed.[93] Over breakfast with editor in chief of the *New-York Tribune* and author of the famous slogan "Go West, young man," Horace Greeley, Gordon revealed that not only did he personally own $30 million in stock of the Erie Railroad but also controlled an additional $20 million on behalf of fellow English stockholders.[94] He conveyed his keenness to reorganize the management of the troubled railroad.[95]

It was enough of a hint to elicit a visit from the embattled president of the Erie Railroad, Jay Gould. Born to a small farmer and dairyman in upstate New York, by 1872, the diminutive, thirty-five-year-old Gould had established a reputation as one of the most brilliant financial minds of his generation.[96] Too short to meet the Union army's five-foot-three height requirement during the war, Gould instead made a career on Wall Street, where he outmaneuvered none other than Cornelius Vanderbilt to win control of the Erie Railroad by diluting the commodore's shares.[97] When Vanderbilt then tried to drive the Erie out of business by slashing his freight rate for transporting cattle from Buffalo to New York, Gould responded by buying up every cow for sale west of Buffalo and shipping them to New York. "Gould," Vanderbilt concluded, "is the smartest man in America."[98]

By 1872, Gould was again under pressure, this time from English investors increasingly impatient for dividends and tiring of the railroad's legal dramas. Without a serious game change, Gould was facing defeat at an upcoming election of directors and repeal of a clause that allowed him to avoid annual reelection contests.[99] He therefore visited Gordon at the Metropolitan. Over the course of a lively meeting, his lordship conveyed that with the sixty thousand shares under his control, he wished to reorganize the directorate of the Erie and resolve outstanding legal matters and the issue of the annual election of directors.[100] For that, he was willing to endorse retaining Gould as president.[101]

However, Gordon claimed his investigations into the railroad's affairs had cost him $1 million, for at least half of which he thought it reasonable the company reimburse him once new management, headed by Gould, was in place.[102] Anxious to lock down the support of the shares purportedly under Gordon's control, within a week, Gould personally delivered $500,000 in cash and railroad shares. When Gordon, upon tallying the notes and securities, noted a deficit, Gould, though disputing the error, returned promptly with additional cash. Asked for a memorandum of receipt, Gordon returned the cash, stating that his word of honor should be sufficient. Satisfied by his lordship's word, Gould set the bundle down before departing.[103]

Two weeks passed, during which time Gordon remained at the Metropolitan. But on March 22, Gould received word from a stockbroker in Philadelphia that Gordon had instructed him to sell some of the railroad shares Gould had delivered as part of the "reimbursement." Smelling a rat, Gould leaped to action.

Rather than proceed through the courts, Gould alerted Boss Tweed and brought a judge and the New York chief of police to a room in the Metropolitan adjoining Gordon's suite.[104] Making use of a connecting door, an intermediary discreetly informed his lordship that either he return the cash and securities, or else the police superintendent next door would escort him to Ludlow Street jail.[105] Gordon relented, returning $200,000 and agreeing to hand over signed instructions to his brokers to cancel the sales in Philadelphia.[106] However, once Gould left, Gordon immediately telegraphed to countermand the order and initiated legal proceedings against Gould.[107] Gould countersued "for felonious conversion" of the railroad shares, claiming Gordon had obtained them through false representations.[108] Arrested on April 9, Gordon avoided jail when two enemies of Gould's posted his $37,000 bail bond.[109]

The bizarre case generated keen public interest, with the press covering developments blow by blow.[110] At a pretrial hearing, Gould's counsel repeatedly subjected Gordon to questions about his family background and relations, which Gordon protested had no purpose other than to insult.[111] As far back as he could recall, his mother, relations, and acquaintances had addressed him as Lord Gordon Gordon.[112] To the court, he claimed that his baptismal name was Gordon Harcourt Gordon, though he had only ever used the Harcourt name in signing family deeds and in his monogram.[113] Regarding said monogram, he stated that it was merely a crest that he and his family had always used on notepaper.[114]

The majority of his alleged shares in the Erie Railroad he claimed to have received from his stepfather and trustee, Count Charles Henri De Crano, who resided in Notting Hill and Florence.[115] He also claimed to have acquired shares through his uncle, Charles Gordon, whose address he gave as the Place Vendôme in Paris, and that he controlled additional shares owned by his sister, the Baroness of Kurl in Italy.[116] Cablegrams sent to the American consulates in Paris, London, and Bern by Gould's legal team revealed no relatives by those names at the stated addresses.[117]

In any event, when the hearing resumed the next day, Gordon was gone, the night before having boarded a train to Canada. After miraculously evading an extrajudicial attempt to capture and extradite him to the United States, in September 1873, Gordon was arrested in Manitoba for giving false information to a magistrate, claiming his name was "Hubert Charles Gordon." But with the Crown declining to prosecute, authorities released him, and Gordon retreated to a small town twelve miles west of Winnipeg, where he stayed as a lodger.[118]

It was there that on August 1, 1874, "Lord" Gordon Gordon was confronted by two detectives operating on warrants for his arrest for larceny and forgery committed in England and Scotland.[119] As he began to dress for the journey, he noted that he required his Scotch cap, and made a dash to the bedroom. It was there, with his back to a wall, that Lord Gordon Gordon held a pistol to his right temple and, in the words of a contemporary report, "blew his brains out."[120]

The Gordon case was not mere curiosity. When news of the Gordon-Gould feud first broke in April 1872, it immediately amplified growing unease among European investors of the probity of investing in American railroads. Already by mid-May, *The Times* of London noted that not only was it cause for alarm that a potential fraud like Gordon could have swindled the president of a major American railroad company out of hundreds of thousands of dollars but also that industry insiders continued to seek the likes of Gordon and Gould at all. "We see," they wrote, "the Vice-President of one of the largest railway combinations in the United States, coming in haste from Philadelphia to introduce [Gould] to Lord Gordon; and Mr. Horace Greeley, the chosen candidate of one large section of the Democracy for the next Presidential election, forming one of the breakfast party" that first facilitated the Gordon-Gould agreement. Indeed, of the Liberal Republican Party's nominee for president in 1872, they wrote that "it does not appear that Mr. Greeley had the slightest improper view in consorting with Gordon and Gould."[121]

Moreover, *The Times* astutely observed that one of the bondsmen bailing Gordon out of jail was a certain Horace F. Clark, who just so happened to be the son-in-law of Gould's archnemesis Cornelius Vanderbilt.[122] To European investors, the whole affair thus appeared quite "wild west." Gould's extrajudicial methods to recoup his securities certainly did not help in the eyes of London observers. "We see," wrote *The Times*, "the New-York Superintendent of Policy and one of the New-York Judges still at [Gould's] service whenever he may 'want a man arrested.'"[123]

Of Gordon and Gould, *The Times* could not help but to conclude that there was a "fatal significance in the existence of a state of society in which association with such persons can be regarded as a matter of course." They advised readers that the situation called for "watchful attention on the part of all interested, not only in the affairs of the Pennsylvania Central Railroad and its multitude of dependent lines, but also in those of the Erie." Only if Gould were fully accountable to the law, and "those who still control the largest railway interests in the United States are no longer found to flock together with him as being of the same feather," might it "become possible for distant shareholders to regard their American investments without distrust."[124]

By August, Northern Pacific bond sales in London had thus slowed to a trickle. Cooke's London agent wrote to him on August 20 to advise that while "now and then" they may manage to sell a few hundred pounds' worth of bonds, "many days" would pass without a single sale. He assured Cooke that they were doing everything they could, declaring that "we are heart and soul with you." Nonetheless, when the Credit Mobilier scandal broke the following month, total bond sales had fallen from a peak of some $1 or $1.25 million per month in 1871 to just $173,000. Meanwhile, work on the St. Paul and Pacific Railroad stopped after Dutch bondholders refused to provide further credit. Northern Pacific, which held a controlling stake in the line, had to issue public statements in both the United States and Europe clarifying that they were not financially responsible for the struggling line.[125]

The federal government exacerbated the situation the following year when, keen to be seen as punishing the Union Pacific, they withheld interest payments on the company's land grant bonds. Cooke lamented the action to his brother, noting that it "is damaging our credit abroad." The bonds had long since been sold by Union Pacific to investors who were completely innocent of the Credit Mobilier scandal. "Who will buy a bond abroad," Cooke asked, if the government had now set the precedent that it could just arbitrarily freeze interest payments.[126]

Whereas Cooke had once hoped to sell $100 million in Northern Pacific bonds in Europe alone, by September 1873, he had managed to move just $25 million.[127] A major source of capital inflows into US railroad securities was then further squeezed when France successfully paid off the last of the five-billion-franc indemnity imposed on them by the German Empire after the latter's victory in the Franco-Prussian War.[128] So important had German capital—and the prospect of German immigration to the plains surrounding the Northern Pacific line—been that Cooke even named the future capital of the northern Dakota territory *Bismarck*, after the victorious Prussian chancellor. But with French indemnity payments concluding two years ahead of schedule, and following the failure of a major Austrian bank, German and Austrian investors grew increasingly reluctant to invest in US railroads.[129]

As railroad bond sales ground to a halt, to cover construction costs the Northern Pacific had to rely ever more on Cooke & Co. for cash advances. Cooke's associates pleaded with him to limit further advances, but to sell bonds, he needed construction of the line to proceed, and for construction of the line to proceed, Northern Pacific needed cash, which required bond sales.[130] By September 1873, Cooke & Co.'s balance sheet was thus effectively frozen with $1.5 million in Northern Pacific overdrafts and $9 million in unsold—and increasingly unsalable—Northern Pacific bonds.[131]

But perhaps the fatal blow came in the form of an odd, dark cloud that appeared in southwestern Minnesota on June 12, 1873.[132] As the cloud drew nearer, farmers could hear a dense roar and realized with horror that it was not a cloud at all but a vast locust swarm stretching for miles. Within hours, the "hoppers"—locusts are simply grasshoppers that have turned gregarious and swarmed—devoured knee-height fields of grass and wheat.[133] By the end of summer, swarms had infested nearly every settled region of Minnesota, Iowa, Dakota Territory, Montana Territory, Wyoming Territory, Colorado Territory, Missouri, Nebraska, Indian Territory (present-day Oklahoma), and Texas, completely decimating gardens and corn crops and destroying at least one-third of the grain crop.[134] Swarms even stretched as far north as Canada.

For an enterprise whose primary pitch to investors was that a railroad through some of the most fertile soil in the world would attract tens of thousands of settler farmers—like the tenants from "Lord" Gordon Gordon's overcrowded Scottish estates—the visitation of the locust plague was an existential shock, regularly covered in the contemporary press.[135] Indeed, over the next few years, the western migration on which Cooke had based his pitch plummeted, and many settlers left.[136] In Minnesota alone, Norwegian immigration plunged from 10,352 in 1873 to 4,601 in 1874, and did not increase again until 1880. The *Nordisk Folkeblad* and other Norwegian newspapers were flooded with letters from settlers to their families back home, explicitly lamenting the grasshopper plague. Many suffered credit foreclosure.[137] Irish immigration plunged from 77,300 in 1873 to 53,700 the following year and just 14,600 by 1877.[138]

With money markets tightening throughout the summer of 1873, cracks began to appear.[139] On September 8, the New York Warehouse and Security Company suspended payment after two of their directors were temporarily unable to repay a large loan they had collateralized with bonds of the Missouri, Kansas & Texas Railway.[140] Five days later, a second New York bank, the highly reputable Wall Street firm Kenyon, Cox & Co., also suspended. Like Cooke with Northern Pacific, Kenyon, Cox & Co. had extended large overdrafts to the Canada Southern Railway, which they needed to finance by selling bonds.[141] Unfortunately, word arrived from London early in the week that "it was impossible, at present, to negotiate more bonds," the difficulty having occurred "very suddenly" and occasioning "much surprise."[142]

Investors were already wary of Cooke's similar Northern Pacific problem as a massive, 275-wagon team made their way up the Yellowstone River to survey the proposed line.[143] Accompanied by the US Army—including four companies from Custer's infamous Seventh Cavalry—the expedition faced intense media interest throughout the summer of 1873.[144] On September 10, the press reported particularly violent encounters with hundreds of Sioux warriors, resulting in four US troops killed in action and two more wounded. Only after several hours of heavy fighting was Custer able to stabilize the situation by ordering a general charge.[145] The next day, *The Times* printed a stark warning about the difficulties facing the Northern Pacific. "If several thousand of our best soldiers," they asked, "can only hold the ground on their narrow line of march for a hundred and fifty or two hundred miles west of the Upper Missouri," then "what will peaceful bodies of railroad workmen be able to do, or what can emigrants accomplish in such a dangerous region?"[146]

Following the failure of Kenyon, Cox & Co. over the weekend, markets opened Monday to uncertainty and unease. As investors digested rumors that short selling by the always-scheming Jay Gould may have played a role in the firm's demise, Cooke entertained President Grant at Ogontz, his palatial north Philadelphia estate.[147] Wednesday morning brought further false rumors that the Chicago and Rock Island Railroad would miss its semiannual dividend payment.[148] Nonetheless, with some market commentators urging confidence, markets even rebounded upon opening on Thursday.[149]

Yet that morning, Fahnestock, Cooke's partner and head of the firm's New York office, invited the managers of three New York City banks to the New York office of Cooke & Co., whereupon he informed them that unless they could provide $1 million in credit by ten o'clock, the firm would have to suspend payment.[150] In the wake of recent developments, the New York branch had faced large drains of deposits, almost all of which were held by other banks (Cooke & Co. had hardly any individual depositors). With the Philadelphia office drawing on the New York branch to fund cash advances to Northern Pacific, the New York office was about to run out of funding.[151] When asked what Fahnestock could offer for collateral, he replied, "Nothing." The firm had no securities left to pledge. Unwilling to lend without security, the gentlemen left.[152] Shortly before 11:00 a.m., Jay Cooke & Co. thus ushered customers from their 20 Wall Street office and closed the doors.[153]

Fahnestock evidently having made the decision without consulting the firm's namesake, the news reached Cooke in Philadelphia via his private telegraph as a complete surprise.[154] Turning away from his colleagues to hide the tears pouring down his face, Cooke instructed the Philadelphia office to close as well. The office was in shock. No one had ever seen this titan of finance, the man who financed the Union war effort, cry.[155] Meanwhile, at the Washington, DC, branch of Jay Cooke & Co., where customers were calmly conducting business as usual, a middle manager suddenly entered the floor and loudly instructed them to "get out, gentlemen, get out—the orders are to close our doors!"[156]

Within minutes, the First National Bank of Washington—the largest bank in Washington—followed suit, as did fourteen banks for which Jay Cooke & Co. was financial agent, including five Freedman's Savings & Trust Company banks for emancipated slaves. A block away at a luncheon at the prestigious Willard Hotel, with General William Tecumseh Sherman holding court, Cooke's brother Henry received a telegram informing him of the Wall Street and Philadelphia suspensions. He thought it was a joke.[157]

To say that the failure of Jay Cooke & Co. sent shock waves through US financial markets would be an understatement. When Fahnestock brought notice of the suspension to the New York Stock Exchange, the president of the exchange initially refused to read it to members, the notice having been written in pencil rather than the requisite ink.[158] Between the time it took for Fahnestock to rewrite the notice, the entire exchange emptied as brokers stampeded to reach their offices.[159] Sell orders flooded the exchange. Within forty-eight hours, no fewer than seven prominent banking houses suspended payment.[160] Call money rates—the interest rates at which banks lent to brokers—surged from a typical 4.6 percent in August to a record 61.2 percent in September.[161] Commercial paper rates spiked from 7.1 percent in August to 14.3 percent in September and an almost unprecedented 16.5 percent in October.[162]

With a complete freeze in credit markets, the US economy would contract by 4.3 percent over the next year—the biggest decline in the US economy to date—with the economy enduring a protracted two- to five-year recession, depending on recession chronology. While the economy returned to growth in 1875, deflation

persisted, exacerbated by the demonetization of silver by the Coinage Act of 1873—
what critics later described as the "Crime of 1873"—and a decline in the number
of banks. From 1873 to 1876, the monetary base of the US economy contracted by
5.5 percent, and by the end of the recession, there were still sixty-nine fewer banks
than in 1873.

Further amplifying banking distress was that locust swarms disastrously
returned in 1874.[163] And again, in even greater numbers, in 1875. Indeed, one
swarm was so dense that it forced an entire Union Pacific train to stop for two
hours near Plattsmouth, Nebraska.[164] In some instances, tracks became so "slick
with grasshopper guts" that trains could not gain traction.[165] A Plattsmouth physician and amateur meteorologist, Dr. Albert Child, estimated that a passing
swarm—possibly the same swarm that stopped the Union Pacific train—spanned
a staggering 198,000 square miles—an area larger than the entire state of California.[166] At an estimated 12.5 trillion grasshoppers, "Albert's swarm" was likely the
greatest concentration of animals ever recorded.[167]

The renowned children's author Laura Ingalls Wilder recalled the locust plague
in her memoir of the pioneer Ingalls family's time in Minnesota. That summer,
Wilder's father had remarked on the dry, warm weather and was puzzled why the
"old-timers" called it "grasshopper weather."[168] But the "old-timers" were perceptive; the combination of dry summer conditions and southerly winds in the
summers of 1873, 1874, and 1875 were ideal for creating swarms of the Rocky
Mountain locust.[169] In wet soil, grasshopper egg pods are vulnerable to fungus,
hence populations can explode following successive dry summers.[170]

Recalling the event, Wilder described a cloud unlike any they had ever seen,
like snowflakes but larger and glittering in the sunlight. As the strange cloud drew
closer, something hit Wilders's head: the largest grasshopper she had ever seen. "The
cloud was hailing grasshoppers," she realized in horror. "The cloud *was* grasshoppers."[171] Another contemporary observer likened the noise of the myriad engaged
jaws to "the low crackling and rasping" of a prairie fire.[172] Families like the Ingallses
tried to cover crops with clothes and blankets, but the grasshoppers devoured the
textiles before consuming the crops. Crop damage in 1874 alone was estimated to
be $200 million—nearly $700 billion in 2024 dollars.[173] According to contemporary gallows humor, the hoppers "ate everything but the mortgage." Their waste
even poisoned wells and streams.[174]

Despite the confluence of unfortunate Acts of man, God, and Church, the
recession beginning in September 1873 has gone down in history as the almost

inevitable consequence of reckless overinvestment in railroads. Within hours of the September 1873 panic, Cornelius Vanderbilt noted to a reporter that "building railroads from nowhere to nowhere at public expense is not a legitimate undertaking."[175] The press generally concurred, lampooning Cooke and the Northern Pacific and describing the endeavor as "a wild scheme to build a railroad from Nowhere, through No-Man's-Land to No Place."[176] If not punishment, recession was at least atonement for prior prodigality.

This is a view largely held by economic historians today. "The railroad industry was by far the most important in generating the depression of the 1870s," reports *Business Cycles and Depressions: An Encyclopedia*. "The collapse of the railroad boom," the encyclopedia reports, "created a banking crisis in October 1873."[177] For the nineteenth century as a whole, Kindleberger makes frequent mention of "railroad booms" and "railroad manias," as do Michael Bordo and Antu Murshid in a 2001 edited volume by World Bank economist Stijn Claessens and future member of President George W. Bush's Council of Economic Advisers and the Bank of England's Monetary Policy Committee, Kristin Forbes.[178] From these and other sources, one might reasonably conclude that "overinvestment" in railroads was the cause of recession in the United States and/or the United Kingdom in 1847, 1853, 1857, 1869, 1873, 1882, 1887, and 1893.[179]

But is it possible that this suspected serial killer of economic expansions during the nineteenth century was in fact falsely accused and convicted? Despite being heavily invested in US railroads, the United Kingdom managed to avoid recession in 1873. Indeed, even the UK affiliate of Jay Cooke & Co., Jay Cooke, McCulloch & Co., survived the crisis without suspending payment.[180]

Moreover, if, as both contemporary and secondary sources would lead one to believe, railroad "booms" or "manias" gone bust were to explain nineteenth-century recessions of which irrational railroad exuberance was a purported cause—then one would logically expect to observe sharp spikes in railroad mileage to be followed by long plateaus of no new railroad mileage. Yet when one plots the cumulative miles of railroad track in the United States, the result is remarkably smooth; there is simply no protracted pause, let alone contraction, in the volume of railroad track in the country.

Quite the contrary, US railroad mileage exhibits a striking fealty to a stable, long-run upward trend that plateaus in the early twentieth century, as shown in Figure 17. Though the pace of building slowed during the recessionary years of 1873 through 1875, by 1876, it had already begun to increase more rapidly, and

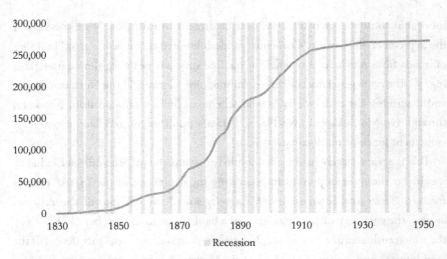

Figure 17: Cumulative Miles of Railroad Built in the United States, 1830–1952.
(National Bureau of Economic Research, "Miles of Railroad Built for United States
(A02F2AUSA374NNBR)," Federal Reserve Bank of St. Louis; National Bureau of Eco-
nomic Research, "NBER Based Recession Indicators for the United States from the Period
Following the Peak through the Trough (USREC)," Federal Reserve Bank of St. Louis.)

in 1879, more than five thousand miles of track were completed. By the end of the
decade, the cumulative mileage of installed railroad track in the United States was
already back to where it would have been had it continued uninterrupted along its
long-run trend. By the early 1880s, it was slightly above trend.

Even looking at railroad bond yields and stock prices, it is not entirely clear
that the run-up to 1873 constituted a speculative boom succeeded by bust.[181]
While railroad equity prices were above their long-term trend, they had already
peaked in September 1872—a full year before the onset of the recession. Bond
yields (inversely related to bond prices) were in fact above trend, consistent with Jay
Cooke struggling to sell Northern Pacific bonds.

If economic fluctuations throughout the latter half of the nineteenth century
were driven by booms and busts in railroad construction, then we would expect
to observe railroad stock and bond prices moving in tandem as part of a general
appetite for railroad securities. But over the sixty-year period since 1857, railroad
bond yields and equity prices were generally positively correlated—bond prices
tended to fall below trend when stock prices rose above trend. This would suggest
that above-trend equity prices were more about shifts in the capital structure—on

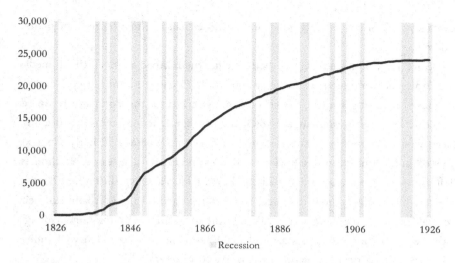

Figure 18: Cumulative Miles of Railroad Built in the United Kingdom, 1826–1926. (National Bureau of Economic Research, "Increases in Length of Railway Line Opened for Traffic for Great Britain (A02085GBA374NNBR)," Federal Reserve Bank of St. Louis; Stephen Broadberry et al., "Dating Business Cycles in the United Kingdom, 1700–2010," *Economic History Review*, January 27, 2023, ehr.13238. For missing years between 1868 and 1872, and 1912 and 1920, I interpolate using the average annual increase during the corresponding number of years on either side of the missing years.)

account of changing preferences for debt versus equity—than broad, irrational railroad manias.

Smooth fealty to trend in railroad construction is even more evident in the United Kingdom, where there is no evidence whatsoever of a stepwise increase in the cumulative mileage of railroad track (Figure 18). Rather, one observes a smooth increase in the volume of installed track that increases slowly at first, then more rapidly, then gradually slows in the early twentieth century. But there is no evidence of the sort of fits and stops that one would associate with a boom-bust cycle of railroad construction.

Indeed, quite the contrary. The recession of 1847 is commonly attributed to a "boom" or "mania" in railroad construction in the 1840s in the United Kingdom. Yet here again, there is evidence of continuity rather than an abrupt and protracted pause after a period of purported overbuilding. In the five years preceding the 1847 crisis, annual railroad construction in the United Kingdom averaged 400 miles per year; in the five years after the crisis, railroad construction was higher, not lower, averaging 678 miles. Hardly what one would expect in the aftermath of manic boom gone bust.

As for Jay Cooke and the Northern Pacific, the railroad survived the immediate panic and continued construction, but by 1875 entered bankruptcy.[182] Expeditiously emerging from a bankruptcy reorganization, the company resumed construction, and in mid-August 1883, the two construction teams approaching from west and east met near Independence Creek in Montana.[183] Early the next month, in the foothills of the Rocky Mountains and ninety-one years after Thomas Jefferson—who both commissioned the Lewis and Clark expedition and floated the idea of a highway from the Great Lakes to the Pacific—the railroad held their formal "golden spike" ceremony.[184] Former President Grant did the honors alongside the Northern Pacific's president, Henry Villard, and surveyor Henry Chandler Davis, who had driven in the first spike thirteen years earlier.[185]

It was a high-profile affair attended by three thousand guests and featuring a traditional war dance by Indigenous Americans from the Crow Reservation.[186] But even as dignitaries gathered to celebrate successful completion, media continued to lampoon the railroad's alleged folly. In a contemporary cartoon for the satirical magazine *Puck*, Villard appeared as a huckster circus promoter enticing unsuspecting investors into his tent for the "Great Northern Pacific R. R. Show," with promotional posters boasting of "a genuine English lord" and a trombonist playing from *New York Sun* sheet music, nods to the Gordon and Credit Mobilier scandals.[187]

Though the railroad reentered bankruptcy reorganization following the recession of 1893, it again reemerged and became a profitable concern after New York banking giant John Pierpont Morgan acquired a controlling stake and amalgamated Northern Pacific with other lines under his control.[188] Indeed, Northern Pacific would eventually merge with the Great Northern Railway and Chicago, Burlington and Quincy Railroad to become the Burlington Northern Railroad, which in turn merged with the Atchison, Topeka and Santa Fe Railway in the 1990s to become the railroad behemoth BNSF Railway.[189] Already a major shareholder, during the 2008–09 recession, Berkshire Hathaway acquired the remaining 77 percent of the combined railroad they did not already own.[190] Thus, the allegedly feckless ambition of Jay Cooke's gamble would not only come to successful completion but also was ultimately acquired by one of the most legendary value investors of all time, Warren Buffett. So much for the notion of a "wild scheme to build a railroad from Nowhere, through No-Man's-Land to No Place."[191]

Cooke himself desperately attempted to avoid relinquishing control of his enterprises. But when he was unable to obtain unanimous consent from creditors, on November 26, 1873, a judge declared him bankrupt. Forced to surrender his beloved palatial estates, he retreated to a cramped little cottage, stung by the world's verdict on him and resigned to seeing out his days in quiet retirement.[192]

Yet after a few years and multiple inquiries from a former associate of the Northern Pacific campaign, Cooke agreed to entertain an unlikely venture.[193] To the considerable surprise of his brother and son, the man who for his entire career had discouraged mining investments now expressed interest in a Utah silver mine and set off to examine the property himself.[194] Though his former associate died en route, Cooke continued the expedition, which involved a 150-mile wagon journey to reach the site of the mine, some 225 miles southwest of Salt Lake City.[195]

With characteristic meticulousness, Cooke engaged engineers to assess the mine and hired lawyers to scrutinize the title to the property.[196] Convinced of the mine's potential should it benefit from a rail link, Cooke obtained from the mine owners—four feuding Irishmen and Scotsmen—an option to buy half the mine in exchange for a pledge to use his financial acumen to secure a railroad connection to Salt Lake City. Persuading the owners to supply a quarter of the capital, Cooke then returned east via Salt Lake, where he convinced the Mormon Church—which owned an existing nearby rail line—to extend that line and invest another quarter of the required capital for the new link to the mine.[197]

For the remaining 50 percent, Cooke then had an ingenious idea. Back east, he visited the office of the president of the Union Pacific, Sidney Dillon. Dillon immediately greeted him warmly, noting that Cooke, back when he was still with E. W. Clark, had once "saved" him with a $20,000 loan at a critical moment during the construction of the drama-filled Erie Railroad. Dillon thus offered whether there was anything he could do now to return the favor.[198]

When Cooke laid out his proposition, Dillon briefly excused himself before returning with none other than the infamous Jay Gould.[199] Spotting a buying opportunity during the depths of the 1873 railroad panic, Gould had quietly bought one hundred thousand shares in the Union Pacific at "crisis prices" of fifteen to thirty dollars per share, which subsequently recovered to seventy-five dollars.[200] The next year, working with Dillon, he became a director.[201]

Remarkably, the two Jays had never met. Now face-to-face with the "Little Wizard," Cooke presented his maps and made the case for laying 176 miles of track to the Horn Silver Mine.[202] He contended that the new line could be constructed at

$10,000 per mile using old iron rails and rolling stock stored by the Union Pacific in Utah.[203] "With us three men," Cooke asserted, "there is not the least occasion for a written agreement." Surprisingly for a man who had been swindled by Gordon's word just a few years prior, Gould agreed, pledging the remaining 50 percent and assuring that the cash would be available "as fast as it is needed."[204]

Both men upheld the verbal contract, and not only was the railroad successfully completed but the mine became a tremendous boon. Nicknamed the "Bonanza mine," according to one contemporary source, it was "unquestionably the richest silver mine in the world."[205] In 1879, Cooke successfully organized a syndicate—anchored by an heir to the Cunard Steamship fortune—to exercise his option to buy half the mine, earning almost $1 million from his commission and share.[206] Through his prescient investment in the Bonanza mine and facilitation of a connecting railroad, Cooke had managed to achieve one of the most remarkable financial comebacks in US history. With his newly regained wealth, he was even able to reacquire his beloved estates.[207]

Living to read about the golden spike ceremony for the Northern Pacific—by which point, creditors of Cooke & Co. had been paid $1.56 for each dollar owed—Cooke would see out his days in semiretirement. He gave readily to charity and led a local Bible class, and in the summer of 1891 finally made a trip over the length of the Northern Pacific. Enjoying farming, hunting, and fishing, and adhering to the end to an outmoded cape cloak and wide-brimmed hat, Cooke died peacefully in February 1905 at the age of eighty-three.[208]

Like Fordyce, Cooke had bounced back spectacularly from a devastating economic setback. Despite the false narrative of an ill-conceived and unsustainable railroad boom, so too had Northern Pacific. As we will find in the next chapter, this is the norm rather than the exception to economic recessions; while busts do not follow booms, sharp rebounds typically follow sharp economic contractions.

Moreover, while the marquee failure of Cooke & Co. and consequent sudden stop of credit in September 1873 may have constituted the precipitate shock of the 1873 recession, as in 1857, that shock was itself the adverse consequence of a series of overlapping and interacting events. It would also in turn be succeeded by subsequent shocks, not least the providential revisitation of locusts. Once again, an unhappy recession was unhappy in its own way.

4

OSCILLATIONS OR PLUCKS

> Everywhere we witness to-day a decided decline of the
> "skyscraper principle," not only in architecture but also
> in the economic sphere. Almost everywhere it becomes
> a fact beyond dispute that dimensions have outgrown
> the optimum size and must now be reduced, by a very
> painful process, to more reasonable proportions.
>
> —WILHELM RÖPKE, 1936

From the Hong Kong office of UK investment bank Kleinwort Benson, Andrew Lawrence had a ringside seat during the 1997–98 Asian financial crisis. The young real estate analyst would later recall that at the time, he could not help but to look around at the various tall buildings under construction in the region.[1] Just a year before the onset of the crisis, construction of the soaring Petronas Towers in Kuala Lumpur concluded; two years later, the Malaysian structures officially became the tallest buildings in the world, breaking the twenty-five-year record of Chicago's Sears (now Willis) Tower.

In a report with a somewhat cheeky title—"The Skyscraper Index: Faulty Towers," a reference to the 1970s Monty Python comedy classic *Fawlty Towers*—Lawrence noted that new world records for building height seemed to eerily correlate with the onset of major economic crises. Construction of the Singer Building and Metropolitan Life Insurance Company Tower—which successively held the title of tallest building in the world from 1908–09 and 1909–13, respectively—seemed to roughly coincide with the US panic and recession of 1907. Completion

of Metropolitan Life's successor as world's tallest building, the Woolworth Building, then preceded by just months the onset of the 1913–14 US recession. But perhaps most spectacularly, Lawrence noted that the Great Depression coincided with
the completion of a slew of record- or near-record-breaking skyscrapers—the Bank
of Manhattan Building (1930), Chrysler Building (1930), and the iconic Empire
State Building (1931).

Even completion of the World Trade Center (1972) and Sears Tower (1974) cor-
responded roughly with the onset of the severe 1973–75 recession. To this igno-
minious list one could then add not only the Petronas Towers but also Dubai's Burj
Khalifa—currently the tallest building in the world—whose completion in October 2009 approximately coincided with the 2008–09 global financial crisis and a
near default by the Dubai government.

Lawrence's Skyscraper Index was not entirely novel. More than half a century
earlier, Ralph Nelson Elliott postulated that stock prices followed a predictable
pattern—what became known as the *Elliott wave principle*, or *Elliott wave theory*—
of collective, periodic waves of optimism and pessimism. Successive "impulse"
and subsequent "corrective" waves, Elliott found, are not only observable but
even predictable using the Fibonacci sequence.[2] The Elliott wave pattern was thus
evocative of Schumpeter's nesting of short-run Kitchin, medium-run Juglar, and
long-run Kondratiev waves. Though Elliott himself focused on meticulous analysis of annual, monthly, weekly, daily, hourly, and half-hourly charts of stock price
movements, subsequent proponents of Elliott wave theory popularized what they
dubbed the "skyscraper indicator," an apparent correlation between construction of
the world's tallest buildings and stock market peaks.[3]

The logic underlying Lawrence's Skyscraper Index or Elliott wave theorists' skyscraper indicator is straightforward—record-breaking construction activity reflects
undue or otherwise excessive investor optimism, which inevitably yields to corrective pessimism. Hence cyclical oscillations of overconstruction followed by crisis.
While acknowledging that his Skyscraper Index was just a correlation, Lawrence,
like Elliott wave proponents before him, suggested there was much to be learned
from the seemingly periodic fluctuations in investment in tall, signature pieces of
real estate investment.

Indeed, later commenting on what he called an "unhealthy correlation," Lawrence explained that the "unhealthy part" was "that skyscrapers seem to mark a
very large economic boom that typically ends in large recession." Their construction thus tended to correlate with bigger, credit-driven economic expansions that

were then succeeded by relatively sharp, deep contractions. Thus, in Lawrence's view, it was not that tall buildings per se were the cause of recessions but rather that they were symptomatic of broader unsustainable booms of which they were merely the proverbial tip of the iceberg.[4]

Despite its intuitive appeal, the prognostic power of the Skyscraper Index as a literal, physical indicator is not borne out by econometric evidence. Analyzing the timing of the announcement and completion dates of record-breaking skyscrapers, recent scholars have found negligible correlation with the peaks or troughs of economic fluctuations. Moreover, they discovered that while record-breaking building height and economic output are cointegrated—both variables change over time, but over the long term, there is a stationary relationship between them—building height does not *cause* output. In fact, they find the exact opposite—it is output that "causes" building height—that is, an expanding economy predicts building height rather than building height predicting a contracting economy.[5]

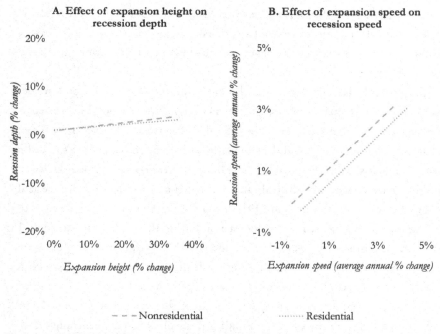

Figure 19: Real Value of Private Buildings at End of Expansion and Subsequent Recession, 1925–2024. (Bureau of Economic Analysis, "Real Net Stock: Private Fixed Nonresidential Structures (Bil. Chn. 2017$) [EPNSH@USECON]," Haver Analytics; Bureau of Economic Analysis, "Real Net Stock: Private Fixed Residential Structures (Bil. Chn. 2017$) [EPRH@USECON]," Haver Analytics.)

Yet though the literal, physical height of an economic expansion may not predict the likelihood or depth of a subsequent contraction, could the underlying logic that bigger or faster expansions in the total volume of building activity precede deeper or faster contractions nonetheless be true? What about economic activity more broadly—do higher or faster economic expansions precede deeper or faster economic contractions? And what about the converse—are faster, deeper contractions succeeded by slower, shallower recoveries?

If the logic underlying the Skyscraper Index is true, then we would expect to observe that a higher trough-to-peak increase in the total stock of buildings in the economy during an economic expansion would be followed by a deeper peak-to-trough decline during the subsequent recession. In Panel A of Figure 19, I therefore plot the trough-to-peak "height" of the increase in the real value of buildings during an economic expansion against the peak-to-trough "depth" of the subsequent contraction for every US recession since 1925. For both residential and nonresidential buildings, I add a dotted trend line that best fits the observed data points. If the logic underlying the Skyscraper Index were true, then we would expect to observe a downward slope to the observed data points—bigger trough-to-peak increases in building values associated with bigger peak-to-trough declines during the succeeding recession.

Surprisingly, the solid lines in Panel A of Figure 19 reveal that, for both residential and nonresidential structures, there is effectively no relationship whatsoever between the cumulative change in the real value of constructed buildings at the end of an economic expansion and the cumulative change by the end of the succeeding recession. Statistically, the slopes of those lines are precisely zero. Moreover, we can see that in most recessions, the real value of private buildings does not decline at all.

As shown in Panel B of Figure 19, nor is a faster growth rate of building activity associated with faster rates of contraction during the succeeding recession. In fact, the upward-sloping lines in Panel B indicate that faster trough-to-peak annual growth rates in the real stock of private residential and nonresidential structures are on average succeeded by *slower* peak-to-trough annual declines, and the results are statistically significant. Here again, we can see that in most recessions, the real value of buildings continues to rise. Building busts simply do not generally succeed building booms.

In contrast, as shown in Figure 20, building *booms* can succeed building *busts*. Though the years preceding the Wall Street crash of 1929 are widely described as the "Roaring Twenties," characterized by Gatsbyesque excess, it is important to

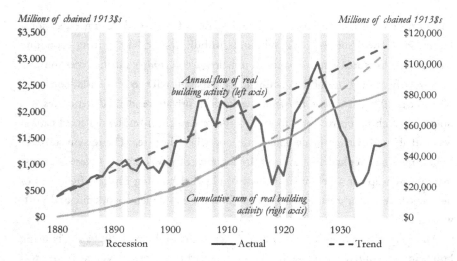

Figure 20: Real Building Activity in the United States, 1880–1939. (National Bureau of Economic Research, "Total Nonfarm Building Activity for United States (A02241US-A398NNBR)," Federal Reserve Bank of St. Louis. Considering the relatively small sample size, I estimate a linear time trend in the level of building activity.)

recognize that the 1920s followed nearly a decade of major armed conflict, post-war depression and a wave of strikes, and a deadly pandemic. Figure 20 reveals that because of these exogenous disruptions, real nonfarm building activity in the United States—which in the thirty years through 1910 had roughly adhered to a long-term trend—plunged after 1914. After bottoming in 1918 at the end of World War I, the level of real building activity in the United States then rebounded sharply, and by 1925–26 had recovered to where it would have been had it continued uninterrupted along its prewar trend. However, thereafter, building activity began to decline, a full three years before the peak of the infamous stock market "bubble."

Moreover, Figure 20 also shows that at no point during the 1920s did the *cumulative* volume of building activity in the United States exceed where it would have been had building activity continued uninterrupted along its prewar trend. In 1927 and 1928, the cumulative volume of real building activity had merely recovered to 90 percent of where it would have been had the pace of building continued at its pre-1914 trend. With the recession beginning in 1929, it then plummeted. By the eve of World War II, following two deep recessions in 1929–1933 and 1937–38, the cumulative volume of building activity in the United States was still 24 percent below prewar trend.[6] Rather than *negative* deviations from trend during recessions constituting error corrections to *positive* deviations from trend during expansions, Figure 20 instead suggests that rebounds in building activity during economic recoveries constituted error corrections to below-trend *troughs* during recessions.

Similarly, though numerous eminent scholars still refer to residential construction in the 1920s as a *housing boom*, the stock of private residential structures was only just catching up to trend in 1929—the real stock of residential fixed capital was still about 2 percent below long-run trend when the Great Depression started.[7] What may have looked like a boom in the *flow* of new housing investment was merely catch-up for a below-trend *stock* of physical housing capital after years of deficient investment during World War I and the subsequent pandemic and post-war recession.

More recently, despite a common characterization of the mid-2000s as a housing boom in the United States, such a boom is not conspicuously evident in the real stock of private residential fixed capital in the run-up to the 2008–09 housing-cum-financial crisis. After rising to a level that was a modest 1.1 percent above long-run trend in 2004, by 2006, the real volume of the US housing stock had returned exactly to trend; by 2007, it was already 0.9 percent below trend. Over the course of the ensuing 2008–09 recession, it would fall almost 3 percent below trend and only recover to trend in 2013. In fact, at no point during the entire century since 1925 was there an instance of the residential, nonresidential, or even overall private capital stock rising above long-run trend during an expansion to a level to which the trend did not subsequently rise and then exceed within a matter of a few years.[8]

Indeed, over the entire century since 1925, not only is the actual stock of private fixed capital barely distinguishable from trend but also was slightly below trend in 1928 and 1929 on the eve of the Great Depression. Similarly, the stock of private business fixed assets specifically was slightly below trend in 1928, and just 0.6 percent above trend in 1929. As we saw with railroad mileage in Chapter 3, the real volume of the private real capital stock—both overall and when broken down into its business and residential components—exhibits remarkable fealty to trend. The same pattern is robust to using alternative statistical techniques for estimating long-run trend.[9]

Thus, while it may have been premature, precocious, or otherwise hasty, one would be mistaken to conclude that the capital stock created by the US economy was ever, in retrospect, "excessive."[10] Indeed, by 2022, purchasing a new home in the United States cost nearly six years of income for the typical household, the highest ratio on record and up nearly 20 percent since the eve of the 2008–09 crisis.[11] Meanwhile, the price of an existing home topped five years of a typical family's income, likewise up by more than a fifth since 2007.[12] Millennials struggling to afford their first home in 2022 would thus hardly conclude that there was too much homebuilding in the 2000s; if anything, they might justifiably conclude there was too little.

But what about economic activity more broadly, beyond just construction? Former US Treasury officials Larry Summers and J. Bradford DeLong once likened economic fluctuations to "symmetric oscillations about a rising trend"[13]—that is, economic fluctuations may be characterized as alternating peaks and troughs in overall economic activity that over time average out to a long-run trend, with higher trough-to-peak expansions balanced proportionately by deeper peak-to-trough contractions. Buildings notwithstanding, is this the essence of economic fluctuations—oscillating periods of above-trend activity followed by periods of proportionately below-trend activity, as shown in Panel A of Figure 21?

Or is Figure 20 more representative not just of construction specifically but of economic activity more generally? In contrast to the notion that phases of contraction and stagnation succeed phases of unsustainable commercial excitement and overbuilding, what if recessions are simply negative deviations from the norm of positive trend growth, rather than corrections of irrational or otherwise unsustainable positive deviations from trend?

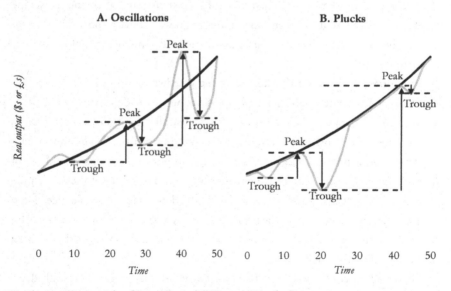

Figure 21: Illustration of "Oscillations" Versus "Plucks."

In contrast to the "oscillationist" view of economic fluctuations, Milton Fried-man suggested that economic fluctuations might instead be akin to random, downward "plucks" of a taut but elastic string. If one were to pluck the string at random points and with random force, then the amplitude of the rebound would be exactly symmetrical to the amplitude of the downward pluck. But the ampli-tude of the downward pluck would be entirely unrelated to the prior position of the string.[14]

Friedman surmised that such plucks might be analogous to economic contrac-tions. In a recession-less world, economic growth would proceed uninterrupted along long-term trend, with trend growth determined simply by growth of available labor, capital, and technological knowledge, corresponding to the upwardly sloping solid black lines in Panels A and B of Figure 21. Long-run trend would thus be analogous to a string stretched tautly upward. But occasionally, that trend may be interrupted by adverse shocks that generate temporary, negative deviations—that is, downward plucks of varying force that are randomly distributed across time, as shown in Panel B of Figure 21.

While the height of the recovery from a downward pluck would thus mirror the depth of the preceding contraction, the same would not be true in reverse; the amplitude of the downward pluck would be entirely unrelated to the amplitude of the preceding expansion. The resulting pattern would thus differ markedly from that generated by the oscillationist view of recessions implicit in the Skyscraper Index, in which periods of rapid, unsustainable growth above trend would be sym-metrically followed by periods of stagnation and underemployment of comparable depth and severity.

In Figures 22 and 23, I therefore examine whether variation in the height and speed of an economic expansion explains variation in the depth and speed of the subsequent contraction. If recessions are fundamentally about oscillations, then we should expect the depth and speed of a recession to mirror the height and speed of the preceding expansion. Higher, faster trough-to-peak expansions should be fol-lowed by deeper, faster peak-to-trough contractions. But if instead they are funda-mentally about plucks, then we should expect the depth and speed of a recession to have no relation whatsoever to the height and speed of the preceding expansion, but that the height and speed of a recovery will be symmetrical to the depth and speed of the preceding contraction.

Figure 22 plots the estimated relationship between the peak-to-trough depth of an economic recession against the trough-to-peak height of the preceding

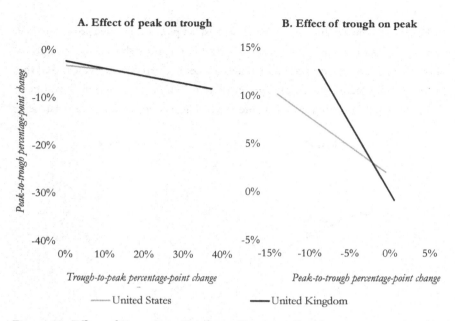

Figure 22: Effect of Expansion Height on Recession Depth, 1700–2020. See data appendix.

expansion for every recession with available data since 1700, looking separately at real GDP, real consumption, real investment, and bank lending. The horizontal axes are scaled to reflect the minimum and maximum observed height for each variable, while the vertical axes are scaled to symmetrically match the horizontal. Under the oscillationist view of recessions, each of the lines relating expansion height to recession depth should be downward sloping from top left to bottom right, reflecting the effect of higher expansions on deeper recessions. If recessions are about plucks, then the lines should be perfectly flat, reflecting no relationship between expansion height and recession depth.

As is clearly visible from the flat lines in Figure 22, the depth of US and UK recessions is entirely unrelated to the height of the preceding expansion. For all four variables, statistically, the effect of a higher peak on the subsequent trough is precisely zero. Indeed, for US investment and bank lending, if anything, higher peaks are on average associated with slightly *shallower* troughs, though the effects are not statistically significant. These results are a stark contrast to the pattern we would expect to observe under the oscillationist theory of recessions, wherein each of the solid lines should instead be sharply downward sloping—higher expansions followed by deeper contractions.

Rather than height and depth, Figure 23 instead plots the average peak-to-trough rate of contraction during an economic recession against the average trough-to-peak growth rate during the immediately preceding expansion. We can see that for the United States, the average growth rate in GDP, consumption, investment, and bank lending during an economic expansion has no relationship whatsoever

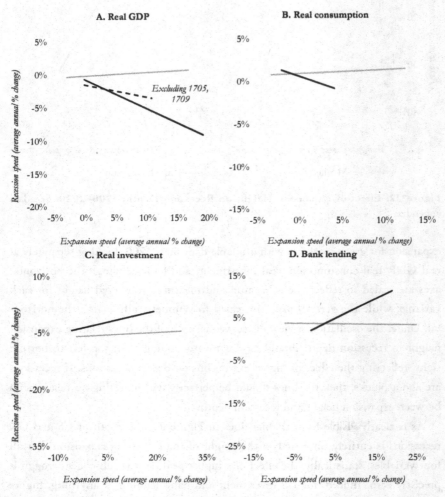

Figure 23: Effect of Expansion Speed on Recession Speed, 1700–2020. Faster expansions of real investment in the United States appear to be associated with modestly faster contractions, though the effect is not statistically significant and is entirely driven by the unique 1945 recession, during which private investment rebounded sharply after contracting during World War II. In Panel C, I therefore exclude the 1945 US recession from the graph and reported trend. See data appendix.

to the average rate of contraction during the subsequent recession. Though faster investment expansions appear to be associated with modestly faster contractions, the effect is not statistically significant and is entirely driven by the 1945 recession at the end of World War II, when private investment rebounded sharply after contracting during war. Excluding 1945, the slope is perfectly flat.

The same pattern holds in the United Kingdom for consumption, investment, and bank lending. While faster contractions in real GDP in the United Kingdom appear to follow faster expansions (Panel A), this is entirely driven by extreme harvest fluctuations during the wartime recessions of 1705 and 1709.[15] Excluding those two unique recessions, for GDP as well, faster UK expansions have no effect on the speed of the subsequent contraction.

Figures 22 and 23 are thus wholly consistent with a plucking model of economic fluctuations and wholly inconsistent with the notion that fluctuations are driven by oscillations. The height and speed of an economic expansion generally have no relation to the depth and speed of the subsequent recession in either the United States or the United Kingdom. In particular, credit "booms" simply do not precede the average recession in either the United States or United Kingdom. Nor is prior "overconsumption" a primary cause of recessionary fluctuations. Indeed, in many recessions, real personal consumption expenditures do not decline at all, as consumers utilize savings and credit to maintain consumption as much as possible in the face of adverse income shocks.

But what about the effect of the depth and speed of a recession on the height and speed of the subsequent expansion? Do long, slow recoveries follow deeper, faster recessions? Or, per Friedman's plucking hypothesis, is the opposite the case?

Figure 24 plots the estimated relationship between trough-to-peak height of an economic recovery against the peak-to-trough depth of the preceding recession for every recession with available data since 1700, again looking at real GDP, consumption, investment, and bank lending. The axes are scaled symmetrically to reflect the minimum and maximum observed heights and depths for each variable. Under the oscillationist view of recessions, each of the lines relating recovery height to recession depth should be flat, reflecting the hypothesis that the height of an expansion explains the depth of a recession, not the other way around. But if recessions are about plucks, then the lines should be downward sloping, reflecting the effect of deeper recessions on steeper recoveries.

In both the United States and United Kingdom, the downward-sloping solid lines in Panel A of Figure 24 indicate that deeper peak-to-trough declines in

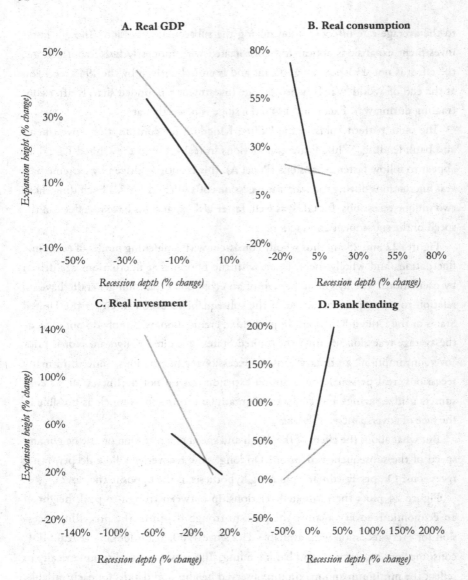

Figure 24: Effect of Recession Depth on Expansion Height, 1700–2020. Reported trends for UK real investment and bank lending in Panels C and D of Figure 24 exclude the atypically long recovery from the long, war-related recession from 1944 through 1947. This unique recession and subsequent expansion was such an extreme outlier that its inclusion even reverses the sign of the estimated trends for consumption and lending and substantially steepens the estimated negative slope for investment. For ease of visual inspection, the vertical axis in Panel A is truncated at a level that excludes the recovery from the 1944–47 UK recession and the wartime recovery from the 1938 US recession; however, both are included in the calculation of the reported trend lines. See data appendix.

real GDP are associated with higher trough-to-peak increases during the subsequent recovery. Indeed, statistical tests indicate that a 1 percent deeper peak-to-trough decline in real GDP is associated with an approximately 1 percent higher trough-to-peak increase during the subsequent recovery—that is, the amplitude of the rebound is symmetrical to the amplitude of the contraction. The same pattern holds for real investment in both economies (Panel C), with a 1 percent decline in real investment in the United States even associated with a greater than 1 percent rebound.

Panel B of Figure 24 reveals that contractions in real consumption are generally much smaller in magnitude than contractions in real investment or real GDP, consistent with households using savings and credit to sustain their level of consumption during recessions. For the United States, the depth of the peak-to-trough contraction in consumption is essentially unrelated to the height of the subsequent recovery.

For the United Kingdom, the relationship between recession depth and expansion height is sharply negative, indicating bigger rebounds following bigger contractions in consumption. However, this is mostly driven by the United Kingdom's atypically long recovery from the protracted, war-related recession from 1944 through 1947, during which—as we will see in Chapter 7—the UK government imposed strict consumer rationing. In 1948, the UK economy then entered an exceptionally long recovery that only ended in 1973 with the Arab oil embargo during the Yom Kippur War. Excluding this outlier, like in the United States, the depth of the peak-to-trough contraction in UK consumption is essentially unrelated to the height of the subsequent recovery.

In contrast to the other three variables, as can be seen in Panel D, deeper contractions in bank lending are associated with shallower recoveries in lending in both economies, though the result is only statistically significant for the United States. Thus, while credit busts generally do not follow credit booms, deeper contractions in bank lending do often precede weaker credit recoveries.

Friedman's plucking model also suggests that faster contractions should generally be followed by faster recoveries. Figure 25 therefore plots the average trough-to-peak growth rate of an economic recovery against the average peak-to-trough rate of contraction during the preceding recession. The downward sloping lines in Panel A of Figure 25 indicate that faster recessions are indeed typically followed by faster recoveries, with faster peak-to-trough rates of decline in real GDP associated with faster trough-to-peak growth rates during the subsequent rebound.

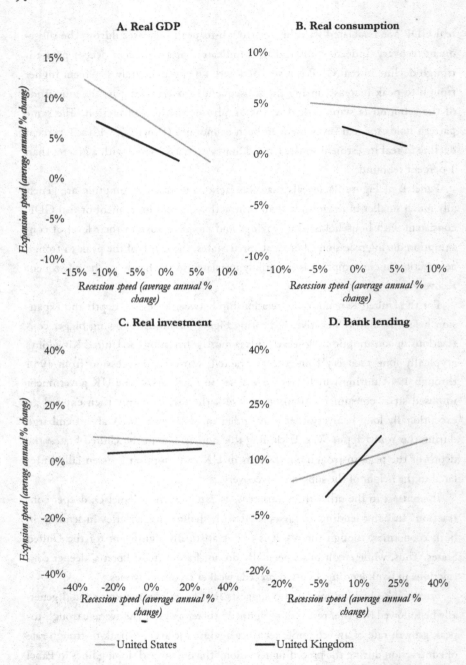

Figure 25: Effect of Recession Speed on Expansion Speed, 1700–2020. Reported trend for US real investment in Panel C of Figure 25 excludes the recovery from the unique 1945 recession, during which private investment rebounded sharply after contracting during World War II.

However, Panels B and C suggest that what holds for the economy overall does not necessarily hold for consumption and investment specifically. While faster contractions in UK consumption are generally followed by faster rebounds (Panel B), statistically the speed of contraction in consumption and investment during recessions on average has no relation to the speed of the subsequent rebound (Panels B and C). Faster declines in bank lending during recessions are in fact typically followed by slower lending growth in both the United States and United Kingdom (Panel D).

Nonetheless, Figures 24 through 25 are generally consistent with a plucking model of economic fluctuations, and again wholly inconsistent with the oscillationist view. Deeper, faster recessions are generally associated with higher, faster rebounds in both the United States and United Kingdom, while higher, faster expansions have no effect whatsoever on the depth or speed of the subsequent recession.[16] Indeed, while on average the height and speed of an economic expansion can explain less than a tenth of the variation in the height and speed of the subsequent recession, the depth and speed of a recession can explain almost a third of the variation in the height and speed of the subsequent recovery.

In the acclaimed 2009 book *This Time Is Different*, Carmen Reinhart and former International Monetary Fund chief economist Kenneth Rogoff found that recoveries from recessions associated with financial crises tend to be slower and more protracted.[17] However, Michael Bordo and Joseph Haubrich more recently

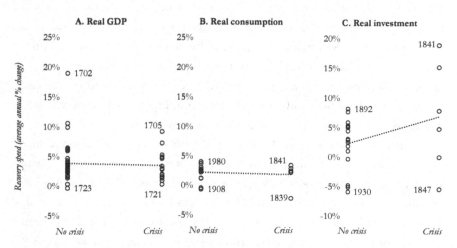

Figure 26: Effect of Financial Crisis on Speed of Recovery, 1700–2019. See data appendix. (Stephen Broadberry et al., "Dating Business Cycles in the United Kingdom, 1700–2010," *Economic History Review*, January 27, 2023, A3–5.)

found that recessions associated with financial crises were generally followed by more rapid recoveries. Bordo and Haubrich identify three exceptions to this general pattern: the recoveries from the Great Depression, the relatively mild recession of the early 1990s, and the 2008–09 financial crisis.[18] But Bordo and Haubrich only looked at the United States, and only back to 1882. So, who is correct, Reinhart and Rogoff or Bordo and Haubrich? Do financial crises result in slower or faster recoveries?

Utilizing new UK data, in Figure 26, I report the trough-to-peak average annual rate of growth during recovery from every UK recession since 1700 through 2019, categorized by whether the recession was accompanied by a financial crisis.[19] Results indicate that contrary to both Reinhart and Rogoff and Bordo and Haubrich, whether a recession was caused by a financial crisis statistically has no effect whatsoever on the speed of the subsequent recovery in either real GDP, real consumption, or real investment. If anything, UK recessions coincident with financial crises were historically associated with faster rather than slower recoveries in real investment (Panel C).

Instead of a simple binary indicator for whether a recession was caused by a financial crisis, one can also estimate the effect of the peak-to-trough decline in bank lending on the speed of the subsequent recovery to see whether slower economic recoveries follow deeper credit contractions. Under the Reinhart and Rogoff thesis, bigger contractions in bank lending during a recession should be followed by slower recoveries in GDP, consumption, and investment, with the opposite pattern prevailing under the Bordo and Haubrich thesis. Yet here again, in contrast to both Reinhart and Rogoff and Bordo and Haubrich, for the United Kingdom, the effect of a faster contraction in lending during a recession on the speed of the subsequent recovery in real GDP, consumption, and investment is precisely zero. In other words, over the long run, bigger credit contractions on average have no effect on the speed of the subsequent recovery.

A final, more nuanced variation of the oscillationist theory of economic fluctuations is that what determines recession severity is not the peak *level* of economic activity but rather distortions between the separate decisions of consumers to save or consume, and of businesses to produce consumer goods for today or to instead invest in capacity to produce a greater volume of consumer goods in the future. This was the essence of various interwar business cycle theories such as Hayek's.[20]

As discussed in Chapter 2, Hayek contended that when the market rate of interest was lower than the real rate of return on capital, it would allow businesses to bid resources away from the production of goods for immediate consumption toward longer-term investment projects capable of producing a greater volume of consumer goods in the future. Because lower rates would inflate the value of longer-term investments, those projects would temporarily be able to bid resources away from projects with shorter lead times. But eventually, scarcity in the supply of consumer goods relative to demand for them would generate inflation in the price of consumer goods.[21] Unless additional credit were forthcoming at an ever-faster rate, the rising price of consumer goods would ultimately pull resources back toward the production of consumer goods today, thereby forcing liquidation of misbegotten longer-term investments.

If Hayek's "concertina effect"—as one contemporary economist dubbed his theory of alternately lengthening and shortening production periods—were characteristic of economic fluctuations, then we would expect to observe that larger increases in the ratio of investment to consumption during expansions are followed by larger decreases during the subsequent contraction.[22]

Panel A of Figure 27 therefore plots the peak-to-trough decline in the ratio of investment to consumption against its trough-to-peak increase during the preceding expansion for every UK recession since 1830 and every US recession since 1925. If recessions constitute remedial declines in the ratio of investment to consumption, then we would expect the lines relating recessionary changes in that ratio to changes during the preceding expansion to be sharply downward sloping; bigger trough-to-peak increases associated with bigger peak-to-trough declines. If recessionary changes in the investment-to-consumption ratio are fundamentally unrelated to changes in that ratio during the preceding expansion, then the lines should be flat.

However, if recessionary declines in the investment-to-consumption ratio are not remedial but instead temporary negative deviations from trend, then we should observe bigger increases in that ratio to follow bigger declines. Panel B of Figure 27 therefore plots trough-to-peak increases in the investment-to-consumption ratio against its peak-to-trough decrease during the preceding recession.

Figure 27 fundamentally contradicts Hayekian theory. Statistically, the effect of a larger increase in the investment-to-consumption ratio during a US expansion on the peak-to-trough decline during the subsequent recession is precisely zero (Panel A). In the United Kingdom, while a larger increase in the investment-to-consumption ratio is associated with a modestly bigger decline during the subsequent recession, the effect is entirely driven by two unique exogenous shocks—the

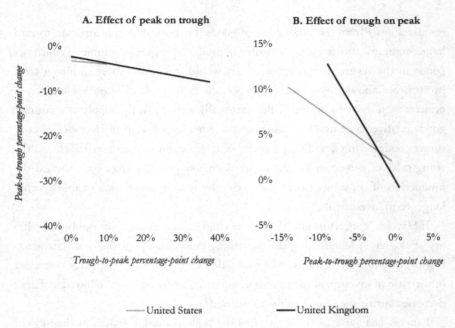

Figure 27: Effect of Investment/Consumption Peak on Investment/Consumption Trough. See data appendix.

wartime recession beginning in 1944 and the recession following the 1973–74 Arab oil embargo. Hardly evidence that there was something inherently flawed in the balance between investment and consumption during the preceding expansions.

In stark contrast, Panel B of Figure 27 indicates that larger recoveries in the ratio of investment to consumption follow deeper recessionary declines. This pattern holds even if one excludes the exceptionally long recovery from the deep 1944 UK recession at the end of World War II. For the United Kingdom, statistical tests even indicate that the true relationship between the decline in the investment-to-consumption ratio during recessions and rebound during the subsequent recovery may in fact be one-for-one. This would imply that all of the increase in the investment-to-consumption ratio during an economic expansion is merely recouping the decline in the ratio during the preceding recession.

Moreover, whereas the increase in the investment-to-consumption ratio during expansions can explain just 0.5 percent (United States) to 14 percent (United Kingdom) of the variation in its decline during the subsequent recession, the opposite is true for recessions. The depth of the peak-to-trough decline in the investment-to-consumption ratio during recessions can explain 34 percent (United Kingdom) to

50 percent (United States) of the variation in its trough-to-peak increase during the subsequent recovery. In short, relative changes in consumption versus investment during economic recessions are not correcting imbalances during the prior expansion; rather, relative changes in consumption versus investment during economic expansions are correcting imbalances during the prior recession. Pluck.

———————

There is a seductive, even physical logic to the Skyscraper Index. It is not just the intuitive appeal to the law of gravity; while height-defying buildings may not literally rise and fall over the course of economic expansions and contractions, groundlessly optimistic valuations and the corresponding pace of activity certainly can. It is also that the index suggests there are observable, measurable dimensions of an economic expansion that can presage the contours of the succeeding recession. Moreover, like apparent asset "bubbles," it lends itself to post hoc reasoning. Over the past century and a half, there have been fewer height records—or, for that matter, conspicuous asset bubbles than recessions—so it is not difficult to find a recession with which to retrospectively pair a new record within a couple of years' proximity.[23]

Like Andrew Lawrence surveying the Hong Kong skyline during the 1997 Asian crisis, prominent interwar economist Wilhelm Röpke thus similarly surmised that an apparent trend toward bigger, taller buildings and bigger economic establishments more generally during the 1920s derived from a certain "megalomania" characteristic of the "'gay twenties.'" Everywhere, Röpke suggested, physical and economic dimensions more broadly had outgrown their optimal size, with the consequences becoming "only too manifest" during the succeeding depression. He even wondered if engineers might be able to testify "as to how far enterprises have been inflated beyond the technical optimum scale by a pathological predilection for mere size, by considerations of prestige and other irrational motives."[24] Hence, for Röpke as for Lawrence, skyscraper height was merely symptomatic of a much broader, deeper iceberg of overinvestment or otherwise unsustainable economic expansion.

Yet as we have seen in this chapter and the previous, there is nothing in the height—physical or otherwise—speed, or duration of an economic expansion that can explain variation in the depth, speed, or duration of the succeeding economic contraction. The contours of economic contraction are completely unrelated to the contours of the preceding expansion. Fundamentally, economic recessions are not about the alternation between positive and negative deviations from a trend but rather temporary, negative deviations from that trend. Plucks rather than oscillations.

But if recessions are fundamentally about plucks rather than oscillations, then who, or what, is doing the plucking? Is it merely coincidental that some of the largest, sharpest contractions discussed in this chapter were the result not of prior economic distortions but of the extreme distortions of war, while some of the biggest, fastest expansions were simply recoveries therefrom? These are all questions we will explore in the next three chapters.

5

TURF, COAL, AND OIL

Many tradesmen [were] frozen out of their trades
and employ, and starved for want of fire; coals and
turf being at double prices, and obliged to wait two
days at the pits or [ere] their turn came to be served.

—WILLIAM STOUT, 1739

While real GDP per capita in the United States declined more than 5 percent in the four years from 1872 through 1876—with a trough of nearly 10 percent in 1875—across the pond, the UK economy powered through, extending what would ultimately be a then-record sixteen-year-long expansion. Though unemployment increased and real GDP per capita grew at an anemic pace, real GDP and consumption both rose continuously throughout. Just seven UK banks failed during the four-year period, during which time, the UK economy expanded by more than 6 percent.

Unfortunately for the British, just as the Rocky Mountain locust plague dissipated and the United States finally entered recovery, the United Kingdom was struck by an environmental shock of their own from a rather unlikely source. Whereas successive dry summers ("grasshopper weather") had brought the locust plague to the United States, it was after two successive cool, wet summers that, in 1879, the British Isles were afflicted by the worst outbreak of the fungus-like oomycete *Phytophthora infestans*—the same blight that catastrophically devastated Ireland in the 1840s—since the Great Famine itself. Indeed, the severity of the 1879 blight was estimated to have been as grave as that of 1845–47, when a quarter of Ireland's population emigrated or died of hunger and disease.[1]

While the British and Irish economies of 1879 were far less vulnerable to a resurgence of blight than they were in 1845, the effects were still devastating. In Ireland, where at least half the potato crop was lost and the remainder was of small and deficient quality, poorhouses were inundated by destitute Irish.[2] Though officials reported no evidence of outright starvation, hunger and privation were extensive, with the Irish population in workhouses jumping 15 percent and those receiving some form of "out-door" relief spiking nearly 30 percent.[3]

Even in England, early estimates indicated that the unusually cool, wet conditions of the summer of 1879 had reduced the wheat harvest by 50–70 percent over the prior year, and the ears that did survive were generally small.[4] While England could afford to import grains, the consequent drain of gold from London to New York generated considerable financial pressure, contracting the UK monetary base and contributing to deflation of nearly 5 percent.[5] For the year as a whole, UK agricultural output plunged 20 percent.[6]

As the UK unemployment rate jumped from under 6 percent in 1877 to nearly 8 percent in 1879, political and social unrest mounted. One Poor Law inspector in Ireland observed that "debts have increased; credits are almost stopped; capital is scared away, and difficulties which might have been surmounted by mutual forbearance and good-will" had instead "been intensified by setting class against class, and giving cause for the general feeling of 'insecurity and uncertainty' which prevails."[7] Though landlords on both sides of the Irish Sea slashed rents amid the economic "depression," the price of imported food rose, and Irish landlords faced mounting threats of rent boycotts and violence.[8] The incumbent UK government of Conservative leader Benjamin Disraeli was shortly routed in the general election of early 1880.

After collapsing during the American locust plagues of 1873–76, UK emigration to North America surged in response to the 1879 UK agricultural depression.[9] Irish emigration to the United States soared 350 percent from its 1878 nadir.[10] As one contemporary press report opined, the rising price of flour "will tend to keep up the tide of emigration which has set in from Great Britain to America, Australia, the Cape, New-Zealand, and Canada." "Herein," they surmised, "lies our safety from riot and revolution," for there was no shortage of "agitators who distinctly charge the present depression upon the landlords and the Government, ignoring bad harvests."[11] Another documented a party of tenant farmers dispatched to Canada from Scotland and the north, east, and west of England "to investigate the advantages of settlement in the Dominion."[12] In retrospect, "Lord" Gordon Gordon's pitch to the Northern Pacific that his over-crowded Scottish tenancies required resettlement was thus hardly far-fetched.

Though on the face of it, the 1879 UK recession was a food supply shock, con-temporary reports tended to emphasize another dimension to the agricultural distress—namely, the dearth of "turf," or peat. Detailing the wholly deficient state of nearly every crop, Irish Poor Law inspectors were relieved by the apparent absence of widespread starvation. Yet what they consistently noted was a "famine" of fuel.

While the harvesting and burning of peat may now be a distant memory in advanced economies, evoking a vague recollection among older generations of a charming and even fragrant fireplace scent, in the eighteenth- and nineteenth-century United Kingdom—and in many emerging economies and some Irish pubs still today—the combustion of decayed turf was a primary source of fuel.[13] A cool, wet summer that impeded the drying out of harvested turf was thus a major adverse energy supply shock for millions of English, Irish, Scottish, and Welsh who still relied on burning turf for cooking and domestic heating, and could not readily substitute coal. Turf or peat was furthermore an important source of fertilizer, as well as fuel for industrial activities such as coking and, in Scotland, distilling.[14]

Though coal was available in Ireland, this was of little relief to rural poor for whom turf was the only accessible and affordable fuel. Citing the "continuous rain," already in October 1879, one inspector observed that the supply of turf was univer-sally deficient, threatening "much suffering and sickness."[15] Another, Dr. Freder-ick MacCabe, surveying the counties of Dublin, Wicklow, and portions of five other Irish counties, observed that "in every union in which turf is used as fuel it is reported that it has been found impossible to save sufficient for the requirements of the coming winter and spring." Of coal, MacCabe noted that the fuel "fortunately can be purchased at lower prices than have prevailed for some years past, but much suffering is on the whole anticipated from the deficient supply of turf."[16]

Two months later, another inspector reported that all in his district concurred that "there is a general want of fuel all through the Union, and I have found in driv-ing through the districts round Tralee, that many of the cottages have not stacks of turf at all, and even those who have some turf have not nearly sufficient for their requirements during the winter." He described the deficit as "such as to amount to a famine." Indeed, he noted that in one town, "the people are burning the heather and bushes, and there is great probability that some families may, in consequence of inability to procure firing, be forced into the Workhouse."[17]

Harvest shocks before the advent of fossil fuels were effectively energy supply shocks not only because of their effect on the supply of turf but also because a primary source of inland transportation was animal draft power. Indeed, as late as the mid-1870s, provender (i.e., livestock feed) and biomass still constituted approximately 30 percent of UK energy expenditure.[18] Even by the turn of the century, provender and biomass accounted for approximately 20 percent of UK energy expenditure, while biomass alone provided 21 percent of US energy supply.[19]

In addition to 1879, UK recessions in 1710, 1731, and 1740 were essentially energy supply shocks triggered by severe cold or harvest failures, with harvest failure also contributing to wartime recessions in 1727 and 1756.[20] The 1710 recession was a direct consequence of the Great Frost of 1709, an extreme winter event across Europe that resulted in famine-level deficits of bread and meat.[21] Oxford professor of botany and superintendent of the university's Botanic Garden, Jacob Bobart, observed that the destruction of wheat constituted "a general Calamity."[22] With the ground in many locations freezing up to several feet deep, in spring there was little grass for livestock and draft animals, many of which had already perished in the long frost. The harvest failure thus "brought depression to industries dependent on grain."[23] A financial crisis ensued later that year as the United Kingdom suffered an acute drainage of gold to finance grain imports.[24]

When severe frost again struck in 1739–40, the Thames fully froze over. Though the event enabled a rare frost fair during which Londoners set up vendor booths, games, and bacchanalian festivities on the frozen artery, it also sealed the Thames to all shipping.[25] According to contemporary ironmonger and merchant William Stout, with the ground covered by frozen snow for a whole month, "many tradesmen [were] frozen out of their trades and employ, and starved for want of fire."[26] Stout described "a dearth of fuel," with coal and turf doubling in price.[27] The fuel deficit "froze up the mills," such that the price of milled grain spiked by a third. Meanwhile at sea, ships "had their sails and rigging so froze that they could not work them, but suffered them to drive on shore where many were lost, particularly coal ships." The price of coal surged, and many starved.[28]

While Charles Kindleberger would later blame the UK recession of 1721 on a "bubble" in South Sea Company stock bursting in the summer of 1720, at the time, Stout noted instead the severity of recent environmental shocks to the supply of energy. Snow and frost covered the ground for an entire month, which, he noted, "went hard with people." Worse, following "the greatest sea-flood that had been in the memory of any man then living," he lamented that the loss of turf in the floods and consequent scarcity of coal "caused great mortality and distempers by the extreme changes in the weather."[29] Despite the scintillating narrative of the boom and bust of the South Sea bubble driving recession, the impact of the company's collapse was largely confined to a relatively small number of goldsmiths and merchants. For the broader English business community, it was by no means catastrophic.[30] But the dearth of energy was.

Frost and blight were not the only threats to the supply of turf and provender. The April 1815 eruption of Mount Tambora in present-day Indonesia constituted the largest volcanic eruption in recorded human history. Spewing huge volumes of ash and sulfur miles into the atmosphere, the eruption triggered a volcanic winter. The following summer—during what became known as the "Year Without a Summer"—was one of the coldest on record, resulting in devastating crop failures across Europe. UK grain production dropped 10–20 percent, while cattle and pig stocks declined 5 percent.

Yet once again, contemporaries specifically noted the impact on the supply of turf. One observer recorded that "it was utterly impossible for the agriculturist, or his labourers to make the usual quantity of turf, and the small portion of that necessary article, which they have been able to save and remove from the bogs, is so extremely wet, that it will scarcely answer." They implored "those benevolent members of society, who feel for the distresses and miseries of their indigent fellow-creatures," to establish funds "for the purchase of coals and cheap grates" for poor households, who otherwise would "suffer most severe from the want of fuel" during the coming winter.[31]

From turf and provender to coal and oil, energy supply shocks have been perennial accomplices to the murder of economic expansions. Why? Is energy unique? As Stout astutely observed, defining characteristics of energy are not only the extent to which it is an essential fuel for almost all aspects of the economy—from transport to heating to industrial power generation—but also that it is an input for which households and businesses have limited ability to substitute in the event of adverse supply shocks. As we have thus just seen, even in the eighteenth century, disruptions to the supply of coal or turf could effectively bring commercial activity to halt. But since we moved away from turf and provender toward coal, oil, and other sources of energy, have we become less susceptible to energy supply shocks?

The short answer is that our vulnerability to adverse energy shocks has varied considerably across time and space. The year 1879 notwithstanding, the impact of energy supply shocks on the UK economy was generally declining over the course of the eighteenth and nineteenth centuries as the United Kingdom diversified away from overwhelming reliance on provender and biomass toward coal.[32] However, by the end of the century, increased dependence on coal and then oil and gas in turn rendered both the UK and US economies once again increasingly vulnerable. But unlike in the eighteenth and early-nineteenth centuries, the proximate causes of those shocks were not environmental Acts of God but rather of distinctly anthropo-morphic origin—specifically, industrial action in the coal industry and oil supply disruptions resulting from geopolitical conflict.

Perhaps the starkest illustration of the former was the short, sharp UK recession of 1926. Just two years prior, the Dawes Plan had permitted Germany to resume exports of coal to satisfy World War I reparation payments, increasing competition for UK coal producers. Compounding the challenge, in 1925, the UK chancellor of the exchequer, Winston Churchill, returned pound sterling to the gold stan-dard at the prewar exchange rate, resulting in a substantially overvalued pound that reduced the competitiveness of UK coal exports at precisely the moment that German coal reentered global markets.

In response to the weaker market, coal mine owners started demanding lon-ger hours and lower pay. When the Miners' Federation of Great Britain refused to accede, in May 1926, approximately 1.75 million workers in the United Kingdom walked off the job in solidarity with the miners. "Not a penny off the pay; not a minute on the day" was the slogan.[33] On the eve of the strike, employment in the UK coal mining industry was still 1.1 million out of a total population of just over 45 million.[34] With an average family size of approximately four, this implied that a staggering one in ten of the UK population were directly tied to the coal industry, not to mention those indirectly connected to the industry through distribution and warehousing, let alone end users.[35]

The strike effectively brought the UK economy to an immediate standstill. In May, coal production plunged from five million long tons to a mere ten thousand, and remained near zero through July and below two million through November.[36] According to *The Economist*, the strike "closed down the iron and steel industry" and "made it impossible for many other industries to make firm contracts and greatly increased unemployment."[37] Real GDP contracted at an annual rate of 22 percent in the second quarter of 1926 and 11 percent in the third quarter.[38] So stark was the loss of income that the British even drank less, with the country's alcohol bill dropping 4.5 percent from its 1925 level.[39]

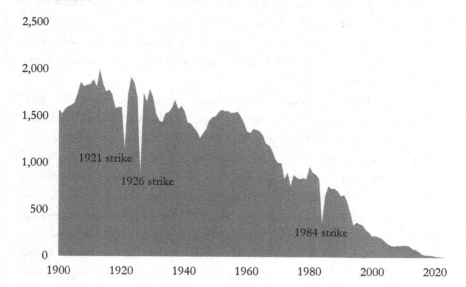

Figure 28: Coal Production in the United Kingdom, 1900–2023. Not even the slumps in coal production during the Great Depression and World War II rivaled the 1921 and 1926 declines. Though the contentious 1984–85 National Union of Mineworkers strike resulted in an even bigger annual percentage decline in UK coal production, by that time, coal accounted for a much smaller share of UK energy consumption. Moreover, with the UK government having stockpiled coal in anticipation of industrial action, the UK economy weathered the shock without recession. (Energy Institute—Statistical Review of World Energy, "Coal Production," Our World in Data, 2024; Energy Institute—Statistical Review of World Energy, "Energy Consumption by Source, United Kingdom," Our World in Data, 2024.)

In opposition to the strike, the Conservative government of Stanley Baldwin launched a new, anti-strike government newspaper, *The British Gazette*. Commandeering scarce paper to rapidly ramp up production—triggering clashes with *The Times* and *Daily Mail*—by the end of the strike, the gazette had reached a circulation of 2.2 million.[40] Churchill, a former journalist, served as editor and even wrote much of the copy himself. On the morning of Thursday, May 6, he boldly declared that "either the country will break the General Strike, or the General Strike will break the country."[41]

In the end, the country broke the general strike. On May 12, the Trades Union Congress capitulated. While the coal mining associations persisted for months longer, by December, desperate, destitute miners had little choice but to return to the pits. Within a month, UK coal production was already above its prestrike level.[42] Real GDP rebounded at an annual rate of 15 percent in the final quarter of 1926 and 32 percent in the first quarter of 1927, by which point, it was back above prestrike level.[43] After spiking in May 1926, by January 1927, the UK unemployment rate was below its prestrike level.[44]

Like the 1879 UK "turf famine," US recessions resulting from coal strikes were explicitly described at the time as "coal famines."[45] One such "famine" occurred during a six-week strike by the United Mine Workers in the autumn of 1900. One New York woman, having received delivery of twelve tons of coal just a few weeks prior, placed an order for fifteen tons more "at once." To the puzzled coal dealer, she responded that the twelve tons "will not last me longer than January. Do you expect me to freeze during February and March?"[46] Long Island farmers resorted to cutting oak and hickory wood.[47] Exacerbating the situation was that large-scale coal strikes in France and Austria-Hungary in early 1900 had already created a coal "famine" in Germany, thereby increasing pressure on American coal supplies just as Europe's usual swing supplier, the United Kingdom, hoarded coal for their war against the Boer Republics in South Africa.[48] But after plunging 83 percent during the six-week strike, coal shipments rebounded sharply upon resolution, surpassing their immediate prestrike level within a month.[49] According to Christina Romer's recession chronology, the relatively short recession ended within two months.[50]

The fuel famine was even more intense two years later when in May 1902 approximately 150,000 US coal workers again went on strike, demanding living wages and union recognition.[51] During the 163-day strike, hard coal could scarcely be found at any price.[52] "Hysterical" demand for any available soft coal thus drove bituminous prices to "top notch" levels, with two tons of less-dense soft coal needed to replace every one ton of hard anthracite.[53]

Already by early August, press reports anticipated a "coal famine" unless the strike ended soon. By October, the wholesale price of soft coal had nearly tripled in real terms.[54] Warning that "a coal famine in the winter, is an ugly thing, and I fear we shall see terrible suffering and grave disaster," in mid-October President Teddy Roosevelt—with assistance from John Pierpont Morgan—managed to convince the mine operators to submit to arbitration.[55] Union leadership called off the strike a few days later.

It was too late. The coal famine Roosevelt feared was already underway. Even before the strike, press reports had warned that severe weather threatened "the largest anthracite coal famine suffered by the country in some time," with blizzards

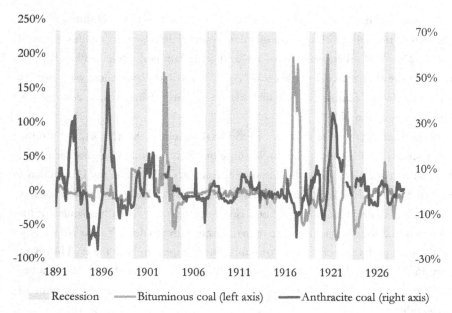

Figure 29: Year-over-Year Percent Change in the Real Price of Coal in the United States. I deflate using seasonally adjusted CPI since 1947, not seasonally adjusted CPI since 1913, and an index of the general price level since 1860. For bituminous coal, I extend the price series back to 1891 by splicing four overlapping soft coal price series of differing time frames. (National Bureau of Economic Research, "Wholesale Price of Anthracite Coal, Chestnut; Tidewater, New York Harbor for New York, NY (M04G4AUS35620M288N-NBR)," Federal Reserve Bank of St. Louis; National Bureau of Economic Research, "Wholesale Price of Bituminous Coal, Mines for United States (M0490CUSM349N-NBR)," Federal Reserve Bank of St. Louis; National Bureau of Economic Research, "Retail Price of Bituminous Coal for United States (M04047USM238NNBR)," Federal Reserve Bank of St. Louis; National Bureau of Economic Research, "Wholesale Price of Bituminous Coal, Mines for United States (M0490AUSM294NNBR)," Federal Reserve Bank of St. Louis; National Bureau of Economic Research, "Wholesale Price of Bituminous Coal, Georges Creek, F.O.B. New York Harbor for New York, NY (M04046US35620M294N-NBR)," Federal Reserve Bank of St. Louis; U.S. Bureau of Labor Statistics, "Consumer Price Index for All Urban Consumers: All Items in U.S. City Average (CPIAUCSL)," Federal Reserve Bank of St. Louis; U.S. Bureau of Labor Statistics, "Consumer Price Index for All Urban Consumers: All Items in U.S. City Average (CPIAUCNS)," Federal Reserve Bank of St. Louis; National Bureau of Economic Research, "Index of the General Price Level for United States (M04051USM324NNBR)," Federal Reserve Bank of St. Louis.)

completely halting freight and coal traffic for nearly two weeks.[56] Within a week of the start of the strike, cities caught off guard found themselves already in short supply. In New York, there was talk of an "anthracite famine," while in Philadelphia, reports were that the coal market was "tight."[57] Just days later, there were further fears of a "water famine" in Philadelphia on account of insufficient coal for the city's pumping stations.[58]

After more than three months of industrial action, by September, the famine was universal.[59] With coal prices in Washington, DC, reaching levels not seen since the Confederate blockade of the Potomac during the Civil War, many DC residents rushed to buy oil stoves.[60] In Connecticut, housewives had to be more creative; they gathered, dried, and burned horse chestnuts for fuel.[61] Their husbands, meanwhile, turned to felling timber, occasionally trespassing to do so.[62] One New Jersey amusement park owner even burned old bowling tenpins to keep his establishment running.[63] While the real price of soft coal had nearly tripled from its October 1901 level, for hard coal, there was effectively no price—there was simply none to be bought.[64]

With autumn turning to winter, rail and tram systems shut down, as did water and electric plants.[65] Steel and flour mills were forced to curtail production and idle workers.[66] In Springfield, Massachusetts, and Schenectady, New York, school closures affected some fifteen thousand students, while in Cambridge, Massachusetts, "wealthy Harvard students, like cats in a woodshed, shivered and swore and suffered in their historic but sievelike old dormitories."[67]

As coal shipments gradually rebounded in early 1903, the famine eased in February, though railcar shortages continued to hamper the flow of fuel through the latter half of 1903.[68] After the shock of the preceding year, many companies took to maintaining coal reserves, or else to conserving coal through the utilization of manufactured coal briquettes made from the previously unused fine coal dust near mines.[69] Early reports of the NBER thus documented the famine persisting through spring of 1903.[70] Though the economy improved through the summer of 1903, it would not be until 1904 until the US economy firmly entered recovery.

But coal lockouts and strikes not only truncated mature economic expansions, they also terminated nascent recoveries—for example, in the United Kingdom in 1893 and 1921 and United States in 1920.[71] During the 1921 event, tentative signs of recovery from a severe postwar UK recession were interrupted by a relatively short strike of a million workers in October 1920 followed by a protracted management lockout of a million miners beginning April 1, 1921. For three straight months, UK coal production was down a staggering 99 percent.[72] Real GDP plunged at an annual rate of 41 percent—a roughly similar order of magnitude to that experienced during the COVID-19 pandemic—while industrial production collapsed at an annual rate of 82 percent and the unemployment rate rose from just under 8 percent to nearly 13 percent. Only in July and August, as miners were finally permitted to return to the pits, did the UK economy firmly reenter recovery. With coal production recovering by more than 6,000 percent in July, industrial production and real GDP in the third quarter rebounded at annual rates of nearly 600 percent and 70 percent, respectively.

Across the pond, the young, ten-month-old US recovery from the postwar, pandemic recession of September 1918 through March 1919 was similarly interrupted in 1920 by industrial action. A wave of 3,630 labor strikes involving 4.2 million workers—more than one in ten of all employed workers in the United States—culminated at the end of 1919 in a strike by nearly 400,000 coal workers and 365,000 steelworkers.[73] During the forty-day coal strike, US coal production plunged 67 percent and was still down by over a third through the first half of 1920.[74] In real terms, the wholesale price of soft coal—which accounted for about 85 percent of US coal production and a third of primary energy consumption—nearly quadrupled.[75]

In the face of such adverse supply shocks, inflation remained stubbornly high. After jumping 40 percent in 1917–18 on the back of a nearly 50 percent increase in base money supply during the war, inflation hit 15 percent in 1919 and 16 percent in 1920. Indeed, the strikes themselves were largely in response to wages failing to keep pace with soaring inflation. In 1920, there were still 3,411 strikes involving 1.5 million workers, or approximately 4 percent of all employed workers nationwide, with the principal cause being the "ever rising cost of living."[76]

In their landmark treatise, *A Monetary History of the United States*, Milton Friedman and Anna Schwartz blamed the severe 1920–21 US recession squarely on the Federal Reserve. Of the Fed's decision to raise short-term interest rates from 4 percent in November 1919 to 7 percent by June 1920, Friedman and Schwartz described it as an extraordinarily and unnecessarily restrictive monetary policy for an economy on the brink of and then in recession.[77] But while Friedman and Schwartz pointed to deflation in the latter half of 1920 and 1921 as unambiguous evidence of the Fed's error, later analysis found that a surge in agricultural production could explain much of the decline in prices during 1920–21.[78] Thus, while an injurious Act of Church likely contributed to and exacerbated the 1920–21 US recession, it is perhaps understandable why the fallible high priests of the Fed may have so erred; while the wartime expansion of the money supply and consequent high inflation were known, future harvest conditions were not.

If coal had succeeded turf and provender as a frequent source of energy supply shocks, by the end of World War II, coal was no longer top energy dog in the United States, having dipped below 50 percent of primary energy consumption in 1940.[79] But as oil replaced coal as the single-largest source of energy, a distinct category of energy supply shocks rose to the fore—those of geopolitical provenance. Examples include the Iraqi invasion of Kuwait in 1990, the Suez Canal crisis of 1956–57, the nationalization and subsequent international boycott of Iranian oil in the early 1950s, and the inability of US oil infrastructure and distribution to keep pace with sharply rebounding oil demand in the aftermath of World War II.[80]

But the quintessential example of these geopolitical shocks was that which murdered record-long economic expansions in both the US and UK economies. In the first three quarters of 1973, both the United States and United Kingdom were expanding healthily; hiring and industrial production rose, while the unemployment rate fell. To be sure, oil supply had increasingly struggled to match demand.[81] At the time, the oil majors—the so-called Seven Sisters Anglo-Persian Oil Company, Shell plc, Standard Oil of California, Gulf Oil, Texaco, Jersey Standard, and Standard Oil of New York—generally managed the price of oil, keeping it stable at a constant level for protracted periods.[82] With the nominal price of a barrel of oil thus fixed at $3.56 since December 1970, by January 1973, there were already shortages of heating fuel in the United States, followed that spring by gasoline.[83] By June, there were more than one thousand US gas stations that closed for lack of gas.[84]

It certainly did not help that US oil production peaked at the start of the decade as mature fields reached geologic maturity. Moreover, when title to Middle East oil passed from international oil companies to sovereign governments, it passed from entities with an incentive to extract as much as possible before losing title to sovereign states that in contrast had an incentive to act as a profit-maximizing cartel.[85] Thus, the transition from a Gulf of Mexico–centric global oil market to a Persian Gulf–centric one had implications for not just the *actual* supply of oil but also for the *perception* of potential supply.[86] At the same time, the 1963 Clean Air Act had induced switching from coal-fired to oil-fired power generation, with oil's share of US electricity generation thus jumping from 6 percent in 1963 to 17 percent by 1973.[87]

The year 1973 also witnessed one of the largest-ever spikes in US food prices, with food inflation topping 20 percent during the fall, having risen at a record annualized rate of 102 percent in August. Widespread drought across Eurasia the prior year, particularly in the Soviet Union, had severely impacted global grain harvests, with the consequent Soviet purchases of US wheat dubbed "the great grain robbery" of 1972. Drought continued in China in 1973, by which time global grain reserves were largely depleted.[88]

This was the context in which on October 17, the Organization of Arab Petroleum Exporting Countries (OAPEC) imposed an oil embargo on countries they considered supportive of Israel during the Yom Kippur War, followed by large production cuts. By November, Arab oil production was down 4.4 million barrels per day, effectively removing 7–8 percent of global supply that additional production by non-Arab oil producers could not immediately replace.[89] Already by December, gasoline shortages in the United States were so pervasive that time spent queueing for gas in urban areas effectively added an additional 12 percent to the cost, rising to 50 percent in March. For rural residents, the cost of queueing added 84 percent to the effective price of gas.[90] As one Citgo gas attendant in Connecticut, Bruce

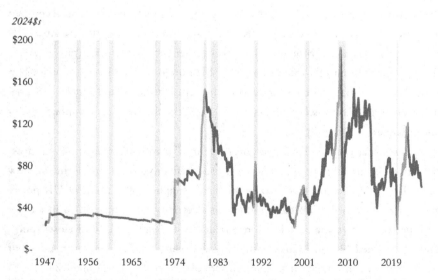

Figure 30: Real Spot Price of West Texas Intermediate Crude Oil. (Federal Reserve Bank of St. Louis, "Spot Crude Oil Price: West Texas Intermediate (WTI) (WTISPLC)," Federal Reserve Bank of St. Louis; US Bureau of Labor Statistics, "Consumer Price Index for All Urban Consumers: All Items in U.S. City Average (CPIAUCNS)," Federal Reserve Bank of St. Louis.)

Faucher, put it, if they didn't ration their gasoline, "we'd be out in a couple of hours and wouldn't have any for our regular customers."[91]

From January 1, 1974, Persian Gulf exporters then doubled the price of oil.[92] For the month overall, even the measured price of oil—exclusive of queueing costs—more than doubled in real terms. Though OAPEC lifted the embargo in March 1974, supplies remained tight, and precautionary buying in anticipation of future supply constraints kept prices extremely elevated. Year over year, the average real price of oil in 1974 was more than double its 1973 level.[93] During the summer of 1974 travel season, the real price of a gallon of gas was still 30 percent above its October 1973 level.[94]

As the cost of living rose and energy prices remained high, on November 12, 120,300 coal miners nationwide struck for almost a month, with the union only fully withdrawing the picket line just before Christmas.[95] An additional 64,500 coal miners in Illinois, Indiana, Kentucky, Pennsylvania, Virginia, and West Virginia went on strike from December 9 to 23, with 11,400 in Virginia, West Virginia, and Ohio striking again for three weeks in February and early March.[96]

Meanwhile in the United Kingdom, the 1973–75 recession was similarly deep and protracted. Whereas from 1947–73, the coal-intensive UK economy was relatively insulated from geopolitical shocks to global oil supply, by 1973, oil accounted for almost 50 percent of primary UK energy consumption and 30 percent of UK electricity generation.[97] Moreover, just weeks after the start of the Arab embargo, the National Union of Mineworkers (NUM) announced an overtime work ban with the aim of halving coal production. It was only the second official UK coal strike since the disastrous general strike of 1926, the first being a 1.5-month walkout in January 1972.

In response, the Conservative government of Edward Heath took the drastic action of enacting a three-day work order, effective from midnight on New Year's Eve 1973. To conserve coal—which still supplied 60 percent of UK power generation—the order limited commercial electricity consumption to just three days per week, terminated television broadcasts at 10:30 p.m., and closed pubs. The state-owned National Coal Board offered miners a 16.5 percent wage hike, but with inflation running at an annualized rate of 17 percent, on January 24, NUM members voted to strike. Hoping to settle the dispute at the ballot box, Heath called a general election, running on a campaign slogan of "Who governs Britain?" The answer of the British electorate—not Ted Heath. In a bruising defeat, Heath's Tories lost their majority and were unable to form a coalition.

Historians would later link the 1973–75 UK recession to the "Barber boom," a period of robust growth following an old-school, deficit-financed Keynesian "dash for growth" via consumption tax cuts and higher pension benefits announced in March 1972 by Heath's chancellor of the exchequer, Anthony Barber. Yet if the consumption-led Barber boom was a prime suspect for the 1973–75 recession, it is odd that the recession was primarily characterized not by a bust in consumption but rather by a sharp fall in fixed capital investment and in the output of the oil and gas construction and distribution industries, the very sectors most adversely impacted by an oil supply shock in the oil-importing United Kingdom.[98] As later analysis concluded of the roughly coincident US recession, "while it is extremely important to view the oil price increases of 1973–1974 in a broader economic context, the specific timing, magnitude, and nature of the supply cutbacks" were more closely associated with geopolitical shocks than boom-bust demand factors.[99]

In a parallel pattern to 1710 and 1721, a crisis among a subset of banks in the United Kingdom from November 1973 into 1974 was likewise more a consequence of the 1973–75 energy price shock and consequent recession than a proximate cause thereof. UK "secondary banks"—so called because they relied primarily on wholesale and secondary money markets instead of deposits—had expanded their assets substantially since the 1960s through loans to property developers and second mortgages. Yet with inflation eroding the real value of mortgage payments on past loans and rising interest rates impairing the value of the underlying collateral, by December 1973, several secondary banks were increasingly struggling to find funding in the secondary money markets. Small depositors even began queueing outside branches.[100]

After a marathon eighteen-hour meeting fueled by ham sandwiches and whiskey, on the morning of December 20, the Bank of England announced a £72 million support package for the troubled secondary bank Cedar Holdings.[101] Yet the announcement that a bank of Cedar's size and prominence required rescue generated panic rather than reassurance, with the share prices of many secondary banks plunging by a third within hours.[102] Working with the "Big Four" banks—Barclays, Lloyds, Midland, and National Westminster—on December 21, the Bank of England thus announced a "lifeboat operation." As depositors withdrew funds from the secondary banks and deposited them in the Big Four clearing banks, the latter would recycle those deposits back to the secondary banks. The operation worked.[103]

Unfortunately, both economies would enjoy little reprieve. During the Iranian Revolution of 1978–1979, Iranian oil production fell from 6.0 million barrels per day to just 0.4 million barrels by January 1979, representing a loss of 9 percent of total world output.[104] Though production recovered somewhat throughout 1979 and Saudi Arabia and other producers were able to offset about two-thirds of the shortfall, by summer, the relative price of oil was already up nearly 20 percent from its prerevolution level and would continue rising through the first half of 1980.[105] Moreover, after a series of border skirmishes and diplomatic incidents throughout 1980, on September 10, Iraq forcibly seized territories promised under the 1975 Algiers Agreement between Iraqi president Saddam Hussein and the deposed shah of Iran Mohammad Reza Pahlavi, but never transferred. A full-scale Iraqi invasion of Iran followed twelve days later, knocking out 2.4 million barrels per day of Iraqi oil production from September 1980 through January 1981.[106]

By the spring of 1980, the price of oil in the United States was already more than double its prerevolution level, while the price of a gallon of gas had spiked more than 50 percent.[107] In many places, stations reverted to rationing by queue. As one expectant Los Angeles grandmother, Beverly Lyons, put it in May, "It's horrible; it's just like it was five years ago." Stuck thirty-second in a line of more than sixty cars outside an LA Mobil station shortly after 8:00 a.m., Lyons reported from her Buick that "I've been here an hour; my daughter expects her baby this weekend . . . I've got to get some gas!"[108] The cost of queueing then effectively added as much as a third again to the sticker price of a gallon of gas.[109]

Indeed, a recurring issue in US recessions during the first four decades after World War II was not just the increase in the *price* of oil following adverse supply shocks but also the non-price *rationing* of oil supply due to the actual existence or implicit threat of reimposition of price controls. Not only did the existence or threat of price controls during the recessionary oil shocks of 1948–49, 1953–54, 1957–58, 1969–70, 1973–75, and 1980 result in inefficient, non-price rationing through shortages and queues, they also impeded supply responses to current or anticipated shortfalls.[110]

The combination of a sharp energy supply shock alongside aggressive monetary policy tightening on both sides of the Atlantic rendered the 1980 and 1981–82 recessions in the United States and 1979–81 recession in the United Kingdom particularly severe. The unemployment rate hit nearly 11 percent in the United States and 9 percent (and rising) in the United Kingdom; then postwar records for both economies.

Yet for all the economic hardship of the oil shocks of the 1970s and early 1980s, the all-time record price of oil in the United States hit not in 1973 or 1979 but in

June 2008. The same month, the real price of US natural gas reached a level only topped during the immediate aftermath of Hurricanes Katrina and Rita.[111]

Though there was no marquee supply disruption, a combination of supply-and-demand shocks in the run-up to 2008 were all factors in the unprecedented price spike. On the geopolitical front, security concerns and political instability exacerbated production challenges in Nigeria and Iraq, the latter still recovering from the US-led invasion and subsequent insurgency. Following labor disputes and general mismanagement at state-owned PDVSA, Venezuelan oil production had been declining since the late 1990s.

Meanwhile, in 2008, US production reached its lowest level since the early 1950s.[112] North Sea production peaked at the turn of the century and declined steadily thereafter, while Indonesian production peaked in the 1990s. By the 2000s, Indonesia, originally a major oil exporter, was a net oil importer. Though Saudi Arabia ramped up production in response to the Iraq War, by 2006, even Saudi production faltered as the kingdom's mammoth Ghawar field—the largest conventional oil field in the world—passed peak production. The cumulative effect of these disruptions was that global oil output barely grew in 2006, and outright contracted in 2007, even as China's exceptionally rapid economic growth following admission to the World Trade Organization generated an insatiable appetite for petroleum.

By the summer of 2008, the real price of a gallon of gasoline in the United States thus reached its all-time high of $5.86 per gallon.[113] For the average US household, in the summer of 2008, real spending on energy goods and services hit $8,466 in 2024 dollars, the highest on record and $2,000 more than they had been paying just three years prior.[114] By comparison, average real household spending on mortgage interest reached an all-time high of $7,498 in the fourth quarter of 2007 and by the summer of 2008 was still over $800 higher than three years prior.[115] In other words, for the average household, the energy price shock was more than double the roughly contemporaneous shock of mortgage rates resetting higher.

But as we saw in earlier recessions, the 2007–08 energy price shock did not confine itself to energy. As the cost of energy soared, so too did the price of highly energy-intensive fertilizer.[116] By the time Lehman Brothers failed in September 2008, nitrogenous fertilizer prices had jumped by an unprecedented 86 percent year over year.[117] The US Department of Agriculture estimated that the volatile and upward trend in US natural gas prices had caused a 17 percent decline in the supply of ammonia in the United States, with US ammonia production falling 44 percent between 2000 and 2006. Ammonia prices paid by farmers more than doubled.[118] Reflecting the sharp run-up in fertilizer costs, food inflation topped 6 percent in the autumn of 2008.[119]

Yet it was not just the direct effect of higher energy prices on the cost of manufacturing fertilizer—which with a requisite temperature of more than nine hundred degrees Fahrenheit consumed nearly 2 percent of global energy production—that drove up food inflation in 2007–08.[120] It was also the indirect effect of policy responses to those higher energy prices. As global energy prices rose throughout the 2000s, farmers increasingly diverted production of crops for food toward biofuel, further incentivized by a spate of new government mandates and subsidies.[121] According to one study, the effects of the diversion of US corn production to biofuels were on par with "the great grain robbery" of 1972–73.[122] A leaked report from the World Bank—then under the leadership of longtime Bush family loyalist Robert Zoellick—found that increased biofuel production had raised global food prices by 70–75 percent.[123] According to senior sources, the Zoellick-led organization quashed publication of the report to avoid embarrassing President George W. Bush.[124]

In any event, it was an awkward situation for a president who, having narrowly lost the corn-producing state of Iowa in the razor-thin 2000 presidential election, in 2005 signed into law a new mandate that 7.5 billion gallons of renewable fuel, mostly corn ethanol, be mixed with gasoline, and in 2007 expanded that mandate to 36 billion gallons.[125] On top of that, federal and state governments were subsidizing biofuel via tax credits to the tune of roughly one dollar per gallon.[126] The mandatory replacement of toxic methyl tert-butyl ether (MTBE) with ethanol as an oxygenate in gasoline only further fueled (no pun intended) the run-up in ethanol demand.[127] As the longtime chief economist of the US Department of Agriculture put it, ethanol was the "foot on the accelerator" of corn demand.[128]

By early 2008, American households were thus simultaneously confronted by not only adjustable-rate mortgage payments that had already been resetting higher for more than a year but even more saliently an energy- and subsidy-induced global food price crisis, and the highest real price of oil on record. Estimates of the macroeconomic effects of just the third of these shocks alone imply that absent the oil-induced decline in consumer spending—in particular, purchases of domestic automobiles—the first three quarters of 2008 would not have been characterized by recession in the United States.[129]

Indeed, real GDP growth in the four quarters through September 2008 would have been 0.5-percentage points higher were it not for the oil-induced decline in real consumer spending on automobiles, expanding by a modest but hardly recessionary 0.8 percent.[130] With no oil shock at all, the US economy would have expanded by nearly 4 percent in the four quarters through September 2008.[131] Instead, the US economy expanded just 0.3 percent during those four quarters while contracting at an annual rate of 1.4 percent in the last three. In other words, similarly to the United Kingdom in 1710, 1721, and 1973, the United States was already more than eight months into an energy-induced recession *before* the collapse of Lehman Brothers and subsequent banking crisis.

Despite a declining role of oil in the US economy, recent studies have found that the macroeconomic effect of oil supply shocks remains largely undiminished since the 1970s. While the effect of oil price increases on economic output has declined over time, the effect of oil supply decreases on the price of oil has risen over time as demand for petroleum and related products has become less elastic, leaving the net effect on output largely constant across time.[132] For sectors that continued to intensively use petroleum and petroleum products even after the oil shocks of the 1970s—for example, plastics and other petrochemicals, aviation fuel, maritime and rail transportation—in the short run, there was simply no substitute.

The large economics literature on the role of energy shocks in generating mac-roeconomic fluctuations identifies three primary channels.[133] The first is a demand transmission channel, which consists of four effects. First, a discretionary income effect; higher energy costs reduce the amount of money households have to spend on other goods and services after paying essential energy bills. Second, large changes in energy prices can raise uncertainty about the future path of energy costs, thereby prompting consumers to postpone irreversible purchases of durable goods like cars. Third, there is a precautionary saving effect; concerned about the higher probability of future employment and income losses as a result of energy shocks, consumers may curtail purchases of all goods and services as they seek to increase savings. Finally, there is an operating cost effect; insofar as consumers expect high energy costs to persist, they may reduce purchases of energy-intensive durable goods, such as motor vehicles and appliances.[134]

The second channel is on the supply side. Multiple studies have identified high complementarities in production between capital and energy above and beyond the direct effect on production of higher input costs. At least as early as 1983, economists observed that a reduction in the supply of complementary factors of production—particularly low-cost energy—during the 1970s lowered the profit-ability of and demand for capital, thereby reducing real investment.[135]

Economists have also found that the employment response to an oil price increase is bigger at more capital- and energy-intensive establishments, with oil price shocks accounting for 20–25 percent of the cyclical variability in manufacturing employment growth—twice as much as monetary shocks.[136] Other studies found that because energy is essential to obtaining the flow of productive services from installed capital, energy price shocks were in effect equivalent to adverse technology shocks.[137] These models thus speak directly to the observations of William Stout following the frost of 1739–40, when he observed those "many tradesmen frozen out of their trades and employ, and starved for want of fire," with the lack of fuel having "froze up the mills."[138]

A third channel is the effect of rising energy costs on the actions of the central bank. A key transmission mechanism of oil price shocks to the broader economy was the consequent tightening of monetary policy. Indeed, this mechanism was on display not only during the postwar US recessions of 1970, 1973–75, 1981–82, 2001, and 2008–09 but also, as we have just seen, during the severe pre–World War II recession of 1920–21. More recent research has found that adverse oil price shocks were less contractionary during periods when advanced economies were operating at 0 percent monetary policy rates, such as during the post-2009 period of unconventional monetary policy.[139]

The monetary policy and various demand channels would explain why inflation typically, but not always, tends to decline during recessions, even though we would conventionally expect adverse supply shocks to amplify rather than attenuate inflation. During the postwar US recessions of 1953–54, 1957–58, 1973–75, 1980, 1981–82, 1990–91, 2001, and 2008–09, inflation rose before it fell. During the interwar recessions of 1920–21 and 1923–24 and the end-of-war recessions of 1918 and 1945, inflation similarly rose before falling. As we have also seen, energy price inflation in earlier postwar US recessions—specifically, 1948–49, 1953–54, 1957–58, 1970, and 1973–75—would have been even greater without price controls (official or unofficial), or had reported energy inflation incorporated the time cost of rationing through queue.

This is not at all to purport a uni-causal theory of any single recession, let alone all recessions. Rather, as we will explore more in the next chapter, most recessions have occurred in the context of a major shock or cluster of shocks of which energy is frequently just one. Indeed, though serial accomplices to the murder of economic expansions, energy price shocks cannot be a universal cause of recessions for the simple reason that there are so many exceptions. In the postwar period, these include the 1960–61 US recession and the 2020 pandemic recession in both economies. During the interwar period, while researchers have identified an energy price shock in 1931, it impacted a US economy that was already two years into the Great Depression and came after a sharp slump in the price of oil over the preceding year.[140] The US recession of 1937–38 similarly appears to have been unrelated to energy prices.

Moreover, energy is not alone among recession-contributing commodity supply shocks. Cotton—like oil, an essential and complementary input across a wide range of industries—could be similarly fatal to economic expansions in the nineteenth century. During the UK "cotton famine" recession of 1862 following the Union blockade of Confederate cotton exports, UK industrial production fell 6 percent while the unemployment rate doubled from 2.6 percent to 5.2 percent.

Indeed, researchers have found that fluctuations in the cotton harvest were important contributors to most major industrial fluctuations in the United States from around 1880 until World War I, particularly in 1883, 1893, 1895, and 1910.[141] Adverse cotton harvests would substantially lower US net exports, resulting in net external drains of gold that would tighten US money market conditions and exacerbate pressure on the fragmented, undercapitalized, and under-diversified US banking system. Large fluctuations in the output of a single agricultural commodity could thus result in higher interest rates and overall deflation through reserve drains and bank failures, thereby generating substantial fluctuations in industrial production in the nonagricultural economy.

More fundamentally, the effects of turf, coal, oil, or cotton shocks on the macroeconomy illustrate that because goods produced by different industries are highly complementary as inputs into production, sectoral or industry-specific shocks may be at least as important as aggregate shocks in generating economic fluctuations.[142] For instance, an economy-wide shock—such as an unanticipated increase in the federal funds rate—would simultaneously lower demand for auto parts (an input into auto assembly), steel manufacturing (an input into auto parts), and final auto assembly.[143] Alternatively, an industrial strike specific to the auto parts manufacturing sector would not only lower auto parts production, it would also reduce demand for steel and disrupt auto assembly.[144]

Both shocks would result in lower output and employment across all three industries. But as the example illustrates, correlated declines in economic activity across multiple industries could thus result either from a relatively high frequency of aggregate shocks that directly impact all industries even if substitutability between inputs is high and linkages between industries low; or from low substitutability between inputs and high linkages between industries transmitting sector-specific shocks even though aggregate shocks are relatively rare.[145]

Quantitatively, a growing body of recent research has found that in the short run, industries' ability to substitute across inputs is limited, with the result that sectoral, rather than aggregate, shocks are the primary source of GDP fluctuations.[146] Case in point, in Chapter 3, we already observed that as the banking sector is highly linked to other sectors in the economy through the provision of credit, and in the short run, firms and households have limited substitutes for bank credit, shocks specific to the banking sector can have macroeconomic implications.

While the quest for grand theories of recessionary shocks that are macroeconomic in nature—money supply, aggregate demand, irrationally exuberant booms and consequent busts—the proximate triggers of episodes of economic contraction are often more mundane and more microeconomic. Low short-term elasticities of substitution between inputs in response to sector-specific shocks may not be the sexiest explanation of economic contractions but, at the end of the day, seem to be at least as important as aggregate shocks, if not more so.

Insofar as sectoral shocks do account for a disproportionate share of economic recessions, there are perhaps grounds for optimism. Given the prevalence of energy supply shocks in past US and UK recessions, the transition to a more diversified energy mix may attenuate the impact on the macroeconomy of supply shortfalls in any one energy source. The oil intensity specifically, and energy intensity generally, of producing a unit of GDP in both economies has also been declining steadily over time with improved productivity. Moreover, the long, gradual transition from a primary (agricultural), to a secondary (manufacturing), and finally to a tertiary (services) economy tends to lower macroeconomic volatility; not because agricultural or manufacturing production is inherently more "cyclical" but rather because their relatively high energy and capital intensity renders them more sensitive to shocks.

Ultimately, while we may not be able to evade history, over time, we can and do learn how to better deal with shocks that historically would have proved fatal to economic expansion. As we have already seen hints of in this chapter, while energy shocks are common contributing factors to the death of economic expansions, they generally do not occur in isolation. As we will see in the next chapter, typically, quite a lot must go seriously wrong for a large, diversified economy like that of the United States or United Kingdom to enter and remain in a protracted state of broad-based contraction.

6

A GREAT DEAL OF RUIN

> Only a foolish optimist can deny the dark realities of
> the moment. Yet our distress comes from no failure
> of substance. We are stricken by no plague of locusts.
> Compared with the perils which our forefathers
> conquered because they believed and were not afraid,
> we have still much to be thankful for. Nature still
> offers her bounty and human efforts have multiplied
> it. Plenty is at our doorstep, but a generous use
> of it languishes in the very sight of the supply.
>
> —President Franklin Roosevelt, 1933

In the summer of 1931—less than two years before Roosevelt's first inaugural address—the eighth plague of Egypt once again descended upon the American Midwest and Plains. In an ominous echo of the 1870s, already in April 1931, press reports warned of favorable conditions for grasshoppers, noting that "a grasshopper epidemic is feared."[1] Though the Rocky Mountain locust that had previously plagued the American plains in the trillions had gone extinct by the early 1900s—the last preserved specimen was collected in 1902—extreme heat and successive droughts in 1930 and 1931 created ripe conditions for a population explosion of the High Plains locust.[2]

Sure enough, by July, from Iowa and Nebraska to the Dakotas, contemporary accounts reported that locust-ridden fields were "denuded of every green blade." In Nebraska, sixty-three of the state's ninety-three counties were infested, while entomologists discovered that a single South Dakotan field of 1,600 acres had been so devastated that there was "not enough grass to feed a single animal."[3] One swarm was said to be so dense that it blocked out the sun and one had to shovel grasshoppers with a scoop.[4] In Union County, South Dakota, more than a thousand farmers "knelt on the spot where sixty years ago their fathers knelt and asked divine aid against the scourge," one of many contemporary references to the catastrophic 1873–76 locust plague.[5] Though the Hoover administration "declared war on the hordes of grasshoppers," there was little they could do.[6]

In a devastating double blow, the extreme heat and drought that were so hospitable to locust reproduction were also devastating to crops. Overshadowed in historical memory by the drought of the mid-1930s that produced the Dust Bowl, contemporaries referred to the 1930 environmental disaster—centered in the Mississippi and Ohio River Valleys—as "the Great Drought," with Secretary of Agriculture Arthur Hyde calling it "the worst drought ever recorded in this country."[7]

While Iowa, Nebraska, and South Dakota were worst affected—with the situation in parts of Nebraska and South Dakota described as "a catastrophe"—the 1931 drought and accompanying locust plague stretched from the Great Lakes to the Rocky Mountains, infesting Michigan, Minnesota, North Dakota, and Montana, and as far south as Missouri, as roughly illustrated in Panel A of Figure 31.[8] In a scene eerily reminiscent of the 1870s plague, in the early summer of 1931, the tracks in Knox County, Nebraska, "were so littered with the pests that section crews could not propel handcars."[9]

To put the scourge in physical perspective, a grasshopper swarm the size of Manhattan can in one day consume as much food as forty-two million people.[10] With a Springfield, Missouri, newspaper reporting in 1931 on a ravenous swarm spanning more than 46,876 square miles—an area over double the size of Manhattan—this implies that just one swarm in the summer of 1931 was consuming the equivalent of nearly ninety million people each day.[11]

Naturally, economic and financial reports from affected Federal Reserve districts regularly covered the unfolding disaster in 1931.[12] Though accounting for only about a fifth of deposits in suspended banks in the latter half of 1931, the sheer number of bank failures in states severely afflicted by the 1931 drought cum locust plague was unique. With less than a third of all US banks in June 1931, worst affected states accounted for more than two in five US bank failures in the second half of 1931.[13] The proportion is even higher if one includes additional states, such

A. 1931 locust infestation

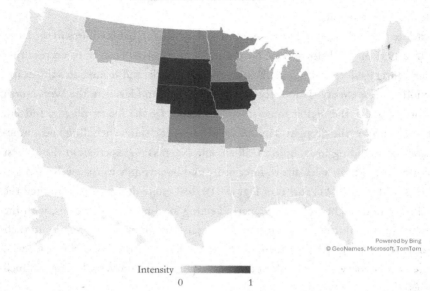

Intensity

0   1

B. Forced farm sales due to foreclosure, bankruptcy, etc., year through March 1932

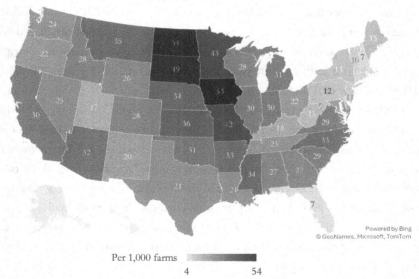

Per 1,000 farms

4   54

Figure 31: 1931 Locust Plague. Panel A is based on contemporary press reports cited in this chapter. The data in panel B is from the *Federal Reserve Bulletins* cited in this chapter.

as Arkansas, that may have been spared the locust plague but nonetheless endured the two-year drought.[14]

Moreover, the geographically concentrated increase in bank failures in the latter half of 1931 mapped closely onto farm distress, with forced farm transfers resulting from mortgage foreclosures, bankruptcy, deeding back, and related defaults nearly doubling from twenty-six to forty-four per one thousand farms in the West North Central region, the region most severely affected by the locust plague. Indeed, ground zero for the drought cum locust plague—the states including and immediately surrounding Iowa, South Dakota, and Nebraska—experienced the highest rates of forced farm sales due to foreclosure and bankruptcy in the twelve months through March 1932 (Panel B of Figure 31). Real estate dealers explicitly cited the incidence of drought and grasshoppers affecting local market conditions, with the decline in the value of farm real estate extinguishing many owners' equity in their farms. Already by 1931, as many as one in six farms in the West North Central states were underwater, the value of owner's equity in the property having declined to less than the mortgage balance.[15]

While farm equity values and average net farm returns declined across the board in 1930, 1931, and 1932 as global commodity prices fell and mortgage rates rose, in no region did they decline more sharply than in the West North Central. Indeed, the region comprising Minnesota, Iowa, Missouri, North Dakota, South Dakota, Nebraska, and Kansas was the only region in the country to experience outright negative net farm returns, with average net farm income falling from $1,684 in 1929 to -$178 in 1931 and -$98 in 1932.[16]

It did not take long for even contemporaries to blame the intense suffering on what in retrospect appeared to be an ill-advised, even irrational, land "boom" during the 1910s and 1920s. A January 1933 report from the US Department of Agriculture declared that an upward trend in commodity prices from the turn of the century through 1920 had led to "the development of a psychology ripe for a boom."[17] Later that year, the department noted that the "land boom" had "appeared in a more aggravated form" in the West North Central states, and even attempted to relate the magnitude of the declines in farm values in 1930–33 to the increase in farm values during the 1910s.[18]

More recent scholars have similarly characterized the 1920s as a period of an agricultural land boom.[19] Well, yes, in hindsight, any appreciation in land values and expansion of mortgage debt may look like a "boom" when succeeded by a

"slump" resulting from historic drought, locusts, and a global commodity deflation. Yet that is hardly a basis on which to define a boom.

This is not at all to suggest that the 1930–31 droughts and locust plague constituted a primary cause for the severe depth and duration of the Great Depression in
the United States.[20] Rather, they serve as a stark reminder that a defining feature
of the Great Depression was not a single, temporally continuous and spatially con-
tiguous cause but rather a succession of overlapping and interacting shocks, often
highly region-specific. Yet though unique in the volume and severity of those overlapping and interacting shocks, the Depression was not unique in featuring a multiplicity of coincident shocks. Indeed, a confluence of overlapping and interacting
shocks, rather than any single or uni-causal factor, is a feature of most recessions.

Following the British defeat at the Battle of Yorktown during the American Revolution, Scottish politician Sir John Sinclair lamented to Adam Smith that "if we
go on at this rate, the nation *must be ruined*." Smith calmly responded, "Be assured,
my young friend, that there is a great deal of ruin in a nation."[21] His point was that
it takes a great deal of misfortune and folly to destroy the accumulated human,
physical, and institutional capital of a national economy. A similar point could
be made about recessions; a lot must go wrong, or go wrong in a big way, to push
a large, diversified economy with sound institutions and a stock of human and
physical capital accumulated over decades, into a period of outright, broad-based
contraction.

In Chapter 1, we observed Eugen Slutsky's striking finding that a moving sum
of random lottery numbers mapped almost impeccably onto an index of British
business cycles over a more than twenty-year period. In this chapter, we will see
that the confluence of random and mutually independent adverse shocks can similarly generate irregularly recurring economic fluctuations.

We will also find in this chapter that Slutsky's use of lottery numbers was an
unintentionally apt one. After all, in any given year, there is a nontrivial chance
that an economy endures a harvest failure, a deep freeze, a war, a strike, or any
number of other potential adverse shocks. Though not all these shocks are necessarily random and independent of one another—for instance, war or industrial action
may be more likely in contexts of preexisting economic hardship—nor are they
predictable or perfectly dependent.

Suppose that in any given year there were a one-in-six chance each of a deep
freeze, war, and a coal strike. In this case, recession-inducing shocks could be

thought of as analogous to simultaneously rolling three standard, six-sided dice, one labeled *deep freeze*, another *war*, and a third *coal strike*. Any die rolling a 1 would then represent the occurrence of the corresponding shock in that year. The outcome of the roll of each die would not affect that of the others, and each roll would have a one-in-six chance of producing a 1.

With many potential shocks, each with different probabilities of occurring in any given year, the exercise would consist of simultaneously rolling many dice, with the number of sides of each die corresponding to the probability of that shock occurring in any given year. For instance, considering the century between the 1918 Spanish flu and 2020 coronavirus pandemic, a *pandemic* die might have one hundred sides. Recessionary shocks like pandemics are thus analogous to negative lotteries—lotteries in which one loses rather than gains money in the event of a "winning" ticket or roll. As we saw in Slutsky's work, the summation of such "chance causes" can generate what appear to constitute undulating patterns of economic activity, even though the underlying process is in fact random.

In addition to ruinous drought and locusts, the US economy was buffeted in the early 1930s by contractionary monetary policy, the sharp decline in the New York stock market beginning in the autumn of 1929, and the June 1930 enactment of the Tariff Act of 1930—the eponymously named Smoot-Hawley Tariff—which brought the average tariff rate on all US imports from approximately 14 percent to 20 percent. But there was also the Revenue Act of 1932, which raised personal income tax rates across the board, including hiking the top marginal rate from 25 percent to 63 percent.[22] The act not only brought the corporate income tax rate from 12 percent to 13.75 percent, it also extended the new rate to all corporate income, eliminating a prior exemption for corporate income under $3,000 (roughly $500,000 in 2024 dollars).[23] The same act imposed a two-cent tax on all bank checks, which resulted in a 12 percent contraction in money supply.[24]

Meanwhile, the banking dimension of the Great Depression in the United States was not one but four distinct and mostly regionally specific banking crises. The first was indeed highly region-specific, relating to the November 1930 failure of Nashville-based Caldwell & Company, then the largest investment bank in the South.[25] Two out of every five bank closures during the 1930 crisis were in the Nashville-adjacent St. Louis Federal Reserve District, while just four of twelve fed districts accounted for 80 percent of all bank suspensions and more than half of deposits in failed banks.[26] Meanwhile, six unaffected districts accounted for fewer than 10 percent of suspensions.[27] Notably, the New York money market, which previously constituted the epicenter for so many pre-1914 US banking crises such as 1857 and 1873, was largely unscathed.[28]

The second crisis, between April and August 1931, was similarly geographically concentrated, with the four Federal Reserve districts of Chicago, Minneapolis, Cleveland, and Kansas City accounting for 75 percent of all bank suspensions.[29] One-third of bank suspensions occurred in the Chicago District alone, and two in five in the Chicago and Cleveland Districts, which together accounted for two-thirds of deposits in suspended banks.[30] Though often related to the May 1931 failure of the Austrian bank Creditanstalt, there is little evidence that the consequent banking troubles in Austria and Germany were a primary cause of this second US banking crisis. If anything, net gold inflows as international investors sought refuge in the perceived safety of the United States was a mitigating rather than exacerbating factor during the summer of 1931 US banking crisis.[31] Again in stark contrast to pre-1914 crises, the New York money market was not a primary source of disturbance and was largely unaffected by a crisis that was largely limited to Toledo and Chicago.[32]

The third banking crisis of the Depression, in the fall of 1931, is conventionally attributed to the UK's departure from the gold standard on September 21 and consequent hoarding of gold out of fear that a devalued pound sterling would result in a decline in US net exports and an external drain of gold.[33] Yet recent scholarship has been unable to find any direct link between the United Kingdom going off gold and specific bank suspensions in the United States.[34] Rather, the US banking crisis in the latter half of 1931 was once again highly regionally variegated, with the increase in suspension rates concentrated among the drought- and locust-infested states in Figure 31 that experienced an exceptionally high incidence of forced farm sales due to foreclosure and bankruptcy. Suspension rates were also high in parts of the Southeast, where falling cotton prices and the lingering effects of earlier boll weevil infestations adversely impacted farmers, particularly in South Carolina and Georgia.[35]

Indeed, the geographic pattern of bank failures throughout the first three banking crises of the Great Depression in the United States is consistent with a growing body of economic research that identifies bank fundamentals, rather than panic, as the primary cause of bank runs.[36] Failed banks typically exhibit some combination of rapid balance sheet expansion via expensive wholesale funding and a deterioration in the value of loan portfolios as a result of adverse shocks to bank borrowers, or else of tight monetary policy lowering prices of banks' holdings of bonds and other securities.[37] The latter variety of shock recently helped undo Silicon Valley Bank in early 2023.

Historically, laws against branch banking meant that the US banking system consisted of thousands of small, unitary banks in more rural areas relying on larger correspondent banks in the major regional reserve cities, such as Chicago, St. Louis, and Cleveland.[38] In the event of a spatially correlated shock, such as drought or locusts, the most central nodes in regional banking networks—systemically important banks in the major regional reserve cities—were thereby exposed to large numbers of peripheral banks simultaneously withdrawing reserves to meet demands of local depositors.[39] A surge in small bank failures in the Midwest and Plains could thus expose larger banks in central reserve cities like Chicago to large-scale drains of reserves.

Considering the regional patterns of bank failures during the banking crises of the Great Depression, there is thus growing academic evidence that the fourth and final of the major banking crises of the Depression ended only when there was a fundamental shift in expectations about the future direction of agricultural commodity prices. Notwithstanding the ongoing struggles in the locust plague states, after dropping 6 percent in 1930, total crop production for the United States as a whole recovered in 1931, limiting upward domestic pressure on agricultural commodity prices.[40] Moreover, with three successive banking crises having resulted in an almost unprecedented decline in the money supply that the Federal Reserve failed to offset, deflation—and deflationary expectations—set in.[41]

Agricultural producers were thus caught in a financial vise. On one side, their debts—particularly mortgages—were nominally fixed, and therefore increasing in real terms as the price level declined. On the other side, with commodity prices typically more flexible than the overall price level, the price of their output was generally declining relative to operating expenses.[42] For many American farmers, it was a financially unsustainable situation.

The denouement arrived in the spring of 1933. On February 14, the governor of Michigan announced a statewide banking moratorium, igniting a cascade of preemptive bank withdrawals as depositors in surrounding states feared similar suspensions of payment. Within a month, banks were closed in thirty-three states, while deposit restrictions were in effect in ten and optional closure in five.[43] It was the first genuinely national banking crisis of the Depression. In response, just thirty-six hours after taking the oath of office, President Roosevelt imposed a week-long, nationwide bank holiday, at the conclusion of which he announced a raft of measures intended to raise prices in the US economy, culminating in the United States' April 1933 departure from the gold standard.[44] The result was a rise in inflation expectations that finally boosted the relative price of agricultural output, raising farm incomes and lowering real farm debt burdens.[45]

According to recent scholarship, higher inflation expectations after persistent deflation over the preceding four years can explain anywhere from 20–60 percent of the rebound in economic growth in the spring of 1933. Interestingly, a perceptive early observer of this dynamic was none other than Yale's disgraced Irving Fisher, who, in an October 1933 article on the "debt-deflation theory of great depressions," recognized that it was precisely the "reflation" since March 1933 that had halted the pernicious spiral of rising real debt burdens.[46]

The turnaround was indeed stark. Having plunged 36 percent and 51 percent, respectively, between the third quarter of 1929 and first quarter of 1933—including a 20 percent annualized decline in 1933:Q1—real GDP and industrial production rebounded at annual rates of 35 percent and 109 percent in the spring and summer of 1933. In 1934, the US economy expanded by 7 percent, followed by 16 percent in 1935 and 14 percent in 1936; a stunning illustration of the "plucking" model. While some might attribute the recovery to a positive policy action—namely, taking the United States off the gold standard—a more accurate reading would rather recognize the preceding contraction as in part a tragic example of the Hoover administration's violation of the economic equivalent of a Hippocratic oath to first do no harm.

Environmental shocks like drought and locust plagues can also interact in devastating fashion with disruptions of war. One of the longest recessions in UK history began with an "unparalleled drought" in the summer of 1762, followed that winter by an "intense frost" beginning on Christmas Day and lasting through the end of January that "put a stop to several handicraft trades."[47] The Thames froze in places, thwarting maritime traffic. In classic British fashion, on New Year's Eve 1762, some curious partygoers / amateur meteorologists placed a glass of red port wine upon a table in the open air; it froze solid in two hours, able to bear five shillings in coin atop it.[48] A glass of brandy upon the same table froze in six. The following summer was then extremely wet across England and Wales, with the Thames even bursting its banks later in the year.[49]

But if drought, deep freezes, and flooding were not enough to contend with, at the end of the Seven Years' War in 1763, the Prussian government decided to dump their wartime grain reserves, triggering a 75 percent collapse in the price of wheat.

At the same time, having debased their coinage during the war, they demonetized the depreciated coinage and reduced the value of new coinage that could be minted per unit of silver.[50] The combination of such a deflationary shock with the collapse of a prominent Berlin-based merchant bank that had been long wheat thus resulted in a severe, Europe-wide financial crisis.[51] Once again, a severe financial crisis thus succeeded and amplified rather than initiated the start of a recession.[52]

But even worse was the winter of 1946–47. Already by late 1946, the UK recession that had begun in 1943 was one of the longest on record, with wartime rationing of food, clothing, soap, fuel, paper, and other products extending well into the postwar period. Indeed, though the United Kingdom managed to avoid wartime rationing of bread and flour, when drought and ongoing recovery from war left the 1945 European wheat harvest at just half its prewar level, from July 1946, the Attlee government decreed bread and flour rations.[53] Continual rain over the next month further devastated the UK wheat harvest, with contemporary reports describing it as "the worst in living memory."[54]

Then, following several cold snaps in December 1946 and early January 1947, from January 21, a high-pressure weather system settled over Scandinavia, blocking warmer, low-pressure systems from progressing across the Atlantic. For nearly two months, temperatures in the British Isles remained at or below freezing, with Kew Observatory in London recording twenty straight days without sunshine.[55] Pack ice in the English Channel blocked the usual ferry service between England and Belgium.[56]

The coldest February on record paralyzed UK coal production, just recently nationalized by the Labour government. Ice floes and hurricane-force winds "lashed coal ships to their piers," while snow trapped seventy-five thousand coal-laden railroad cars. Stockpiles froze solid at pits and railroad depots.[57] After confidently boasting the preceding autumn that "there will be no fuel crisis, I am the Minister for Fuel and Power and I ought to know," Labour minister Manny Shinwell resorted to cutting electricity supplies to industry and turning off domestic electricity supply for five hours each day.[58] London's central electricity board, like Buckingham Palace, worked in overcoats and by candlelight, while television and radio programming was cut, newspapers reduced in length, and magazines suspended to conserve paper.[59] Industrial production plunged at an annual rate of 33 percent.

But it was the human toll that really characterized the climactic conclusion to the 1943–47 UK recession. In the "bomb-scarred slums" of east London, Mrs. Sophie Chimes collapsed after queueing for two hours in "bone-chilling wind."

When neighbors carried her to her small, prefabricated home in Whitechapel, Mrs. Chimes managed to break up two empty wooden crates of sadly ironic Sunkist oranges to generate a small fire in her stove.[60] Her husband—like two million other Brits, now unemployed—had gone to queue for potatoes, which were for the first time subject to rationing after the freeze destroyed some seventy thousand tons.[61]

With fields frozen and under heavy snow, farmers responded to the vegetable shortage by employing pneumatic drills to dig up parsnips.[62] In a desperate attempt to relieve the situation, the Royal Navy even deployed all available submarines to the nation's ports, using their onboard diesel generators for domestic power generation, code-named Operation Blackcurrant. Though the freeze finally broke in mid-March, the combination of melting snow, the wettest March on record in many parts of the country, and still-frozen ground that could not absorb surface runoff resulted in catastrophic flooding.[63]

Yet if large, coincident shocks like wartime rationing and extreme weather and other environmental events could generate long, deep recessions, so too could multiple smaller shocks generate relatively short, shallow recessions. Though innocent, it is not uncommon for economic expansions to be executed by *lingchi*—"death by a thousand cuts."

We have already seen coal strikes—for example, in 1902 in the United States and 1926 in the United Kingdom—of sufficient scale to trigger recession on their own. But when two hundred thousand US coal miners walked out on strike on April 1, 1927, market observers expected the economic impact to be relatively modest.[64] Though US soft coal production plunged by nearly half through July, preemptive stockpiling and continued production by nonunionized mines mitigated the impact.[65] Nonetheless, the strike was a particularly bitter one, with almost daily clashes between police and picketers.[66] In a preview of energy price shocks to come, *The New York Times* even observed that, in response to the strike, oil was increasingly becoming a competitor to hard coal.[67]

According to Romer's improved methodology, the 1927 US recession began in April and extended through December, coincident with the onset and conclusion of the nine-month-long coal strike.[68] But further hitting industrial output during the relatively mild recession was Henry Ford's December 1926 decision to shut down all his factories and idle two hundred thousand workers as Ford transitioned from the Model T to the new Model A automobile in the face of increased competition from Chevrolet. Having peaked at almost 50 percent of all cars produced in the United States in 1924, by 1926, the Model T still accounted for about 40 percent of US auto production.[69] The six-month closure thus saw total US auto production drop 22 percent in 1927, with new passenger car registrations down nearly 20 percent.[70] After eking out a 0.5 percent annualized gain in the first quarter of 1927, industrial production dropped 6 percent over the rest of the year.

Meanwhile, in the American South, a severe boll weevil infestation damaged 3 percent of the 1927 cotton crop in Texas to as much as 40 percent in Georgia and Florida.[71] Overall, the weevil-infested US cotton crop dropped by nearly 30 percent in 1927.[72]

A more recent example of expansion death by a thousand cuts was the relatively short, mild recession beginning April 2001, conventionally attributed to the collapse of the late 1990s dot-com bubble in technology stocks. To be sure, after peaking at $6.2 trillion in March 2000, by March 2001, the market capitalization of the tech-heavy NASDAQ composite had declined to just $2.7 trillion.[73] Yet empirical estimates of the short-run effect of changes in financial wealth on consumer spending imply that the decline in tech stocks lowered US consumer spending by at most about $30 billion; a drop in the bucket for a then $10.5 trillion economy.

Even higher, longer-run estimates that consumer spending responds by three to five cents for every one-dollar change in financial wealth implies a hit to US consumption of just 1 percent. In either case, the true effect was likely even smaller given the high concentration of NASDAQ equity wealth among higher-net-worth households, whose spending behavior tends to be less responsive to changes in financial wealth.[74] Moreover, US equity markets had already started to recover in April 2001, with the market capitalization of the NASDAQ rebounding 17 percent in the three months through June.

A bigger shock to labor demand in the United States was the October 2000 establishment of permanent normal trade relations (PNTR) with the People's Republic of China. Enacted by Congress to allow China's accession to the World Trade Organization, PNTR granted permanent most-favored-nation tariff rates to the then-$2 trillion (in 2024 dollars), 1.3-billion-person Chinese economy.[75] Previously, since 1980, Congress had to annually renew China's most-favored-nation status. Without renewal, US tariffs on imported Chinese goods would have jumped to the higher tariff rates—originally established under none other than the Smoot-Hawley Tariff Act of 1930—applied to nonmarket economies such as China's. Though ultimately always renewed, renewal was uncertain and politically contentious. With removal of that uncertainty, US manufacturing thus entered a period of unexpectedly rapid decline.[76]

The same month that Congress passed PNTR, the MIT-educated CEO of Lexmark—then the second-largest computer printer manufacturer in the world—announced that the Kentucky-based company would lay off 10 percent of their US workforce by the end of the year as they outsourced production to southern China. Between October 2000 and April 2001, more than eighty major US employers would follow suit, accounting for as many as thirty-five thousand lost jobs.[77] But more important than manufacturing *layoffs*—which increased by seventy thousand between late 2000 and the late summer of 2001—was that manufacturing *hires* dropped by more than double that, accounting for 70 percent of the decline in overall hiring.[78] Excluding manufacturing, US layoffs actually *decreased* by seventy-five thousand in the first eight months of 2001.

Scholars would later attribute the "jobless recovery" after 2001 in part to what became known as "the China shock," which could explain 26–55 percent of the staggering and historically sudden loss of 3.4 million US manufacturing jobs between 2000 and 2007.[79] Indeed, after remaining largely constant for the entire postwar period through 2000, from the start of the recovery in December 2001 through the end of the expansion in December 2007, manufacturing employment in the United States shed 2.1 million jobs. Not only were most of these workers unable to find reemployment in other, nonmanufacturing sectors, but the loss of manufacturing jobs also had adverse effects on demand for complementary non-manufacturing workers in local labor markets.[80]

Underscoring the nontrivial impact of the China shock on the US economy was that the UK economy skated through the two-quarter-long US recession. Though, as we will see in Chapter 8, there were several reasons the United Kingdom was spared recession in 2001, among them was that as a member of the European Union they had already had permanent normal trade relations with China since 1980. With the 1980 Chinese economy both substantially smaller and less globally integrated than the Chinese economy of 2000, this meant the United Kingdom had a much longer runway for economic adaptation, in contrast to the sudden, large shock inflicted on the US economy.[81]

But if the China shock was not enough, the US economy had an additional, more familiar challenge with which to contend in early 2001. Driven largely by a strong rebound in economic activity in east and southeast Asia following the Asian financial crisis of 1997–98, global oil demand rose sharply in 1999–2000.[82] By the end of 2000, the real price of oil had risen to its highest level since the 1990 Iraqi invasion of Kuwait, with the price of a gallon of gasoline similarly reaching levels not seen since the war. As a share of disposable personal income, US expenditures on energy goods and services jumped by more than a percentage point, to nearly 5 percent. Throughout 2000, overall energy inflation in the United States ran in the double digits, peaking at 21.3 percent midyear and still clocking in at 18 percent at the start of 2001.[83]

For California, the largest economy in the union, a combination of rising wholesale gas prices, the disruption of hydropower by drought, and government controls on retail electricity prices resulted in a critical mismatch between energy supply and demand, the consequence of which was rolling blackouts throughout the first half of 2001.[84] Into the teeth of this US energy crisis, in early 2001, the Organization of the Petroleum Exporting Countries (OPEC) twice voted to further cut production.[85]

Yet despite the multiplicity of adverse shocks, the 2001 recession was, as noted above, a relatively mild affair. Over the course of the eight-month recession from April through November, real GDP expanded, albeit by a paltry 0.2 percent. Though the unemployment rate spiked, its November 2001 level of 5.5 percent remained well below non-recession levels observed throughout most of the 1980s. While initial estimates of US GDP indicated slight expansion in the first two quarters of 2001 followed by contraction in the third, later revisions had the US economy contracting in all three quarters, before revisions to the revisions identified discrete contractions in the first and third quarters, interrupted by healthy expansion in the second.

Ultimately, all the GDP contraction during the two-quarter recession was during the quarter that included the terrorist attacks of September 11, a period that witnessed the complete closure of North American airspace, a massive stock market sell-off, direct physical harm to the then-second-largest state economy in the United States, and widespread fear and uncertainty. As the NBER acknowledged at the time, were it not for the economic consequences of September 11, it was entirely possible that the relatively modest decline in economic activity during the year would not have been sufficiently broad, deep, and protracted for them to conclude that a recession began in March–April of that year.[86] So, while the parable of the "dot-com recession" may have a certain moral clarity, the reality was that a lot had to go wrong—even tragically so—in 2000–01 for the US economy to enter outright recession.

The passage of time can easily erase historical memory. Few alive today remember the postwar rationing and extreme winter weather events that the postwar UK economy endured. Fewer still could remember the visitation of boll weevils and Ford shutdowns in 1927 or bank check taxes and locusts in the early 1930s in the United States. None experienced the coal famines of the early twentieth century, let alone the eighteenth-century turf famines and frosts to which we heard William Stout refer in Chapter 5.

And yet we have also seen that the passage of time is not alone culpable for eroding memory of recessionary shocks and their historical contexts. In 2001, as in 1857, 1873, 1929, 2008, and many recessions, even contemporary narrative gravitates toward a penitent, uni-causal boom-bust explanation of present economic predicament over the more prosaic and multifaceted. Indeed, even the 1772 recession made immediately infamous by the spectacular failure of Alexander Fordyce occurred in the context of broader European economic hardship following yet another extreme eighteenth-century winter in 1771–72.[87]

It is not just moral clarity that such accounts of historical recessions offer. It is also simplicity. It is far easier to ex post facto pick out some subjectively excessive boom than it is to painstakingly consult the historical record for both qualitative and quantitative primary evidence of the actual shocks to which economies were subjected during recessionary episodes. Even such classic works as Charles Kindleberger's *Manias, Panics, and Crashes* at times reads like the work of an armchair historian, with references to sundry, vaguely defined booms, sometimes specific, sometimes broad-based. Meanwhile, economists continue to construct models of the endogenous or self-generating economic cycle.[88] Yet recessions occur and have always occurred in actual history, in which people and economies endure war, weather, pandemics, strikes, and accidents of interminable variety, any one or several of which can strike in any given year.

However, while the notion that each year we are automatically enrolled in a sort of negative economic lottery may be disheartening, we should draw assurance from the observation that typically quite a few recessionary "dice" need to roll a 1 for large, diversified economies like the United States' and United Kingdom's to enter outright recession. As Adam Smith reassured his concerned friend, there is indeed a great deal of ruin in a nation. In the next chapter, we will examine whether the public sector is an effective source of insurance in the event of a recession or if instead government itself is as or more likely to cause one.

7

FIREFIGHTERS AND ARSONISTS

Everyone is a Keynesian in a foxhole.
—ROBERT LUCAS, 2008

Ulysses S. Grant was hardly a man of fear. The victor of Vicksburg, the man
whose armies slugged it out against General Robert E. Lee and the Army of
Northern Virginia across the bloody trenches of Petersburg, was dogged and
unflinching to the point of callousness. Some contemporaries even called him a
butcher.[1] During the Battle of Cold Harbor, he controversially ordered a disastrous assault on Lee's entrenched Confederate forces, suffering 13,000 casualties
to Lee's 4,500.[2]

But in September 1873, the eighteenth president did something he had rarely
done before—he blinked. Following news of Jay Cooke & Co.'s suspension of payment on September 18, President Grant canceled his planned return to Washington
from Cooke's mansion at Ogontz in Philadelphia.[3] Instead, he proceeded to New
York, where he and Treasury secretary William Richardson held court at the Fifth
Avenue Hotel as frantic New York financiers pled for the federal government to
relieve pressure in money markets by releasing millions of dollars' worth of previously retired currency.[4]

To finance the Union war effort during the Civil War, Congress had authorized
the Treasury to issue $450 million in paper currency that was backed only by the
faith and credit of the US federal government and thus could not be redeemed
for gold.[5] But with the end of the war, concerned that the continued circulation
of these fiat "greenback" notes would be inflationary, Congress authorized the

Treasury to contract the supply of money by taking back or "redeeming" green-backs in exchange for US government bonds.[6]

Holders of greenbacks thus received federal bonds in exchange for their green-backs, which the Treasury then retired from circulation. Over the next two years, Treasury accordingly retired from circulation $44 million (approximately $140 billion in 2024 dollars) worth of greenbacks, before alarm at the deflationary effects of such a contraction in the supply of currency prompted Congress to halt further redemptions in 1868.[7]

Treasury was thus left with a "reserve" of $44 million in previously issued currency, along with ambiguous authority to release it back into circulation. They exploited that ambiguity in October 1872—as the Grant reelection campaign was in full swing—when then–Assistant Secretary of the Treasury Richardson, in Secretary George Boutwell's absence, reissued approximately $4.5 million in green-backs from "the reserve" to facilitate "relief of the business of the country, then suffering from the large demand for currency employed in moving the crops from the South and West." The situation, according to Richardson, seemed "to have warranted the issue upon grounds of public policy."[8]

Though Boutwell approved of Richardson's actions, Congress did not, with a majority of the Senate Committee on Finance maintaining that reissuance violated the policy of contraction that the 1868 legislation had merely halted rather than reversed. Both Boutwell and Richardson had to testify before the committee. But as Congress had neither explicitly granted discretion to the Secretary of the Treasury in the use of the "reserve," nor did they now retroactively resolve the issue with clarifying legislation forbidding its use, the putative existence of a greenback "reserve" persisted.[9]

Thus, as "bankers, brokers, business and professional men" thronged the halls and vestibules of the Fifth Avenue Hotel in September 1873, the key question on everyone's mind was whether the president and Treasury secretary could and would deploy the $44 million reserve to relieve the worsening cash crunch.[10] Already on Friday evening, September 19, Grant telegrammed Richardson to instruct him to purchase $10 million in government bonds to relieve stress in financial markets.[11] Yet as emergency discussions dragged on through the weekend, Grant's advisors warned him that any purchase of bonds using the greenback reserve would likely be unconstitutional.[12]

To the disappointment of the lords of finance gathered at the Fifth Avenue Hotel, late Sunday afternoon, the president and Richardson concluded that financing bond purchases through the reissuance of retired greenbacks would be unconstitutional.[13] Richardson's bond purchases would therefore have to rely on cash from the preceding months' sales of Treasury gold.[14] While both Grant and Richardson stressed that purchases would draw not one cent from the reserve, during Sunday morning's discussions, Grant intimated that "if financial disaster should threaten the ruin of the best business interests of the country" and existing Treasury resources prove inadequate, he would consider it, constitutional or not.[15]

By the end of the day on Thursday, September 25, Richardson announced that he would make no further bond purchases; he had exhausted the entirety of Treasury's approximately $14 million in cash reserves.[16] However, while insisting that he had not touched the $44 million greenback reserve, in the coming weeks and months, Grant and Richardson quietly tapped the reserve for $26 million (equivalent to $85 billion in 2024 dollars) to fund government expenditures, effectively releasing greenbacks into circulation.[17] It was simply reissuance via purchases of goods and services rather than bonds.

In fact, it was not the first time that Grant blinked in the face of financial turmoil. Just four years previously, during the relatively mild recession from July 1869 through December 1870, Grant instructed Boutwell to unload $4 million in federal government gold to break the diminutive financial genius Jay Gould's attempt to corner the market for gold. The government's intervention drove down the price of gold and stemmed the panic that had triggered "Black Friday" on September 24, 1869, and nearly ruined Gould.[18]

Even before the Grant administration, it was not without precedent for the United States federal government to intervene at moments of acute economic and financial crisis. During 1857, as panic gripped the country in August 1857, President Buchanan's Treasury secretary and future president of the Provisional Congress of the Confederate States of America, Howell Cobb, drew down the federal government cash reserve by $7 million (approximately $50 billion in 2024 dollars) to purchase financial securities, including approximately $3 million in direct purchases of government and private securities.[19]

Almost exactly 150 years later, as the US economy descended into its worst economic crisis since the Great Depression and the Federal Reserve and US Treasury ballooned their balance sheets in a frantic attempt to stem the rapidly deteriorating situation, Nobel laureate in economics Robert Lucas remarked to a journalist, "Well I guess everyone is a Keynesian in a foxhole."[20] Just a few weeks prior, Congress had passed and President George W. Bush signed into law the Emergency

Economic Stabilization Act of 2008, appropriating $700 billion (over $1 trillion in 2024 dollars) for the US Treasury to purchase impaired assets from US banks. Meanwhile, the Federal Reserve's balance sheet had doubled from $900 billion at the end of August to $1.8 trillion, and before the end of the year would peak at $2.3 trillion.[21]

Lucas's quip was ironic gallows humor from a man who in 1980 had remarked that "one cannot find good, under-forty economists who identify themselves or their work as 'Keynesian.' Indeed, people even take offense if referred to as 'Keynesians.' At research seminars, people don't take Keynesian theorizing seriously anymore; the audience starts to whisper and giggle to one another."[22] Over the preceding decade, the phenomenon of concurrently high inflation and high unemployment had discredited notions, associated with the late British economist John Maynard Keynes, that government could effectively dampen fluctuations in unemployment without generating rising rates of inflation.

Yet historically, Grant and Richardson, and Buchanan and Cobb, were by no means alone in their Damascene conversions to faith in monetary and fiscal intervention in the event of economic contraction. While 1945 is often viewed as an inflection point after which the newly expanded role of the state and increased reliance on automatic government stabilizers attenuated economic fluctuations, historically, there has often been public sector intervention in the event of recession. Indeed, the average peak-to-trough percentage changes in the monetary base and real public spending in the United States were statistically no different after 1945 versus before. In real terms, the monetary base in the United States actually expanded by 5 percent *more* during prewar versus postwar recessions, though this may simply reflect the fact that prewar recessions were more likely to be accompanied by falling prices, thereby raising the real value of the existing base money supply.

Similarly in the United Kingdom, the average peak-to-trough percentage changes in the monetary base and real public spending were statistically no different after 1945 versus before. The general continuity in the average response of the monetary base is especially striking considering that, for most of the prewar period, the Bank of England was a privately held company, while US coinage and paper currency in circulation was determined not by the Federal Reserve, established in 1913, but by the US Mint and private banks issuing bond-backed notes.

However, while the average *percentage change* in public spending during postwar economic recessions may have been similar, the absolute *level* of spending has been substantially higher in both countries since 1945, and thus the same percentage change during recessions has been off a substantially higher base. Indeed, in September 1873, federal government spending was just 3.4 percent of US GDP. On the eve of the Great Depression, federal spending was still only about 3 percent of GDP, while overall federal, state, and local spending was not even 11 percent. In contrast, since 1945, it has averaged just over 30 percent.

Meanwhile, though public spending in the United Kingdom was generally higher than in the United States before the war—13 percent in 1900 and 25 percent on the eve of the Great Depression—it was still substantially lower than during the period since the end of World War II, when public spending in the United Kingdom averaged 40 percent of GDP. Thus, since the 1930s and 1940s, in both economies, there has been a substantial expansion of the public sector's economic footprint.

This development was certainly not lost on Columbia professor, Wesley Clair Mitchell protégé, former chairman of President Eisenhower's Council of Economic Advisers, and future chairman of the Federal Reserve, Arthur Burns. In his 1959 presidential address to the American Economic Association (AEA), the bespectacled, pipe-smoking Burns noted that not only had federal, state, and local government expenditures nearly quadrupled as a share of the economy over the preceding half century but also that both government revenue and transfer payments had become substantially more responsive to economic conditions.[23]

Compared to previous decades, when governments relied overwhelmingly on customs revenues, postwar US governments increasingly relied on revenue from personal and corporate income taxation, the collection of which operated progressively and countercyclically. When the economy was strong, government tax revenue went up and after-tax income increased by less than pretax income; whereas when the economy was contracting, government tax revenue declined and after-tax income declined by less than pretax incomes. After-tax income thereby fluctuated by less than pretax income. Moreover, Burns noted that a sophisticated, nationwide system of unemployment insurance and social security meant that fluctuations in personal incomes were increasingly untethered from fluctuations in overall economic activity.[24]

More than a quarter century, he noted, had passed since the financial panics of the Great Depression, and more than twenty years since the country had experienced what could reasonably be described as a severe recession. The four recessions between 1945 and 1959 were each relatively brief and mild, with the longest lasting eleven months. Despite acknowledging that the economy nonetheless continued to be "swayed" by economic fluctuations, the central thesis of Burns's address was that the severity of those swings had been very much attenuated by the spectacular growth in government over the preceding quarter century.[25]

In 1977, eighteen years after Burns's AEA presidential address, Yale economist and future chairman of the Council of Economic Advisers under President Clinton, Martin Baily, published an influential paper at the Brookings Institution. While carefully caveating the results of his analysis, Baily developed a model demonstrating that the apparent increase in economic stability in the postwar period could, per Burns's hypothesis, be explained by the evolved role of government economic policy, particularly the rise of automatic, countercyclical macroeconomic stabilization policies.[26]

Though Baily's paper generated spirited discussion at the time, by the mid-1980s, the thesis had become conventional wisdom. In a 1984 working paper and follow-up chapter in a marquee 1986 conference and subsequent edited volume for the NBER, Harvard economists Brad DeLong and future Treasury secretary Larry Summers found that the increasing "institutionalization" of the US economy had rendered the economy substantially less volatile than in the pre–World War II period. In particular, they noted that the increased role of a tax-and-transfer system that automatically stabilized posttax household incomes had effectively decreased the share of households that would have to substantially curtail spending in the event of shocks to pretax incomes. Such institutional features could thereby attenuate the amplitude of fluctuations in overall consumer spending.[27]

But is the conventional, received wisdom that increased government intervention since the Great Depression has effectively smoothed fluctuations in economic activity correct? Has the state tamed the business "cycle"? Conversely, can governments contribute to the onset of recession as much as or more than they contribute to their resolution?

In an ironic counterpoint to Burns's thesis, just one month after the AEA published Burns's celebration of the triumph of fiscal policy over the business cycle in his 1959 presidential address, the US economy entered recession. Adding to the irony, the 1960 recession ended one of the shorter expansions in US history. So much for having tamed economic fluctuations. Already by the late 1980s, future Council of Economic Advisers chair Christina Romer began to challenge the Burns thesis that institutional changes since the 1930s had effectively attenuated economic volatility. Romer found that the appearance of higher prewar volatility was likely a consequence of measurement error and statistical artifact.[28] Nonetheless, Romer's was a minority view.[29]

However, as we have already learned in Chapter 2, "Peter Pan Versus Dorian Gray," prewar US and UK expansions were no more likely to die of old age than postwar expansions and prewar US and UK recessions were no less likely to die of old age than postwar recessions. These two observations alone complicate the theory that state intervention is necessary to reduce the frequency and duration of recessions.[30]

Unfortunately, testing whether automatic stabilizers and an increased level of public spending have attenuated the depth and duration of recessions is confounded by the fact that government intervention both affects the level of economic activity and is the consequence of it. Deeper, longer recessions may be accompanied by larger increases in public spending, but that does not necessarily mean that larger increases in spending cause longer or deeper recessions.

A better test of the potential role of public spending in mitigating recessions is thus to simply evaluate whether the duration and depth of economic recessions is a function of historical time. If the expanding role of the state over time has reduced the expected duration and depth of a recession, then we should observe that recession durability and depth are decreasing over time.

As can be seen in Panel A of Figure 32, contrary to the Burns hypothesis, recession duration has been essentially constant across time in both the United States and United Kingdom. Statistically, the passage of time has had precisely no effect on average recession duration in either country. Though US recessions since 1945 were, on average, shorter than prewar recessions, the estimated effect disappears using the improved Davis-Romer chronology. The average duration of a post-1945 US recession of 1.2 years is statistically no different from the prewar average of 1.4 years. In the United Kingdom, the average postwar recession persisted for 1.6 years, statistically no different from the 1.5-year prewar average.

As can also be seen in Panel A, in both countries, the longest recessions on record were associated with major wars, a stark warning that actions of the state can cause or contribute to recession as easily as they can mitigate them. All three of the longest UK recessions followed world wars—namely, the recessions of 1944–47, 1919–21, and 1762–65, respectively, corresponding to World War II, World War I, and the Seven Years' War, the latter often regarded as the first truly global or "world war."

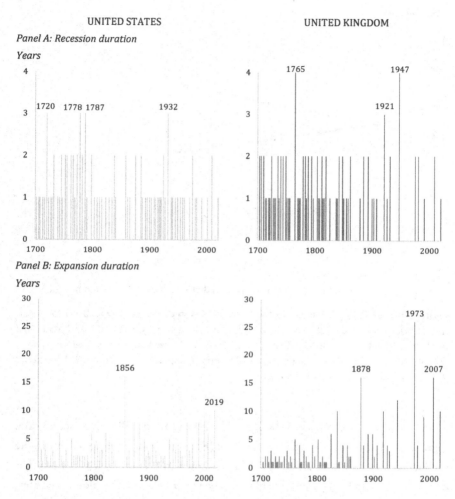

Figure 32: Recession and Expansion Age at Time of Death, 1700–2020.

Similarly, outside the Great Depression, two of the four longest US recessions were during and immediately following the American Revolution. In fact, the effect of that war on the American economy was on par with the Great Depression. While aggregate statistics are limited, real wages in the United States fell by almost half between 1775 and 1779, and as late as 1786 were still nearly 10 percent below their 1775 level. Between 1774 and 1789, GDP per capita may have contracted by as much as 30 percent. By comparison, during the Great Depression, real GDP per capita contracted by 33 percent.[31]

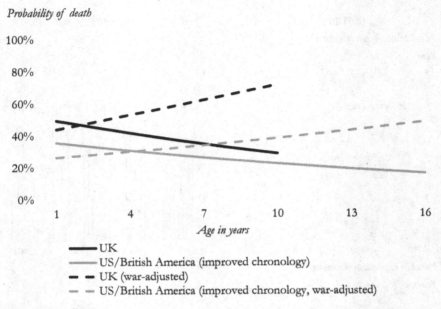

Probability of death

Figure 33: Probability a UK or US Expansion Ends in the Next Year, 1700–1854. (Patrick O'Brien and Nuno Palma, "Not an Ordinary Bank but a Great Engine of State: The Bank of England and the British Economy, 1694–1844," *Economic History Review* 76, no. 1 [2023]: 305–29. Underlying data through 1844 kindly shared by the authors. I then extend the annual indicators through 1854 here.)

In Chapter 2, we observed the rather surprising result, albeit not statistically significant, that economic expansions before 1855 were if anything less likely to die the longer they had been alive. However, as shown in Figure 33, it turns out that this result is entirely driven by the high frequency of episodes of major armed conflict before 1855, with which recessions were highly correlated—that is, recessions were statistically much more likely during or in the immediate aftermath of major wars. Thus, the probability that an economic expansion died in the next year only appeared to decrease as an expansion aged for the simple reason that expansion duration was positively correlated with peace.

Accordingly, as shown in Figure 33, if we simply account for the duration of any ongoing major war in which the United Kingdom was engaged in any given year before 1855—which either directly or indirectly involved the United States as well—the apparent phenomenon that pre-1855 expansions were slightly less likely to die the longer they had survived disappears.[32] Like post-1855 UK and

US expansions, pre-1855 expansions were simply no more or less likely to die than younger expansions. But the persistence of major international armed conflict *was* likely to murder economic expansions in both economies during the eighteenth and nineteenth centuries.

One can also assess the Burns hypothesis by statistically testing whether average recession duration shifted systematically after specific points in time.[33] If shorter-duration recessions were associated with an expanded role of the state in both economies since the 1930s or 1940s, then we would expect to observe a sharp break toward shorter recessions sometime between the Great Depression and the end of World War II. Yet again, results are inconsistent with the timing of the Burns hypothesis. Using the Davis-Romer recession chronology, statistical tests reveal no evidence of a break toward shorter US recessions after those ending in 1932, 1938, 1945, or even 1914, a year after the establishment of the Federal Reserve.[34] The only break toward shorter US recessions was in 1785, at the end of the Revolutionary War. The same tests indicate no systematic break toward shorter UK recessions after those ending in 1931 and 1947, despite the advent of comprehensive social welfare in 1946 under the Atlee government.

Another dimension of the Burns hypothesis is that not only did postwar macroeconomic policies and institutions shorten the average duration of recessions, they also rendered the postwar economy less volatile and less susceptible to recession in the first place, implying longer economic expansions. To be sure, expansions have indeed become more durable over time. Using both the NBER and Davis-Romer chronologies extended back to 1700, one finds that with the passage of each decade the average duration of an economic expansion in the United States increased by 0.1 years. For the United Kingdom, the passage of each decade is associated with a 0.4-year increase in the average duration of an economic expansion.

Since World War II, the average US expansion has thus endured 2.7 years longer (2.1 years longer using the Davis-Romer chronology) than the average pre-1946 US expansion, while the average UK expansion has endured 10 years longer, driven in part by the exceptionally long recovery from World War II. Even excluding that expansion—which was, for all its impressiveness, shorter than Australia's unbroken 30-year expansion from 1991 until the COVID-19 pandemic—the average postwar UK expansion was still almost 7 years longer than the average prewar expansion.

Yet the increased durability of post–World War II expansions in both economies is not a discontinuity in either 1945 or the 1930s but rather the continuation of a much longer-term trend toward more durable expansions. Indeed, according to the Davis-Romer chronology, one of the longest US expansions on record was that which ended in 1856, while one of the longest UK expansions in history ended in 1878. Notably, the longest expansions in both US and UK history occurred during periods of relative peace.[35]

Using the Davis-Romer recession chronology, there is no systematic shift toward longer expansions after those ending in 1929, 1937, or 1944. If there were any sharp break, statistical tests suggest it occurred in 1883, decades before any dramatic expansion of the US public sector. The same tests for a single break toward longer expansions in the United Kingdom indicate a potential break in 1907. Thus, statistically, there is no evidence whatsoever of a structural shift toward shorter recessions and longer expansions specifically after the 1930s or 1940s.

Moreover, the provision of palliatives is only one side of the ledger. Governments can also generate adverse shocks just as often as they may attempt to alleviate them; they can be arsonists as well as firefighters. The 1949 US recession was unlikely to have occurred had the US government not reimposed wartime credit controls on consumer lending just two months prior.[36] In an attempt to suppress postwar inflation, President Truman requested, and Congress granted, the presidential authority to impose broad controls on banks' provision of consumer credit. From September 20, 1948, through June 30 the following year, the president thus exercised that authority to instruct the Federal Reserve to raise minimum down-payment requirements and impose minimum monthly installments and maximum maturities on various types of consumer loans.[37] Within two months, the US economy—but not the UK economy—was in recession.

Though Congress—with the signed support of four hundred economists—reauthorized the presidential imposition of credit controls in 1951 during the Korean War, a congressional subcommittee subsequently found the 1948 and 1951 controls to have adversely impacted the provision and allocation of credit. Congress thus repealed the president's authority to impose credit in 1953.

Yet two decades later, the mere threat of a return of credit controls was sufficient to generate a credit shortage in late 1969. Again concerned by elevated inflation, in the summer of 1969, the Nixon administration began jawboning banks to voluntarily restrict credit through nonprice mechanisms.[38] At the same time, two Democratic members of Congress, Leonor Sullivan and Henry Reuss, concerned that interest rate hikes were too blunt an instrument for curtailing inflation, attached to an existing financial regulation bill an amendment that would grant the president discretionary authority to impose credit controls.[39]

Caught between pressure from the administration and the now credible threat that Congress would reauthorize presidential authority to impose mandatory credit controls, from July, US banks began engaging in voluntary credit rationing, restricting certain types of loans.[40] Overall bank credit thus contracted outright that month, and the following, and again in October, and would end the year down more than 2 percent in real terms. Indeed, a large economics literature has since found that uncertainty and fear about economic policy can have an even greater effect than the policies themselves.[41]

Meanwhile, with Congress racing to pass the bill before recessing for Christmas, there was no time to hold hearings on the economic rationale or potential macroeconomic effects of consumer credit controls versus interest rate hikes. The House and Senate therefore passed a compromise version of the bill on December 19, including Sullivan and Reuss's amendment, without holding any formal hearings. President Nixon signed the legislation into law on Christmas Eve 1969.[42] The then-record-long economic expansion that had begun in March 1961 came to an end that month, with bank credit contracting a further 2 percent in real terms in the first two months of the new year.

Just a decade later, keen during an election year to demonstrate that he was taking bold action to combat inflation, President Jimmy Carter invoked the authority that the 1969 act granted him to direct the Federal Reserve to impose consumer credit controls in March 1980. Though the NBER would later determine that the relatively short recession of 1980 began in February, rumors were swirling for months that the administration was contemplating the reimposition of controls.[43] On February 15, *The New York Times* even reported that Alfred Kahn, President Carter's designated "Advisor to the President on Inflation," was strongly pushing for the imposition of credit controls on consumer loans in an effort to curb inflation.[44] Markets were thus keenly aware that the policy was baking, if not already baked.

But misguided government policies over money and credit extend much further back in time. To curb speculation in land, in the summer of 1837, outgoing US President Andrew Jackson issued an executive order instructing the secretary of the

Treasury to accept only gold and silver as payment for sales of public lands, much of which the US government had only recently acquired through the forced displacement of Indigenous Americans under the Indian Removal Act of 1830. The order had the unintended effect of draining specie reserves from New York, Philadelphia, and New Orleans to the interior at the very moment that interest rate hikes by the Bank of England and an infestation of Hessian flies were generating external drains of gold.[45] The result was a severe credit crisis culminating in the Panic of 1837, among the worst US recessions of the nineteenth century.

Examples abound, but one of the most important and grave powers of government— namely, the decision to go to war—is also one of the most destructive economic forces over the past four centuries in both the United States and United Kingdom. As we have just seen, the longest recessions on record in the United States and United Kingdom have generally occurred in wartime contexts, while the longest economic expansions occurred in periods of relative peace. War and war-related disruptions truncate economic expansions, lengthen economic recessions, and amplify economic volatility to appalling extremes. On the question of war, it could thus be said that the state is more Napoleon III than Florence Nightingale.

If the Burns hypothesis that the expanded role of automatic stabilizers and countercyclical demand management since 1945 were true, then we would also expect to observe smaller average peak-to-trough declines in macroeconomic aggregates and smaller peak-to-trough increases in the unemployment rate during recessions. Yet peak-to-trough fluctuations in real GDP, real consumer spending, real investment, and the unemployment rate have been strikingly consistent across time. As indicated by the dotted trend lines in Figure 34, the passage of time can explain almost none of the variation in peak-to-trough changes in real GDP, consumption, investment, or unemployment.

Statistically, peak-to-trough declines in real GDP (since 1790), consumption (since 1834), and investment (since 1901), and peak-to-trough increases in the unemployment rate (since 1890) in the United States were on average no different after 1945 versus before. In the United Kingdom, the average peak-to-trough decline in real GDP (since 1700) and peak-to-trough increase in the unemployment rate (since 1760) were likewise statistically no different after 1945 versus before. Average peak-to-trough declines in real consumption and real investment (both since 1830) in the United Kingdom were in fact *greater* after 1945 versus before. If average peak-to-trough changes in output, unemployment, consumption, and

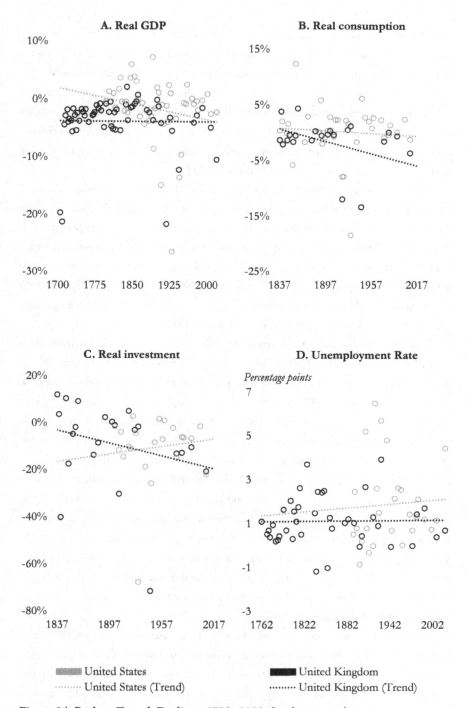

Figure 34: Peak-to-Trough Declines, 1700–2020. See data appendix.

investment were no more moderate in the period since the rise of more interven-
tionist states versus the period before, then the argument that increased government
intervention has attenuated economic fluctuations becomes difficult to sustain.

We can also explore the variance in the unemployment rate and growth rates of
real GDP, real consumer spending, and real investment to determine whether institutional changes since the 1930s have dampened expansion peaks and recession
troughs. If they have, then we would expect to observe a decline in within-cycle
variance of the unemployment rate and economic growth rates.

Figure 35 reveals that while the variance of real GDP growth over the course of
the average sequence of US expansion and contraction has indeed declined since the
first half of the twentieth century, it has merely declined to a level consistent with
its variance throughout much of the nineteenth century. Meanwhile, after very
high volatility in real GDP growth in the war-intensive early-eighteenth century
and during the Napoleonic Wars, the variance of within-cycle real GDP growth in
the United Kingdom has remained consistently low and stable by historical standards since Napoleon's final defeat at Waterloo in 1815.

Real consumer spending has consistently been considerably less volatile than
overall GDP, and that volatility has generally been declining over time in the
United States in a trend extending back to the first half of the nineteenth century.
Statistical tests indicate 1857 as a possible break toward lower average variance in
within-cycle real consumption growth in the United States, almost a hundred years
before the advent of the automatic stabilizers that Burns et al. highlighted as the
primary source of greater stability in postwar real consumer spending.

Meanwhile in the United Kingdom, the variance of real consumer spending
growth over the course of expansions and contractions has been consistently low
and stable since the first half of the nineteenth century, only spiking during the
cycles ending in the postwar recessions following World Wars I and II and the 2020
COVID pandemic recession. The long-run stability of UK consumption growth is
a stark contradiction of the notion that an expanded role for automatic stabilizers
and countercyclical demand management has attenuated the volatility of consumer
spending since the 1930s or 1940s.

Within-cycle real investment growth in both countries has consistently been
considerably more volatile than both real consumption and real GDP, though again
roughly constant over time. The notable exceptions were the Great Depression and
World War II. The most volatile cycle for real investment in the United States was

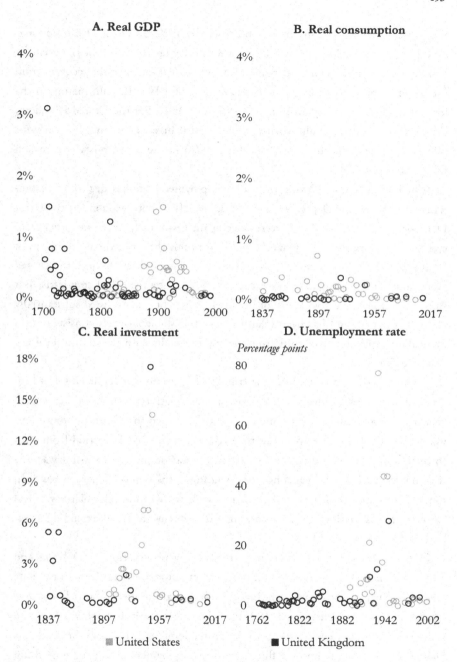

Figure 35: Peak-to-Trough Variance, 1700–2020. See data appendix.

that which included the sharp rebound from the 1929–32 Great Depression and then return to recession in 1937–38. Meanwhile, by far the most volatile cycle for real investment in the United Kingdom was that which included the recovery from the Great Depression through the first half of World War II, culminating in the long, deep wartime recession from 1943 through 1947. For the United Kingdom, the only other exceptionally volatile cycle for real investment since the early-to-middle nineteenth century was that which ended in the severe postwar recession following World War I.

While within-cycle volatility in the unemployment rate has declined substantially since the Great Depression and World War II in both economies, the Great Depression and World War II were once again historically aberrant rather than typical. From approximately World War I through the immediate aftermath of World War II, within-cycle variance in the unemployment rate in both the United States and United Kingdom was exceptionally high by historical standards. But since 1945, the cyclical volatility of the unemployment rate declined substantially in both countries and has been relatively low and stable at levels consistent with cyclical unemployment volatility from the mid-late eighteenth century until the eve of World War I.

In short, rather than marking the triumph of government stabilization of economic fluctuations, the decline in macroeconomic volatility since the mid-twentieth century in both economies has merely marked a return to historically more normal levels of volatility compared to the extremes of the martial period from 1914 through 1945. For consumption in particular, outside periods of world war, the within-cycle volatility of real consumer spending in the United Kingdom has been roughly constant for the past two centuries, while the within-cycle volatility of real US consumer spending has been on a long-run downward trend extending as far back as the 1850s.

In part, this could simply reflect another key observation of DeLong and Summers—namely, that one should only expect automatic stabilizers to generate greater stability in consumer spending if a substantial number of households were otherwise liquidity constrained. If households can effectively borrow or rely on savings to maintain their consumption at desired levels even in the event of adverse income shocks, then temporary fluctuations in employment and income need not translate into fluctuations in consumer spending. Indeed, DeLong and Summers found evidence that at least some of the observed decline in US output volatility during the twentieth century could be attributed to a decline in the fraction of households that were liquidity constrained as improvements in financial intermediation expanded the volume of and access to consumer credit.[46]

Consistent with this hypothesis, in 1840, the total volume of money circulating in the United States, including deposit accounts with overdraft facilities, could cover just five weeks of income, versus nearly twenty weeks of income in the United Kingdom.[47] By the turn of the century, that had risen to about twenty-four weeks in both countries, whereafter the two remained roughly on par through the 1980s, by which point, broad money supply in both countries was equal to about thirty weeks of nominal income. Since the late 1980s, the broad money supply of the United States has then risen even further, to about forty weeks of nominal income, while in the United Kingdom it has surpassed fifty weeks' equivalent, even as nominal incomes continued to rise in both economies. As the supply of money is merely the liability side of bank balance sheets, such growth is consistent with an expanding provision of credit and increased financial sophistication.

However, though long-run macroeconomic data may reject the hypothesis that increased state macroeconomic intervention has prevented the incidence and decreased the duration of recessions, that rejection is by no means a critique of the *normative* responsibility to provide the first of President Franklin Roosevelt's "three R's"—relief, recovery, and reform. The evident irrelevance of policy to recession depth and duration, expansion longevity, or macroeconomic volatility is not an argument for inaction, let alone for austerity.

Faced with a bond market revolt over legacy debts from the Napoleonic Wars—which alone consumed 56 percent of UK government expenditure—and additional borrowing to relieve famine-stricken Ireland, in 1847, the government of Lord Russell reluctantly curtailed spending by approximately 1 percent of GDP and shifted more of the burden of relief onto Irish landowners.[48] At the same time, to stem outflows of gold as the blighted British Isles imported foreign corn and the US government mandated that all payments to and by the US government must be transacted in specie or Treasury notes, the Bank of England hiked interest rates.[49] The consequent contractionary fiscal and monetary impulses thus impacted a UK economy that was already desperately struggling with economic and demographic catastrophe.

Moreover, in any event, there are compelling social welfare arguments for attenuating the adverse impact of recessionary shocks on households and families. The impact of adverse economic shocks is not evenly distributed across households, nor equitably distributed by ability to withstand those shocks. That economies in the aggregate can recover from adverse shocks does not mean that every individual household can or does. Recent research has found that a relatively modest UK unemployment insurance program effectively reduced earnings inequality and materially mitigated poverty in the United Kingdom during the Great Depression.[50] Even before the advent of public unemployment insurance, many UK workers who could afford to would insure themselves against income losses due to sickness or lost employment through paid membership of mutual benefit societies.[51]

As observed most recently during the 2020 COVID-19 pandemic, despite increased financialization over time, there remains a nontrivial number of liquidity-constrained households and firms, particularly at moments of severe economic contraction and elevated credit risk. There can thus be a moral case to mitigate human suffering at the individual level even if, in the aggregate, an expanded role of the state has not evidently attenuated the depth or duration of recessions, nor dampened cyclical economic volatility.

Indeed, while praising Secretary Cobb for deficit-spending the 2024 equivalent of nearly $50 billion on stock and bond purchases during September and October 1857, one newspaper article at the peak of the panic noted that such support ought to have "removed all cause of aggravation had the simple scarcity of Gold been at the bottom of the difficulty, instead of the sudden and senseless withdrawal of all financial trust and confidence."[52] It did not.

At the end of the day, Cobb could do little to counter the "indiscriminate slaughter of railway securities" and the withdrawal of "all support from the further prosecution of the [financial] system." While acknowledging that there may have been "some few instances" of mismanagement that would justify prudent hesitation, *The New York Times* concluded that the present situation had simply "struck dumb the credit of all the lines, old and new, bonds and shares."[53] They might then have quite appropriately presaged President Roosevelt's opening to his first inaugural address by asserting that "the only thing we have to fear is fear itself."

Newspaper reports in 1873 echoed the same sentiment, with *The New York Times* writing that Grant and Richardson's purchases of $12 million in bonds had been in vain, as the released currency "has been immediately withdrawn" and "the prevailing want of confidence has had the effect practically to neutralize the action of the Government."[54] To put it in medical terms, while the state may provide palliative care, it cannot cure; the patient can only recover on their own. Fortunately, at least, patients "U. S." and "U. K." have never failed to recover—every recession has eventually ended—though some illnesses have lingered substantially longer than others.

In their autobiographical retrospective on the 2008–09 recession, former Federal Reserve and Treasury Department officials Ben Bernanke, Tim Geithner, and Hank Paulson likened themselves to firefighters, putting out the flames of crisis and recession. But as we have seen, there is little evidence that increased state intervention has attenuated either the frequency of recessions or their depth and length.

Moreover, we have also seen that the state can instigate as well as palliate recessionary shocks, not least by unleashing arguably the single-most devastating shock that can be inflicted on economies—namely, war. Though the notion that the adversities of war may increase innovation, engender productive interstate economic competition, or even end an economic calamity like the Great Depression offers eucharistic comfort, the reality is that war is an unambiguous economic net negative. In short, the state can be economic arsonist as well as firefighter. Thus, the overwhelming lesson for economic policymakers aspiring to mitigate the adverse effects of economic fluctuations should perhaps be an economic analog of the Hippocratic Oath—first, do no harm.

8

THE PATRIOTIC RECESSION

When America sneezes, the world catches a cold.

—Unattributed

On the morning of Sunday, September 14, 2008, as Lehman Brothers' fate hung in the balance, senior officials at the Federal Reserve and US Treasury were cautiously optimistic that they could still facilitate a merger of the troubled investment bank with the healthier British bank Barclays. The night before, they had learned that Bank of America was working toward an acquisition of the similarly troubled Merrill Lynch, raising the prospect that Barclays, under the leadership of a hard-charging American, Bob Diamond, could likewise pull together a deal to absorb Lehman.[1]

Keen to ensure that Lehman could open for business Monday morning, the US Treasury and Federal Reserve insisted that any buyer guarantee Lehman's trades. But UK securities regulations required that unless the UK Financial Services Authority (FSA) issued a waiver, such a guarantee would require a vote of Barclays shareholders. Unfortunately, such a vote would take time.[2] When Sir Callum McCarthy, the soon-to-retire chairman of the FSA, bluntly informed New York Fed president Tim Geithner and SEC chairman Chris Cox that he was not authorized to grant such a waiver, Treasury secretary Hank Paulson frantically put in a call to the UK chancellor of the exchequer, Labour MP Alistair Darling.[3] Darling was similarly blunt. "He didn't want to import our cancer," Paulson would tell Geithner after the call.[4] To major US bank CEOs assembled downstairs at the New York Federal Reserve, Paulson would be even more explicit—the British "grinf***ed us," he declared.[5]

Darling ended up importing the US cancer anyway. With no private buyer, US officials proceeded to plan B—preparing for a Lehman bankruptcy filing.[6] At the same time in London, directors of Lehman's European subsidiary, Lehman Brothers International (Europe) Ltd. (LBIE), alarmed by the deteriorating situation of their parent company, Lehman Brothers Holdings Inc. (LBHI), sought assurances that LBHI would make payments on their behalf to honor liabilities coming due on September 15.[7] As LBHI essentially managed all cash resources of Lehman's global operations centrally in New York, any failure on the part of LBHI to make payments on behalf of LBIE would render the latter immediately insolvent and in default. After close of business on Friday, LBHI had already pulled $8 billion out of London in its daily sweep.[8]

When, shortly after midnight on Monday morning, LBIE learned from their parent that LBHI would be filing for Chapter 11 bankruptcy protection in the United States, directors immediately raced to obtain the protection of an administration order, which a judge granted at 7:56 a.m. that morning—just four minutes before London markets opened.[9] From that point, four accountants from PricewaterhouseCoopers, led by Tony Lomas, a fifty-one-year-old veteran of the bankruptcies of the disgraced US energy giant Enron and the British auto icon MG Rover, had executive authority over the bank's entire European operations.[10] Under UK bankruptcy procedures, the primary responsibility of Lomas and his team was henceforth their fiduciary obligation to realize LBIE assets for the benefit of all creditors, without preference. Thus, all LBIE's liabilities were immediately frozen.

Unfortunately, those assets included collateral of LBIE's clients that LBIE had "rehypothecated"—that is, used as collateral for the bank's own borrowing. Whereas US securities regulation limited rehypothecation to 140 percent of the loan amount, in the United Kingdom, banks faced no such limit. As a result, dozens of hedge funds and wealth management firms that relied on LBIE's prime brokerage services—the bank processed 12 percent of all trades on the London Stock Exchange—could not access the assets they had deposited as collateral.[11] Reports indicated that anywhere from $40 billion to $70 billion of client assets were instantly frozen.[12] Moreover, the administrators had to unwind more than 140,000 failed trades—trades that Lehman clients had initiated but which were still in the process of settlement at 7:56 a.m. London time.[13]

As hedge funds raced to pull collateral from other prime brokers on both sides of the Atlantic lest they find additional funds similarly impounded during potential administration proceedings, the cost of interbank borrowing surged, and banks that were particularly reliant on wholesale markets for short-term funding quickly came under pressure from concerned investors and creditors.[14] The British banking giant HBOS lost over a third of its equity value on Monday, September 15, as analysts noted its heavy reliance on wholesale funding.[15] Through its founding merger of Halifax and the Bank of Scotland in 2001, HBOS could lay claim to being the fifth-oldest bank in the United Kingdom, with Bank of Scotland having been established by the Parliament of Scotland in 1695, just one year after William III granted a royal charter to the Bank of England.[16] But by Thursday, HBOS had little choice but to sell itself to Lloyds TSB for just a quarter of its equity valuation a year earlier.

Within weeks, the cancer had spread further, with the chairman of the venerable Royal Bank of Scotland—established by royal charter in 1727 as a counterweight to the perceived Jacobite sympathies of the older Bank of Scotland—informing Darling that his bank was within hours of running out of funding.[17] Brown and Darling now had a full-blown banking crisis on their hands—the worst in the United Kingdom since 1825—prompting them to frantically insist on a £50 billion recapitalization package for eight UK banks and building societies.[18]

In reality, the United Kingdom had already imported the US cancer a year earlier, when a depositor run on the Newcastle-based Northern Rock marked the first bank run in the United Kingdom since 1866. Ironically for a financial crisis universally associated with subprime real estate, Northern Rock engaged in almost no subprime mortgage lending whatsoever, let alone subprime US mortgage lending; almost 90 percent of their assets were prime UK residential mortgages. The problem, much like for HBOS, was on the liability side. To fund expansion of their lending portfolio, Northern Rock had increasingly relied on wholesale markets, both through short-term borrowing and by securitizing their mortgage assets for use as collateral for longer-term loans.[19] Just 23 percent of "the Rock's" funding came from stabler retail deposits.[20]

The shock came on August 9, 2007, when the French bank BNP Paribas announced it was freezing three investment funds due to losses in its US housing portfolio, triggering a spike in short-term interbank interest rates—what Northern Rock traders noted at the time as a "dislocation in the market" for their funding.[21] Northern Rock's senior leadership, including their PhD zoologist chairman, the future 5th Viscount Ridley, had reasoned that their increasing reliance on securitized wholesale borrowing would in fact insulate them from a global credit crunch, as investors and creditors would likely flee to the relative safety of low-risk, prime

UK mortgages.[22] Instead, with surging short-term rates and a widespread aversion to mortgage-backed securities generally after several high-profile fund failures, Northern Rock could no longer fully fund its portfolio with new liabilities. Unable to find another bank willing to acquire it, leadership reluctantly turned to the Bank of England for emergency assistance.

Though the Bank of England determined that Northern Rock "is solvent, exceeds its regulatory capital requirement and has a good quality loan book," and therefore agreed to support it by lending, at a penalty rate, against eligible collateral provided by Northern Rock, the decision leaked before a formal announcement. With rumors circulating of a pending intervention, officials decided to pull forward the announcement from Monday, September 17—which had been Northern Rock's preferred date to allow time to prepare their website—to Friday, September 14, at 7:00 a.m..[23] But it was already too late—at 8:30 p.m. on Thursday, BBC News 24 and later other BBC outlets reported that the Bank of England would be providing emergency financial support to Northern Rock.[24]

Despite BBC business editor Robert Peston noting that "the firm remains profitable," he added that "the fact that it has had to go cap in hand to the Bank is the most tangible sign that the crisis in financial markets is spilling over into businesses that touch most of our lives."[25] In any event, retail depositors immediately began to withdraw deposits, with a retail depositor run developing that evening and continuing through Monday when, after frantic discussions over the weekend, Darling announced that the government would be extending its full guarantee of deposits from its standard £2,000 limit to instead cover all existing deposits in Northern Rock.[26]

The phrase "When America sneezes, the rest of the world catches a cold" has a persistent habit of popping up whenever the United States enters a period of economic or financial disturbance. The aphorism appears to have first entered common use in 1907. A month after the Panic of 1907, a visiting Belgian official in New York, commenting on the relationship between American and European financial conditions, remarked that "when America has a cold, Europe sneezes."[27] At the tail end of the relatively short and mild 1960–61 US recession, Fed governor Abbot Low Mills Jr. similarly remarked at a meeting of the Open Market Committee that "if it is true that history repeats itself, it seemed not at all improbable that the country was moving into a situation that would find its friends abroad again saying that 'when America sneezes, Europe and other parts of the world have pneumonia.'"[28]

Despite its modern provenance in relation to the spread of financial contagion from New York in the early twentieth century, the phrase's origins are in fact distinctly European—Austrian, to be precise. Reflecting on the recent tendency for France to export political upheaval to the rest of the continent, the eminent and wily Austrian chancellor Klemens von Metternich noted, "When France sneezes, the whole of Europe catches a cold."[29]

During the pandemic recession of 2020 in both the United States and United Kingdom, it was in some sense quite literally the case that economic contraction ultimately proved to be as transmissible across international borders as the coronavirus itself. In this very particular sense, it bore at least some passing resemblance to the otherwise quite different 2008–09 recession, in which banks rather than airline passengers were international vectors, and vectors of a credit market infection rather than upper respiratory infection.

The two most recent recessions in both economies would therefore seem to provide testament to the idea that recessions are, if not contagious, then at least clear manifestations of the butterfly effect. First formally articulated by the mathematician and meteorologist Edward Norton Lorenz, though with a much older lineage, it is the proposition that even small, remote perturbations—such as the gentle flapping of a butterfly's wings—can set in motion atmospheric dynamics that eventually generate large storms in quite distant locations.[30]

Yet is it in fact generally true that recessions are inherently international phenomena? In contrast to the 2008–09 and 2020 recessions, the recession that inaugurated the twenty-first century was a rather patriotic affair, limiting itself to the United States. The UK economy powered through the eight-month US recession with growth of 1.3 percent (1.9 percent for the year as a whole) and with the UK labor market adding twenty thousand jobs per month.[31]

According to the latest recession chronology from Stephen Broadberry et al. and the National Bureau of Economic Research (NBER), the United Kingdom also avoided recession in 1829, 1865–67, 1869–70, 1887–88, 1913–14, 1923–24, 1937–38, 1948–49, 1953–54, 1957–58, 1960–61, and 1970—US recessions each.[32] Since the end of the Great Depression, fewer than half of recessions have been shared between the two economies, with the United Kingdom avoiding eight US recessions while enduring no UK-only recessions.

This differential frequency of recessions cannot be chalked up to differential methodology for determining recessions, as movements in the unemployment rate and real GDP in the two economies moved in parallel during shared recessions but diverged during identified US-only recessions. Specifically, during the shared recessionary periods of 1973–75, 1979–82, 1990–91, 2008–09, and 2020, both economies experienced outright year-over-year declines in real GDP. In contrast, with the exceptions of the relatively mild recessions of 1960 and 1970, all US-specific recessions between the end of World War II and the 1973–75 oil embargo recession presented year-over-year declines in real GDP, during which time, real GDP in the United Kingdom continued to expand.

The same is true of real GDP per capita, which grew continuously in the United Kingdom from 1948 through 1973, subsequently declining only during the shared recessionary years of 1974–75, 1980–81, 1991, 2008–09, and 2020.[33] In contrast, real GDP per capita in the United States also declined during the US-only recession years of 1949, 1954, 1958, and the second halves of 1960, 1970, and 2001.[34]

A similar pattern is evident in unemployment data. Whereas the United States experienced sudden, sharp jumps in the unemployment rate during each of its solo postwar recessions between 1945 and 1973, the United Kingdom experienced much more muted unemployment responses throughout the period. During the 2001 US recession, the UK unemployment rate remained essentially flat at approximately 5 percent as the labor market added a healthy sixty thousand jobs per quarter. This was in stark contrast to the shared recessionary periods of 1973–75, 1979–82, 1990–91, 2008–09, and 2020, when unemployment rates in both economies moved suddenly and sharply higher together.

When the US economy reentered recession in mid-1937 after four years of recovery from the Great Depression, it contracted by more than 3 percent. Real business investment declined by a fifth, the unemployment rate jumped almost 5 percentage points, and employment declined by two million workers. But on the other side of the Atlantic, real GDP continued to expand in 1937–38, while real investment rose. Though the unemployment rate ticked up 1.5 percentage points, employment also expanded by fifty-four thousand workers. The pattern of similar movements in macroeconomic variables during shared recessions and divergent movements during US-only recessions is therefore compelling evidence that the greater frequency of recession in the United States cannot be attributed merely to measurement error.

Among the thirty-four episodes of recession in the United States since 1854, the United Kingdom also experienced recession in just half of those cases. Among the seventeen instances of shared recessions, on a quarterly basis, just three have been exactly coincident in both economies; in nine instances, the United States led the United Kingdom into recession, whereas in only five instances did the United Kingdom enter recession before the United States.

Of those five instances of the United Kingdom leading and the United States lagging, three have occurred since 1970, and all three coincided with large oil price shocks—1973, 1979, and 1990—with two also coinciding with international wars (1973, 1990) and the third with a major revolution (1979). A fourth instance was during the Second World War, when the war-ravaged UK economy entered recession nearly two years before the United States.

But before the oil shocks of 1973–90—by which point, reliance on oil in the two economies had generally converged—for much of the postwar period, a key source of UK macroeconomic stability relative to the United States was their more intensive reliance on an abundant supply of domestic coal. At the time of the 1948–49 US recession, coal accounted for less than half of US primary energy consumption generally and electricity generation specifically, while oil—of which the United States was already a net importer—accounted for nearly two-fifths of energy consumption overall and a tenth of electricity generation.[35]

In stark contrast, 90 percent of the UK's overall energy consumption and 98 percent of its electricity generation came from coal, of which the United Kingdom was a prolific net exporter to the tune of twenty million tons per year. Just 0.4 percent of UK power generation came from oil.[36] Coal would continue to dominate the UK energy mix until the early 1970s, when oil finally surpassed it as the largest source of primary energy consumption, even hitting 30 percent of electricity generation. Fortuitously for the United Kingdom, as we saw in Chapter 5, from 1926 until 1972, the United Kingdom went without a single official coal strike. Unfortunately, oil would thereafter almost continuously remain the UK's primary source of energy during the oil-crisis intensive years from 1971 through 1995, when it was in turn surpassed by natural gas.

While oil and coal are both tradable international commodities, they are not perfect substitutes. Over the short term, they are not really substitutes at all; US power plants relying on oil or gas could not immediately and costlessly switch to burning coal in the event of an adverse geopolitical shock to oil or gas supply. A common global oil supply shock could therefore have differential economic impact depending on differing levels of reliance on oil versus coal in domestic power generation and energy consumption overall.

Whereas US electricity prices thus spiked during successive recessionary oil price shocks between 1948 and 1970, UK electricity prices remained flat or even fell.[37] Indeed, UK coal production and domestic consumption generally rose or remained roughly constant during the US recessions between 1948 and 1970.[38] In contrast, US coal production and consumption actually fell during or immediately preceding the oil-induced US recessions of 1948–49, 1953–54, and 1970 as domestic coal workers went on strike to secure higher wages in the face of high domestic energy prices.[39]

More recently, the United Kingdom also powered through the eight-month 2001 US recession, to which energy inflation was once again a major contributor, as discussed in Chapter 6. Reflecting the highly fragmented, regional nature of pipeline-reliant natural gas markets, whereas natural gas prices doubled in the United States during the year preceding the 2001 recession, the UK price of natural gas—now the UK's largest source of energy as North Sea oil and gas output peaked and the United Kingdom net-exported gas—actually declined 5 percent.[40]

Overall energy inflation in the United Kingdom thus averaged less than half that in the United States during 2000. In the first three months of 2001, energy inflation in the United Kingdom even turned negative, while averaging 12 percent in the United States.[41] In January, the price of natural gas in the United States posted the largest increase ever measured by the Bureau of Labor Statistics, with the spot price having already more than tripled during 2000.[42]

But what about before the oil shocks of the decades following World War II? During the entire pre-Depression period from 1854 through 1933—before the ascent of oil—the United States was a prolific net exporter of recession, leading the United Kingdom into recession on seven occasions. In contrast, the United Kingdom led the United States into recession on just two occasions, in 1892–93 and 1926. The latter coincided with the short, sharp recession resulting from the 1926 strike, while the former similarly resulted from strike activity in the cotton and coal mining industries, as well as harvest failures.[43] Just two recessions during this period were exactly coincident, while in nine instances, the United States endured recession alone.

Using less precise but longer-term annual recession chronologies, since independence in 1776, the United States led the United Kingdom into recession in seven instances, the United Kingdom led on four occasions, the two economies shared nineteen annually coincident recessions, and twenty-one recessions were US-specific. Just six UK recessions since 1776 were specific to the United Kingdom.

Even before independence, the British North American colonies were more likely to lead than lag the home country into recession. From 1700 through 1776, the colonies led the United Kingdom into recession on six occasions, the United Kingdom led on two occasions, and they shared ten coincident recessions. However, while the colonies were part of the British Empire, just three recessions were specific to the colonies, while five were specific to the home country.

Though precise comparisons of economic size are subject to measurement error, the US economy may have surpassed that of the United Kingdom in overall size as early as 1862, when the latter suffered severe recession owing to the US blockade of Confederate cotton exports.[44] So it is not inconceivable that the United States' status as a net exporter of recession is in part merely a function of size. But even when the UK's was the larger economy, it was not the case that when the United Kingdom sneezed, the United States (or the thirteen colonies) caught pneumonia; if anything, the smaller US/colonial economy from 1700 through 1862 was still more than twice as likely to lead the United Kingdom into recession than to follow.

However, whereas during the 160 years since the American Civil War the United Kingdom was substantially less recession-prone, during the 160 years from 1700 through the start of the American Civil War, the United Kingdom was slightly more recession-prone than the United States and its colonial predecessors. Though most recessions during this period were shared—with nineteen coincidental recessions, the United States leading the United Kingdom into ten recessions, and the latter leading the former into just four—twelve recessions were unique to the United Kingdom, compared to just seven for the United States and its predecessor thirteen colonies. As we saw in the previous chapter, statistically, the greater recessionary proclivity of the UK economy before 1860 can be attributed to the country's frequent involvement in major international conflict.

Another way to look at the interrelation of US and UK recessions is to calculate whether the start of a recession in the United States is correlated with the start of a recession in the United Kingdom and whether the United States being in recession is correlated with the United Kingdom being in recession. By this measure, on a quarterly basis, the start of a recession in the United Kingdom is uncorrelated with the start of a recession in the United States. This low correlation has been roughly constant since 1854 and was even slightly negative in the decade through 1863. On an annual basis since 1700, the start of a recession is more correlated between the two economies and has risen since the Great Depression, though the overall correlation is still weak to modest.

On a quarterly basis, *being* in recession is somewhat more correlated between the two economies, though the correlation remains weak. Moreover, on an annual basis, being in recession is no more correlated between the two economies than entering a recession. In short, historically, more often than not, recessions are patriots.

Of course, recession chronologies are just one dimension along which economic fluctuations in one economy may correlate with fluctuations in another. More revealing, perhaps, is whether changes in observable macroeconomic measures in one country move substantially in tandem with changes in the same measures in another country. At quarterly frequency, changes in inflation (as measured both by consumer price indices and overall GDP price deflators), nominal GDP, and nominal government bond yields are highly positively correlated between the United States and United Kingdom since 1875. Since the end of the Great Depression, changes in stock market indices are also moderately correlated between the two countries.

In contrast, changes in physical variables—real GDP, the unemployment rate, industrial production, and employment—are very weakly correlated or even uncorrelated since 1875. Though changes in real variables in the two economies have generally become more correlated over time, the correlations remain weak even in more recent decades. Changes in various monetary variables, including money supply, the monetary base, commercial paper rates, and corporate bond yields are likewise uncorrelated or very weakly correlated between the two economies.

We observe a similar pattern in annual data. Here again, changes in nominal ten-year government bond yields are strongly positively correlated between the United States and United Kingdom, as are changes in overall inflation and, less strongly, nominal GDP. Employment growth in the two countries is moderately correlated, though this likely reflects historically similar growth rates in the annual working-age (fifteen to sixty-four) population in both countries.[45] Since 1933, consumer price inflation has been strongly correlated in both countries, while changes in industrial production, stock market indices, unemployment rates, long-term government bond yields, and real GDP have been moderately correlated.

Consistently the least correlated variable between the two countries is the annual rate of change in the number of banks. This correlation has been effectively zero continuously since 1700, meaning that, on average, bank populations in the two economies move wholly independently of one another. Chancellor Darling may have imported the 2008 subprime mortgage crisis from the United States, with several brand-name high street British banks enduring their consequent fates, but historically, the British banking population was largely immune to annual fluctuations in the population of their American counterparts.

In short, for major macroeconomic variables for which long-run time series data exists, it appears that fluctuations from year to year in one economy are only moderately positively related to fluctuations in the other, and for some key variables, fluctuations in one economy are essentially unrelated to fluctuations in the other. Strikingly, though fluctuations in macroeconomic variables in the two countries have become more related over time, the same pattern of only moderate positive correlation holds even in more recent decades.

How is it that annual macroeconomic fluctuations in two broadly similar, open, and deeply integrated economies can be only moderately interrelated? Part of the explanation lies in the fact that historically the US economy was simply more volatile. In general, volatility—as measured by the standard deviation of annual rates of change—was higher in the United States than in the United Kingdom. This is particularly evident for key *real* variables—namely, industrial production, real GDP, and employment. The exceptions to the general pattern of greater US volatility appear to have been wages and prices, which were generally more variable in the United Kingdom than in the United States. Implicitly this means that any common shock to the willingness to spend versus save a unit of money in the two economies was more likely to translate into changes in prices in the United Kingdom rather than changes in real output.

More importantly, however, the United States historically also experienced much larger swings in the supply of money and bank lending, particularly real estate lending. Though the United Kingdom experienced even greater volatility in their monetary base—the volume of notes and coinage in circulation or held as bank reserves—than the United States, this did not translate into larger shifts in the broader supply of money—bank deposits and other demand accounts— and overall bank credit. Despite higher volatility and larger fluctuations in the UK monetary base, broad money was substantially less volatile, with the range between the largest annual decline and largest annual increase in broad money supply in the United States almost double that in the United Kingdom.

We see a similar pattern on the asset side of bank activity in the two countries. The maximum annual decline in total bank lending in the United States, -25.2 percent in the peacetime year of 1933, was more than double the maximum lending decline in the United Kingdom (-12.5 percent), which occurred in 1915 during World War I. The difference in bank real estate lending volatility is similarly stark, with the range between the biggest annual decline and biggest annual increase in real estate lending in the United States almost double that in the United Kingdom.

As early as 1913, Wesley Clair Mitchell observed the "striking" stability of UK banking, noting that whereas the US national banks contracted lending during financial crises, English banks were often able to expand their lending. While deposits fell sharply during US crises as fearful depositors withdrew funds, in the United Kingdom, Mitchell noticed that deposits even tended to rise "a trifle" during crises.[46]

Why was British banking historically so much stabler than American banking? The most important difference between the two banking sectors was that whereas in most states for most of US history not only were banks prohibited from operating branches across state lines, but most were also prohibited from operating more than one branch even within the state. By 1900, the United States thus had 12,427 banks with just 117 branches. A mere 87 US banks operated branches; the rest were single-establishment institutions known as *unit banks*.[47] In contrast, since 1826, UK banks were able to merge and operate a broadly diversified network of nationwide branches; by the end of the nineteenth century, the United Kingdom thus had 363 banks operating nearly 6,000 branches.[48]

Many banks with few branches pose unique challenges to financial stability. First and foremost, small, single-location banks tend to lack sufficient capital to absorb drains of deposits following adverse shocks. Second, such entities are often insufficiently diversified on both the asset and liability sides of their balance sheets. The former is more obvious—if a bank has a single location, its lending portfolio will tend to be geographically and sectorally concentrated and therefore vulnerable to large local shocks that can adversely impact most of the bank's borrowers simultaneously. Crop failure or local real estate price declines were common historical examples of such spatially correlated shocks.

In contrast, in a nationwide banking system with geographically dispersed branches, adverse local shocks in one region can be offset by stability in other regions. In this sense, a large, diversified economy is analogous to a large, diversified investment portfolio. Like investors, banks that lend broadly across sectors and regions can effectively hedge against region- or sector-specific shocks. Moreover, a broadly diversified, branched bank can cross-subsidize establishments experiencing adverse shocks by shifting reserves from unaffected establishments.[49]

But an arguably even more important problem in a unit banking system is lack of diversification on the liability side. The nature of local or otherwise spatially correlated shocks is that they adversely impact not only the value of a bank's assets but also the financial situation of their depositors and other creditors. Multiple creditors experiencing an adverse income shock at the same time can trigger simultaneous withdrawals, straining bank reserves. Moreover, since the personal wealth of shareholders in small, local banks was often highly correlated with the state of the local economy, in the event of failure, the assets of shareholders could be insufficient to cover losses, even when shareholder liability extended beyond their subscribed capital.[50]

Consequently, the failure rate of US banks, particularly before and during the Great Depression, was substantially much higher during US recessions than during non-recessionary years. In contrast, the bank failure rate in the United Kingdom on average was not only much lower than in the United States but also essentially no different in recessionary versus non-recessionary years. Moreover, the UK banking system achieved this stability without public deposit insurance; whereas various US states provided public deposit insurance off and on since 1829, and the federal government since 1933, the United Kingdom did not have public deposit insurance until 1979, and even then imposed a lower ceiling for insured deposits.[51]

Before 1826, however, the United Kingdom suffered all the pathologies of many small banks with few branches, along with, as we have just seen, more frequent recessions. Under the Bank of England Act of 1709, no bank in England or Wales except the Bank of England could have more than six partners. The rule effectively meant that the provision of a sufficient volume banking services for the growing British economy required a rising number of small banking institutions, which peaked in 1810 at 897. But though mandating that no other bank could have more than six partners achieved the political objective of protecting the privileged position of the Bank of England, it came at a cost. With no more than six partners, many English banks were substantially undercapitalized both in absolute terms and relative to their Scottish peers, who had no such limit on the number of partners.[52]

With hundreds of small, undercapitalized and under-diversified institutions, the pre-1826 English banking system was thus prone to runs and stoppages when adverse shocks impaired bank balance sheets. Such shocks hit with force in, for example, 1816, the "Year Without a Summer" following the eruption of Mount Tambora. Simultaneously confronting postwar fiscal austerity and Bank of England tightening, the UK economy entered a deep recession that claimed the lives of one hundred UK banks. One hundred more banks failed during the severe financial crisis of 1825–26, when 12 percent of the UK banking system failed.[53] One contemporary observer, William Huskisson, president of the Board of Trade, declared that England "was within four-and-twenty hours of a state of barter."[54]

Writing about the banking carnage in *The Edinburgh Review*, the eminent Scottish economist John Ramsay McCulloch noted that there was "little doubt that the repeal of the injurious and absurd restriction by which more than *six* individuals are prevented from joining in any copartnery for the issue of notes, would be a considerable improvement on the existing system." With each partner in those banks, McCulloch noted, "bound to the whole extent of their fortunes for the debts of the copartnery, security would be afforded to the public against ultimate loss."[55]

McCulloch did not believe that lifting the six-partner rule would alone be sufficient to attenuate the risk of bank failures in an economy exposed to as much commercial hazard as England's.[56] But when after considerable debate Parliament finally eliminated the restriction for banks located at least sixty-five miles outside of London (the Bank of England's turf) through the May 1826 Country Bankers Act, and seven years later eliminated the restriction for banks within London as well, the results were striking.[57] Almost immediately, the most common exit route from the UK banking population switched from failure or closure to merger, acquisition, or amalgamation.[58]

But even as the number of UK banks declined through consolidation, the number of bank *branches* across the country rose substantially. By 1873, there were 564 banks operating 2,945 bank branches in the United Kingdom.[59] In that year— the year of Jay Cooke's failure and the start of the US "long depression"—the nineteenth-century London banker and editor in chief of *The Economist*, Walter Bagehot, published his classic analysis of the London financial system, *Lombard Street: A Description of the Money Market*. Bagehot marveled at the delicate balance of UK credit markets. "There is," he noted, "no country at present, and there never was any country before, in which the ratio of the cash reserve to the bank deposits was so small as it is now in England." Indeed, he observed that "the amount of that cash is so exceedingly small that a bystander almost trembles when he compares its minuteness with the immensity of the credit which rests upon it."[60] With broadly diversified, nationwide branch banking, the UK banking system could provision such immense credit while achieving an enviable level of banking stability.

Bagehot's own bank, Stuckey's Banking Company, was a product of the post-1826 consolidation and diversification of the UK banking sector. Founded around 1772—as we saw in Chapter 3, the year of one of the worst UK banking crises of the eighteenth century—in Langport in the west of England, by the early nineteenth century, Stuckey's partners had opened additional banking companies in Bridgewater and Bristol under separate deeds of partnership. However, in response to the Country Bankers Act, the three enterprises along with a fourth promptly merged.[61]

Born the year of the amalgamation, Walter would, like his father, eventually join Stuckey's, becoming secretary to the Committees of Management at Langport and Bristol in 1855 and vice chairman in 1875, a position his father had occupied for thirty years.[62] By 1873, Stuckey's had already acquired ten more banks in Somerset and Devon, and Bagehot himself had been supervising the bank's London business since 1861. The firm would eventually merge with the Lancashire-based Parr's Bank Limited, by which point, it had grown to forty-seven branches and twenty-four subbranches.[63] Parr's itself would in turn be acquired in 1918 by the London County & Westminster Bank, whose predecessor, London & Westminster Bank, had also previously incorporated Lord Overstone's former bank of Jones, Loyd & Co., bringing the combined entity to seven hundred branches.[64] London County & Westminster Bank would eventually merge with the National Provincial Bank in 1968 to become National Westminster Bank, or NatWest, which in 2000 was then acquired by Royal Bank of Scotland (RBS).[65]

The contrast between an increasingly national, branched UK banking system and a highly fragmented, unbranched US one is dramatically illustrated by the number of people per bank in each country. In 1873, there were just over 50,000 Britons for every British bank; in the United States, on average each bank served just 13,000 Americans. The US figure would decline almost continuously until a 1920 nadir of a mere 3,500 Americans per bank, by which point, the average British bank was serving almost 165,000 Britons.

Despite three recessions and numerous bank failures throughout the 1920s, the US population per bank would remain under 5,000 until successive clusters of bank failures during the Great Depression. Even then, on the eve of World War II, the average UK bank was serving 240,000 Britons compared to the average US bank serving just 8,700 Americans. The same pattern holds if one expands the definition of a bank to include not only commercial banks but also UK building societies and thrift savings banks and US savings and loan institutions.[66]

Marvellous and *delicate* were the terms Bagehot used to describe a situation in which "there never was so much borrowed money collected in the world as is now collected in London."[67] A marvel it certainly was; from 1864 through 1938, there were no fewer than nineteen thousand bank failures in the United States, compared to just over two hundred in the United Kingdom. Even when we express bank failures as a percentage of the overall bank population, while bank failures occurred in the United Kingdom, one sees nothing like the large waves of concurrent bank failures in the United States. Though a recession-less UK banking crisis in 1866 was still very much on Bagehot's mind when he wrote *Lombard Street*, the incidence of bank failure in the United Kingdom during that crisis was still lower than in the United States in 1878, 1893, 1930, 1931, 1932, and 1933.

Ostensibly, the establishment of the Federal Reserve System in 1913 should have provided an effective remedy for such fragility by enabling temporarily illiquid banks in adversely impacted regions to access liquidity through the Fed's discount window. In principle, the Fed could adhere to Bagehot's "rule" that in the event of a liquidity crisis, the ultimate reserve bank should lend early and without limit to solvent institutions, against good collateral, and at penalty rates of interest, as the Bank of England attempted to do with Northern Rock in 2007.[68] However, not only did the Federal Reserve System as a whole, and individual regional Federal Reserve banks specifically, often fail to adhere to this dictum, but even if they had, it could not have resolved crises of insolvency versus mere illiquidity.[69]

Whereas in the United Kingdom, stronger banks or consortia of banks—often coordinated by the still wholly private Bank of England—could acquire weaker institutions, such amalgamations of multiple banking establishments would have violated unit banking laws in the United States. As late as the 1970s and 1980s, US bank regulators frequently struggled to deal with bank failures as state laws often prohibited the acquisition of an in-state bank by an out-of-state bank, while rules concerning market concentration prevented bank mergers that might result in high market concentration within the state.[70] Paradoxically, Darling and Sir Callum's decision to effectively block Barclays' Lehman acquisition in September 2008 was thus distinctly un-British; instead, they imported an American tradition of regulatorily tying their hands on one bank amalgamation and then publicly bailing out other institutions.

With the vast majority of US states maintaining restrictions on both inter- and intrastate branching until the 1980s, the average US bank was still serving fewer than twenty thousand Americans as late as 1989.[71] However, with double-digit interest rates under Volcker and federal tax policy lurching from dramatically lowering the effective tax rate on real estate investment in 1981 to sharply raising it in 1986, the US banking sector found itself in its worst crisis since the Great Depression. In 1989, the failure rate for US banks hit 4.1 percent—worse than during any period outside the Great Depression itself. In response, states reluctantly loosened restrictions not only on branching but also on the ability of out-of-state banks to acquire in-state banks. If troubled institutions could not grow their way out of delinquent mortgages, then the second-best option was for them to be liberated to merge or sell themselves out.

American economic policy officials had long been aware of the relative strengths of the UK's nationwide, branched banking system. In 1932, an expert committee appointed by the Federal Reserve produced a ninety-nine-page report on branch banking in England. Explicitly referencing the 1826 elimination of the six-partner rule, the committee found that "losses to depositors because of bank failures have been negligible in England since the rise of the great branch banking organizations." Writing in the depths of the Great Depression, they noted that in England "there were less than ten failures among commercial joint stock banks from 1900 to 1925, and since that date there have been none." Even more striking, they found that "since 1914 the ratio of deposits of suspended banks in England to the average yearly deposits of active banks has been less than one-fiftieth of the same ratio for the State and national banks of the United States."[72]

Not only did the committee observe that "these large branch systems of England serve a wide geographical area and are in contact with a variety of business interests" and thus "have a wide diversification in their portfolios" but also that the many branches and subbranches of British banks were "spread over practically all of England and Wales in competition with each other." In other words, concentration at the national level masked fierce competition between banks at the local level, such that government commissions concluded that not only had there been "little or no attempt on the part of the amalgamated banks to exercise any monopoly power" but also that "concentration so far has been accompanied by increased competition . . . in the spread of banking facilities through new offices."[73]

More recent research has found a similar pro-competitive effect of the limited instances of branching during the Great Depression in the United States, with positive implications for bank stability.[74] Single-establishment unit banks that were exposed to the competition of branched banks were more likely to survive the Great Depression than banks that were not exposed to competition from branches.

Curiously, the 1932 commission found that in stark contrast to the US banking system, British banking was governed by "a very small body of law compared to the voluminous banking codes of the federal and state jurisdictions here." US reserve and minimum capital requirements, interest rate restrictions, unit banking laws, and public supervision and examination of banks were "things wholly unknown in British law and practice," they observed. Whereas in the United States, aspiring banks had to apply to public authorities for an official charter, in the United Kingdom, "any persons meeting a few pro forma requirements have the right to set up in the banking business."[75] The superior stability of UK banking simply did not require the application of regulatory palliatives.

The US commissioners further found that in the United Kingdom, "governmental agencies publish no material comparable to the extensive information as to condition and income collected by the supervisors of banks in the various jurisdictions in this country."[76] Indeed, to reconstruct historical statistics as basic as the number of banking institutions operating in the United Kingdom in any given year requires that one rely on a private publication, the Bankers' *Almanac Register of Bank Name Changes and Liquidations*, as no such public register exists.[77] Once again in contrast to the United States, the superior stability of the UK banking system meant there was simply no compelling reason for public authorities to collect vast volumes of UK bank data.

It is tempting, after the contagiousness of the 2008–09 financial crisis and 2020 pandemic recession, to presume that recessions are inherently international phenomena, but for most of the past four centuries, recessions have often been distinctly patriotic affairs. But though that patriotism has declined somewhat in more recent decades, with the United States and United Kingdom sharing common shocks in 1973, 1979, 1990, 2008, and 2020, not only has the United States always been more recession-prone than the United Kingdom, it has also always been more likely to export than to import recession.

The frequently patriotic nature of recessions contradicts the universalist implications of the manias, panics, and crashes or cyclical overinvestment view of recessions. If mania and panic are inherent to economic fluctuations, or if the tendency to overinvest during economic expansions inheres in a market economy, then we should expect two broadly similar and deeply integrated economies such as the United States and United Kingdom to share similar recessionary experiences. That they do not reflects the fundamentally idiosyncratic and conditional nature of recessionary shocks and the propagation thereof.

In particular, whereas the fragmented, under-diversified US banking system historically tended to amplify adverse shocks to the US economy, the diversified, nationwide UK banking system tended to absorb rather than amplify adverse shocks. Hence, though the two economies often share the same nominal shocks such as inflation or spikes in bond yields, the same is not true of the supply of money, bank lending, the number of banks, real GDP, and unemployment, changes in which are either weakly correlated or outright uncorrelated between the two economies.

Despite consolidation and diversification over the past four decades, the US banking system still retains hallmarks of its regional, unit banking heritage. That legacy was perhaps most notably on display during the early 1990s recession, when 1,043 (approximately one-third) of US savings and loan institutions failed. More recently, it manifested with the 2023 failure of Silicon Valley Bank, whose Silicon Valley–heavy depositor base, increasingly unable to secure financing as the Federal Reserve tightened financial conditions, withdrew deposits to fund operations. Even many of the signature bank failures of 2008—Washington Mutual, IndyMac, and Downey Savings and Loan—had a distinctly regional flare, reflecting geographic variation in home foreclosure rates.

The differential recessionary experiences of the United Kingdom and United States over the past two centuries is thus a stark illustration that while adverse shocks may not discriminate across economic jurisdictions, vulnerability to those shocks can vary substantially across time and space depending on institutions and dependence on key inputs. Fundamentally, the United Kingdom was historically more recession-proof than the United States—not because they were relatively lucky or less prone to cycles of mania and panic. Rather, it was for the far more mundane reasons that, since 1826, the United Kingdom enjoyed a broadly diversified banking system and their more coal-intensive economy was less susceptible to geopolitical shocks to the supply of oil.

PURGE THE ROTTENNESS

Liquidate labor, liquidate stocks, liquidate
the farmers, liquidate real estate . . . It will
purge the rottenness out of the system.

—SECRETARY OF THE TREASURY ANDREW MELLON, 1929

Andrew William Mellon was just eighteen years old when the 1873 failure of Jay Cooke & Co. plunged the US economy into what was then commonly referred to as *the great depression*—that is, until an even greater one hit in 1929, by which time, Mellon was secretary of the US Department of Treasury and the second-longest serving Treasury secretary in US history. At least according to the official business cycle chronology of the National Bureau of Economic Research, the recession that followed the September 1873 panic remains the longest on record.[1]

Not surprisingly, it was a formative experience for the young and shy Andy—or AW, as he was also known—who had only recently joined his father's bank, the Pittsburgh-based T. Mellon & Sons' Bank, as a full-time employee. In successive waves of suspensions and failures, close to half of Pittsburgh's banks failed, and T. Mellon & Sons nearly met the same fate, even suspending payments in November of 1873. It was initiation by fire for Andy, to whom his father, Judge Thomas Mellon, delegated increasing responsibility at the bank. Resuming payments in early 1874, Judge Mellon and his son spotted opportunity if they could simply weather the "cyclone."[2]

The problem, Judge Mellon would later recall in a private autobiography for his family, was that while property was widely available for sale, an opportunistic buyer first had to set off "in search of its true owners, who could only be discovered through the tedious process of judicial sales in the bankrupt and other courts," so much having been mortgaged, assigned, or hypothecated. "Nothing," the elder Mellon concluded, "but a process of general liquidation could determine what any man owned or was worth." More colorfully, he added that "the stock had to be boiled down to evaporate the water from it. Real and fictitious wealth had become so mixed up that the refining process or bankruptcy and sheriff's sales became necessary to separate the dross from the true metal."[3]

But the Mellons invested the time and effort in scooping up good assets at bargain prices during the crisis and its immediate aftermath. They foreclosed on mortgages, bought extensively at sheriff sales of bankrupt estates, and evicted tenants who were delinquent on their rent.[4] By his own admission, such ruthlessness imbued the senior Mellon with a reputation as a "hard, practical man, disposed to acquire wealth by every fair means." But by the early 1880s, that harsh disposition had generated considerable returns for the family enterprises.[5]

For the economy overall, in Pittsburgh and elsewhere, the 1870s were a time of inexorable pressure to cut costs, innovate, and find new markets. For firms as for assets, it was a period during which market pressures relentlessly sorted dross from true metal. The Mellons, father and son, were experts at just that sorting.

More than his brothers, Andy acquired his father's uncompromising business acumen during the 1870s. Throughout his adult life, he would often ask, "What would Father do?" in response to confrontation with a difficult challenge. But whereas the judge had been "hard, cold, and forbidding," with a "downright mean streak" and a deeply held belief that "life was a perpetual battle," the son was similarly disciplined but less severe. According to Andy's own son, the younger Mellon "reached adulthood as a thin-voiced, thin-bodied, shy and uncommunicative man," lacking either interest in or aptitude for forging personal relationships.[6]

It was this quiet and unostentatious man who, as secretary of the Department of the Treasury, was confronted in the autumn of 1929 by the worst crisis to hit the US economy since the financial cyclone of his youth. Whereas Judge Thomas Mellon had been haunted by the childhood memory of the panic of 1819, when his own father's farm "was not worth half the deferred payments that remained against it," it was to 1873 that Andy turned in 1929.[7]

According to President Hoover, "At great length, Mr. Mellon recounted to me his recollection of the great depression of the seventies." Mellon, Hoover recalled, "told of the tens of thousands of farms that had been foreclosed; of railroads that had almost wholly gone into the hands of receivers; of the few banks that had come through unscathed; of many men who were jobless and mobs that roamed the streets." And yet, Mellon noted, when his father returned early from England upon learning that steel orders were beginning to pour into closed furnaces, the panic had ended, and within a year, "the whole system was working again."[8]

Thus, likely once again asking himself, "What would Father do?" Secretary Mellon's advice to the president was typical of his father's: "Liquidate labor, liquidate stocks, liquidate the farmers, liquidate real estate . . . It will purge the rottenness out of the system." Echoing his father almost verbatim, he added that "there is a mighty lot of real estate lying around the United States which does not know who owns it." The only solution, in his mind, was to force those mortgages into liquidation. "Values will be adjusted, and enterprising people will pick up the wrecks from less competent people," as indeed he and his father had done in the aftermath of 1873.[9]

Though Hoover ultimately rejected Mellon's advice, instead nearly doubling federal expenditure in real terms by the end of 1932—a bigger increase even than during his successor's first term—the "liquidationist" assessment was not uncommon. Reflecting the view of many prewar economic theorists, the eminent Harvard economist Joseph Schumpeter was broadly in agreement with Mellon.

Writing in the immediate wake of the Depression, Schumpeter argued that "depressions are not simply evils, which we might attempt to suppress," but rather "forms of something which has to be done, namely, adjustment to previous economic change." Reflecting on the earlier depressions of 1825 and 1873 and the "recuperative powers of our industrial system," Schumpeter further noted that "recovery came of itself" and, indeed, that "recovery is sound only if it does come of itself." In contrast, "any revival which is merely due to artificial stimulus leaves part of the work of depressions undone." Though Schumpeter viewed *relief* as "imperative on moral and social grounds," he saw attempts to "artificially" *remedy* depression as counteracting the constructively destructive function of recessions.[10]

Schumpeter would later expand his "recuperative" or cleansing view of recessions into a broader theory of economic growth in which waves of technological innovation would result in "the perennial gale of creative destruction." "The fundamental impulse that sets and keeps the capitalist engine in motion," he argued, "comes from the new consumers' goods, the new methods of production or transportation, the new markets, the new forms of industrial organization that capitalist enterprise creates." But that process of "industrial mutation" inevitably involves the revolutionization of the entire structure of an economy, a relentless destruction of the old and creation of the new.[11] Recurrent economic troubles are thus "the means to reconstruct each time the economic system on a more efficient plan." Though Schumpeter acknowledged that "they inflict losses while they last, drive firms into the bankruptcy court, throw people out of employment," eventually "the ground is clear and the way paved for new achievement."[12]

In one respect, Mellon and Schumpeter's view of recessions as performing a cleansing, reallocative function is merely another restatement of the boom-bust, manias, panics, and crashes theory of recessions. As their British contemporary, London School of Economics professor and economics department chair Lionel Robbins put it, while "nobody wishes for bankruptcies" and "nobody likes liquidation," when "the extent of mal-investment and over-indebtedness has passed a certain limit," liquidation becomes both inevitable and essential.[13]

But in another important respect, the notion that recessions are performing a valuable reallocative function, sorting the "dross from the true metal," constitutes a fundamentally novel proposition. It suggests that recessions are not just inevitable and remedial, they are also necessary and a feature of the growth process itself, irrespective of past potential excesses or malinvestments.

Despite their undeniable collateral damage, do recessions ultimately serve a growth-enhancing, reallocative purpose, purging less productive firms and economic arrangements to release inefficiently employed labor and capital? Does an economy look substantively different at the end of a recovery, relative to how it would have looked had the preceding recession never happened?

The search for "Schumpeterian growth"—economic growth through perennial gales of cleansing, creative destruction—has certainly been exhaustive and remains ongoing. More recent theories generally postulate that, fundamentally, recessions are periods when the economy is called upon to engage in an abnormally high level of reallocation of resources from less- to more-productive enterprises and uses. In many of these neo-Schumpeterian models, an economy faces a choice between producing and reorganizing. When an economy is rapidly expanding, it may be costly for firms to sacrifice the production of goods and services that are presently in high demand to instead invest more in reorganization and restructuring that will raise productivity and output only in the future.

In a highly relatable analogy during the 1990–91 US recession, one early proponent of this "recessions-as-reorganizations" view, longtime NBER recession dating committee chair Robert Hall, noted that "during periods of intense effort, one's office becomes more and more disorganized. Piles of unsorted materials develop first on desks and tables and later on the floor." But "as disorganization cumulates and the office's level of organizational capital deteriorates further and further, the professional's productivity begins to suffer."[14] In contrast, when the opportunity cost of investing time and resources in reorganizing is low—for example, during a recession, when the lost sales from sorting one's desk instead of selling product are smaller—then more workers and firms will engage in productivity-enhancing reorganization and restructuring.

Valerie Ramey, a former doctoral student of Hall's and his eventual successor as chair of the NBER recession dating committee, at the time similarly suggested that recessions might be analogous to pit stops. In an auto race, a raised yellow flag requires all drivers to reduce speed due to a hazard on the track, which makes it the ideal time to take a pit stop for deferred maintenance. Ramey thus suggested that economic slowdowns might be the economic equivalent of yellow flag events—opportunities when enterprises in need of a quick overhaul can take advantage of the rest of the economy proceeding at a slower speed to "invest" in reorganization and rightsizing, resulting in layoffs clustering at specific points in time.[15]

Supporting this "pit stops" or "recessions-as-reorganizations" conception of recessions were two then-recent findings. First, recent research seemed to suggest that recessions are times when job losses are concentrated in a relatively small number of firms making relatively large employment cutbacks, thereby releasing an abnormally large number of job seekers into the labor market.[16] Second, future IMF chief economist Olivier Blanchard and future Nobel laureate Peter Diamond found that employment losses during recessions were driven by high rates of job destruction rather than low rates of job creation, while economic expansions were driven by low rates of job destruction rather than high rates of job creation.[17] Like Schumpeter, Blanchard and Diamond concluded that their results were most consistent with a theory of recessions as "periods of cleaning up."[18]

Thus, Hall concluded that during recessions, for the most part, labor markets seemed to carry on as if it were "business as usual." For most business establishments, it seemed that employment growth proceeded normally; pushing unemployment higher was instead sharp contractions in employment among a minority of establishments.[19] As a result, during recessions, the labor market still appeared to match unemployed workers to vacant jobs at the same or higher volume as during economic expansions; it was just called upon to process a much larger number of unemployed workers during the former than the latter.

Around the same time, in 1991 economists at Stanford and Harvard found evidence in support of the Schumpeterian thesis that the Great Depression constituted a gale of creative destruction. Using 1929 manufacturing plant size as a crude proxy for adoption of new mass production technology on the eve of the crash, they found that there was a large shakeout in the motor vehicle industry as exits from operation were dominated by smaller, lower-productivity plants.[20] This left an industry populated by more productive firms employing new mass-production technology. The researchers interpreted this shakeout as evidence of an accelerated diffusion of new production technologies to a greater fraction of motor vehicle production.

Analyzing the more recent 2008–09 financial crisis, scholars have found that skill requirements in job vacancy postings increased in areas that were hit harder by the recession relative to in areas that were hit less hard. They interpreted this result as evidence consistent with firms treating the recession "as a time of 'cleansing,' enabling them to restructure their production" toward routine-biased technology that economizes on routine labor while expanding utilization of higher-skilled cognitive labor.[21]

In 2016, researchers also found that on average, the 1981–82, 1990–91, and 2001 recessions were associated with increased productivity-enhancing reallocation across US manufacturing establishments. But at the same time, they observed that during the 2008–09 recession, the intensity of reallocation declined, and the reallocation that did occur was less productivity-enhancing than reallocations during the three earlier recessions. Moreover, their estimates of the productivity-enhancing reallocations of the three recessions preceding 2008–09 were substantially attenuated when they excluded the 1981–82 recession. The 1981–82 recession was characterized by a particularly strong surge in job destruction and exits by low-productivity establishments followed by a particularly large surge in job creation in 1984 as interest rates and energy prices declined.[22] It is typically not a good sign for the validity of an empirical result when the result is driven by the outlier or exception.

This highlights a key challenge for recent tests of the cleansing view of recessions. Even a sample period of thirty years, spanning the early 1980s through the Great Recession of 2008–09, only includes four or five recessions. As we have seen, unlike happy expansions, each recession is unhappy in its own way; four or five data points is thus hardly a foundation for strong statistical inference.

Moreover, it is not even clear that the economic evidence available in the early 1990s supported the "recessions-as-reorganizations" hypothesis. Commenting on

Hall's reorganizations hypothesis, future chairman of President Clinton's Council of Economic Advisers, Martin Baily, questioned whether it was indeed the case that during recessions firms are "deciding to produce less because reorganization is so profitable."[23] Then–chief economist of the World Bank and future Treasury secretary Larry Summers was blunter. There was, he recalled, an old discussion joke to describe his reaction to Hall's paper: "how it contains much that is new and much that is true, but, unfortunately, what is new is not true and what is true is not new." But in this case, Summers declared that he "did not think there was very much that was true in this paper," so the joke did not apply.[24]

Summers's skepticism was certainly merited. Already at the time, Baily noted that in contrast to the "reorganization" hypothesis, economic productivity often declined during a recession, which at least in the short term was hardly consistent with managers streamlining or otherwise cleaning up their production processes. Another contemporary commentator also objected to Ramey's pit stop metaphor, noting that typically after a pit stop, drivers "get going right away," whereas the immediate aftermath of a recession sometimes lacked a similar spike in employment.[25] Indeed, discussants of Hall's paper were at that very moment in 1991 on the cusp of what economists would dub a "jobless recovery," characterized by weak job growth.[26]

More importantly, in the 1990s, economists lacked comprehensive data on labor market flows. But with the availability of new data on job openings and labor market turnover ("JOLTS") from December 2000 onward, the "cleaning up" or "pit stop" theory increasingly seems at odds with what the labor market tells us about recessions. While the unemployment rate surged during each of the past three recessions in the United States, the rate at which workers experienced separation from their jobs was essentially flat or even declined during the 2001 and 2008–09 recessions.

A major reason for this is that the rate at which workers quit their jobs declines markedly during recessions, offsetting the relatively modest rise in the rate of layoffs and discharges. Meanwhile, both the rate at which firms hire new workers and the overall *level* of job hires declined during each of the past three US recessions. Thus, in contrast to earlier studies and common misperception, in the first instance, most recessions are characterized not by a surge in the rate at which firms lay off workers but rather by a sharp decline in the rate at which they hire new workers.[27]

A declining rate of job hires and flat or falling rate of job separations is not exactly what one would expect during an episode of intense reallocative churn.

Moreover, with less hiring and a relatively modest but nontrivial uptick in the rate at which workers are involuntarily separated from their jobs through layoffs and discharges, the average and median duration of an unemployed worker's time out of employment surges during a recession and then comes down only gradually.[28] Again, hardly the portrait of an efficient reorganization.

Historical data on manufacturing employment from 1919 through 1930 indicates that the same pattern observed since 2000 prevailed in earlier periods as well. The job separation rate through discharges declined during interwar recessions, while the separation rate through layoffs rose modestly, and only after recession was already well underway. With quit rates plummeting, the real driver of rising unemployment during interwar recessions, as during more recent recessions, was thus a collapse in the rate of gross hiring.[29]

An additional problem with the "cleansing" view of recessions is that while there is evidence that recessions may hasten the net destruction of less efficient matches between workers and jobs, unfortunately, they also hinder the creation of the most efficient matches by impeding the job-to-job transition of workers into better, more productive jobs through quitting. Indeed, leaving one job for a better one is an essential element of productivity-enhancing labor market dynamism. Thus, while recessions may "cleanse" by killing off marginal production arrangements that are no longer viable when profitability declines, they also "sully" by deterring entrepreneurs from creating new job openings, such that workers have fewer opportunities to quit and migrate to higher-quality jobs for which they are better suited.[30]

During economic expansions, higher-productivity businesses expand primarily by attracting workers away from lower-productivity businesses. In contrast, during recessions, this job "ladder" essentially collapses, such that though there is some cleansing early on as low-productivity firms reduce hiring and increase separations, as unemployment rises, the "sullying" effect dominates and lingers.[31] During the Great Recession of 2008–09, there was consequently a "deep freeze in job-to-job upgrading and attrition up the job ladder."[32]

Jobs created during recessions are also of lower average quality and more likely to be destroyed later than jobs created during economic expansions.[33] Specifically, jobs created during recessions tend to offer lower wages, and workers who lose their jobs during mass-layoff events when the unemployment rate is high experience cumulative earnings losses equal to nearly 3 years of their pre-displacement earnings, versus 1.4 years if the unemployment rate is low.[34] And what drives that higher earnings loss is not that laid-off workers are unable to find another job but rather that they are only able to do so in lower-skill occupations.[35] Insofar as higher wages reflect higher productivity, these results imply that not only are job-finding rates lower during recessions but also that jobs created during recessions are of lower rather than higher average productivity.[36]

Part of the problem is that recessions tend to murder potentially high-productivity firms in their infancy.[37] Recessions are perennially guilty of rampant reverse age discrimination. More likely to encounter financial constraints during recessions, young firms account for a disproportionate share of employment losses and business exits versus older, more established firms.[38] It is hard for "perennial gales" of creative destruction to clear the way for younger, more dynamic firms when those very gales discriminate against younger firms in favor of maturer incumbents. Indeed, during the severe UK recession of 1979–81 and its immediate aftermath, many of the steel casing plants that closed were *not* the least profitable.[39]

Jobs added during recessions furthermore tend to be shorter in duration; facing fewer job options during and immediately following recessions, workers often have little choice but to accept lower-quality matches.[40] This is in fact a central feature of every labor market recovery—after losing a job during a recession, many workers enter a protracted period of successive short-term jobs punctuated by further episodes of unemployment as they search for a stable job match.[41]

But while we might not be able to observe evidence of cleansing and reallocative churn in the labor market, can we at least observe it at the broader sectoral level? If recessions are fundamentally about reallocation—destroying existing economic arrangements to create new ones—then it would be reasonable to expect that the economy at the end of an economic recovery would exhibit substantive, observable differences from the counterfactual economy that would have emerged had the preceding expansion proceeded uninterrupted by a recessionary cleanse. Is that the case?

If there is cleansing and reallocation that occurs during recessions, then we would expect to observe that a sector whose share of the economy had risen above (or fallen below) its long-term trend during the preceding expansion should subsequently experience a large contraction (or expansion) of its share of the economy during the succeeding recession.[42] In Figure 36, I therefore plot the deviation of each GDP component's share of total output at the end of each recession against its deviation from trend at the end of the preceding expansion, and label notable recession outliers.

As shown in Panel A of Figure 36, since 1947, each component of GDP as a share of overall GDP at the end of a US expansion and at the end of the subsequent recession has exhibited remarkable fealty to long-run trend. Indeed, at the end of an

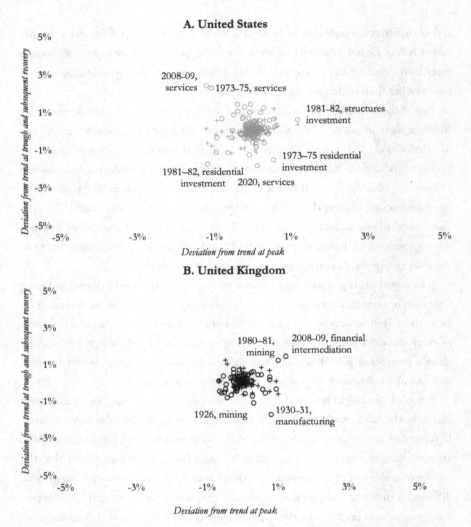

Figure 36: Deviation of GDP Components from Trend Shares of Output. US GDP shares are from Tables 3A and 3B of the Bureau of Economic Analysis' GDP press release, accessed via Haver Analytics. UK GVA shares are from the Bank of England's "A Millennium of Macroeconomic Data."

expansion, the typical component's share of overall output has deviated just 0.003 percent from trend, and the same at the end of a recession. Moreover, there is no relationship whatsoever between positive deviations from trend share of GDP at the end of an expansion and negative deviations from trend at the end of the subsequent recession. As can be seen, deviations from trend at both peak and trough simply cluster randomly around zero.

The biggest negative deviations from trend at the end of a recession were for residential investment during the oil-shock recession of 1973–75 and the oil-shock cum interest-rate shock of the early 1980s. But as can be seen in Panel A, residential investment had already been below trend at the end of the expansion preceding the 1981–82 recession, so the recession was hardly correcting for prior excess allocation. Consumption of services jumped from slightly negative to slightly positive during the 1973–75 and 2008–09 recessions, but this was not because of any great reallocation toward services consumption, which actually declined in real terms during both recessions. Rather, it was that consumption of services merely declined by less than other components of economic output.

Meanwhile, the biggest positive deviation from trend at the end of an expansion was just before the 1981–82 recession, when investment in structures was approximately 1 percent above its long-term trend share of GDP. This was predominantly the result of a surge of investment in mining exploration, shafts, and wells following the oil price shocks of the 1970s, as well as recovery from the relatively short, sharp recession in 1980. As a result, structures investment as a share of GDP would remain about 1 percent *above* trend throughout the duration of the 1981–82 recession and subsequent recovery, further boosted by large tax incentives in President Reagan's 1981 tax cuts.[43]

We see similar results in the United Kingdom in Panel B. Since 1921, at the end of an economic expansion and succeeding recession, the typical UK industry's share of total gross value added has deviated just 0.2 percent from long-run trend. Outside financial intermediation, the largest deviations were typically negative divergences for mining and manufacturing during recessions. The Great Depression especially impacted UK manufacturing, whose share of gross value added (GVA) ended the two-year recession nearly 2 percent below trend.

Not surprisingly, during the 1926 UK coal strike, mining's share of GVA plunged from slightly above trend to about 1 percent below. In contrast, mining's share rose over 1 percent above trend during the deep recession of 1979–81 as new North Sea oil production came on line and ramped up in response to the oil price shocks of the 1973–74 Arab oil embargo and 1979 Iranian Revolution. Though financial services were about 1 percent above trend as a share of the UK economy on the eve of the 2008 financial crisis, their share rose rather than fell during the subsequent recession.

But perhaps reallocation is not just an outcome of recessions themselves but of recessions and the subsequent recovery process that gradually churns out a new, more efficient allocation of resources? In Figure 36, I therefore also plot the deviation of each GDP component's share of total output at the end of every expansion against its deviation from trend at the end of the succeeding recovery. Yet here again we see remarkable fealty to trend; there is no relationship whatsoever between deviation from trend at the end of one expansion and deviation at the end of the subsequent recovery in either the United States or United Kingdom.

One can observe an even more pronounced fealty to trend in US employment data.[44] At the end of a US economic expansion, succeeding recession, and subsequent recovery, the typical industry's share of total employment deviates just 0.1 percent from long-run trend. Two of the largest divergences from trend were for employment in leisure and hospitality (3.5 percent below trend share) and government employment (1.8 percent above trend share) during the unique pandemic recession of March–April 2020, when nationwide lockdowns generated large private employment losses in leisure and hospitality while government employees generally remained on payrolls.

Besides the coronavirus pandemic, since 1939, the only other large divergence from trend was for employment in durable goods. During the wartime expansion that ended in February 1945, employment in the durable goods industry as a share of total employment rose 2.4 percent above trend. It then fell to 2.6 percent below trend by the end of the postwar recession. While the wartime reallocation of resources toward the production of durable military equipment may have been unnatural and unsustainable, the subsequent reallocation away from durable goods is a testament more to the extreme distortions of war and demobilization than to any generally natural, salutary function of recessions.

Unfortunately, looking even further back in time, it is not possible to compute sectoral or industry shares, as earlier output estimates are indexed volumes rather than output measured in currency units. However, for the nearly two centuries from 1700 through 1870, it is at least possible to examine whether broad economic sectors (agriculture, industry, services) whose level of output was above trend at the peak of a UK economic expansion subsequently returned to or dipped below trend during the subsequent recession.[45]

Here again, one can observe no systematic tendency across sectors for the level of output to decline relative to trend during a recession if production in that sector was above trend during the preceding expansion. Indeed, for the agricultural and services sectors, the sign is wrong—for every 1 percent above trend at the end of an expansion, output in those sectors is still 0.4 percent and 0.2 percent above trend by the end of the succeeding recession, respectively. Looking at a more detailed industry level, the same pattern holds, with no systematic tendency across all industries for output to decline relative to trend during a recession if production in that industry was above trend during the preceding expansion. For metals and mining, financial services, domestic services, and "other industry," the sign is wrong—if output is above trend at an expansion peak, it is more rather than less likely to remain elevated relative to trend at the trough of the succeeding recession.

Domestic services exhibit particularly strong persistence of trend deviation—for every 1 percent above trend at the end of an expansion, output of domestic services is still 0.8 percent above trend at the trough of the subsequent recession—consistent with services being one of the least volatile components of the economy. The only industry that on average experiences a decline relative to trend during recession after rising above trend during the preceding expansion is textiles and leather; for every 1 percent above trend at the end of an expansion, textile and leather output is 0.6 percent below trend at the trough of the subsequent recession. This, however, likely reflects the more discretionary nature of demand for such goods. Ultimately, some industries, such as certain manufacturing industries, are simply more responsive to shifts in aggregate economic activity. Other sectors, particularly services, are less discretionary and less responsive to aggregate shocks.

But even if recessions are not periods of intensified reorganization and reallocation, might it still be the case that recessions are periods of elevated investment in future productivity-enhancing activities, per Bob Hall's desk metaphor? If recessions are periods that lower the opportunity cost of investing in restructuring activities that will raise future productivity and output at the expense of current output, then we should expect recessions to be periods of increased spending on research and development. Yet examining the period from 1958 to 2003, far from rising during recessions, economists have found that entrepreneurs concentrate their innovation during economic expansions.[46] Over the near century from 1929 through 2024, I find the same; real investment in research and development tends to rise above trend during economic expansions and fall below trend during recessions.[47] Precisely the opposite of what one would expect in the recessions-as-reorganizations view.

Like the penitent's notion that busts must follow booms, the idea that recessions serve a salutary, cleansing purpose has a certain palliative appeal. For all the pain and suffering wrought by periods of economic decline—lost jobs, lost income and health insurance, foreclosed homes, adverse health effects—it is comforting to think that the discomfort is at least medicinal, albeit with side effects. Or, to revisit a metaphor from Chapter 2, perhaps we might draw consolation from the notion that recessions are the economic equivalent of intermittent wildfires required to clear out deadwood so that younger, healthier redwoods might thrive and their pine cones unleash new seeds.

Hence we observe the recurring search for proof that recessions are periods during which the low-opportunity cost of reorganization serves as a coordinating mechanism for efficiency-enhancing liquidation and reallocation. Even many who purport to critique the "liquidationist" views of Schumpeter or the austere Andrew Mellon nonetheless presume that constituting new, more efficient economic arrangements may require breaking existing arrangements. Some firms will fail, some workers will lose jobs, and some investors will incur losses, in order that capital and labor otherwise trapped in lower-productivity firms can by force of necessity migrate to higher-productivity enterprises.

But was there a large population of unproductive firms at the end of 2019 that required systematic liquidation by a once-in-a-century pandemic to facilitate the constructive flow of people and capital to more productive endeavors? Even if there were people and investment dollars trapped in inefficient enterprises or sectors, why should their reallocation to more efficient enterprises require that the economy overall, on net, lay off workers? In any event, most workers laid off in 2020 returned to the same job from which they were involuntarily separated in March and April.

Of course, 2020 was unique; most recessions do not consist of economy-wide shutdowns and temporary stay-at-home orders. But similarly during the 1926 mining strike, it would be hard to argue that the UK economy had to shrink by more than 3 percent and the unemployment rate spike by almost 2 percentage points because the UK economy had an inefficient allocation of resources. After all, a year later, UK coal production was already back above its prestrike level. While few would argue that the US savings and loan industry was the epitome of good health at the end of the 1980s, did "cleansing" really require an Iraqi invasion of Kuwait and consequent removal of 4.3 million barrels of daily oil production from global markets?

Unfortunately, at the end of the day, recessions are pain without gain. Though economists have developed sophisticated Schumpeterian models in which creative destruction is concentrated during recessions—when the opportunity cost of reallocation is lowest—the historical record reveals that while creative destruction is an important source of long-run growth, recessions are on net counterproductive to the process.[48] In contrast to "conventional wisdom," economic restructuring falls rather than rises during recessions. While job destruction abates and job creation improves during initial stages of economic recovery, it is not enough to offset the initial surge in destruction and decline in creation during recession.[49]

Thus, though over the long run Schumpeterian creative destruction may account for more than half of productivity growth, that is despite rather than because of recessions.[50] On net, recessions simply do not accelerate or otherwise augment it. Worse, rather than expedite the natural flow of workers and capital up the productivity ladder from less to more efficient firms, they tend to sabotage the ladder itself, which then requires steady restoration. The result is that several years on from a recession, employment, output, and productivity typically look roughly the same as if they had continued uninterrupted on pre-recession trend. So too does the allocation of labor and output across sectors and industries. Recessions are not salutary episodes of intensified creative destruction—they are costly deviations from trend growth, with lost output and employment in the interim.

10

AN OBJECT IN MOTION

In a condition of this kind, the thing
to be feared most is fear itself.

—JULIUS BARNES, 1931

If recessions are fundamentally about shocks, then one might reasonably assume that the recession ends when the shock, or shocks, end. To be sure, that is often the case, particularly when the shocks are of the Act of God or Act of Man varieties. As we saw in Chapter 5, the recession associated with the 1926 UK coal strike was short and deep, but also succeeded by an equally steep and rapid rebound. The severe postwar UK recession of 1919–21 might have ended as much as a year earlier were it not for the intercession of the coal lockout of 1921. After effectively grinding to a halt during the three-month lockout, the UK economy then rebounded rapidly when management allowed miners back to the pits.

In this respect, historical strike-driven recessions tended to resemble the 2020 pandemic recession, in which millions of workers were furloughed or otherwise temporarily laid off from their employers without permanent separation. As during a strike, there was no requirement for a lengthy search and matching process for unemployed employees to match with new employers.[1] The 2020 pandemic recession was thus sharp and deep, but also short and succeeded by a correspondingly sharp and steep rebound.

Yet it is not always, or even typically, the case that recessions end when the most proximately culpable shocks dissipate. For one thing, random shocks can randomly multiply; as we have seen, most recessions involve a succession of overlapping and interacting adverse events. But also, any given shock can persist at lower intensity long after inception. Though energy prices eased following the termination of the 1973–74 Arab oil embargo, they remained substantially elevated relative to pre-recession levels, not least due to the consequent increase in the perceived risk of future supply disruptions. Similarly, as we saw in Chapter 6, the US economy continued to hemorrhage manufacturing jobs following the shock of permanent normal trade relations with the nonmarket People's Republic of China, contributing to the 2001–07 recovery's common moniker, "the jobless recovery."[2]

Though labor going on strike may trigger relatively short, sharp recessions, the shock of capital effectively going on strike can have far more pernicious, persistent effects. As we saw in Chapters 1 and 6, a defining feature of the Depression and other long recessions was an extreme reluctance on the part of creditors to lend capital at any price but to the safest, most reliable and short-term borrowers.[3] Few creditors dare to lend against collateral—whether farms in the 1930s or home mortgages in 2009—when gripped by the expectation that the value of that collateral is both uncertain and presently and foreseeably declining.

Indeed, there is another, even more important reason why recessions may not end even after the triggering shocks dissipate—fear. In his 2017 presidential address to the American Economic Association, Nobel laureate Robert Shiller noted the viral nature of stories of business failures during the Great Depression, with frequent accounts of businessmen dying by suicide. President Roosevelt's first inaugural thus included the classic line that "the only thing we have to fear is fear itself."[4] The famous invocation echoed a remark two years earlier by Julius Barnes, president of the US Chamber of Commerce. Noting that "the thing to be feared most is fear itself," Barnes warned that the "retarding effect of a sense of insecurity is promptly communicated from worker to consumer, from consumer to producer and the whole machine stalls, and the anticipated evil becomes real."[5]

Though difficult to quantify, shifts in collective confidence can be both sudden and highly correlated with the death of economic contraction and birth of economic recovery, when stories and economic narratives begin to shift from ruin to renewal. The intensity of Google searches for the word *layoff* jumped in January 2008—just as the 2008–09 commenced—before surging later in the year. Peaking at its all-time high in January 2009, search intensity remained substantially elevated throughout early 2009.

But as winter turned to spring, Americans began to seek out more optimistic stories and information. As search intensity for *layoff* returned to normal, pre-recession levels, in May 2009, search interest in *green shoots* spiked from essentially zero in February–March 2009 to more than ten times its prior record. The NBER later concluded that the recession ended the following month. Similarly, after soaring during the pandemic shutdowns of March and April 2020, searches for *layoff* fell sharply while search intensity for *reopening* shot from near-zero to its all-time maximum in May. The NBER later concluded that recovery from the pandemic recession had commenced that month.

While expansions do not and never have died of old age, recessions do and always have, with the probability of death rapidly increasing with a recession's age. Moreover, by comparison to expansions—which in the United Kingdom have even lived to the ripe old age of twenty-six years—the life expectancy of a recession is short. In both the United States and United Kingdom, most recessions since 1700 have died aged just one year old, and those rare recessions that lived longer than two years were exceptional, their longevity generally attributable first and foremost to war.

Indeed, as we saw in Chapters 6 and 7, the oldest recessions on record in either the United States or United Kingdom were wartime UK recessions in 1944–47 and 1763–65, both of which lived to be four years old. Yet as we saw in Chapter 6, both were extended on either end by extreme winter weather events that froze transportation, created industrial fuel shortages, flooded towns and cities, and devastated livestock and the following year's crop harvests.[6] The United Kingdom's sole three-year recession, meanwhile, was that which occurred at the end of World War I, coinciding not only with demobilization of the UK economy but also with a wave of industrial action, particularly in the vital coal industry.

According to the improved Davis recession chronology, the United States has never experienced a recession lasting longer than three years. Yet the four three-year-old US recessions were similarly exceptional. Aside from the Great Depression, all three of the other US recessions enduring longer than two years occurred during the eighteenth century. Two—the deep recessions of 1776–78 and 1785–87—occurred during and in the immediate aftermath of the American Revolution, with the latter coinciding with continued British-sponsored wars between the United States and Indigenous North American peoples and the exodus of some eighty thousand British loyalists. During the former, real wages in the new country plunged by nearly half.

The only other American recession lasting longer than two years was that which ended in 1720. Though the reliability of recession dating in the colonial period is low, this recession coincided with the War of the Quadruple Alliance of Spain against Britain, France, Austria, and the Dutch Republic from 1718 to 1720. But a far worse, enduring, and material shock came from a more unlikely martial source—pirates. With the end of the earlier War of the Spanish Succession in 1714 and consequent unemployment of thousands of former sailors and privateers, North American piracy entered the climactic peak of its golden age. Indeed, by May 1718, the menace had grown so pervasive that the legendary and feared pirate Edward Teach—better known as Blackbeard—even managed to blockade the key trading port of Charleston, South Carolina.[7]

Contemporary reports lamented gangs of pirates "that have infested our Coast; one Crew being no sooner gone off, but another hath appeared, to the great Destruction of Trade in general." In August of 1718, observers in Charleston noted that "we have now 8 Sail lying ready to depart, but dare not venture out; and it is almost impossible for any inward Bound Vessel to escape them [the pirates]."[8] Of the Carolinas, another remarked that "the Trade of this Place was totally interrupted," adding that "what made these Misfortunes heavier to them, was a long expensive War . . . which was but just ended when these Robbers infested them."[9]

And it was not just the Carolinas, with pirates also ravaging trade up and down the mid-Atlantic colonies.[10] Brigands were even known to intercept ships bound from Jamaica to Salem, Massachusetts, off the coast of Long Island, and to launch raids in the mouth of the Delaware River.[11] The contemporary concern that "*America* Trade will suffer very much" is thus borne out by available colonial statistics; imports from England plunged nearly 30 percent between 1717 and 1720, while Charleston exports of pitch, tar, turpentine, and lumber dropped sharply.[12] For the maritime trade on which the North American colonies depended heavily, the pirate scourge was devastating. With ships, cargo, and even life and limb exposed to such hazard, maritime trade simply ceased.

Relief came only gradually, beginning when Benjamin Hornigold, a titan of North American piracy's golden age and founder of the Bahamian "Republic of Pirates," accepted a king's pardon and became a paid pirate hunter.[13] Six months after his daring blockade of Charleston, in November 1718, Blackbeard met a dramatic death following a violent battle with sailors of the Royal Navy, with the triumphant captain Robert Maynard ordering Blackbeard's severed head mounted afront his ship *pour encourager les autres*. In December, Charleston authorities then executed the infamous "Gentleman Pirate" Stede Bonnet, having captured and tried the former Barbados landowner the prior month.[14]

Two years later, in the autumn of 1720, the Royal Navy finally managed to capture John Rackham, known as "Calico Jack" for his flamboyant dress, alongside notorious cross-dressing female pirates Anne Bonny and Mary Read.[15] Though Jamaican authorities executed Calico Jack by hanging in November 1720, his erstwhile partners—and possible lovers—Bonny and Read "pleaded their bellies," gaining temporary stays from execution until their pregnancy claims could be verified.[16] Read was "found quick with Child," but was "seiz'd with a violent Fever, soon after her Tryal" and died in prison in April 1721.[17] Bonny, meanwhile, when offered to see Calico Jack on the day of his hanging, refused, remarking that "had he [Jack] fought like a Man, he need not have been hang'd like a Dog."[18] She remained in prison until evidently delivering her child, whereupon she was "reprieved from Time to Time."[19]

Just before Read's death, in March 1721, Jamaican authorities also tried, convicted, and hanged the ruthless and dreaded pirate captain Charles Vane, infamous for his brutal assaults on the crews of captured merchant ships.[20] Like Captain Maynard with Blackbeard's severed head, Jamaican authorities similarly exhibited Vane's corpse in a cage to warn other pirates.[21] Meanwhile, by early 1721, two additional pirate legends, Bartholomew "Black Bart" Roberts and Frenchman Olivier Levasseur, had shifted away from North America to Africa, granting the thirteen North American colonies a reprieve from their predations on commerce.[22] Indeed, the well-dressed, sober Black Bart's North American raids—whose tally of four hundred captured ships by 1721 was unmatched—had previously extended as far north as Newfoundland.[23] But even Black Bart met his demise in February 1722, killed by a single bullet to the throat during an engagement off the Guinea Coast with a Royal Navy man-of-war.[24]

With the pirate threat thus abating as one after another legendary brigand either met execution or accepted the king's pardon, confidence—and, as a result, colonial trade—finally began to recover. Having fallen continuously from 1717 through 1720, in 1721, colonial imports from England rebounded. Imports jumped 4 percent in 1721 and almost 30 percent the following year. Money in circulation, which had contracted for three years straight and was down 15 percent since 1717, rebounded sharply, and the exchange rate recovered.

But such protracted periods of economic contraction are rare. Since 1700, just over 70 percent of US recessions have endured for approximately one year or less, while 94 percent have endured for two years or fewer. For the United Kingdom, 55 percent of recessions since 1700 have lived to the age of a year or less, while 95 percent have lived for two or fewer years. Every recession has ultimately ended in renewed economic expansion, with most doing so within about a year and the overwhelming majority within about two years. And that short life expectancy of recessions is not a recent phenomenon but an august pattern extending at least as far back as 1700.

Thus, though it may be difficult to see the light at the end of the tunnel when in the grip of recession, fear of its longevity is not only unfounded, it is also injurious. For if recessions do not end when their proximate triggers dissipate, then they end when narratives of hope displace those of loss, and when we—households, businesses, consumers, investors—collectively replace defensive fear with cautious confidence. Indeed, as we saw in Chapter 6, the single-most decisive factor in the recovery from the Great Depression in the spring and summer of 1933 was the substitution of more optimistic price expectations for continued, grinding deflation.

But while fear of the longevity of recessions may be without just cause, so too is optimism in the potential immortality of economic expansions. Indeed, it is the very human lurch from hope to fear and back again that renders the narrative of boom and bust so instinctive and seductive.

Reports of the death of economic fluctuations are often subject to exaggeration toward the end of long expansions, particularly as policymakers seek to congratulate themselves on the apparent holiday from history. Celebrating the then-longest US economic expansion on record, in their 1969 *Economic Report of the President* (ERP), President Lyndon Johnson's Council of Economic Advisers (CEA) lauded the economic policy achievements of the Kennedy and Johnson administrations. "No longer," they declared, "is the performance of the American economy generally interpreted in terms of stages of the business cycle. No longer do we consider periodic recessions once every 3 or 4 years an inevitable fact of life." Instead, "the forces making for economic fluctuations have been contained through the active use of fiscal and monetary policies to sustain expansion."[25]

At a 1969 conference titled "Is the Business Cycle Obsolete?," MIT professor, former Kennedy advisor, and future Nobel laureate Paul Samuelson echoed the administration's hubris, remarking that the NBER had "worked itself out of one of its first jobs—namely, the business cycle."[26] Ironically, by the end of the year, the record-long expansion would not only come to an end but would also usher in a twelve-year period during which the average economic expansion in the United States would survive for fewer than three years.

Nearly thirty years later, as the US economy approached a new record-long expansion, top officials in the Clinton Treasury Department privately boasted that government policy could, in the absence of external shocks, prolong the ongoing expansion indefinitely. Like Francis Diebold and Glenn Rudebusch, they concluded from then-nascent research that the age independence of postwar expansions reflected countercyclical demand management successfully counteracting endogenous economic shocks, not yet knowing that the apparent age dependence of prewar expansions was a statistical figment.[27] In the final ERP of the Clinton administration in January 2001, the CEA concluded that "the current situation of low inflation, high productivity growth, and lean inventories reveals no sign of an end to the expansion," which, as of November 2000, had broken the 1961–69 record.[28] Two months later, the expansion ended in recession.

The temptation toward confidence in the ability of policy to attenuate or even eliminate economic fluctuations is particularly pronounced during periods of extended economic expansion and moderate volatility. Shortly after the then-longest US expansion on record and relatively short, mild recession of 2001, Nobel laureate Robert Lucas confidently declared in his presidential address to the American Economic Association that macroeconomics' "central problem of depression prevention has been solved," noting that the stability of aggregate production and consumption in postwar decades "must be seen in part as an achievement of the economists, Keynesian and monetarist, who guided economic policy over these years."[29] A year later, then–Federal Reserve governor and future chairman Ben Bernanke attributed the decline in the volatility of economic output over the preceding two decades to "improved monetary policy."[30]

Former UK prime minister and chancellor of the exchequer Gordon Brown was even more hubristic. Midway through the second-longest expansion in UK history, the then-chancellor lamented that "for 40 years, our economy has had an unenviable history under Governments of both parties of boom and bust."[31] In stark contrast, Brown expressed pride that "against a background of mounting uncertainty and instability in the global economy, we set about establishing a new economic framework to secure long-term economic stability and put an end to the damaging cycle of boom and bust."[32] Ironically, the UK expansion then underway would in 2008 end in the deepest UK recession since the end of World War II.

However, as noted in Chapter 7, this is not at all to suggest that the evident irrelevance of policy to recession depth and duration, expansion longevity, or macroeconomic volatility is an argument for inaction. Quite the contrary; with the impact and ability to absorb adverse economic shocks unevenly distributed across households, there are compelling social welfare arguments for attenuating the adverse impact of recessionary shocks on people and families.

Moreover, while expansionary fiscal and monetary policy may not remediate recession, contractionary policy in the face of recession can make recessions much worse, as we saw with contractionary fiscal policy during the UK recession of 1847 or contractionary monetary policy during the Great Depression in the United States.[33] Rather, history simply offers a warning that we cannot look to the state to arrest episodes of economic contraction ex post, let alone to prevent them ex ante, except in both instances by way of the Hippocratic advice to first do no harm.

Nonetheless, though the long-run macroeconomic data contradicts the hypothesis that increased state intervention has tempered the frequency and depth of economic contractions in the United Kingdom and United States, many eminent economists have long argued—and continue to argue—that recessions are unique phenomena of market economies.

While recognizing that state-directed, planned economies suffer from their own economic pathologies and misallocations of resources, the distinguished Harvard economist Gottfried Haberler maintained that the maladjustment, overinvestment, and "overexpansion" he believed constituted the root cause of recessions in market economies was inapplicable to planned economies.[34] A planned economy, he contended at a 1936 conference, would simply "not allow" depressions to develop, and if one did threaten "to develop in the private sector, the planned economy would be in a good position and would surely not hesitate to counteract vigorously."[35]

Commenting on Haberler's work, one of Arthur Burns's Columbia colleagues went further still, concluding that the business cycle of market economies was nonexistent in planned economies such as that of the Soviet Union.[36] Echoing the point, the renowned growth economist Evsey Domar suggested that the primary challenge for planned economies was likely to be one of inflation rather than stability. "If a capitalist society may be compared with an airplane, whose inherent tendency is to fall down unless supported by the work of its motor," he postulated, then "a socialist society might be likened to a ballon, which, were it not for its cables or ballast, would fly off into the air altogether."[37]

Another conference participant was more skeptical of the proposition that planned economies were immune to the types of disturbances that appeared to generate economic fluctuations in market economies.[38] Four years earlier, their short monograph on the subject, *The Economics of Disturbance*, had been savaged in a brutally critical review by future economics Nobel laureate and pioneer of large-scale macroeconomic forecasting Lawrence Klein. In a scathing assessment, Klein asserted that "a strong case can be made for the position that it is the capitalist mode of production that gives rise to crises." "One of the main points of this position," he continued, "is that capital accumulation in relation to the profit motive, a purely capitalist phenomenon, is the root of all economic evil." Acknowledging that at least some of the most serious economic disturbances were exogenous in nature—in particular, war—Klein then proceeded to ask, "Can socialism be honestly accused, as can capitalism, of bringing such critical disturbances on the world?"[39]

Yet the notion that planned or otherwise nonmarket economies are somehow immune to recession is not borne out by the historical record. Following severe recession during the 1917–22 Russian Civil War, the Soviet Union endured a deep recession in the early 1930s as the policy of agricultural collectivization created a devastating famine that claimed the lives of anywhere from five to eleven million Soviet citizens.[40] In addition to wartime recessions in 1941–42 and 1945–46, the Soviet economy also experienced recession in the late 1970s, as well as an ultimately fatal recession from 1989 to 1991.[41] According to the Maddison Project historical economic database, the Soviet economy also contracted in 1959 and 1963, though it is unclear whether these episodes of contraction could be characterized as outright recessions.[42]

Indeed, as one participant in the same 1936 NBER conference at which Haberler presented his paper on business cycles in planned economies pointed out, "Soviet planning has been so poor that the government-controlled press is full of complaints about frequent shutdowns of manufacturing plants for lack of raw materials and consequent layoffs of workers." Moreover, the participant observed, "There is extremely bad coordination among industries that depend on one another for their materials or parts, such that "it is a common occurrence for plant managers to be dismissed, indicted, and sentenced to jail or forced labor camps for failure to fulfill impossible tasks laid down by the planners in Moscow."[43] Planned economies, like market ones, are thus just as if not more susceptible to microeconomic, sector-specific shocks, which, as we have seen, can generate recessionary impacts at the macroeconomic level.

Nonetheless, in the aftermath of the 2008–09 global financial crisis, the nonmarket economy of the People's Republic of China (PRC) appeared to be a beacon of economic stability. Yet like the former Soviet Union, the economic history of the PRC also includes multiple episodes of economic contraction, often severe. In addition to contracting in 1954, the Chinese economy experienced a devastating recession from 1958 to 1962 during the Great Leap Forward—an experience that generated mass famine and the deaths of up to forty-five million Chinese—with Chinese living standards falling by more than a fifth.[44] Less than a decade later, the

Chinese economy again endured severe recession during the Cultural Revolution, with Chinese living standards dropping by 10 percent between 1966 and 1968, and again at the tail end of the Cultural Revolution in 1976, when real GDP contracted by 3 percent and real GDP per capita by 5 percent.[45]

China also may have experienced recession in 1989–90, with real GDP eking out a 0.8 percent expansion in 1989 and just 0.1 percent in 1990 while falling by more than 2 percent in per capita terms, contributing to mass protests in Tiananmen Square.[46] In more recent memory, the PRC's economy was the first to enter recession during the COVID-19 pandemic, with the Chinese economy plunging in the first quarter of 2020 as the country entered the first stage of what would ultimately be three years of on-again, off-again pandemic lockdowns. There is simply no abolishing, or otherwise planning away, recessions.

The primary basis for the erroneous belief that nonmarket economies are somehow immune to recession is the mistaken notion that recessions are endogenous, the inevitable consequence of the excesses and imbalances of the preceding expansion. Yet as we saw in Chapters 3 and 4, while sharp recoveries typically follow sharp recessions, it is simply not the case that busts follow booms. In the absence of a change in economic policy regime, several years after a recession, economies typically look quite like how they would have looked had they continued uninterrupted along pre-recession trend.

The apophany that some excess or misallocation appeared in retrospect to precede a painful stimulus like recession appeals to another of our evolved behaviors as a social species—namely, our organization and transmission of patterns through moral-laden stories. There is a reason that parables and their anthropomorphized analogue, fables, remain among the most enduring and most recognized of stories. From the parables of Jesus to Aesop's fables, they convey a moral lesson, a maxim by which to live better and freer from harm and guilt.

In his presidential address to the American Economic Association, Shiller wondered aloud how the narrative of the October 1929 stock market crash as the defining event of a recession that was already over a month old became so powerful and enduring. Part of that strength, he concluded, was a "certain moralizing." "The fact," Shiller noted, "that the 1920s had been not only a time of economic superabundance but also of sexual liberation—a morality viewed negatively by some, though they were unable to make a case against it until the new story of the stock market crash appeared." Sermons on the Sunday following the great crash moralized the event, attributing it to "excesses, moral and spiritual." As Shiller observed, the penitent, boom-and-bust narrative framed the crash as "a sort of day-of-judge-ment on the 'Roaring Twenties,'" a term that in fact only came to prominence in the 1930s.[47]

Perceived patterns encoded and transmitted through parables can provide us with a certain sense of comfort, even control over bad events. If we can identify past actions that appeared to precede harm and avoid repetition of those harm-inducing actions, then it grants us some agency over the future. Stories about boom and bust, moreover, encode these moral lessons with the five essential elements of a successful narrative. They have characters—protagonists and antagonists, heroes and villains. They have a setting—a time and place of excess—and plot—the sequence of events occurring through a process of cause and effect, culminating in resolution.

But apophanous stories are not always innocuous. As one contemporary writer during the Great Depression, Catherine Hackett, remarked, whereas "in the old Boom era," one could conspicuously consume without a sense of guilt, "Now it was different." Stories of business failures, suicides, and penury were contagious. In such a context of fear and "revulsion" against the perceived excesses of the 1920s, it is no wonder that households tightened their belts. Yet as Hackett, observing housewives sitting tight and waiting for prices to fall further "before buying anything but actual necessities," remarked, "I do not need to be an economist to realize that if all the twenty million housewives do that, business recovery will be indefinitely delayed."[48]

Government too can overreact to its perceived accessory to past sins through acts of atonement. Surveying one hundred years of Federal Reserve history, the late Harvard macroeconomist Julio Rotemberg observed a strong tendency on the part of the Fed "to act as if it were penitent when critics successfully argue that 'bad out-comes' are a product of Fed 'mistakes.'" Indeed, the essence of penitence is regret and repentance for past wrongdoing. If it is genuine, then the sinner must first and foremost avoid repeating the sin.[49]

According to Rotemberg, one such episode of penitence on the part of the Federal Reserve was the institution's conduct of monetary policy during the Great Depres-sion. Having contentiously abandoned a prior commitment to extend credit only for "productive" and not "speculative" purposes in 1927, within two years, the Fed repented their decision after taking blame for an intervening run-up in equity prices. With their consequent hawkish turn in 1928–29 likely contributing to the declines in industrial production in the late summer and early autumn of 1929 that possibly precipitated the Great Crash, the Fed's penitence led them to restrict monetary policy at precisely the wrong moment.[50] Milton Friedman, Anna Schwartz, Allan Meltzer, and Ben Bernanke would later lay primary blame for the Depression squarely on the conduct of exceedingly restrictive monetary policy by the Federal Reserve.[51]

More recently, after the 2008–09 recession, policymakers on both sides of the Atlantic effectively demanded through new regulation that their economies produce goods and services with less of a key input for which, over any meaningful time horizon, there are few substitutes—namely, bank credit to the private nonfinancial sector.[52] Effectively, postcrisis regulatory changes on both sides of the Atlantic mandated that banks substitute public lending to the state for private lending to households and businesses. Especially in the United Kingdom, where businesses were historically more reliant on banks for external financing and banks were on average bigger and therefore more likely to be subject to new requirements under postcrisis rules, the regime change after 2010 rendered the 2008–09 credit shock semipermanent.[53]

Adjusted for inflation, as of 2025, total credit to the private nonfinancial business sector in the United Kingdom had thus still never recovered to its pre-2010 level.[54] In the United States, it eventually recovered, but not to pre-2010 trend. In both economies, economic output never fully recovered to the level that would have prevailed had both economies continued uninterrupted along pre-recession trend, thus constituting one of the rare exceptions to the "plucking" pattern of economic fluctuations. Unfortunately, no economic policy is without trade-offs.

While our pattern-seeking nature may often lead us to protect ourselves against harm, it can thus also lead us to mistakenly avoid otherwise innocuous behavior or, worse, engage in ostensibly remedial behavior that is in fact counterproductive. The perception that the pain of an economic contraction is somehow the direct and proportionate consequence of the gains of the preceding economic expansion can lead us on an errant mission to identify what was so "wrong" in the latter that it inflicted upon us the former. An essential conclusion of this book is that there is nothing "wrong" with an economic expansion that requires, as its remedy, an economic contraction.

Moreover, the instinctual but ultimately ill-conceived quest to identify what was "wrong" with an economic expansion can lead us to misdiagnose what are ultimately the decisive determinants of economic prosperity over the long term. As documented in Chapter 8, the United Kingdom has historically been substantially less recession-prone than the United States. Yet the United Kingdom is also—and has since 1935 consistently been—substantially poorer per person than the United States.

Indeed, after the United States first achieved UK levels of per capita GDP in 1880, output per person in the two economies remained roughly even through the turn of the century, whereupon US GDP per capita gradually pulled ahead of that in the United Kingdom. By the eve of the Great Depression, the United Kingdom was nearly 30 percent poorer per capita than the United States. Though by avoiding the economic catastrophe that devastated the United States during the Depression, the United Kingdom briefly surpassed the United States in 1933 in GDP per capita terms, since 1935, GDP per capita in the United Kingdom persistently declined relative to the United States. Since 1970, the United Kingdom has been roughly 30 percent poorer per capita than the United States, a gap that if anything has only widened in the past decade.

Thus, though our risk-averse minds tend to fixate on the minority of years in which the economy contracts, we ought to be at least, if not more, concerned about the majority of years in which the economy expands. Because if, as we saw in Chapter 4, recessions are at the end of the day temporary deviations—downward plucks—from long-run trend, then what ultimately matters much more to human flourishing than the downward plucks is the long-run trend. Though it may seem odd for a book about economic contractions to so conclude, an unambiguous lesson of the past four centuries of US and UK economic history is that the more than 80 percent of years that do not end in recession matter more to long-term economic prosperity than the fewer than 20 percent of years that do.[55]

Worse than that, our apophanous search for patterns may lead us to erroneously identify that which we perceive to have been "wrong" in an expansion and therefore in need of remedy. Like the hypochondriac, we are forever identifying illnesses in an otherwise generally healthy economic host. But as we have seen, busts do not follow booms, expansions do not die of old age, and recessions serve no cleansing, therapeutic function. The determination to inhibit economic expansion, to over-medicate an otherwise healthy patient in the belief that doing so will inoculate against economic contraction may thus be worse than ineffective. Rather, insofar as it impairs long-run trend, it could be consigning millions to a poorer future and doing so under the hubristic pretense that we can, in effect, evade history.

Yet while the recognition that recessions are not only inevitable but also unrelated to any potentially remediable defect in the preceding expansion is a depressing admission of powerlessness, we should be heartened by the undeniable fact that we are, over time, becoming better at avoiding recessions. Indeed, not only was the economic expansion that ended with the pandemic shock of 2020 the longest in US history but also, were it not for that two-month, virus-induced recession, then as of July 2026, the US economy would have entered its seventeenth year of economic expansion—roughly double the duration of the previously record-long 1960s expansion that elicited such triumphal hubris from academics and policymakers. The UK expansion that ended in March 2008 was tied for the second-longest on record; the longest ending with the oil embargo of 1973.

Thus, as it pertains to economic fluctuations, it could be said that Newton's first law of motion is half-right. Just as an object in motion stays in motion unless acted upon by an external force, so too do economic expansions endure unless interrupted by shocks that are external to the growth process itself. But the inverse does not hold. An economy at rest does not remain at rest in the absence of an external force propelling it into motion; unlike expansions, recessions *do* die of old age. Thus, if economic expansions are Peter Pan, never growing old, perhaps recessions are Benjamin Button. Frail and infirm at inception, they age in reverse, ending their time-limited existence as healthy, infant expansions.

Recessions will keep happening. Unless we somehow banish history, economies will continue to sustain adverse shocks that they can neither perfectly foresee nor wholly hedge against. Yet the knowledge that recessions are deviant interruptions of growth rather than inevitable salutary products of it ought to assure us against the fear and commercial revulsion that attends and amplifies those episodes of interrupted growth. It should also caution policymakers that recessions are neither the symptom of underlying illness in the preceding expansion that requires the administration of remedial treatment, nor an injunction to austere penance for past sin. Palliative and pastoral care may be required, but not prophylactic surgery and puritan ascetism.

Perhaps above all, while we can and have learned over time how to better hedge and diversify risk to absorb adverse economic shocks, we must also be ever on guard against hubris. Apophanies offer the illusory presumption that traumatic events like recessions follow a predictable, manageable pattern. But as we have seen, like unhappy families, each recession is unhappy in its own way. More important for long-term human flourishing are happy economic expansions. Fortunately, though still mortal, the life expectancy of expansions is higher than that of recessions, and rising over time.

ACKNOWLEDGMENTS

An undertaking of this scope and scale naturally accrues quite a few debts of gratitude. The intellectual conception and framing of the book benefited immensely from early conversations with and feedback from my former Stanford colleagues, in particular John Cochrane, Michael Boskin, and Ran Abramitzky. Bob Hall also had very helpful ideas for translating monthly and quarterly recession chronologies into annual chronologies. Mike Bordo, Rich Clarida, Jason Furman, and Valerie Ramey kindly offered to read the completed manuscript.

The project and manuscript also benefited enormously from numerous discussions with two intellectual giants of the field—namely, Mike and my friend and mentor Niall Ferguson. I further owe a particularly large thanks to George Selgin, who has not only been a longtime friend and mentor but also first directed my attention to the hitherto obscure role of locusts in the 1873 recession. Across the pond, John Turner, Nuno Palma, and Jason Lennard generously shared historical data they had collected—along with coauthors, including my friends Stephen Broadberry and Patrick O'Brien—on the UK bank population, war chronologies, and quarterly GDP estimates. Seminar participants—especially Valerie Ramey and Robert Hodrick—in the Economic Policy Working Group at the Hoover Institution at Stanford University helpfully probed the arguments and evidence.

Innumerable conversations and discussions with current and former colleagues in the White House and at Greenmantle LLC and ExxonMobil Corporation likewise informed and provoked. In particular, Chris Birdsall and Darrin Talley brought invaluable perspective on the dynamics and microeconomic implications of historical energy price shocks. Discussions with my former White House colleague Andrew Olmem always provided fresh perspective on the legal dimensions of US financial history. Steven Braun kindly shared some of his vast reserve of US macroeconomic knowledge.

The manuscript also benefited from exceptional feedback from my former colleague on the Council of Economic Advisers, Joe Sullivan, who diligently read and offered comments on every chapter draft. Considering the sheer scale of the data universe for a project of this nature, gaining an initial beachhead was critical. To that end, early research assistance from Reade Ben and Britt Nordquist to help compile colonial American economic statistics and identify key biographical figures was a big boost.

One of the first essential steps toward bringing a project like this to ultimate fruition is securing a publishing contract. To that end, I am grateful that my agent, Andrew Wylie, took a chance on me and helped to greatly enhance the scope and framing of the proposal and, for that matter, entire book. He was also a genuine pleasure and privilege to work with. Chris Miller, friend and author of the rightly acclaimed monograph *Chip War*, kindly shared his proposal as motivation.

Another who took a chance on me was Clive Priddle of PublicAffairs. My discussions with Clive were both probing and engaging as he expertly and curiously nudged me to be bolder and to embrace the narrative form. While I was sad that with Clive moving on to new endeavors we were unable to see the project through to publication together, I was thankfully guided to the finish line by the expert hands of Emily Taber. Through multiple drafts, Emily patiently helped me to hone the narratives and intellectual arguments to present a more succinct, accessible, and hopefully persuasive thesis. It was a real pleasure and privilege to be able to work with her, and the manuscript that emerged from her editorial supervision was vastly improved from that which first crossed her desk. To Emily, I must extend a most heartfelt thank-you.

Though I began this project as a Kleinheinz Fellow at the Hoover Institution at Stanford University, I completed most of it while working a full-time, nonacademic job. The study of recessions therefore consumed evenings, weekends, and pretty much any other spare time. I therefore owe an enormous debt of gratitude to my husband, Oliver, for his patience and support. Even more than that, Ollie was an intellectual companion and partner on the journey, bringing to bear not only his profound expertise in energy and political economy but also his unparalleled ability to construct and deconstruct an argument. This book would not have happened without him.

DATA APPENDIX

RECESSION DATES

Annual UK recession dates are from Broadberry et al.[1] Quarterly UK recession dates are also from Broadberry et al. back to 1926:Q1. I extend quarterly UK recession dates back to 1854:Q4 using macroeconomic time series from the Bank of England's comprehensive historical UK macroeconomic dataset, "A Millennium of Macroeconomic Data."[2]

To identify peaks and troughs at quarterly frequency, I take as a starting point the annual recession indicators in Broadberry et al. and then apply the National Bureau of Economic Research's (NBER) definition of a recession—namely, "a significant decline in economic activity that is spread across the economy and that lasts more than a few months."

Following the approach of the NBER, I then determine the quarters of peaks and troughs based on a range of monthly and quarterly measures of aggregate real economic activity published in "A Millennium of Macroeconomic Data," in particular real GDP and the unemployment rate. I also incorporate nominal variables, including narrow and broad money supply, long-term bond yields, commercial paper rates, and an index of historical share prices.[3] I also cross-reference these quantitative indicators with narrative evidence reported in Thorpe (1926).[4] Results are reported in Table A1.

Quarterly US recession dates back to 1854:Q4 are from the NBER. For robustness, between 1887:Q1 and 1940:Q2, I also substitute an alternative quarterly recession chronology based on the monthly recession chronology derived in Romer (1994).[5]

The NBER does not maintain an annual chronology. However, I derive an annual chronology back to 1854 from the NBER's monthly and quarterly chronologies using the monthly and quarterly turning points, unless otherwise indicated

PEAK	TROUGH
	1955:Q2
1857:Q3	1858:Q2
1861:Q2	1862:Q3
1878:Q1	1879:Q2
1883:Q3	1885:Q3
1892:Q1	1893:Q3
1900:Q3	1901:Q1
1902:Q4	1904:Q2
1907:Q2	1908:Q3
1918:Q4	1921:Q2

Table A1: Quarterly UK Peaks and Troughs, 1855–1921

by known historical events. Annual US recession dates from 1790 to 1854 are from Moore and Zarnowitz (1986), also reported in Sutch (2006).[6]

I then extend the annual recession chronology for the United States and British North America from 1790 back to 1700 using colonial American statistics from *Historical Statistics of the United States: Millennial Edition*. Because trade statistics are generally the most reliable and consistent, for recession dating, I place particular weight on imports from England and, to a lesser extent, exports to England, both of which are available continuously since 1693. From 1740 on, I am also able to incorporate imports from and exports to Scotland, which was an important importer of North American tobacco.[7] Imports correlate with domestic consumption and investment, while exports correlate with domestic output, as well as demand in the economy of a principal trading partner.

Additional variables that are available continuously since 1700 or before are foreign exchange rates (1649–1790), an index of commodity prices (1665–1790), and money in circulation (1703–1775).[8] I treat price deflation, contractions in money in circulation, and large exchange rate depreciations as recessionary signals, the latter typically occurring during moments of acute financial stress.

Variables that are available irregularly and discontinuously since 1700 include:

- Inbound and outbound vessels and tonnage for Boston, Charleston, James River, Philadelphia, and New York.[9]
- Imports and exports of bar, cast, and pig iron.[10]

- Pitch, tar, turpentine, and lumber exports from Charleston.[11]
- Timber exports from Savannah.[12]
- Indigo and silk exports from Georgia and the Carolinas.[13]
- Tobacco exports.[14]
- Coal imports and exports.[15]

Results are reported in Table A2.

PEAK	TROUGH
	1700
1701	1702
1705	1706
1707	1708
1712	1713
1715	1716
1717	1720
1722	1723
1726	1727
1728	1729
1730	1732
1738	1739
1741	1742
1743	1745
1746	1747
1750	1752
1753	1755
1760	1762
1764	1766
1768	1769
1771	1773
1775	1778
1780	1782
1784	1787
1789	1790

Table A2: Annual US Peaks and Troughs, 1700–1790

To construct consistent time series for relevant macroeconomic variables, I assume that the most recent estimates, particularly of official data, are accurate in levels. To extend those series further back in time using earlier estimates, I then assume that earlier estimates may have misestimated the levels but were accurate in the growth rate. I thus splice earlier series to later by decrementing the first observation of the later series by the growth rate observed in the earlier series.

$$Y_{t-1}^{spliced} = Y_t^{latest} * \left(\frac{Y_{t-1}^{earlier}}{Y_t^{earlier}} \right) \qquad\qquad [A1]$$

I then recursively extend the spliced series by similarly decrementing each newly spliced observation by the growth rate observed in the earlier series.

ANNUAL MACROECONOMIC DATA

UNITED STATES

Nominal GDP: For 1929–present, I import nominal US GDP from the Bureau of Economic Analysis via Haver Analytics (GDPA@USECON).[16] I then extend this back to 1790 in accordance with equation (A1) using nominal GDP data from Sutch (2006).[17]

Real GDP: For 1929–present, I import real US GDP from the Bureau of Economic Analysis via Haver Analytics.[18] I then extend this back to 1790 in accordance with equation (A1) using real GDP data from Sutch (2006).[19]

GDP deflator: I compute the GDP deflator by dividing nominal GDP by real GDP and multiplying by 100.

Real fixed investment: For 1929–present, I import real private and public fixed investment from the Bureau of Economic Analysis via Haver Analytics, summing private, federal defense and nondefense, and state and local.[20] Per equation (A1), I extend the series back to 1925 using real fixed investment from the Bureau of Economic Analysis via Haver Analytics.[21]

Real private fixed investment: For 1929–present, I import real private fixed investment from the Bureau of Economic Analysis via Haver Analytics.[22] Per equation (A1), I extend the series back to 1925 using real private fixed investment from the Bureau of Economic Analysis via Haver Analytics.[23] Per equation (A1),

I also extend the series in indexed form back to 1901 using a chained quantity index for private fixed investment from the Bureau of Economic Analysis via Haver Analytics.[24]

Real private nonresidential fixed investment: For 1929–present, I import real private nonresidential fixed investment from the Bureau of Economic Analysis via Haver Analytics.[25] Per equation (A1), I then extend the series back to 1925 using annual estimates of real private nonresidential fixed investment from the Bureau of Economic Analysis via Haver Analytics.[26]

Real private residential fixed investment: For 1929–present, I import real private residential fixed investment from the Bureau of Economic Analysis via Haver Analytics.[27] Per equation (A1), I then extend the series back to 1925 using annual estimates of real private residential fixed investment from the Bureau of Economic Analysis via Haver Analytics.[28]

Employment: For 1948–present, I import civilian employment among those aged sixteen and over from the Bureau of Labor Statistics via Haver Analytics.[29] For 1901–1947, I import civilian employment among those aged fourteen and over from the US Census Bureau via Haver Analytics.[30] Per equation (A1), I then extend the series back to 1890 using civilian employment among those aged fourteen and over from Carter (2006).[31]

Population: For 1900–present, I import annual estimates of the resident population from the US Census Bureau via Haver Analytics.[32] Per equation (A1), I then extend the series back to 1790 using annual resident population estimates from Sutch (2006).[33] Per equation (A1), I then extend the series back to 1700 using annual population estimates from McCusker (2006).[34]

Unemployment rate: For 1948–present, I import the unemployment rate among those aged sixteen and over from the Bureau of Labor Statistics via Haver Analytics.[35] For 1901–1947, I import civilian unemployment rate among those aged fourteen and over from the US Census Bureau via Haver Analytics.[36] I then extend the series back to 1890 using civilian employment among those aged fourteen and over from Carter (2006).[37]

Unemployment level: For 1948–present, I import the unemployment level among those aged sixteen and over from the Bureau of Labor Statistics via Haver Analytics.[38] For 1901–1947, I import civilian unemployment level among those aged fourteen and over from the US Census Bureau via Haver Analytics.[39] Per equation (A1), I then extend the series back to 1890 using civilian unemployment among those aged fourteen and over from Carter (2006).[40]

Labor force: For 1948–present, I import the civilian labor force among those aged sixteen and over from the Bureau of Labor Statistics via Haver Analytics.[41] For 1901–1947, I import civilian labor force among those aged fourteen and over from the US Census Bureau via Haver Analytics.[42] Per equation (A1), I then extend the series back to 1890 using civilian employment among those aged fourteen and over from Carter (2006).[43]

Average wage: For 1964–present, I import average hourly earnings of private production and nonsupervisory employees from the Bureau of Labor Statistics via FRED.[44] Per equation (A1), I then extend the series back to 1926 using an index of money wages for unskilled labor from Margo (2006).[45] Per equation (A1), I then extend the series back to 1901 using probably hourly rates for unskilled labor from the US Census Bureau via Haver Analytics.[46] Per equation (A1), I then extend the series back to 1774 using an index of money wages for unskilled labor from Margo (2006).[47]

Consumer price inflation: For 1921–present, I import the not seasonally adjusted consumer price index for all urban consumers from the Bureau of Labor Statistics via Haver Analytics.[48] Per equation (A1), I then extend the series back to 1774 using a consumer price index for all items from Lindert and Sutch (2006).[49] I then extend the series back to 1665 using a commodity price index from McCusker.[50]

Real consumption: For 1929–present, I import real personal consumption expenditures from the Bureau of Economic Analysis via Haver Analytics.[51] I then extend the series back to 1900 using real consumption data from Craig (2006).[52] Per equation (A1), I then extend the series back to 1834 using real consumption data from Gallman and Rhode (2020).[53] To bridge a gap between 1859 and 1869, I decrement the 1869 value in the spliced series by the ratio of 1859 to 1869 values in the Gallman and Rhode (2006) series, and then per equation (A1) extend the series back to 1834.

Industrial production: For 1919–present, I import an index of industrial production from the Board of Governors of the Federal Reserve System via FRED.[54] Per equation (A1), I then extend the series back to 1915 using an index of industrial production and trade from the NBER.[55] Per equation (A1), I then extend the series back to 1790 using an index of industrial production from Sutch (2006).[56]

Federal government expenditures: For 1954–present, I import federal receipts from the US Department of the Treasury via Haver Analytics.[57] I extend the series back to 1879 by importing federal government budget expenditures from the NBER via FRED.[58] Per equation (A1), I extend the series back to 1792 using federal budget data in Wallis (2006).[59]

Federal government receipts: For 1954–present, I import federal receipts from the US Department of the Treasury via Haver Analytics.[60] I extend the series back to 1931 by importing federal government budget receipts from the NBER via FRED.[61] Per equation (A1), I extend the series back to 1792 using federal budget data in Wallis (2006).[62]

Federal government gross debt: For 1952–present, I import total public debt outstanding from the US Department of the Treasury via Haver Analytics.[63] I extend the series back to 1939 by importing federal government gross debt from the Council of Economic Advisers via FRED.[64] Since the latter is reported on an annual fiscal year basis, which runs from October 1 of the prior year through September 30 of the current year, to translate into calendar-year values, I compute a weighted average of the current and subsequent fiscal year with weights of 0.75 and 0.25, respectively.

Federal government net debt: For 2001–present, I import total public debt outstanding held by the public from the US Department of the Treasury via Haver Analytics.[65] I extend the series back to 1939 by importing federal government debt held by the public from the Council of Economic Advisers via FRED.[66] Since the latter is reported on an annual fiscal year basis, which runs from October 1 of the prior year through September 30 of the current year, to translate into calendar-year values, I compute a weighted average of the current and subsequent fiscal year with weights of 0.75 and 0.25, respectively. Per equation (A1), I then extend the series back to 1792 using federal budget data in Wallis (2006).[67]

State and local government expenditures: For 1929–present, I import state and local government expenditures from the Bureau of Economic Analysis via FRED.[68]

State and local government receipts: For 1929–present, I import state and local government budget receipts from the Bureau of Economic Analysis via FRED.[69]

State and local government debt: For 1945–present, I import state and local government budget debt from the Board of Governors of the Federal Reserve System via FRED.[70]

Commercial bond yield: For 1996–present, I import the S&P Global Fixed Income Research industrials BBB ten-year average bond yield via Haver Analytics.[71] I extend the series back to 1945 by importing the S&P 500 Industrials BBB bond yield via Haver Analytics.[72] Because data for January 1996 is missing, I splice the two series by calculating the 1996 value as the annual average with January 1996 interpolated between December 1995 and February 1996. I then extend the series back to 1875 using the average corporate bond rate from Balke and Gordon (1986).[73]

Commercial paper rate: For 1972–present, I import the three-month nonfinancial commercial paper rate from the Federal Reserve Board via Haver Analytics.[74] I extend the series back to 1875 using the average commercial paper rate from Balke and Gordon (1986).[75] Per equation (A1), I then extend the series back to 1831 using data on commercial paper rates in James and Sylla (2006).[76]

Stock market: For 1921–present, I import the S&P 500 composite index via Haver Analytics.[77] I extend the series back to 1900 using the index of all common stock from Balke and Gordon (1986).[78] Per equation (A1), I extend the series back to 1871 using the index of all common stock prices from the Cowles Commission and Standard and Poor's Corporation.[79] Per equation (A1), I then extend the series back to 1802 using Schwert's indexes of US stock prices via Rousseau (2006).[80] To link the Schwert stock market series, which ends in 1870, with the spliced S&P–Balke and Gordon–NBER series, which begins in 1871, I use the average of the 1870 to 1871 percent changes in Boston bank and industrial stocks in Rousseau (2006) to decrement the 1871 spliced value to an 1870 starting value.[81]

Long-term government bond yields: For 1954–present, I import nominal ten- and twenty-year Treasury constant maturities from the Federal Reserve Board via Haver Analytics, and the same since 1978 for thirty-year Treasuries.[82] I extend the ten- and twenty-year yields back to 1950 and the thirty-year yield back to 1954 using average yields by maturity in James and Sylla (2006).[83] I compute a simple arithmetic average of the yields for the years for which they are available. Per equation (A1), I then extend this back to 1798 using data on long-term US bond yields from James and Sylla (2006).[84]

Ten-year government bond yield: For 1954–present, I import nominal ten-year Treasury constant maturity from the Federal Reserve Board via Haver Analytics.[85] I then extend the series back to 1950 using average ten-year Treasury yields in James and Sylla.[86]

Twenty-year government bond yield: For 1954–present, I import nominal twenty-year Treasury constant maturity from the Federal Reserve Board via Haver Analytics.[87] I then extend the series back to 1950 using average twenty-year Treasury yields in James and Sylla.[88]

Thirty-year government bond yield: For 1954–present, I import nominal thirty-year Treasury constant maturity from the Federal Reserve Board via Haver Analytics.[89] I then extend the series back to 1950 using average twenty-year Treasury yields in James and Sylla.[90]

Number of banks: For 2006–present, I import the number of FDIC-insured commercial banks from the FDIC via Haver Analytics.[91] For 1834–1980, I use the number of commercial banks in Bodenhorn (2006).[92] Because the FDIC series does not include uninsured banks, from 1980, I augment the FDIC bank count using a linear time forecast of the difference between the FDIC bank count and the Bodenhorn count, with an estimation period of 1956–1980. With the population of uninsured banks declining over time, the linear forecast projects the two series converging in 2005–2006.

Bank failures: For 1934–present, I import the number of failures of all institutions from the FDIC via FRED.[93] I then extend the series back to 1864 using bank failure counts from the *Historical Statistics of the United States* bicentennial edition.[94]

Bank assets: For 1973–present, I import the value of all commercial banks' assets from the Federal Reserve Board via Haver Analytics.[95] Per equation (A1), I then extend the series back to 1834 using annual estimates of bank assets in Bodenhorn (2006).[96]

Bank liabilities: For 1973–present, I import the value of all commercial banks' assets from the Federal Reserve Board via Haver Analytics.[97] Per equation (A1), I then extend the series back to 1834 using annual estimates of bank liabilities in Bodenhorn (2006).[98]

Bank loans: For 1947–present, I import the value of all commercial banks' loans from the Federal Reserve Board via Haver Analytics.[99] Per equation (A1), I then extend the series back to 1834 using annual estimates of bank loans in Bodenhorn (2006).[100]

Bank real estate loans: For 1947–present, I import the value of all commercial banks' real estate loans from the Federal Reserve Board via Haver Analytics.[101] Per equation (A1), I then extend the series back to 1896 using annual estimates of bank real estate loans in Bodenhorn (2006).[102]

Bank securities: For 1947–present, I import the value of all commercial banks' real estate loans from the Federal Reserve Board via Haver Analytics.[103] Per equation (A1), I then extend the series back to 1834 using annual estimates of bank investments in Bodenhorn (2006).[104]

Bank cash assets: For 1973–present, I import the value of all commercial banks' cash assets from the Federal Reserve Board via Haver Analytics.[105] Per equation (A1), I then extend the series back to 1834 using annual estimates of bank cash assets in Bodenhorn (2006).[106]

Bank deposits: For 1973–present, I import the value of all commercial banks' deposits from the Federal Reserve Board via Haver Analytics.[107] Per equation (A1), I then extend the series back to 1834 using annual estimates of bank deposits in Bodenhorn (2006).[108]

Monetary base: For 1959–present, I import currency in circulation and the monetary base (currency in circulation plus reserve balances) from the Federal Reserve Board via Haver Analytics.[109] Per equation (A1), I extend the series back to 1875 using estimates of the monetary base in Balke and Gordon (1986).[110] Per equation (A1), I then extend the series back to 1867 using estimates of the monetary base in Anderson (2006).[111] Per equation (A1), I then extend the series back to 1859 using estimates of the monetary base in Rockoff (2006), summing specie in the form of coin and paper currency held by the public.[112] I link the Rockoff (2006) series to the spliced series by decrementing the 1867 value of the spliced series by the ratio of the sum of specie in the form of coin and paper currency held by the public in 1866 to the spliced value in 1867.

M1 money supply: For 1959–present, I import the M1 money supply from the Federal Reserve Board via Haver Analytics.[113] Per equation (A1), I extend the series back to 1915 using estimates of the M1 money supply in Balke and Gordon (1986).[114]

M2 money supply: For 1959–present, I import the M2 money supply from the Federal Reserve Board via Haver Analytics.[115] Per equation (A1), I extend the series back to 1875 using estimates of the monetary base in Balke and Gordon (1986).[116] Per equation (A1), I then extend the series back to 1867 using estimates of M2 money supply in Anderson (2006).[117] Per equation (A1), I then extend the series back to 1859 using estimates of M2 money supply in Rockoff (2006).[118] I link the Rockoff (2006) series to the spliced series by decrementing the 1867 value of the spliced series by the ratio of the 1866 estimate to the spliced value in 1867.

UNITED KINGDOM

Nominal GDP: For 1955:Q1–present, I import nominal UK GDP from the Office of National Statistics via FRED.[119] Per equation (A1), I then extend the series back to 1700 using quarterly nominal GDP data from the Bank of England via FRED.[120]

Real GDP: For 1955–present, I import real UK GDP from the International Monetary Fund via FRED.[121] Per equation (A1), I then extend the series back to 1700 using real GDP data from the Bank of England via FRED.[122]

GDP deflator: I compute the GDP deflator by dividing nominal GDP by real GDP and multiplying by 100.

Real consumption: For 1995–present, I import real UK private final consumption expenditure from the Organisation for Economic Co-operation and Development via FRED.[123] Per equation (A1), I then extend the series back to 1830 using real consumption expenditures from the Bank of England via FRED.[124]

Real investment: For 1995–present, I import real gross capital formation from the Organisation for Economic Co-operation and Development via FRED.[125] Per equation (A1), I then extend the series back to 1830 using real investment expenditures from the Bank of England via FRED.[126]

Industrial production: I index to 2017 = 100. For 1948–present, I then import seasonally adjusted growth rates for total industry excluding construction from the Organisation for Economic Co-operation and Development via FRED, and increment or decrement the index accordingly.[127] Per equation (A1), I then extend the series back to 1946 using an index of industrial production from the Bank of England via FRED.[128] To bridge a gap between 1938 and 1946, I decrement the spliced series by the ratio of 1938 to 1946 values in the Bank of England series, and then per equation (A1) extend the series back to 1920. Per equation (A1), I then extend the series further back to 1790 using an index of physical volume of industrial production from the National Bureau of Economic Research via FRED.[129]

Unemployment rate: For 1983–present, I import the unemployment rate for persons aged fifteen years or over from the Organisation for Economic Co-operation and Development via FRED.[130] I then extend the series back to 1760 using annual unemployment rate estimates from the Bank of England via FRED.[131]

Employment: For 1971–present, I import employment of persons aged fifteen years or over from the Organisation for Economic Co-operation and Development via FRED.[132] I then extend the series back to 1760 using annual employment estimates from the Bank of England via FRED.[133]

Labor force: For 1955–present, I import the total labor force of those aged fifteen years or over from the Organisation for Economic Co-operation and Development via FRED.[134] Per equation (A1), I then extend the series back to 1950 using data on the number of persons engaged from the University of Groningen and University of California, Davis, via FRED.[135]

Average wage: For 1963–present, I import an index of weekly labor compensation from the Organisation for Economic Co-operation and Development via FRED.[136] Per equation (A1), I then extend the series back to 1209 using average weekly earnings per person from the Bank of England via FRED.[137]

Bank lending: For 1880–2016, I import aggregate bank and building society credit from the Bank of England via FRED.[138] I then advance lending from 2016 to present using December year-over-year growth rates of UK resident monetary financial institutions' (excluding Central Bank) sterling net lending to the private sector excluding intermediate offshore financial centers.[139]

Bank real estate lending: For 1880–2016, I import secured bank and building society credit from the Bank of England via FRED.[140]

Monetary base: For 2016–present, I import currency in circulation and reserve balances from the Bank of England.[141] Per equation (A1), I then extend the series back to 1833 using quarterly M0 data from the Bank of England.[142]

M2 money supply: For 2016–present, I import the level of UK resident monetary financial institutions' sterling M4 liabilities to the private sector (excluding intermediate offshore financial centers) from the Bank of England.[143] Per equation (A1), I then extend the series back to 1844 using quarterly broad money data from the Bank of England.[144]

Number of banks: For 2004–present, I import the number of commercial banks from the International Monetary Fund via FRED.[145] From 1750–1938, I use the bank population from Kenny et al.[146] For an expanded universe of commercial banks, building societies, and trustee savings banks, and new banks by year, I also use bank population data from Michie (2016).[147]

Bank failures: For 1750–1938, I use the bank population from Kenny et al.[148]

Bank failure rate: For 1750–1938, I use the bank population from Kenny et al.[149]

Stock market: For 1958–present, I import an index of financial market share prices for the United Kingdom from the Organisation for Economic Co-operation and Development via FRED.[150] Per equation (A1), I then extend the series back to 1700 using share price data from the Bank of England via FRED.[151]

Consumer price inflation: For 1955–present, I import the not seasonally adjusted consumer price index from the Organisation for Economic Co-operation and Development via FRED and compute year-over-year rate of consumer price inflation.[152] I then extend the CPI and year-over-year CPI inflation back to 1209 and 1210, respectively, using the not seasonally adjusted CPI from the Bank of England's macroeconomic database.[153]

Commercial paper rate: For 1718–2016, I import the discount rate on short-term commercial paper from the Bank of England via Fred.[154]

Commercial borrowing rate: For 1922–2016, I import the corporate borrowing rate from banks from the Bank of England via FRED.[155]

Population: For 1960–present, I import the annual population of the United Kingdom from the World Bank via FRED.[156] I then extend the series back to 1700 using annual population estimates from the Bank of England via FRED.[157]

Net general government debt: For 1966–present, I import nominal total credit to the general government from the Bank for International Settlements via FRED.[158]

I then extend the series back to 1691 using public debt data from the Bank of England via FRED.[159]

Public expenditure: For 1900–2016, I import public sector total managed expenditure from the Bank of England via FRED.[160]

Public receipts: For 1900–2016, I import public sector total receipts from the Bank of England via FRED.[161]

Long-term government bond yields: For 1703–2016, I import consol (long-term bond) yields from the Bank of England via FRED.[162]

Ten-year government bond yield: For 1960–present, I import the ten-year government bond yield from the Organisation for Economic Co-operation and Development via FRED.[163] I then extend the series back to 1929 using ten-year government bond yields from the Bank of England via FRED.[164]

Nominal USD-GBP exchange rate: For 1971–present, I import the nominal USD-GBP exchange rate from the Board of Governors of the Federal Reserve System via FRED.[165] I then extend the series back to 1791 using foreign exchange data from the Bank of England via FRED.[166]

Real USD-GBP exchange rate: For 1791–present, I import the real USD-GBP exchange from the Bank of England via FRED.[167]

QUARTERLY MACROECONOMIC DATA

UNITED STATES

Nominal GDP: For 1947:Q1–present, I import nominal US GDP from the Bureau of Economic Analysis via Haver Analytics.[168] I then extend this in accordance with equation (A1) using quarterly nominal GNP data from Balke and Gordon (1986), converted to nominal GDP by subtracting net factor income from abroad assuming annual estimates of net factor income from abroad in Sutch (2006) were evenly distributed across quarters.[169] I am thus able to extend quarterly nominal GDP estimates back to 1875:Q1.

Real GDP: For 1947:Q1–present, I import real US GDP from the Bureau of Economic Analysis via Haver Analytics.[170] I then extend this in accordance with equation (A1) using quarterly real GNP data from Balke and Gordon (1986), converted to real GDP by subtracting real net factor income from abroad assuming annual estimates of real net factor income from abroad in Sutch (2006) were evenly distributed across quarters.[171] I am thus able to extend quarterly real GDP estimates back to 1875:Q1.

GDP deflator: I compute the GDP deflator by dividing nominal GDP by real GDP and multiplying by 100.

Consumer price inflation: For 1921:Q1–present, I import the not seasonally adjusted consumer price index for all urban consumers from the Bureau of Labor Statistics via Haver Analytics and compute year-over-year rate of consumer price inflation by quarter.[172]

Employment: For nonfarm payroll employment, 1939:Q1–present, I import seasonally adjusted nonfarm payroll employment from the Bureau of Labor Statistics via Haver Analytics.[173] For total payroll employment, 1948:Q1–present, I import seasonally adjusted payroll employment from the Bureau of Labor Statistics via Haver Analytics.[174]

Unemployment rate: For 1948:Q1–present, I import the seasonally adjusted civilian unemployment rate from the Bureau of Labor Statistics via Haver Analytics.[175]

Industrial production: For 1919:Q1–present, I import the Federal Reserve's monthly index of industrial production from the Bureau of Economic Analysis via FRED.[176] Per equation (A1), I then extend this back to 1915:Q1 using the index of industrial production and trade from the NBER Macrohistory Database.[177] Per equation (A1), I then extend this back to 1899:Q1 using the American Telephone and Telegraph Company Index of Industrial Activity for the United States.[178]

Commercial paper rate: For 1971:Q2–present, I import the three-month non-financial commercial paper rate from the Federal Reserve Board via Haver Analytics.[179] From 1857:Q1 until 1971:Q1, I then substitute commercial paper rates for New York from the NBER Macrohistory Database.[180]

Commercial bond yield: For 1996:Q2–present, I import the S&P Global Fixed Income Research industrials BBB ten-year average bond yield via Haver Analytics.[181] From 1875:Q1 through 1996:Q1, I then substitute the average corporate bond rate from Balke and Gordon (1986).[182]

Stock market: For 1921:Q1–present, I import the S&P 500 composite index via Haver Analytics (SP500@USECON). Per equation (A1), from 1900:Q1 through 1920:Q4, I use the index of all common stock from Balke and Gordon (1986).[183] Per equation (A1), from 1871:Q1 through 1899:Q4, I then use the index of all common stock prices from the Cowles Commission and Standard and Poor's Corporation.[184]

Long-term government bond yields: For 1953:Q2–present, I import nominal ten- and twenty-year Treasury constant maturities from the Federal Reserve Board via Haver Analytics and the same since 1977:Q2 for thirty-year Treasuries.[185] I compute a simple arithmetic average of the three yields for the quarters for which they are available. I then extend this back to 1919:Q1 using data on long-term US bond yields from the NBER Macrohistory Database.[186]

Ten-year government bond yield: For US ten-year Treasury yields specifically, I use the ten-year yield from the Federal Reserve Board via Haver Analytics back to 1953:Q2.[187]

Monetary base: For 1959:Q1–present, I import currency in circulation and reserve balances from the Federal Reserve Board via Haver Analytics.[188] Per equation (A1), I then extend the series back to 1875:Q1 using quarterly monetary base data from Balke and Gordon (1986).[189]

M1 money supply: For 1959:Q1–present, I import M1 money supply from the Federal Reserve Board via Haver Analytics.[190] Per equation (A1), I then extend the series back to 1915:Q1 using quarterly M1 data from Balke and Gordon (1986).[191]

M2 money supply: For 1959:Q1–present, I import M2 money supply from the Federal Reserve Board via Haver Analytics.[192] Per equation (A1), I then extend the series back to 1875:Q1 using quarterly M2 data from Balke and Gordon (1986).[193]

Federal government receipts: For 1954:Q1–present, I import federal receipts from the US Department of the Treasury via Haver Analytics.[194] I then extend this back to 1939:Q3 using federal budget receipts imported from the National Bureau of Economic Research via FRED.[195] I extend the series further back to 1930:Q3 using federal budget receipts from the National Bureau of Economic Research via FRED.[196] I extend the series further back to 1879:Q1 using federal budget receipts from the National Bureau of Economic Research via FRED.[197]

Federal government expenditures: For 1954:Q1–present, I import federal receipts from the US Department of the Treasury via Haver Analytics.[198] I then extend this back to 1945:Q3 using federal budget receipts imported from the National Bureau of Economic Research via FRED.[199] I extend the series further back to 1939:Q3 using federal budget receipts from the National Bureau of Economic Research via FRED.[200] I extend the series further back to 1937:Q3 using federal budget receipts from the National Bureau of Economic Research via FRED.[201] I extend the series further back to 1932:Q1 using federal budget receipts from the National Bureau of Economic Research via FRED.[202] I extend the series further back to 1915:Q1 using federal budget receipts from the National Bureau of Economic Research via FRED.[203] I extend the series further back to 1879:Q1 using federal budget receipts from the National Bureau of Economic Research via FRED.[204]

State and local government receipts: For 1947:Q1–present, I import state and local government total receipts from the Bureau of Economic Analysis via FRED.[205]

State and local government expenditures: For 1947:Q1–present, I import state and local government total expenditures from the Bureau of Economic Analysis via FRED.[206]

UNITED KINGDOM

Consumer price inflation: For 1955:Q1–present, I import the not seasonally adjusted consumer price index from the Organisation for Economic Co-operation and Development via FRED and compute year-over-year rate of consumer price inflation by quarter.[207] I then extend the CPI and year-over-year CPI inflation back to 1914:Q3 and 1915:Q3, respectively, using the not seasonally adjusted CPI from the Bank of England's macroeconomic database.[208]

Nominal GDP: For 1955:Q1–present, I import nominal UK GDP from the Office of National Statistics via FRED.[209]

Real GDP: For 1955:Q1–present, I import real UK GDP from the International Monetary Fund via FRED.[210] Per equation (A1), I then extend the series back to 1938:Q3 using preliminary and tentative quarterly real GDP estimates from Broadberry et al. (2023).[211] Per equation (A1), I then extend the series back to 1920:Q1 using monthly real GDP estimates from the Bank of England via FRED.[212]

GDP deflator: I compute the GDP deflator by dividing nominal GDP by real GDP and multiplying by 100.

Unemployment rate: For 1983:Q1–present, I import the monthly unemployment rate for persons aged fifteen years or over from the Organisation for Economic Co-operation and Development via FRED.[213] I then extend the series back to 1855:Q1 using monthly unemployment rate estimates from the Bank of England via FRED.[214]

Employment: For 1971:Q1–present, I import quarterly employment of persons aged fifteen years or over from the Organisation for Economic Co-operation and Development via FRED.[215] I then extend the series back to 1950:Q2 using quarterly employment estimates from the Bank of England via FRED.[216]

Stock market: For 1958:Q1–present, I import a quarterly index of financial market share prices for the United Kingdom from the Organisation for Economic Co-operation and Development via FRED.[217] Per equation (A1), I then extend the series back to 1709:Q2 using share price data from the Bank of England via FRED.[218]

Industrial production: I index to 2017:Q1 = 100. For 1948:Q1–present, I then import seasonally adjusted growth rates for total industry excluding construction from the Organisation for Economic Co-operation and Development via FRED, and increment or decrement the index accordingly.[219] Per equation (A1), I then extend the series back to 1946:Q1 using a monthly index of industrial production from the Bank of England via FRED.[220] To bridge a gap between 1938:Q4 and 1946:Q1, I decrement the spliced series by the ratio of 1938:Q4 to 1946:Q1 values in the Bank of England series, and then per equation (A1) extend the series back to 1920:Q1 using the Bank of England series.[221]

Commercial paper rate: For 1718:Q1–2016:Q4, I import the discount rate on short-term commercial paper from the Bank of England via FRED.[222]

Commercial borrowing rate: For 1977:Q2–2016:Q4, I import the corporate borrowing rate on loans from banks from the Bank of England via FRED.[223]

Long-term government bond yields: For 1753:Q3–2016:Q4, I import consol (long-term bond) yields from the Bank of England via FRED.[224]

Ten-year government bond yield: For 1960:Q1–present, I import the ten-year government bond yield from the Organisation for Economic Co-operation and Development via FRED.[225] I then extend the series back to 1935:Q1 using ten-year government bond yields from the Bank of England via FRED.[226]

Monetary base: For 2016:Q1–present, I import currency in circulation and reserve balances from the Bank of England.[227] Per equation (A1), I then extend the series back to 1870:Q1 using quarterly M0 data from the Bank of England.[228]

M2 money supply: For 2016:Q1–present, I import the level of UK resident monetary financial institutions' sterling M4 liabilities to the private sector (excluding intermediate offshore financial centers) from the Bank of England.[229] Per equation (A1), I then extend the series back to 1870:Q1 using quarterly broad money data from the Bank of England.[230]

NOTES

Introduction: The Anna Karenina Principle

1. Board of Governors of the Alms House, *Ninth Annual Report of the Governors of the Alms House, New York, for the Year 1857* (New York, 1858), 104–5; Mason Brothers, *The New York Almanac and Yearly Record for the Year 1858, Being the Eighty-Third Year of the Independence of the United States of America* (New York, 1858), 37.

2. Regents of the University of the State of New York, "Seventy-First Annual Report of the Regents of the University, of the State of New-York" (Albany, 1858), 364–65.

3. Treasury Investigating Commission, "Report of the Investigating Commission Appointed to Enquire into the Causes of the Defalcation in the State Treasury, and Other Matters Specially Named in the Act of the General Assembly of the State of Ohio" (Columbus, March 7, 1859), 845.

4. Austin E. Hutcheson, "Philadelphia and the Panic of 1857," *Pennsylvania History: A Journal of Mid-Atlantic Studies* 3, July 1936: 185.

5. Hugh Rockoff, "Oh, How the Mighty Have Fallen: The Bank Failures and Near Failures That Started America's Greatest Financial Panics," *Journal of Economic History* 81, no. 2 (2021): 347–48, https://doi.org/10.1017/S0022050721000176.

6. Timothy J. Riddiough and Howard E. Thompson, "When Prosperity Merges into Crisis: The Decline and Fall of Ohio Life and the Panic of 1857," *American Nineteenth Century History* 19, no. 3 (2018): 296, https://doi.org/10.1080/14664658.2018.1540113; Treasury Investigating Commission, "Report of the Investigating Commission."

7. Riddiough and Thompson, "When Prosperity Merges"; Timothy J. Riddiough and Howard E. Thompson, "When Prosperity Merges into Crisis: The Decline and Fall of Ohio Life, Political Economy of Bank Suspension, and the Panic of 1857," SSRN, December 21, 2016, 27, https://papers.ssrn.com/sol3/papers.cfm?abstract_id=2888689.

8. Riddiough and Thompson, "When Prosperity Merges," *American Nineteenth Century History*, 299–300.

9. Riddiough and Thompson, 302.

10. Treasury Investigating Commission, "Report of the Investigating Commission," 764–65.

11. Rockoff, "Oh, How the Mighty Have Fallen," 348.

12. "Commercial Affairs," *New York Daily Times*, August 25, 1857.

13. William Graham Sumner, "A History of Banking in the United States," in *A History of Banking in All the Leading Nations; Comprising the United States; Great Britain, Germany;*

Austro-Hungary; France; Italy; Belgium; Spain; Switzerland; Portugal; Roumania; Russia; Holland; The Scandinavian Nations; Canada; China; Japan, vol. 1 (New York, 1896), 426; "The Great Failure," *New York Daily Times*, September 3, 1857; "The Money Panic," *New York Daily Times*, September 2, 1857; J. S. Gibbons, *The Banks of New-York, Their Dealers, the Clearing House, and the Panic of 1857. With a Financial Chart* (New York, 1858), 350–51; Riddiough and Thompson, "When Prosperity Merges."

14. Gibbons, 352.

15. Gibbons, 348–51, 354.

16. "Arrival of the Central America," *New York Times*, August 13, 1857; Samuel Williamson, "Seven Ways to Compute the Relative Value of a U.S. Dollar Amount, 1790 to Present" (Measuring Worth, 2025), https://measuringworth.com/calculators/uscompare/. Contemporary reports stated that the vessel carried just over $1.8 million of gold. I compute the 2024 value as the relative labor or income value of a commodity, and alternatively as relative labor earnings or relative income or wealth, considering gold's status as a financial asset.

17. "Central America Foundered," *New York Times*, September 18, 1857.

18. "The Loss of the Central America," *New York Times*, September 19, 1857; "News of the Day," *New York Times*, September 17, 1857; "No Insurance on the Central American Losses of the Company," *New York Times*, September 19, 1857; "Heavy Storm at the South," *New York Times*, September 17, 1857; "Commercial Affairs," *New York Times*, September 17, 1857.

19. Hutcheson, "Philadelphia and the Panic of 1857," 187.

20. Hutcheson, 188.

21. Charles W. Calomiris and Larry Schweikart, "The Panic of 1857: Origins, Transmission, and Containment," *Journal of Economic History* 51, no. 4 (December 1991): 819.

22. "The Financial Panic," *New York Daily Times*, September 10, 1857.

23. Calomiris and Schweikart, "The Panic of 1857," 819–20.

24. Davis R. Dewey, "State Banking Before the Civil War," National Monetary Commission, United States Senate, 61st Congress, 2d Session (Government Printing Office, 1910), 73–79; "Third Constitution of the State of New York," 1846, New York State Archives, https://digitalcollections.archives.nysed.gov/index.php/Detail/objects/57721; J. S. M'Calmont Speaker of the House of Representatives, V. Best Speaker of the Senate, and WM. F. Johnston Governor, "AN ACT Regulating Banks," Pub. L. No. No. 322, Laws of the General Assembly of the Commonwealth of Pennsylvania (1850); *The Banking Laws of the State of New York, Complete, from the Original Law of 1838 to the Close of the Session of 1854, in Relation to Banks, Banking Associations, and Individual Bankers Doing Business Under the Same; Arranged in the Order in Which They Were Passed, with Marginal Notes and References* (Albany, 1854), 40–41.

25. Dewey, 73–79; "Third Constitution of the State of New York"; M'Calmont Speaker of the House of Representatives. Though New York legislation in 1849 allowed for a judge to determine whether a bank was "clearly solvent or otherwise," the judge was still obligated to sustain any injunction granted until the demand of the noteholder was fully paid. In any event, there was general uncertainty as to the financial and legal implications of suspending payment, and so no bank wanted to be the first to find out what, exactly, would happen in the event they suspended. See: *The Banking Laws of the State of New York*, 40–41; Riddiough and Thompson, "When Prosperity Merges," *American Nineteenth Century History*, 308.

26. Hutcheson, "Philadelphia and the Panic of 1857," 188–90.

27. Gibbons, *The Banks of New-York*, 354–57; Sumner, "A History of Banking in the United States," 426–27.

28. Sumner, 426.

29. Sumner, 427.

30. "Third Constitution of the State of New York"; Sumner, 427.

31. Sumner, 427.

32. "Hard Times in the City," *New York Times*, October 8, 1857.

33. "Hard Times in the City," *New York Times*, October 9, 1857.

34. "Hard Times in the City," *New York Times*, October 7, 1857.

35. "Have We Been Living Too Fast?," *New York Times*, October 6, 1857.

36. "Causes of the Late Panic," *New York Times*, December 7, 1857.

37. James L. Huston, "Western Grains and the Panic of 1857," *Agricultural History* 57, no. 1 (1983): 20; Calomiris and Schweikart, "The Panic of 1857," 816; "The Grasshopper Plague of Minnesota," *New York Daily Times*, July 15, 1857; "A Plague of Grasshoppers," *New York Times*, July 29, 1873; Charles V. Riley, *The Locust Plague in the United States: Being More Particularly a Treatise on the Rocky Mountain Locust or So-Called Grasshopper, as It Occurs East of the Rocky Mountains, with Practical Recommendations for Its Destruction* (Chicago: Rand, McNally & Co., 1877), 35–36.

38. Riley, 35–36.

39. Christina D. Romer and David H. Romer, "NBER Business Cycle Dating: Retrospect and Prospect," in *NBER and the Evolution of Economic Research, 1920–2020* (Allied Social Science Associations Annual Meeting, San Diego, CA, 2019), 19.

40. John Maynard Keynes, *The General Theory of Employment, Interest, and Money* (Macmillan, 1936), 314. Quoted in: Victor Zarnowitz, *Business Cycles: Theory, History, Indicators and Forecasting*, Studies in Business Cycles 27 (University of Chicago Press, 1992), 256.

41. Romer and Romer, "NBER Business Cycle Dating," 19.

42. Peter Coy, "Do Economic Booms Die of Old Age?," *Bloomberg*, January 10, 2019, https://bloomberg.com/news/articles/2019-01-10/do-economic-booms-die-of-old -age?sref=ojq9DljU.

43. National Bureau of Economic Research, "US Business Cycle Expansions and Contractions," August 18, 2023, https://nber.org/research/data/us-business-cycle-expansions -and-contractions.

44. I discuss the methodology in a data appendix.

45. Samuel Jones-Loyd, *Reflections Suggested by a Perusal of Mr. J. Horsley Palmer's Pamphlet on the Causes and Consequences of the Pressure on the Money Market* (London, 1837), 44.

46. Robert Z. Aliber and Charles P. Kindleberger, *Manias, Panics, and Crashes: A History of Financial Crises*, 7th ed. (Palgrave Macmillan, 2015), 20, 104.

47. William Petty, *The Economic Writings of Sir William Petty*, vol. 1, ed. Charles Henry Hull, (Cambridge, England, 1899), 43.

48. Victoria Albert, "Carlyle Group's David Rubenstein: 'We're Due for a Recession,'" CBS News, August 15, 2019, https://cbsnews.com/news/ recession-2019-carlyle-groups-david-rubenstein-were-due-for-a-recession/.

49. Romer and Romer, "NBER Business Cycle Dating"; Christina Romer, "Spurious Volatility in Historical Unemployment Data," *Journal of Political Economy* 94, no. 1 (1986): 1–37, https://doi.org/10.1086/261361; Christina D. Romer, "Changes in Business Cycles: Evidence and Explanations," *Journal of Economic Perspectives* 13, no. 2 (1999): 23–44.

50. Ben Bernanke, Timothy F. Geithner, and Henry M. Paulson, *Firefighting: The Financial Crisis and Its Lessons* (Penguin Books, 2019).

51. Robert Shiller, "Narrative Economics," *American Economic Review* 107, no. 4 (2017): 990, 993.

52. "The 1988 Piper Alpha Explosion," Lloyd's, https://lloyds.com/about-lloyds/history /catastophes-and-claims/piper-alpha; "The Day 167 Men Perished in the Piper Alpha Oil Platform Disaster," BBC, July 6, 2018, https://bbc.co.uk/programmes/articles/2Zzmc qPgyWLrDRWP6tfBbnt/the-day-167-men-perished-in-the-piper-alpha-oil-platform -disaster.

53. "The Day 167 Men Perished."

54. "Federal Funds Effective Rate (FEDFUNDS)," Federal Reserve Bank of St. Louis, https://fred.stlouisfed.org/series/fedfunds; "30-Year Fixed Rate Mortgage Average in the United States (MORTGAGE30US)," Federal Reserve Bank of St. Louis, https://fred .stlouisfed.org/series/MORTGAGE30US.

55. Home Builders Association of Mississippi, "Wood 2x4 Mailed to Paul Volcker [Photograph]," circa 1980, Federal Reserve Bank of St. Louis, https://fraser.stlouisfed.org /archival-collection/federal-reserve-bank-st-louis-centennial-5182/wood-2x4-mailed-paul -volcker-photograph-527430; US Department of Commerce, Bureau of the Census, "New One-Family Homes Sold [HN1US@USECON]," Haver Analytics.

56. Robert Hall et al., "Business Cycle Dating Committee Announcement November 26, 2001," NBER, November 26, 2001, https://nber.org/news/business-cycle-dating-committee -announcement-november-26-2001.

57. "Causes of the Late Panic."

Chapter 1: Epiphanies or Apophanies

1. Henry Mance, "Nouriel Roubini: 'I Hope I Didn't Depress You Too Much,'" *Financial Times*, December 18, 2022, https://ft.com/content/b86825e3-5e34-4817-801f-0e0c 190bcbbb.

2. Emily Smith, "'Dr. Doom' Economist Nouriel Roubini Forced to Remove Giant Hot Tub," *New York Post*, Page Six, September 3, 2013, https://pagesix.com/2013/09/03 /dr-doom-economist-nouriel-roubini-forced-to-remove-giant-hot-tub/.

3. Justin Fox, "What Exactly Is Nouriel Roubini Good For?," *Harvard Business Review*, May 26, 2010; Eddy Elfenbein, "Roubini: Not Exactly a Prophet," *Seeking Alpha*, August 20, 2009; "Does Overseas Appetite for Bonds Put the U.S. Economy at Risk?," *Wall Street Journal*, Econoblog, March 29, 2005, https://wsj.com/public/resources/documents/econo blog03292005.htm. Elfenbein (2009) was quoting an online piece by Damien Hoffman that is no longer available.

4. Fox, "What Exactly Is Nouriel Roubini Good For?"; Elfenbein, "Roubini"; Dudley Baker, "Ominous Warnings and Dire Predictions of World's Financial Experts—Part 1," *Safehaven*, February 28, 2006, https://safehaven.com/article/4660/ominous-warnings -and-dire-predictions-of-worlds-financial-experts—part-1; David Ignatius, "Taste of the Future," *Washington Post*, February 24, 2006, https://washingtonpost.com/wp-dyn /content/article/2006/02/23/AR2006022301412.html; John Cassidy, "Moneyman," *New Yorker*, January 29, 2006, https://newyorker.com/magazine/2006/02/06/moneyman.

5. Edmund Andrews, "Economy Often Defies Soft Landing," *New York Times*, August 11, 2006; Rex Nutting, "Recession Will Be Nasty and Deep, Economist Says,"

MarketWatch, August 23, 2006, https://marketwatch.com/story/coming-recession
-will-be-nastier-than-2001s-economist-says.

6. Nouriel Roubini, "Have We Learned the Lessons of Black Monday?," *Foreign Policy*, October 16, 2007, https://foreignpolicy.com/2007/10/16/have-we-learned
-the-lessons-of-black-monday/.

7. Walter A. Friedman, *Fortune Tellers: The Story of America's First Economic Forecasters* (Princeton University Press, 2014), 51.

8. Robert W. Dimand and John Geanakoplos, "Celebrating Irving Fisher: The Legacy of a Great Economist," *American Journal of Economics and Sociology* 64, no. 1 (2005): 3–4; George J. Stigler and Claire Freidland, "The Pattern of Citation Practices in Economics," *History of Political Economy* 11, no. 1 (1979): 1–20, https://doi.org/10.1215/00182702-11-1-1.

9. Friedman, *Fortune Tellers*, 51.

10. Robert Shiller, "The Yale Tradition in Macroeconomics" (Economic Alumni Conference, New Haven, CT, April 8, 2011).

11. Friedman, *Fortune Tellers*, 65–66.

12. Friedman, 75, 78.

13. Friedman, 79; Samuel Williamson, "Seven Ways to Compute the Relative Value of a U.S. Dollar Amount, 1790 to Present," Measuring Worth, 2025, https://measuringworth
.com/calculators/uscompare/. I compute the 2024 value as the relative cost of a project.

14. "Babson Predicts 'Crash' in Stocks; Says Wise Investors Will Pay Up Loans and Avoid Margin Trading," *New York Times*, September 6, 1929.

15. "Babson Predicts 'Crash.'"

16. "Fisher Sees Stocks Permanently High; Yale Economist Tells Purchasing Agents Increased Earnings Justify Rise," *New York Times*, October 16, 1929.

17. "Says Stock Slump Is Only Temporary; Professor Fisher Tells Capital Bankers Market Rise Since War Has Been Justified; Economic Reasons Cited," *New York Times*, October 24, 1929.

18. John Kenneth Galbraith, *The Great Crash, 1929* (Houghton Mifflin Harcourt, 2009).

19. Samuel Williamson, "Daily Closing Value of the Dow Jones Average, 1885 to Present," Measuring Worth, 2025, https://measuringworth.com/datasets/DJA/index.php.

20. Williamson.

21. "Calls Fear a Trade Peril: Prof. Fisher Says No Permanent Ill Need Follow Stock Crash," *New York Times*, December 3, 1929.

22. Richardson et al., "Stock Market Crash of 1929," *Federal Reserve History* (blog), November 22, 2013, https://federalreservehistory.org/essays/stock-market-crash-of-1929.

23. "Babson Predicts Election of Hoover; Tells Business Conference That Democratic Victory Would Bring Depression in 1929," *New York Times*, September 18, 1928.

24. "The Prohibition Amendment: Hearings Before the Committee on the Judiciary House of Representatives" (Government Printing Office, 1930); Friedman, *Fortune Tellers*, 65.

25. "Nicholson Relates Dry Law Benefits," *New York Times*, February 25, 1929, sec. 21.

26. "Says Stock Slump Is Only Temporary."

27. Walter A. Friedman, "The Harvard Economic Service and the Problems of Forecasting," *History of Political Economy* 41, no. 1 (2009): 58, 62–65, 67–75, https://doi
.org/10.1215/00182702-2008-037; Warren M. Persons, "Construction of a Business Barometer Based Upon Annual Data," *American Economic Review* 6, no. 4 (1916): 739–69; Warren

M. Persons, "Indices of General Business Conditions," *Review of Economics and Statistics* 1, no. 1 (1919): 5–107; Warren M. Persons, "An Index of General Business Conditions," *Review of Economics and Statistics* 1, no. 2 (1919): 111–205.

28. Alan O. Ebenstein, *Friedrich Hayek: A Biography* (University of Chicago Press, 2003), 32–33; John Baynard Guerard, *The Leading Economic Indicators and Business Cycles in the United States: 100 Years of Empirical Evidence and the Opportunities for the Future* (Palgrave Macmillan, 2022), 23, https://doi.org/10.1007/978-3-030-99418-1; F. A. Hayek, *The Fortunes of Liberalism: Essays on Austrian Economics and the Ideal of Freedom*, vol. 4, Collected Works of F. A. Hayek, ed. Peter G. Klein (University of Chicago Press, 1992), 36–37; Friedrich A. von Hayek, *Contra Keynes and Cambridge: Essays, Correspondence*, vol. 9, Collected Works of F. A. Hayek, ed. Bruce Caldwell (University of Chicago Press, 1995), 11–12; Friedman, "Harvard Economic Service," 74.

29. Ebenstein, 32.

30. Friedman, "Harvard Economic Service," 71.

31. Kathryn M. Dominguez, Ray C. Fair, and Matthew D. Shapiro, "Forecasting the Depression: Harvard Versus Yale," *American Economic Review* 78, no. 4 (1988): 606.

32. Ben Bernanke, "Nonmonetary Effects of the Financial Crisis in the Propagation of the Great Depression," *American Economic Review* 73, no. 3 (1983): 266. Similar credit dynamics have been observed in quite different contexts. See: Tyler Beck Goodspeed, *Famine and Finance: Credit and the Great Famine of Ireland* (Palgrave Macmillan, 2017), https://doi.org/10.1007/978-3-319-31765-6; Tyler Beck Goodspeed, "Environmental Shocks and Sustainability in Microfinance: Evidence from the Great Famine of Ireland," *World Bank Economic Review*, August 31, 2016, lhw043, https://doi.org/10.1093/wber/lhw043.

33. "Records of President Abbott Lawrence Lowell, Series 1930, Folder 265, UAI 5.160," Harvard University Archives, Cambridge, MA; Friedman, "Harvard Economic Service," 82; Dominguez, Fair, and Shapiro, "Forecasting the Depression," 606.

34. Friedman, 83; "Harvard Denies Onus For Trade Predictions: Officials Note That University and Economic Society Separated Three Years Ago," *New York Times*, January 11, 1931.

35. Friedman, 82–84.

36. Dominguez, Fair, and Shapiro, "Forecasting the Depression," 605.

37. Dominguez, Fair, and Shapiro, 606; James D. Hamilton, "Monetary Factors in the Great Depression," *Journal of Monetary Economics* 19, no. 2 (1987): 145–69, https://doi.org/10.1016/0304-3932(87)90045-6.

38. Dominguez, Fair, and Shapiro, 606. Caldwell notes that many other institutes like the HES suffered a similar fate after failing to predict the Depression. See Hayek, *Contra Keynes and Cambridge*, 11.

39. Sir William Petty, *The Economic Writings of Sir William Petty*, vol. 1, ed. Charles Henry Hull, (Cambridge, England, 1899), 43.

40. "Sir William Petty, 1623–1687," History of Economic Thought Website, https://hetwebsite.net/het/profiles/petty.htm.

41. Petty, *The Economic Writings*, 1:13, 15–16.

42. "Sir William Petty, 1623–1687"; Laura Gowing, *Common Bodies: Women, Touch and Power in Seventeenth-Century England* (New Haven: Yale University Press, 2003), 49. Evidently the father was Jeffrey Read, grandson of Sir Thomas Read, in whose house

Greene worked as a maid. According to contemporary reports, Jeffrey was "a youth of about 16 or 17 years of age, but of a forward growth and stature." Greene had been "often solicited by faire promises and other amorous enticements" from Jeffrey, and "at last consented to his unlawfull pleasure," and it was thus that Greene became pregnant. It is unclear if the intercourse was indeed consensual or in fact rape. Upon intense interrogation by Sir Thomas—himself a justice of the peace and former high sheriff of Berkshire, Oxfordshire, and Hertfordshire—Greene initially volunteered only that the father was "a Gentleman of good birth, and kinsman to a justice of Peace," though she appears upon further examination to have revealed Jeffrey to be the father. When brought before a justice, Greene claimed that she had been unaware of her status prior to delivering the "dead born" fetus following overexerting herself turning malt, though the account of a fellow servant suggested she may have been aware. In any event, at least one midwife testified that Greene had suffered a miscarriage, and Petty treated Greene as innocent. See: A Scholler in Oxford for the satisfaction of a friend, who desired to be informed concerning the truth of the business, *Newes from the Dead, Or, A True and Exact Narration of the Miraculous Deliverance of Anne Greene, Who Being Executed at Oxford Decemb. 14. 1650, Afterwards Revived, and by the Care of Certain Physitians There, Is Now Perfectly Recovered : Together with the Manner of Her Suffering, and the Particular Meanes Used for Her Recovery / Written by a Scholler in Oxford : Whereunto Are Prefixed Certain Poems, Casually Written upon That Subject* (Oxford, England, 1651), https://wellcomecollection.org/works/ct2hx-kqk; W. Burdet, "A Wonder of Wonders, &c.," Oxford Text Archive, January 13, 1651, https://ota.bodleian.ox.ac.uk/repository/xmlui/bitstream/handle/20.500.12024/A77839/A77839.html?sequence=5; *A Declaration from Oxford, of Anne Greene* (London, 1651), https://proquest.com/docview/2240920366/99895664?sourcetype=Books.

43. A Scholler in Oxford; Burdet; *A Declaration from Oxford.*

44. A Scholler in Oxford; Burdet; *A Declaration from Oxford.*

45. Greene's father charged visitors for admission to see Anne during her recovery. After her pardon, her fame continued, and she kept the coffin in which she had been placed after hanging. She eventually married, had three children, and lived another fifteen years. J. Trevor Hughes, "Miraculous Deliverance of Anne Green: An Oxford Case of Resuscitation in the Seventeenth Century," *British Medical Journal (Clinical Research Edition)* 285, no. 6357 (1982): 1792–93.

46. "Sir William Petty, 1623–1687."

47. Charles H. Hull, "Petty's Place in the History of Economic Theory," *Quarterly Journal of Economics* 14, no. 3 (1900): 307, https://doi.org/10.2307/1882563.

48. Hull.

49. Dan Dixon, "Analysis Tool or Research Methodology: Is There an Epistemology for Patterns?," in *Understanding Digital Humanities*, ed. David M. Berry (Palgrave Macmillan UK, 2012), 191–209, https://doi.org/10.1057/9780230371934_11.

50. Clément Juglar, *Des Crises Commerciales et de Leur Retour Périodique En France, En Angleterre et Aux États-Unis* (Paris, 1862), vii.

51. Juglar, vii, 142.

52. *Oxford English Dictionary*, s.v. "crisis," accessed September 2023, https://oed.com/dictionary/crisis_n.

53. For a discussion of the use of medical metaphors in the works of Juglar and his contemporaries, see: Daniele Besomi, "Clément Juglar and his contemporaries on the causes of

commercial crises," *Revue européenne des sciences sociales*, no. XLVII–143 (March 1, 2009): 36–38, https://doi.org/10.4000/ress.110.

54. Clément Juglar, *Des Crises Commerciales et de Leur Retour Périodique En France, En Angleterre et Aux Etats-Unis*, 2nd ed. (Paris, 1889), 403–4.

55. Juglar, 164; "Joseph Clément Juglar, 1819–1905," History of Economic Thought Website, https://hetwebsite.net/het/profiles/juglar.htm; Clément Juglar, *A Brief History of Panics and Their Periodical Occurrency in the United States* (New York, 1893), 22. Schumpeter would later associate Juglar with a narrower, nine-to-ten-year cycle. See: Joseph A. Schumpeter, Elizabeth Schumpeter, and Mark Perlman, *History of Economic Analysis*, ed. Elizabeth B. Schumpeter (Routledge, 1997), 1124n.

56. Schumpeter, Schumpeter, and Perlman, 1123, 1123n, 1124.

57. Joseph Kitchin, "Cycles and Trends in Economic Factors," *Review of Economics and Statistics* 5, no. 1 (1923): 10, https://doi.org/10.2307/1927031.

58. Nikolaj D. Kondrat'ev et al., *The Long Wave Cycle* (Richardson & Snyder, 1984); N. D. Kondratieff and W. F. Stolper, "The Long Waves in Economic Life," *Review of Economics and Statistics* 17, no. 6 (1935): 105, https://doi.org/10.2307/1928486. The Kondratiev wave had historical antecedents in the work of Russian Marxist Israel Lazarevich Gelfand (pseudonym Alexander Lvovich Parvus) and Dutch Marxist Jacob van Gelderen. See: Solomos Solomou, *Phases of Economic Growth, 1850–1973: Kondratieff Waves and Kuznets Swings* (Cambridge University Press, 1990), 3–4.

59. "Nikolai Dmitrievich Kondratiev, 1892–1938?," History of Economic Thought Website, https://hetwebsite.net/het/profiles/kondratiev.htm.

60. "Nikolai Dmitrievich Kondratiev."

61. Joseph A. Schumpeter, *Business Cycles: A Theoretical, Historical and Statistical Analysis of the Capitalist Process*, 2 vols. (McGraw-Hill, 1939).

62. Schumpeter, 172.

63. Simon Kuznets, *Secular Movements in Production and Prices. Their Nature and Their Bearing upon Cyclical Fluctuations* (Houghton Mifflin, 1930); Simon Kuznets, "Long Swings in the Growth of Population and in Related Economic Variables," *Proceedings of the American Philosophical Society* 102, no. 1 (1958): 25–52.

64. Simon Kuznets, "Random Events and Cyclical Oscillations," *Journal of the American Statistical Association* 24, no. 167 (1929): 258–75, https://doi.org/10.1080/01621459.1929.10503048.

65. Eugen Slutsky, "The Summation of Random Causes as the Source of Cyclic Processes," *Problems of Economic Conditions* 3, no. 1 (1927): 34–64; Eugen Slutsky, "The Summation of Random Causes as the Source of Cyclic Processes," *Econometrica* 5, no. 2 (1937): 105, https://doi.org/10.2307/1907241.

66. Slutsky, "The Summation of Random Causes," *Econometrica*, 108–10.

67. Mary S. Morgan, *The History of Econometric Ideas* (Cambridge University Press, 1990), 79–83, https://doi.org/10.1017/CBO9780511522109.

68. Steven Pinker, *The Better Angels of Our Nature: Why Violence Has Declined* (Penguin, 2012), 203.

69. Wesley C. Mitchell, *Business Cycles* (University of California Press, 1913), vii; Wesley C. Mitchell, *Business Cycles: The Problem and Its Setting* (National Bureau of Economic Research, 1927).

70. Mitchell, *Business Cycles* (1913), 581.

71. Arthur Burns and Wesley C. Mitchell, *Measuring Business Cycles* (National Bureau of Economic Research, 1946), 3, 6.

72. Burns and Mitchell, 6, 12.

73. Wesley C. Mitchell and Arthur Burns, *Statistical Indicators of Cyclical Revivals* (National Bureau of Economic Research, 1938), 1–2.

74. Julius Shiskin, *Signals of Recession and Recovery: An Experiment with Monthly Reporting*, Occasional Paper 77 (National Bureau of Economic Research, 1961), ix, xi.

75. Saul H. Hymans et al., "On the Use of Leading Indicators to Predict Cyclical Turning Points," *Brookings Papers on Economic Activity* 1973, no. 2 (1973): 339–40, https://doi .org/10.2307/2534095. In November 1968, the publication was renamed *Business Conditions Digest*.

76. Chris Stone, "Conference Board: Composite Index of Leading Indicators," Investopedia (via Internet Archive), https://web.archive.org/web/20190331042704/https://investo pedia.com/university/conferenceboard/conferenceboard2.asp#axzz1tSSqJlKQ.

77. Hymans et al., "On the Use of Leading Indicators"; Alan J. Auerbach, "The Index of Leading Indicators: 'Measurement Without Theory,' Thirty-Five Years Later," *Review of Economics and Statistics* 64, no. 4 (1982): 589, https://doi.org/10.2307/1923943; Francis X. Diebold and Glenn D. Rudebusch, "Scoring the Leading Indicators," *Journal of Business* 62, no. 3 (1989): 369–91; Francis X. Diebold and Glenn D. Rudebusch, "Forecasting Output with the Composite Leading Index: A Real-Time Analysis," *Journal of the American Statistical Association* 86, no. 415 (1991): 603–10, https://doi.org/10.1080/01621459.1991. 10475085; Francis X. Diebold and Glenn D. Rudebusch, "Turning Point Prediction with the Composite Leading Index: An Ex Ante Analysis," in *Leading Economic Indicators: New Approaches and Forecasting Records*, ed. Kajal Lahiri and Geoffrey H. Moore (Cambridge University Press, 1991), 231–56; Arturo Estrella and Frederic Mishkin, "The Predictive Power of the Term Structure of Interest Rates in Europe and the United States: Implications for the European Central Bank," *European Economic Review* 41, no. 7 (1997): 1375–401.

78. Hymans et al., 376.

79. Kajal Lahiri and Geoffrey H. Moore, introduction to *Leading Economic Indicators: New Approaches and Forecasting Records*, ed. Kajal Lahiri and Geoffrey H. Moore (Cambridge University Press, 1991), 7.

80. James H. Stock and Mark W. Watson, "A Probability Model of the Coincident Economic Indicators," in *Leading Economic Indicators: New Approaches and Forecasting Records*, ed. Kajal Lahiri and Geoffrey H. Moore (Cambridge University Press, 1991), 63–89; James H. Stock and Mark W. Watson, "A Procedure for Predicting Recessions with Leading Indicators: Econometric Issues and Recent Experience," in *Business Cycles, Indicators and Forecasting*, Studies in Business Cycles 28 (University of Chicago Press, 1993), 95–156.

81. Francis X. Diebold and Glenn D. Rudebusch, "Measuring Business Cycles: A Modern Perspective," *Review of Economics and Statistics* 78, no. 1 (1996): 67, https://doi. org/10.2307/2109848; Chang-Jin Kim and Charles Nelson, "Business Cycle Turning Points, a New Coincident Index, and Tests of Duration Dependence Based on a Dynamic Factor Model with Regime Switching," *Review of Economics and Statistics* 80, no. 2 (1998): 188–201; Marcelle Chauvet, "An Econometric Characterization of Business Cycle Dynamics with Factor Structure and Regime Switching," *International Economic Review* 39, no. 4 (1998): 969, https://doi.org/10.2307/2527348; Marcelle Chauvet and Jeremy Piger, "A Comparison of the Real-Time Performance of Business Cycle Dating Methods," *Journal*

of Business & Economic Statistics 26, no. 1 (2008): 42–49; James D. Hamilton, "A New Approach to the Economic Analysis of Nonstationary Time Series and the Business Cycle," *Econometrica* 57, no. 2 (1989): 357, https://doi.org/10.2307/1912559.

82. J. D. Hamilton, "Macroeconomic Regimes and Regime Shifts," in *Handbook of Macroeconomics*, vol. 2, ed. John B. Taylor and Harald Uhlig (Elsevier, 2016), 163–201, https://doi.org/10.1016/bs.hesmac.2016.03.004.

83. Christina D. Romer and David H. Romer, "NBER Business Cycle Dating: Retrospect and Prospect," in *NBER and the Evolution of Economic Research, 1920–2020* (Allied Social Science Associations Annual Meeting, San Diego, CA, 2019).

84. Glenn D. Rudebusch and John C. Williams, "Forecasting Recessions: The Puzzle of the Enduring Power of the Yield Curve," *Journal of Business & Economic Statistics* 27, no. 4 (2009): 492–503.

85. For example, when the yield curve inverted in the late 1980s, numerous studies examined the predictive power of the yield curve for recessions and future economic activity. See, for example: Frederick Thomas Furlong, "The Yield Curve and Recessions," *FRBSF Weekly Letter*, March 10, 1989, https://fraser.stlouisfed.org/title/economic-letter-federal-reserve-bank-san-francisco-4960/yield-curve-recessions-517824; James H. Stock and Mark W. Watson, "New Indexes of Coincident and Leading Economic Indicators," in *NBER Macroeconomic Annual 1989*, ed. Olivier Jean Blanchard and Stanley Fisher, NBER Macroeconomic Annual 4 (MIT Press, 1989), 351–409; Campbell R. Harvey, "Forecasts of Economic Growth from the Bond and Stock Markets," *Financial Analysts Journal* 45, no. 5 (1989): 38–45; Howard Keen, "The Yield Curve as a Predictor of Business Cycle Turning Points," *Business Economics* 24, no. 4 (1989): 37–43; Arturo Estrella and Gikas A. Hardouvelis, "The Term Structure as a Predictor of Real Economic Activity," *Journal of Finance* 46, no. 2 (1991): 555–76; E. J. Stevens, "Is There a Message in the Yield Curve?," *Federal Reserve Bank of Cleveland Economic Commentary*, March 15, 1989; Campbell R. Harvey, "The Real Term Structure and Consumption Growth," *Journal of Financial Economics* 22, no. 2 (1988): 305–33, https://doi.org/10.1016/0304-405X(88)90073-6.

86. Michael D. Bauer and Thomas M. Mertens, "Economic Forecasts with the Yield Curve," *FRBSF Economic Letter*, March 5, 2018; Michael D. Bauer and Thomas M. Mertens, "Information in the Yield Curve about Future Recessions," *FRBSF Economic Letter*, August 27, 2018; Michael D. Bauer and Thomas M. Mertens, "Current Recession Risk According to the Yield Curve," *FRBSF Economic Letter*, May 9, 2022.

87. Estrella and Mishkin, "The Predictive Power." While Estrella and Mishkin found that yield curve spreads did have predictive power across France, Germany, Italy, the United Kingdom, and the United States, the relationship between spread and the probability of recession was strongest for Germany and the United States, and weakest for the United Kingdom.

88. John H. Wood, "Do Yield Curves Normally Slope Up? The Term Structure of Interest Rates, 1862–1982," *Federal Reserve Bank of Chicago Economic Perspectives*, August 1983, 17–23.

89. Stevens, "Is There a Message?"

90. Gertjan Vlieghe, "The Yield Curve and QE" (Imperial College Business School, September 25, 2018), 2, 5, https://bankofengland.co.uk/-/media/boe/files/speech/2018/the-yield-curve-and-qe-speech-by-gertjan-vlieghe.pdf.

91. Board of Governors of the Federal Reserve System (US), "Federal Funds Effective Rate (FEDFUNDS)," Federal Reserve Bank of St. Louis, https://fred.stlouisfed.org/series /fedfunds; "Official Bank Rate History Data from 1694," Bank of England, https:// bankofengland.co.uk/-/media/boe/files/monetary-policy/baserate.xls; Bank of England, "Bank of England Policy Rate in the United Kingdom (BOERUKM)," Federal Reserve Bank of St. Louis, https://fred.stlouisfed.org/series/BOERUKQ. Through January 2017, Bank rate data is from the Bank of England Database, "A Millennium of Macroeconomic Data." Since January 2017, I construct the monthly bank rate series as a daily weighted average of bank rate during that month.

92. Claudia Sahm, "Direct Stimulus Payments to Individuals," in *Recession Ready: Fiscal Policies to Stabilize the American Economy*, ed. Heather Boushey, Ryan Nunn, and Jay Shambaugh (Brookings, 2019), 76. Note that there is both a "real-time" Sahm indicator and a "current-time" Sahm indicator. The former uses unemployment rates from initial data releases; the latter uses unemployment rates from subsequent revision estimates. The two track each other very closely. For Figure 6, I use the current time indicator to allow apples-to-apples comparisons with the UK data in Figure 7.

93. Jim Reid, Henry Allen, and Galina Pozdnyakova, *Long-Term Asset Return Study: The History (and Future) of Recessions* (Deutsche Bank, September 18, 2023), 19.

94. Mitchell, *Business Cycles*, 573.

Chapter 2: Peter Pan versus Dorian Gray

1. Luke Kawa, "Jim Rogers: There's a 100% Probability of a U.S. Recession Within a Year," Bloomberg, March 4, 2016, https://bloomberg.com/news/articles/2016-03-04 /jim-rogers-there-s-a-100-probability-of-a-u-s-recession-within-a-year?sref=ojq9DljU#x j4y7vzkg.

2. For a discussion of some of these theories, see: Tyler Beck Goodspeed, *Rethinking the Keynesian Revolution: Keynes, Hayek, and the Wicksell Connection* (Oxford University Press, 2012).

3. Friedrich A. von Hayek, *Contra Keynes and Cambridge: Essays, Correspondence*, vol. 9, Collected Works of F. A. Hayek, ed. Bruce Caldwell (University of Chicago Press, 1995), 20.

4. P. M. Toms, quoted in Alan O. Ebenstein, *Friedrich Hayek: A Biography* (Palgrave, 2001), 75.

5. Friedrich A. von Hayek, *Prices and Production and Other Works: F.A. Hayek on Money, the Business Cycle, and the Gold Standard*, ed. Joseph T. Salerno (Ludwig von Mises Institute, 2008).

6. Hayek, *Contra Keynes and Cambridge*, 24, 25n.

7. Gottfried Haberler, *Prosperity and Depression: A Theoretical Analysis of Cyclical Movements* (League of Nations, 1937), 361.

8. Wesley C. Mitchell, *Business Cycles* (University of California Press, 1913), 475, 573.

9. Matthew O. Jackson and Pietro Tebaldi, "A Forest Fire Theory of the Duration of a Boom and the Size of a Subsequent Bust," Mimeo, February 2019.

10. Jackson and Tebaldi, 1, 20, 28.

11. The Peter Pan analogy for economic expansions is mentioned in Glenn D. Rudebusch, "Will the Economic Recovery Die of Old Age?," *Federal Reserve Bank of San Francisco Economic Letters* 2016-03, February 4, 2016, https://frbsf.org/economic-research/publications

/economic-letter/2016/february/will-economic-recovery-die-of-old-age/. It was too apt of a metaphor not to borrow here.

12. Peter Coy, "Do Economic Booms Die of Old Age?," Bloomberg, January 10, 2019, https://bloomberg.com/news/articles/2019-01-10/do-economic-booms-die-of-old-age?sref =ojq9DljU.

13. Francis X. Diebold and Glenn D. Rudebusch, *Business Cycles: Durations, Dynamics, and Forecasting* (Princeton University Press, 1999).

14. Stephen Broadberry et al., "Dating Business Cycles in the United Kingdom, 1700–2010," *Economic History Review*, January 27, 2023, ehr.13238, https://doi.org/10.1111 /ehr.13238; "A Millennium of Macroeconomic Data," Bank of England, https://bankofeng-gland.co.uk/statistics/research-datasets. Broadberry et al. provide a quarterly chronology for the United Kingdom back to 1926:Q1. Using the annual chronology from Broadberry et al., which extends back to 1700, along with quarterly and monthly data from the Bank of England's "A Millennium of Macroeconomic Data," I then extend a quarterly chronology back to 1854.

15. Christina D. Romer, "Remeasuring Business Cycles," *Journal of Economic History* 54, no. 3 (1994): 573–609; Joseph Davis, "An Improved Annual Chronology of U.S. Business Cycles Since the 1790s," *Journal of Economic History* 66, no. 1 (2006): 103–21; Mark W. Watson, "Business-Cycle Durations and Postwar Stabilization of the U.S. Economy," *American Economic Review* 84, no. 1 (1994): 24–46.

16. Davis, 103.

17. Romer, "Remeasuring Business Cycles," 592.

18. Davis, "An Improved Annual Chronology."

19. For survival analysis, I use a Kaplan–Meier nonparametric estimator of expansion survival as a function of age.

Chapter 3: The Penitent Expansion

1. "Fordyce, Alexander," in *The Dictionary of National Biography* (Oxford University Press, 1917); Leslie Stephen and Sidney Lee, eds., "Fordyce, David," in *The Dictionary of National Biography* (Oxford University Press, 1917); Leslie Stephen and Sidney Lee, eds., "Fordyce, George," in *The Dictionary of National Biography* (Oxford University Press, 1917); Leslie Stephen and Sidney Lee, eds., "Fordyce, James, D.D.," in *The Dictionary of National Biography* (Oxford University Press, 1917).

2. Ray Perman, *The Rise and Fall of the City of Money: A Financial History of Edinburgh* (Birlinn, 2019).

3. Frederick George Hilton Price, *The Signs of Old Lombard Street* (Leadenhall Press, 1902), 169; Perman.

4. Frederick George Hilton Price, *A Handbook of London Bankers: With Some Account of Their Predecessors, the Early Goldsmiths* (London, 1876), 15–16, 104–5; "Memoirs of Mr. Fordyce, a Late Celebrated Banker," *Gentleman's Magazine*, July 1772, 310.

5. Frederick Martin, *Stories of Banks and Bankers* (Macmillan and Co., 1865), 108.

6. Martin, 109–10; "Memoirs of Mr. Fordyce," 311; "Five Ways to Compute the Relative Value of a UK Pound Amount, 1270 to Present," Measuring Worth, 2025, https:// measuringworth.com/calculators/ukcompare/index.php. I compute the 2024 value as the relative labor or income value of a commodity, and alternatively as relative labor earnings or relative income.

7. Martin, 110.

8. Martin, 110; "Five Ways to Compute." I compute the 2024 value as the relative labor or income value of a commodity, and alternatively as relative labor earnings or relative income.

9. Martin, 110.

10. "Memoirs of Mr. Fordyce," 311.

11. Martin, *Stories of Banks and Bankers*, 111; "Five Ways to Compute"; Stephen and Lee, "Fordyce, Alexander." I compute the 2024 value as the relative labor or income value of a commodity, and alternatively as relative labor earnings or relative income.

12. "Memoirs of Mr. Fordyce, a Late Celebrated Banker," 311; Martin, 112–13.

13. "Five Ways to Compute." I compute the 2024 value as the relative labor or income value of a commodity, and alternatively as relative labor earnings or relative income.

14. Paul Kosmetatos, *The 1772–73 British Credit Crisis*, Palgrave Studies in the History of Finance (Springer International, 2018), 2–3, https://doi.org/10.1007/978-3-319-70908 -6; L. Neal, *Course of the Exchange, London, 1698–1823 and Amsterdamsche Beurs, Amsterdam, 1723-1794*, UK Data Service data collection, 1994, SN: 3211, http://doi.org/10.5255 /UKDA-SN-3211-1.

15. Tyler Beck Goodspeed, *Legislating Instability: Adam Smith, Free Banking, and the Financial Crisis of 1772* (Harvard University Press, 2016), 3; "Some Account of the Present Stagnation of Public Credit," *Scots Magazine*, June 1772, 311. Reports differ as to whether he absconded on the eighth or tenth, or whether the latter dates was when his disappearance became known.

16. "Some Account of the Present Stagnation," 311.

17. Price, *A Handbook of London Bankers*, 105; Martin, *Stories of Banks and Bankers*, 113.

18. "Some Account of the Present Stagnation," 311.

19. Richard Saville, *Bank of Scotland: A History, 1695–1995* (Edinburgh University Press, 1996), 161.

20. "Some Account of the Present Stagnation," 312.

21. Goodspeed, *Legislating Instability*, 4, 174.

22. William Forbes, *Memoirs of a Banking-House* (Edinburgh, 1859), 41; Martin, *Stories of Banks and Bankers*, 115; Goodspeed, 146; Kosmetatos, *The 1772–73 British Credit Crisis*, 4n.

23. "Some Account of the Present Stagnation," 314–15; Charles Boase, *A Century of Banking in Dundee* (Edinburgh, 1867), 88.

24. "Some Account of the Present Stagnation," 311–12.

25. Horace Walpole, *Journal of the Reign of King George the Third From the Year 1771–1783*, vol. 1, ed. John Doran (London, 1859), 122.

26. Goodspeed, *Legislating Instability*, 5, 26.

27. David Hume, "David Hume to Adam Smith, 27 June 1772," in *The Correspondence of Adam Smith*, vol. 6, ed. Ernest Mossner and Ian Ross (Oxford University Press, 1987), 161–63; Goodspeed, *Legislating Instability*, 131.

28. Henry Hamilton, "The Failure of the Ayr Bank, 1772," *Economic History Review* 8, no. 3 (1956): 413–15, https://doi.org/10.2307/2598492.

29. E. M., "The Evils Attending Excessive Credit," *London Magazine*, June 1772.

30. Adam Smith, *The Glasgow Edition of the Works and Correspondence of Adam Smith. 1: An Inquiry into the Nature and Causes of the Wealth of Nations*, ed. R. H. Campbell (Liberty Fund, 2009), 310, 316.

31. Hamilton, "The Failure of the Ayr Bank, 1772," 417.

32. Robert Z. Aliber and Charles P. Kindleberger, *Manias, Panics, and Crashes: A History of Financial Crises*, 7th ed. (Palgrave Macmillan, 2015), 74.

33. Goodspeed, *Legislating Instability*, 140.

34. Alex Warden, *The Linen Trade, Ancient and Modern* (London, 1867), 480.

35. "A Millennium of Macroeconomic Data," Bank of England, https://bankofengland.co.uk/statistics/research-datasets; Stephen Broadberry et al., "Dating Business Cycles in the United Kingdom, 1700–2010," *Economic History Review*, January 27, 2023, ehr.13238, https://doi.org/10.1111/ehr.13238.

36. "An Account of the Examinations of Mr Alexander Fordyce, Banker in London, before the Commissioners of Bankruptcy," *Scots Magazine*, September 1772, 473.

37. Stephen and Lee, "Fordyce, Alexander."

38. "Affairs in England," *Scots Magazine*, May 1774, 268; "Cupid's Auction," *Westminster Magazine, or, The Pantheon of Taste*, April 1773; *Garrick's Complete Jester; or, A Library of Fun and Laughter* (London, 1779), 37; G. K., *The Festival of Wit; or, Small Talker, Being a Collection of Bon Mots, Anecdotes, &c, of the Most Exalted Characters* (London, 1793).

39. Kosmetatos, *The 1772–73 British Credit Crisis*, 3–4; Stephen and Lee, "Fordyce, Alexander."

40. Hugh Rockoff, "Oh, How the Mighty Have Fallen: The Bank Failures and Near Failures That Started America's Greatest Financial Panics," *Journal of Economic History* 81, no. 2 (2021): 331–58, https://doi.org/10.1017/S0022050721000176.

41. "Some Account of the Present Stagnation of Public Credit," 311.

42. Rockoff, "Oh, How the Mighty Have Fallen."

43. Neal, *Course of the Exchange.*

44. Ellis Paxon Oberholtzer, *Jay Cooke: Financier of the Civil War*, vol. 1 (George W. Jacobs, 1907), 8–9.

45. Oberholtzer, 1:28–29, 33.

46. M. John Lubetkin, *Jay Cooke's Gamble: The Northern Pacific Railroad, the Sioux, and the Panic of 1873* (University of Oklahoma Press, 2006), 6.

47. Oberholtzer, *Jay Cooke*, 1:53–57.

48. Quoted in Oberholtzer, 1:57.

49. Lubetkin, *Jay Cooke's Gamble*, 6; Samuel Williamson, "Seven Ways to Compute the Relative Value of a U.S. Dollar Amount, 1790 to Present," Measuring Worth, 2025, https://measuringworth.com/calculators/uscompare/. I compute the 2024 value as the relative income value of a commodity, and alternatively as relative income or wealth.

50. Oberholtzer, *Jay Cooke*, 1:101–4.

51. Oberholtzer, 1: 105–6.

52. Oberholtzer, 1:110.

53. Oberholtzer, 1:115; Lubetkin, *Jay Cooke's Gamble*, 8.

54. Lubetkin, 8.

55. Lubetkin, 8–11.

56. Lubetkin, 11.

57. Quoted in Lubetkin, 13.

58. Lubetkin, 5, 12–14.

59. H. W. Brands, *The Money Men* (W. W. Norton, 2010), 161.

60. Eugene Smalley, *History of the Northern Pacific Railroad* (New York, 1883), 3.

61. Smalley, 109–12; Williamson, "Seven Ways to Compute." I compute the 2024 value as the economy cost of a project, and alternatively as the relative output value of income or wealth and the economic share of a commodity.

62. Lubetkin, *Jay Cooke's Gamble*, 9, 14.

63. Lubetkin, 15–16.

64. Ellis Paxon Oberholtzer, *Jay Cooke: Financier of the Civil War*, vol. 2 (Philadelphia: George W. Jacobs & Co., 1907), 157–59; Williamson, "Seven Ways to Compute." I compute the 2024 value as the economy cost of a project, and alternatively as the relative output value of income or wealth and the economic share of a commodity.

65. Oberholtzer, 2:158–59.

66. Smalley, *History of the Northern Pacific Railroad*, 166; Oberholtzer, 2:167.

67. Oberholtzer, 2:244, 337–38.

68. Robert Marshall Utley, *The Lance and the Shield: The Life and Times of Sitting Bull* (Ballantine, 1994), 91–92.

69. Lubetkin, *Jay Cooke's Gamble*, xvii; "The Hostile Savages: Seven Mexicans Murdered by Apaches in Arizona," *New York Times*, September 10, 1872.

70. Oberholtzer, *Jay Cooke*, 2:277–79.

71. Lubetkin, *Jay Cooke's Gamble*, 164.

72. Christopher P. Munden, "Jay Cooke: Banks, Railroads, and the Panic of 1873," *Pennsylvania Legacies* 11, no. 1 (2011): 5, https://doi.org/10.5215/pennlega.11.1.0003.

73. Stephen E. Ambrose, *Nothing Like It in the World: The Men Who Built the Transcontinental Railroad, 1863–1869* (Simon & Schuster, 2001), 373.

74. J. B. Crawford, *The Credit Mobilier of America* (Boston, 1880), 25, 34–35.

75. Crawford, 34, 74; John Patterson Davis, *The Union Pacific Railway: A Study in Railway Politics, History, and Economics* (Chicago: S. C. Griggs and Company, 1894), 163–65.

76. Crawford, 15–16; Davis, 165.

77. Crawford, 30–35; Ambrose, *Nothing Like It in the World*, 93.

78. Crawford, 35.

79. Ambrose, *Nothing Like It in the World*, 98–99.

80. Quoted in Ambrose, 99.

81. "Act of July 1, 1862 (Pacific Railroad Act)," Pub. L. No. 12 STAT 489 (1862), National Archives, https://archives.gov/milestone-documents/pacific-railway-act; Maury Klein, *Union Pacific*, vol. 1, 1862–1893 (University of Minnesota Press, 1987), 300.

82. Ambrose, *Nothing Like It in the World*, 227; Klein, *Union Pacific*, 1, 1862–1893:300.

83. Oberholtzer, *Jay Cooke*, 2:402–7.

84. "'Lord' Gordon Gordon: The Career of a Pseudo Nobleman," *New York Times*, August 5, 1874; Edward Harold Mott, *Between the Ocean and the Lakes: The Story of Erie* (New York, 1899), 184. Later accounts placed Gordon's arrival in Minnesota in September or the summer of 1871, but a more contemporary *New York Times* article placed his arrival in the summer of 1870.

85. "'Lord' Gordon Gordon."

86. An avid sailor, the earl died unmarried and without issue. As his younger brother James had died of rifle wounds two years earlier in a likely suicide, after some uncertainty, the Earldom passed to the third son of the 5th Earl. "The Missing Scottish Nobleman— Effort to Clear Up a Doubt," *New York Times*, December 12, 1870; "Railroad Accident in Massachusetts—New Treasurer of the Union Pacific Railroad—News of the Missing Earl

of Aberdeen—He Is Supposed to Have Washed Overboard from a China Schooner," *New York Times*, April 9, 1871; James Henry Hamilton Gordon, *A Canoe Voyage in the "PoΘion"* (Cambridge, reprinted from *The Light Blue: A Cambridge University Magazine*, 1868); "Case on Behalf of the Right Honourable John Campbell Earl of Aberdeen in the Peerage of Scotland, Claiming a Writ of Summons to Parliament as Viscount Gordon of Aberdeen in the Peerage of the United Kingdom" (Edinburgh, March 22, 1872).

87. Mott, *Between the Ocean*, 184; William Watts Folwell, *A History of Minnesota*, vol. 3 (Minnesota Historical Society, 1926), 364.

88. Folwell, 364–65.

89. "'Lord' Gordon Gordon"; Folwell, 364.

90. Folwell, 364.

91. "'Lord' Gordon Gordon."

92. Mott, *Between the Ocean*, 184; Folwell, *A History of Minnesota*, 363; "'Lord' Gordon Gordon."

93. Mott, 184.

94. Folwell, *A History of Minnesota*, 367; "'Lord' Gordon Gordon"; Mott, 185.

95. "'Lord' Gordon Gordon."

96. Murat Halstead and J. Frank Beale, Jr., *Life of Jay Gould: How He Made His Millions* (Philadelphia, 1892), 17.

97. Greg Steinmetz, *American Rascal: How Jay Gould Built Wall Street's Biggest Fortune* (Simon & Schuster, 2022), 93.

98. Robert Irving Warshow, *Jay Gould: The Story of a Fortune* (Greenberg, Publisher, 1928), 83–84.

99. "The Erie Bill: Report of the Senate Judiciary Committee—A Bill to Repeal Classification and Provide for an Election," *New York Times*, March 8, 1872; Marshall P. Stafford, *The Life of James Fisk, Jr.* (New York, 1872), 153–55; Folwell, *A History of Minnesota*, 367.

100. Mott, *Between the Ocean*, 185.

101. Mott, 185; Folwell, *A History of Minnesota*, 368.

102. Mott, 185; Folwell, 368–69.

103. Folwell, 369.

104. "'Lord' Gordon Gordon."

105. Folwell, *A History of Minnesota*, 369–70; Mott, *Between the Ocean*, 185–86.

106. Folwell, 370.

107. "'Lord' Gordon Gordon."

108. Folwell, *A History of Minnesota*, 370.

109. "Gordon Gordon: New Developments Promised Jay Gould and the Oil Creek and Alleghany Railroad Company," *New York Times*, April 14, 1872.

110. "Gordon and Gould: Some Further Developments in This Remarkable Case," *New York Times*, April 24, 1872; "The Gordon-Gould Case: Argument on the Motion to Vacate the Order of Arrest Against Gordon," *New York Times*, May 8, 1872; "The Gordon-Gould Case: Cross-Examination of the Parties to the Action," *New York Times*, May 18, 1872; "The Gordon-Gould Controversy: Each Asking an Attachement Against the Other," *New York Times*, April 27, 1872; "The Gordon-Gould Case," *New York Times*, May 24, 1872.

111. "Gordon vs. Gould: Reappearance and Examination of the Former Yesterday," *New York Times*, June 21, 1872; "The Gordon-Gould Case: Failure of the Defendant to Appear,"

New York Times, May 23, 1872; "The Gordon-Gould Case: Motion to Dismiss the Complaint," *New York Times*, May 25, 1872.

112. "The Gordon-Gould Case: Cross-Examination"; Folwell, *A History of Minnesota*, 387.

113. "The Gordon-Gould Case: Cross-Examination."

114. "Gordon Gordon: Order of Arrest for $100,000 Against Him," *New York Times*, June 22, 1872; "The Gordon-Gould Case: Cross-Examination." In earlier testimony, Gordon Gordon had indicated that "the coronet on my letters might indicate that I belonged to a noble family."

115. Whether Cambridge Square could be considered as being located in Notting Hill is questionable.

116. "Gordon vs. Gould: Reappearance and Examination"; "The Gordon-Gould Case: Cross-Examination."

117. Folwell, *A History of Minnesota*, 370.

118. Folwell, 370–71, 385.

119. "'Lord' Gordon Gordon"; Mott, *Between the Ocean*, 186; Folwell, *A History of Minnesota*, 385.

120. "'Lord' Gordon Gordon"; Folwell, 385.

121. "The Gordon-Gould Case: Foreign Opinion of the Affair," *New York Times*, May 16, 1872.

122. "The Gordon-Gould Case: Foreign Opinion"; "'Lord' Gordon Gordon."

123. "The Gordon-Gould Case: Foreign Opinion."

124. "The Gordon-Gould Case: Foreign Opinion."

125. Oberholtzer, *Jay Cooke*, 1:239, 344, 380, 384, 392–93.

126. Oberholtzer, 1: 408–9.

127. "The Panic: Excitement in Wall Street. Suspension of Jay Cooke & Co.," *New York Times*, September 19, 1873; "Jay Cooke and His Crash: The Cause, and the Parallel Readings," *Chicago Daily Tribune*, September 26, 1873; Oberholtzer, 1:226.

128. Foreign Office, *Indemnities of War*, Handbooks Prepared Under the Direction of the Historical Section of the Foreign Office (Foreign Office, November 1918).

129. "Excitement on the Vienna Bourse," *New York Times*, May 10, 1873; "Foreign News: The Financial Disturbance," *New York Times*, May 13, 1873.

130. Oberholtzer, *Jay Cooke*, 1:381–88.

131. "The Panic"; "The Contract Between Cooke & Co. and the Northern Pacific," *New York Times*, September 21, 1873; Oberholtzer, 1:398, 418; Lubetkin, *Jay Cooke's Gamble*, 279. When the bank suspended payment, Fahnestock told reporters that $5 million remained to sell, though it is unclear whether this referred to Northern Pacific bonds or a US government bond issue Cooke & Co. were participating in. Contemporary reports suggested public confusion regarding the volume of Northern Pacific bonds on Cooke & Co.'s balance sheet, with estimates ranging from $60 to $85 million, of which the bank had managed to sell $11–$18 million. However, secondary sources suggest a figure of $30 million, of which in the months preceding a maximum of $9 million remained on Cooke & Co.'s books.

132. R. L. Cartwright, "Grasshopper Plagues, 1873–1877," in *MNopedia* (Minnesota Historical Society, November 17, 2011), https://mnopedia.org/event/grasshopper -plagues-1873-1877.

133. Cartwright; "Grasshoppers in Texas," *New York Times*, May 21, 1873. The swarm followed reports of large numbers of grasshoppers as far south as Texas three weeks prior.

134. Harold E. Briggs, "Grasshopper Plagues and Early Dakota Agriculture, 1864–1876," *Agricultural History* 8, no. 2 (1934): 55; Cartwright; "A Plague of Grasshoppers," *New York Times*, July 29, 1873; "The Destitute in Iowa: Previous Reports Confirmed the Relief Already Furnished," *New York Times*, December 12, 1873.

135. In addition to the above, see also: "The Crops: The September Agricultural Report," *New York Times*, September 28, 1873.

136. J. Briggs, "The Grasshopper Plagues in Iowa," *Iowa Journal of History and Politics* 13, no. 3 (1915): 367; Chuck Lyons, "1874: The Year of the Locust," HistoryNet, February 5, 2012, https://historynet.com/1874-the-year-of-the-locust/.

137. Carlton C. Qualey, "Pioneer Norwegian Settlement in Minnesota," *Minnesota History* 12, no. 3 (1931): 262–63.

138. "A Millennium of Macroeconomic Data."

139. "New York: Suspension of a Prominent Firm of Brokers—Daniel Drew One of the Partners," *Chicago Daily Tribune*, September 14, 1873; "Failure in Wall Street: Suspension of Kenyon Cox & Co., Daniel Drew's Brokers," *New York Times*, September 14, 1873; "Trouble in Wall Street: Suspension of the New-York Warehouse Company," *New York Times*, September 9, 1873.

140. "Trouble in Wall Street."

141. "New York: Suspension"; "Failure in Wall Street."

142. "New York: Suspension."

143. "The Yellowstone Expedition: The Command on the March," *New York Times*, July 17, 1873.

144. "The Yellowstone Expedition: The Command"; "The Yellowstone River: Gen. Stanley's Expedition," *New York Times*, August 10, 1873; "The Yellowstone Expedition: Report of Gen. Rosser, in Charge of the Railroad Survey," *New York Times*, August 16, 1873; "The Northern Pacific: Gen. Stanley's Expedition," *New York Times*, June 30, 1873.

145. "The Yellowstone Expedition," *New York Times*, September 10, 1873.

146. "The Yellowstone Expedition," *New York Times*, September 11, 1873.

147. "Daniel Drew's Brokers," *New York Times*, September 16, 1873; Lubetkin, *Jay Cooke's Gamble*, 278.

148. "Chicago and Rock Island Railroad," *New York Times*, September 17, 1873; Lubetkin, 279.

149. "Money Market," *The Independent*, September 18, 1873; "The Panic."

150. Lubetkin, *Jay Cooke's Gamble*, 280.

151. "The Panic."

152. Lubetkin, *Jay Cooke's Gamble*, 280.

153. Oberholtzer, *Jay Cooke*, 1:422; "Bankers and Brokers," *The Commercial & Financial Chronicle: Bankers' Gazette, Commercial Times, Railway Monitor, and Insurance Journal*, January 1, 1870.

154. Lubetkin, *Jay Cooke's Gamble*, 281–82.

155. Oberholtzer, *Jay Cooke*, 2:422.

156. Lubetkin, *Jay Cooke's Gamble*, 283.

157. Lubetkin, 283.

158. Lubetkin, 281–82.

159. "The Panic"; Lubetkin, 281–82.

160. "The Panic."

161. National Bureau of Economic Research, "Call Money Rates, Mixed Collateral for the United States (M13001USM156NNBR)," Federal Reserve Bank of St. Louis, https://fred.stlouisfed.org/series/M13001USM156NNBR.

162. National Bureau of Economic Research, "Commercial Paper Rates for New York, NY (M13002US35620M156NNBR)," Federal Reserve Bank of St. Louis, https://fred.stlouisfed.org/series/M13002US35620M156NNBR.

163. Charles V. Riley, *The Locust Plague in the United States: Being More Particularly a Treatise on the Rocky Mountain Locust or So-Called Grasshopper, as It Occurs East of the Rocky Mountains, with Practical Recommendations for Its Destruction* (Chicago, 1877).

164. "An Episode of the Grasshopper Pest," *Frank Leslie's Illustrated Newspaper*, August 7, 1875.

165. Tammy Partsch, *It Happened in Nebraska: Stories of Events and People That Shaped Cornhusker State History*, 2nd ed., It Happened in . . . Series (Globe Pequot, 2019), 56; Lyons, "1874."

166. Jeffrey A. Lockwood, *Locust: The Devastating Rise and Mysterious Disappearance of the Insect That Shaped the American Frontier* (Basic Books, 2009), 19–21.

167. Helmut Satz, *The Rules of the Flock: Self-Organization and Swarm Structure in Animal Societies* (Oxford University Press, 2020), 8.

168. Laura Ingalls Wilder and Garth Williams, *On the Banks of Plum Creek* (HarperCollins, 1994), 66.

169. Lockwood, *Locust*, 21–23.

170. "South Dakota Governor Begs for Federal Assistance over Grasshopper Plague," History, November 13, 2009, https://history.com/this-day-in-history/grasshoppers-bring-ruin-to-midwest; W. H. Larrimer, "Grasshoppers Ravage Vast Farm Areas: Their Destructive Onslaught in the West Is Said to Be the Worst Since 1876," New York Times, August 9, 1931"; "Enlist States' Aid on Grasshoppers: Federal Officials Urge Governors to Cooperate in the Relief Program," *New York Times*, August 2, 1931.

171. Wilder and Williams, *On the Banks of Plum Creek*, 194–95.

172. Riley, *The Locust Plague*, 87.

173. Lyons, "1874"; Williamson, "Seven Ways to Compute." I compute the 2024 value as the economy cost of a project, and alternatively as the relative output value of income or wealth and the economic share of a commodity.

174. Lyons.

175. Lubetkin, *Jay Cooke's Gamble*, 287.

176. Smalley, *History of the Northern Pacific Railroad*, 204.

177. David Glasner and Thomas F. Cooley, *Business Cycles and Depressions: An Encyclopedia* (Garland Publishing, 1997), 148.

178. Stijn Claessens and Kristin J. Forbes, *International Financial Contagion* (Springer, 2001), 372–74.

179. Willard Thorpe, *Business Annals* (National Bureau of Economic Research, 1926).

180. "Great Britain: Run on Jay Cooke, M'Culloch & Co., of London," *New York Times*, September 20, 1873; "Jay Cooke & Co.," *New York Times*, September 22, 1873; "Great Britain: The Financial Situation—The Run on Jay Cooke, McCulloch & Co. Ended," *New York Times*, September 23, 1873; Broadberry et al., "Dating Business Cycles"; Joseph Davis, "An

Improved Annual Chronology of U.S. Business Cycles Since the 1790s," *Journal of Economic History* 66, no. 1 (2006): 103–21; Oberholtzer, *Jay Cooke*, 2:435–36, 537.

181. National Bureau of Economic Research, "Railroad Bond Yields Index for United States (M1319AUSM156NNBR)," Federal Reserve Bank of St. Louis, https://fred.stlouis-fed.org/series/M1319AUSM156NNBR; National Bureau of Economic Research, "American Railroad Stock Prices for United States (M1105AUSM505NNBR)," Federal Reserve Bank of St. Louis, https://fred.stlouisfed.org/series/M1105AUSM505NNBR; National Bureau of Economic Research, "NBER Based Recession Indicators for the United States from the Period Following the Peak through the Trough (USREC)," Federal Reserve Bank of St. Louis, https://fred.stlouisfed.org/series/USREC.

182. "The Northern Pacific Railroad," *New York Times*, September 20, 1873; Smalley, *History of the Northern Pacific Railroad*, 206–10.

183. "The Last Spike Driven Home," *New York Times*, September 1, 1883; Ed Nolan and Chas. V. Waldron, "NPS Form 10-900: National Register of Historic Places Inventory—Nomination Form: Site of the Completion of the Northern Pacific Railroad, 1883," National Archives, July 20, 1983, https://catalog.archives.gov/id/71976486. *The New York Times* indicates the teams met on August 21, though the official nomination for the addition of the site to the National Register of Historic Places reports August 22, 1883.

184. "The Last Spike Driven: Completion of the Northern Pacific Railroad," *New York Times*, September 10, 1883.

185. "The Last Spike Driven"; "Davis, Henry Chandler" in *The National Cyclopædia of American Biography; Being the History of the United States* (James T. White & Company, 1918).

186. "Affairs of Railroads: The Opening of the Northern Pacific," *New York Times*, August 15, 1883; "The Last Spike Driven"; Nolan and Waldron, "NPS Form 10-900"; "The Northern Pacific Excursion," *New York Times*, August 2, 1883; "The Northern Pacific: Formal Completion of Henry Villard's Railroad," *New York Times*, September 9, 1883; "North Pacific: The Gold Spike Driven Home at Half-Past Three Yesterday Afternoon," *Chicago Daily Tribune*, September 9, 1883; "That Gold Spike: Driven Home Amid Enthusiasm after Much Talk," *Washington Post*, September 10, 1883. *The New York Times* on September 10 indicated the ceremony had taken place on September 9, though the official nomination for the addition of the site to the National Register of Historic Places reports September 8, 1883, as did an August 2 preview and September 9 report from *The New York Times* and reports in the *Chicago Daily Tribune* and *The Washington Post*.

187. Bernhard Gillam, *The Great Rival Adverting Shows to "Boom Up" Stocks*, September 5, 1883, illustration in *Puck* 14, no. 339 (September 1883), centerfold, AP101.P7 1883, Case X, Library of Congress Prints and Photographs Division, Washington, DC.

188. "The Morganization of Industry," *New York Financier*, September 15, 1902.

189. *Encyclopaedia Britannica*, "Northern Pacific Railway Company," July 5, 2013, https://britannica.com/topic/Northern-Pacific-Railway-Company.

190. Scott Patterson and Douglas Blackmon, "Buffett Bets Big on Railroad," *Wall Street Journal*, November 4, 2009.

191. Smalley, *History of the Northern Pacific Railroad*, 204.

192. Oberholtzer, *Jay Cooke*, 2:512, 522.

193. Oberholtzer, 2:523; Writers' Program of the Work Projects Administration for the State of Utah, *Utah: A Guide to the State* (Hastings House, 1941), 324.

194. Oberholtzer, 2:523.

195. Oberholtzer, 2:523; Writers' Program, *Utah*, 324.

196. Oberholtzer, 2:523.

197. *United States Annual Mining Review and Stock Ledger* (Mining Review Publishing Company, 1879), 112; Writers' Program, *Utah*, 323–25; Utah State Historical Society, "When the Fabulous Horn Silver Mine Caved In," *History Blazer: News of Utah's Past from the Utah State Historical Society*, January 1996; Oberholtzer, 2:523–26.

198. Oberholtzer, 2:524; Writers' Program, 325.

199. Oberholtzer, 2:524; Writers' Program, 325.

200. Warshow, *Jay Gould*, 137–42; Halstead and Beale Jr., *Life of Jay Gould*, 75–77.

201. Warshow, 142.

202. Steinmetz, *American Rascal*, xiii.

203. Oberholtzer, *Jay Cooke*, 2:524–25; Writers' Program, *Utah*, 325.

204. Oberholtzer, 2:525.

205. *United States Annual Mining Review*, 112.

206. Oberholtzer, *Jay Cooke*, 2:525; Meade Minnigerode, *Certain Rich Men: Stephen Girard—John Jacob Astor—Jay Cooke—Daniel Drew—Cornelius Vanderbilt—Jay Gould—Jim Fisk* (G. P. Putnam's Sons, 1927), 79–80; Williamson, "Seven Ways to Compute."

207. Oberholtzer, 2:527–28.

208. Oberholtzer, 2: 534–37, 541–47.

Chapter 4: Oscillations or Plucks

1. Andrew Lawrence, "Talking Tall: The Skyscraper Index: An Interview with Andrew Lawrence with Kevin Brass," *CTBUH Journal: International Journal on Tall Buildings and Urban Habitat*, no. 2, 2012: 43.

2. Ralph Nelson Elliott, *The Wave Principle* (Snowball Publishing, 2012).

3. John Downes and Jordan Goodman, *Dictionary of Finance and Investment Terms: More than 5,000 Terms Defined and Explained* (Barrons Educational Series, 2018).

4. Lawrence, "Talking Tall," 43–44.

5. Jason Barr, Bruce Mizrach, and Kusum Mundra, "Skyscraper Height and the Business Cycle: Separating Myth from Reality," *Applied Economics* 47, no. 2 (2015): 148–60, https://doi.org/10.1080/00036846.2014.967380.

6. The nominal series is converted to real, chained 1913 dollars using an index for the general price level of the United States from the NBER Macrohistory Database. I then estimate time trends that are linear in the level of the volume of real building activity and the cumulative volume of real building activity. Unfortunately, these series are only available from 1850 through 1939. I exclude years prior to 1880 to avoid distorting time trends with the effects of the Civil War and the "long depression" of the 1870s. National Bureau of Economic Research, "Nonfarm Residential Building Activity for United States (A02239USA398NNBR)," Federal Reserve Bank of St. Louis, https://fred.stlouisfed.org/series/A02239USA398NNBR; National Bureau of Economic Research, "Index of the General Price Level for United States (M04051USM324NNBR)," Federal Reserve Bank of St. Louis, https://fred.stlouisfed.org/series/M04051USM324NNBR.

7. Real residential investment and capital stock estimates from the Bureau of Economic Analysis (BEA) are available since 1925. I then extend the capital stock estimates

back to 1901 by decrementing the level of real residential investment using annual growth rates in a chained quantity index of residential investment and applying long-run average depreciation rates to recursively calculate net stocks. I then log-transform the series, estimate long-run trend using a Hamilton filter, and transform the filtered trend back into levels. Bureau of Economic Analysis, "Real Net Stock: Private Fixed Residential Assets (Bil. Chn. 2017$) [EPRH@CAPSTOCK]," Haver Analytics; Bureau of Economic Analysis, "Investment: Private Fixed Residential Assets (Bil. Chn. 2017$) [ZPRH@CAPSTOCK]," Haver Analytics; Bureau of Economic Analysis, "Investment: Res Fixed Assets: Private: Chn Qty Idx (2017 = 100) [ZPRQ@CAPSTOCK]," Haver Analytics; Bureau of Economic Analysis, "Depreciation: Private Residential Fixed Assets (Bil. Chn. 2017$) [KPRH@CAPSTOCK]," Haver Analytics. Examples of references to the 1920s as a housing boom include Eugene White, "Lessons from the Great American Real Estate Boom and Bust of the 1920s" (National Bureau of Economic Research, December 2009), https://doi.org/10.3386/w15573; Michael Brocker and Christopher Hanes, "The 1920s American Real Estate Boom and the Downturn of the Great Depression: Evidence from City Cross Sections" (National Bureau of Economic Research, February 2013), https://doi.org/10.3386/w18852; Steven Gjerstad and Vernon Smith, "Consumption and Investment Booms in the 1920s and Their Collapse in 1930," in *Housing and Mortgage Markets in Historical Perspective*, ed. Eugene White, Kenneth Snowden, and Price Fishback (University of Chicago Press, 2014), 81–114; Raghuram Rajan and Rodney Ramcharan, "The Anatomy of a Credit Crisis: The Boom and Bust in Farm Land Prices in the United States in the 1920s," *American Economic Review* 105, no. 4 (2015): 1439–77, https://doi.org/10.1257/aer.20120525.

8. To estimate trends, I again log-transform the series and use a Hamilton filter before transforming the filtered trend back into levels.

9. For robustness, I also use a Hodrick–Prescott filter with a high smoothing parameter (λ) of 125 to avoid mistaking cyclical movements for trend. Gebhard Flaig, "Why We Should Use High Values for the Smoothing Parameter of the Hodrick–Prescott Filter," *Jahrbücher Für Nationalökonomie Und Statistik* 235, no. 6 (2015): 518–38, https://doi.org/10.1515/jbnst-2015-0602; James D. Hamilton, "Why You Should Never Use the Hodrick–Prescott Filter," *Review of Economics and Statistics* 100, no. 5 (2018): 831–43, https://doi.org/10.1162/rest_a_00706.

10. Tyler Cowen recently made a similar observation about the 2000s housing "boom." Tyler Cowen, "What Economists Got Wrong About the Great Recession," Bloomberg, October 24, 2023, https://bloomberg.com/opinion/articles/2023-10-24/the-great-recession-is-now-more-relevant-than-the-great-depression?utm_source=website&utm_medium=share&utm_campaign=twitter&sref=htOHjx5Y.

11. Census Bureau, "Median Income of Households (Current $) [HI@USECON]," Haver Analytics; Census Bureau, "New 1-Family Houses: Median Sales Price ($) [HN1PMA@USECON]," Haver Analytics.

12. Census Bureau, "Median Income of Households"; Census Bureau, "NAR Median Sales Price: Existing 1-Family Homes, United States ($) [HX1PM@USECON]," Haver Analytics.

13. J. Bradford DeLong and Lawrence Summers, "Are Business Cycles Symmetric?" (National Bureau of Economic Research, September 1984), 18, https://doi.org/10.3386/w1444; J. Bradford DeLong and Lawrence H. Summers, "Additional Contribution: Are

Business Cycles Symmetrical?" in *The American Business Cycle: Continuity and Change*, ed. Robert J. Gordon (University of Chicago Press, 1986), 176.

14. Milton Friedman, "Reports on Selected Bureau Programs: The Monetary Studies of the National Bureau," in *The National Bureau Enters Its Forty-Fifth Year* (National Bureau of Economic Research, 1964), 17.

15. Both the 1705–06 and 1709–10 wartime recessions were characterized by dramatic output swings surrounding extremely poor agricultural harvests. Agricultural output dropped by 24.8 percent in 1705–06 and 20.9 percent in 1709–10; Stephen Broadberry et al., "Dating Business Cycles in the United Kingdom, 1700–2010," *Economic History Review*, January 27, 2023, A3–5, https://doi.org/10.1111/ehr.13238; "A Millennium of Macroeconomic Data," Bank of England, https://bankofengland.co.uk/statistics/research-datasets.

16. Recent research looking at fluctuations in the unemployment rate in the United States have observed the same result, finding that "increases in unemployment are followed by decreases of similar amplitude, while the amplitude of a decrease does not predict the amplitude of the following increase." See Stephane Dupraz, Emi Nakamura, and Job Steinsson, "A Plucking Model of Business Cycles," *Journal of Monetary Economics* 152, June 2025: 103766, https://eml.berkeley.edu/~enakamura/papers/plucking.pdf.

17. Carmen M. Reinhart and Kenneth Rogoff, *This Time Is Different: Eight Centuries of Financial Folly* (Princeton, NJ: Princeton University Press, 2009); Carmen M. Reinhart and Kenneth S. Rogoff, "Recovery from Financial Crises: Evidence from 100 Episodes," *American Economic Review* 104, no. 5 (2014): 50–55, https://doi.org/10.1257/aer.104.5.50; IMF Research Department, *World Economic Outlook, April 2009: Crisis and Recovery*, World Economic Outlook (Washington, DC: International Monetary Fund, 2009), https://doi.org/10.5089/9781589068063.081.

18. Michael D. Bordo and Joseph G. Haubrich, "Deep Recessions, Fast Recoveries, and Financial Crises: Evidence from the American Record," *Economic Inquiry* 55, no. 1 (2017): 527–41, https://doi.org/10.1111/ecin.12374.

19. I exclude the recovery from the 2020 pandemic recession because at the time of writing, that recession remains ongoing.

20. F. A. von Hayek, "Capital and Industrial Fluctuations," *Econometrica* 2, no. 2 (1934): 152, https://doi.org/10.2307/1906898; F. A. von Hayek, "[Professor Hayek and the Concertina-Effect]: A Comment," *Economica* 9, no. 36 (1942): 383, https://doi.org/10.2307/2550327; F. A. von Hayek, "The Ricardo Effect," *Economica* 9, no. 34 (1942): 127, https://doi.org/10.2307/2549806; F. A. Hayek, "Three Elucidations of the Ricardo Effect," *Journal of Political Economy* 77, no. 2 (1969): 274–85; Friedrich A. von Hayek et al., *Prices and Production and Other Works: F.A. Hayek on Money, the Business Cycle, and the Gold Standard* (Ludwig von Mises Institute, 2008).

21. Tyler Beck Goodspeed, *Rethinking the Keynesian Revolution: Keynes, Hayek, and the Wicksell Connection* (Oxford University Press, 2012), 51–58.

22. Nicholas Kaldor, "Professor Hayek and the Concertina-Effect," *Economica* 9, no. 36 (1982): 359–82.

23. Jason Barr, "The Myth of the Skyscraper Index," *History News Network* (blog), December 12, 2012, https://historynewsnetwork.org/article/the-myth-of-the-skyscraper-index.

24. Wilhelm Röpke, *Crises and Cycles*, adapted from the German and revised by Vera C. Smith (William Hodge, 1936), 7.

Chapter 5: Turf, Coal, and Oil

1. W. D. Davidson, "History of Potato Varieties," *Journal of the Department of Agriculture, Republic of Ireland* 33 (1935): 57–81; P. M. Austin Bourke, "The Extent of the Potato Crop in Ireland at the Time of the Famine," *Journal of the Statistical and Social Inquiry Society of Ireland* 20, no. 3 (1960): 1–35; P. M. Austin Bourke, "The Potato, Blight, Weather and the Irish Famine" (PhD thesis, Department of Ireland, National University of Ireland, 1965); Tyler Beck Goodspeed, "Environmental Shocks and Sustainability in Microfinance: Evidence from the Great Famine of Ireland," *World Bank Economic Review*, August 31, 2016, lhw043, https://doi.org/10.1093/wber/lhw043; Tyler Beck Goodspeed, *Famine and Finance: Credit and the Great Famine of Ireland* (Palgrave Macmillan, 2017), https://doi.org/10.1007/978-3-319-31765-6.

2. *Annual Report of the Local Government Board for Ireland, Being the Seventh Report Under "The Local Government Board (Ireland) Act," 35 & 36 VIC., c. 69; with Appendices*, Presented to both Houses of Parliament by Command of Her Majesty (Dublin, 1879); *Annual Report of the Local Government Board for Ireland, Being the Eighth Report Under "The Local Government Board (Ireland) Act," 35 & 36 VIC., c. 69*, Presented to both Houses of Parliament by Command of Her Majesty (Dublin, 1880).

3. *Annual Report of the Local Government Board for Ireland, Being the Eighth*, 6.

4. "The British Grain Interests," *New York Times*, July 30, 1879; "Foreign Grain Prospects," *New York Times*, August 13, 1879; "Business and Crop Prospects," *New York Times*, September 10, 1879.

5. "England's Financial Problem," *New York Times*, August 28, 1879; "English Trade and Labor," *New York Times*, September 27, 1879; "A Millennium of Macroeconomic Data," Bank of England, https://bankofengland.co.uk/statistics/research-datasets.

6. Stephen Broadberry et al., "Dating Business Cycles in the United Kingdom, 1700–2010," *Economic History Review*, January 27, 2023, ehr.13238, https://doi.org/10.1111/ehr.13238; "The British Grain Outlook," *New York Times*, October 1, 1879.

7. *Annual Report of the Local Government Board for Ireland, Being the Eighth*, 71.

8. "The Outlook in England: Condition and Prospects of the Farmer," *New York Times*, October 24, 1879; "Irish Agitators on Trial: A Great Crowd at Sligo, But No Disturbances," *New York Times*, November 25, 1879; "England's Beef and Beer: Preparations for Christmas. The Fare of Olden and Modern Times—Dinners for Destitute Children—Famine Threatened in Ireland," *New York Times*, December 15, 1879; "The English Christmas: What Is There to Be Merry Over?," *New York Times*, December 20, 1879.

9. "English Trade and Labor"; "The Outlook in England."

10. "A Millennium of Macroeconomic Data."

11. "The Outlook in England."

12. "English Trade and Labor."

13. "Ceylon Peat Deposits and Their Possibilities," *Tropical Agriculturist*, October 1, 1903; Freya Barnes, "Turf War! Irish Pub's Brutal Reply to 'Virtue-Signalling' Tourist Centre After It Told Them Off for Using a Peat Fire," *Daily Mail*, September 16, 2024, https://dailymail.co.uk/news/article-13855183/irish-family-pub-turf-war-tourist-centre-virtue-signalling-troll-carbon-footprint.html.

14. Samuel W. Johnson, *Peat and Its Uses, as Fertilizer and Fuel* (Orange Judd & Company, 1866).

15. *Annual Report of the Local Government Board for Ireland, Being the Seventh*, 53.

16. *Annual Report of the Local Government Board for Ireland, Being the Eighth*, 58.

17. *Annual Report of the Local Government Board for Ireland, Being the Seventh*, 121, 124.

18. Dirk Jan van de Ven and Roger Fouquet, "Historical Energy Price Shocks and Their Changing Effects on the Economy," *Energy Economics* 62 (2017): 211, https://doi .org/10.1016/j.eneco.2016.12.009.

19. Van de Ven and Fouquet, 211; U.S. Energy Information Administration, *Estimated Primary Energy Consumption in the United States, Selected Years, 1635–1945*, Annual Energy Review 2011 (US Energy Information Administration, September 2012), https://eia.gov /totalenergy/data/annual/pdf/aer.pdf.

20. Van de Ven and Fouquet, 211; Broadberry et al., "Dating Business Cycles in the United Kingdom, 1700–2010," 10, 20; W. G. Hoskins, "Harvest Fluctuations and English Economic History, 1620–1759," *Agricultural History Review* 16, no. 1 (1968): 15–16.

21. T. S. Ashton, *An Economic History of England* (Taylor and Francis, 2013), 54.

22. William Derham, "I. The History of the Great Frost in the Last Winter 1703 and 1708/9," *Philosophical Transactions of the Royal Society of London* 26, no. 324 (1709): 469–71, https://doi.org/10.1098/rstl.1708.0073.

23. Broadberry et al., "Dating Business Cycles," A4.

24. Julian Hoppit, "Financial Crises in Eighteenth-Century England," *Economic History Review* 39, no. 1 (1986): 49, https://doi.org/10.2307/2596100; Broadberry et al., A5.

25. Broadberry et al., A15.

26. William Stout, *Autobiography of William Stout, of Lancaster, Wholesale and Retail Grocer and Ironmonger, A Member of the Society of Friends. A.D. 1665–1752*, ed. J. Harland (London, 1851), 135.

27. Stout, 135; Broadberry et al., "Dating Business Cycles," A15. Stout also noted that ice had "sealed up the Thames to shipping," with the UK economy accordingly suffering a "slump in textiles of all kinds."

28. Stout, 135.

29. Stout, 96–98.

30. Hoppit, "Financial Crises," 47–48.

31. "Agricultural Report," *Newry Magazine; or, Literary & Political Register for 1816*, 431.

32. Van de Ven and Fouquet, "Historical Energy Price Shocks," 204–5.

33. *Parliamentary Debates: Official Report* (His Majesty's Stationery Office, 1927), 616.

34. "Employment in the Coal Industry in the United Kingdom," Our World in Data, https://ourworldindata.org/grapher/employment-in-the-coal-industry-in-the-united -kingdom; "Population, 10,000 BCE to 2023," Our World in Data, https://ourworldindata .org/grapher/population?tab=chart&country=GBR.

35. Office for National Statistics, "Average Household Size (Persons) in England and Wales, 1911–2011," https://ons.gov.uk/generator?uri=/peoplepopulationandcommunity /birthsdeathsandmarriages/families/articles/householdsandhouseholdcompositionin englandandwales/2014-05-29/b5b5cf21&format=xls.

36. National Bureau of Economic Research, "Coal Production for Great Britain (M0133CGBM418NNBR)," Federal Reserve Bank of St. Louis, https://fred.stlouisfed.org/ series/M0133CGBM418NNBR.

37. Broadberry et al., "Dating Business Cycles," A55–56.

38. "A Millennium of Macroeconomic Data."

39. "British Drank Less in 1926 Than in 1925: 4 1/2 Per Cent. Reduction in Bill Is Attributed to Curtailed Incomes and High Taxes," *New York Times*, May 16, 1927.

40. Roy Jenkins, *Churchill: A Biography* (Farrar, Straus and Giroux, 2001), 409; Martin Gilbert and Randolph S. Churchill, *The Prophet of Truth: 1922–1939*, vol. 5, 1st American ed., (Houghton Mifflin, 1977).

41. Gilbert and Churchill.

42. National Bureau of Economic Research, "Coal Production for Great Britain."

43. "A Millennium of Macroeconomic Data."

44. Bank of England, "Unemployment Rate in the United Kingdom (AURUKM)," Federal Reserve Bank of St. Louis, https://fred.stlouisfed.org/series/AURUKM.

45. "New Haven Fears a Coal Famine," *New York Times*, September 14, 1900; "Danger of a Coal Famine: Mr. Pangburn Says That Warm Weather Prevents Distress," *New York Times*, October 3, 1900.

46. "Coal Strike's Funny Side," *New York Times*, September 23, 1900.

47. "Cutting Wood for Fuel: Long Island Farmers Prepare for Threatened Coal Famine," *New York Times*, September 24, 1900. By December, there were reports of actual "coal famine": "Coal Famine in Alabama: Mines Unable to Meet the Demand from Railroads and Industries," *New York Times*, December 20, 1900. By December there were also reports of a "timber famine": "The End of the Lumber Supply," *New York Times*, December 31, 1900.

48. "American Coal in France," *New York Times*, February 24, 1900; "Germany Suffers from Coal Famine," *New York Times*, February 8, 1900; "Coal Trade Revolution," *New York Times*, February 11, 1900; "Coal as an Arbiter of Industry and Trade," *New York Times*, March 25, 1900; "Coal in Demand Abroad," *New York Times*, February 17, 1900; "Great Austrian Mine Strike," *New York Times*, January 23, 1900; "Austrian Miners Strike," *New York Times*, March 4, 1900; "Idle Toilers in Germany. Lack of Fuel and Raw Material Deprives 1,000,000 of Work," *New York Times*, March 25, 1900; Frederick E. Saward, "Will This Country Become a Larger Exporter of Bituminous Coal," *New York Times*, April 1, 1900; "Causes of the Turn in the Stock Market," *New York Times*, March 24, 1900.

49. National Bureau of Economic Research, "Anthracite Coal Shipments for United States (M0117AUSM576NNBR)," Federal Reserve Bank of St. Louis, https://fred.stlouisfed.org/series/M0117AUSM576NNBR. During the strike, the price of coal spiked from $5.50 per ton to $6.75 per ton. See: Frank Julian Warne, "The Anthracite Coal Strike," *Annals of the American Academy of Political and Social Science* 17, January 1901: 15. Of 1900 in the United Kingdom, which experienced a mild recession in the same year, Thorpe reports "coal prices extremely high." See: Willard Thorpe, "The Annals of England," in *Business Annals* (National Bureau of Economic Research, 1926), 173.

50. Christina D. Romer, "Remeasuring Business Cycles," *Journal of Economic History* 54, no. 3 (1994): 592. The Burns and Mitchell recession chronology reports a recession beginning in July 1899 and continuing through December 1900, but this is inconsistent with available macroeconomic data; real GDP continued to expand throughout 1899, as did industrial production.

51. "Mitchell Predicts Victory. Judge Jackson of the United States Court Issues Injunction Against Strikers," *New York Times*, June 12, 1902; Craig Phelan, *Divided Loyalties: The Public and Private Life of Labor Leader John Mitchell*, SUNY Series in American Labor History (State University of New York Press, 1994), 166–67; Jonathan Grossman, "The Coal Strike of 1902—Turning Point in U.S. Policy," *Monthly Labor Review* 98, no. 10 (1975):

22; Robert H. Wiebe, "The Anthracite Strike of 1902: A Record of Confusion," *Mississippi Valley Historical Review* 48, no. 2 (1961): 238–39, 241, 243.

52. National Bureau of Economic Research, "Anthracite Coal Shipments."

53. "Restrict Soft Coal Supply," *New York Times*, June 23, 1902; Frederick E. Saward, "Soft Coal Expansion," *New York Times*, August 31, 1902.

54. "Hard-Coal Famine Faces Householders: Serious Problem Threatens Unless Strike Ends Soon. Dealers Declare That the Anthracite Supply Is Nearly Exhausted—Elevated Road Buying Up Fuel in Small Towns," *New York Times*, August 5, 1902; National Bureau of Economic Research, "Wholesale Price of Bituminous Coal, Georges Creek, F.O.B. New York Harbor for New York, NY (M04046US35620M294NNBR)," Federal Reserve Bank of St. Louis, https://fred.stlouisfed.org/series/M04046US35620M294NNBR; National Bureau of Economic Research, "Index of the General Price Level for United States (M04051USM324NNBR)," Federal Reserve Bank of St. Louis, https://fred.stlouisfed.org/series/M04051USM324NNBR.

55. Herbert Croly, *Marcus Alonzo Hanna: His Life and Work* (Macmillan Company, 1912), 399; Grossman, "The Coal Strike of 1902," 24–25.

56. "Storm Ties Up Coal Mines," *New York Times*, March 6, 1902; "Coal Shortage at Elizabeth, N.J.," *New York Times*, March 6, 1902.

57. "Anthracite Famine in New York," *New York Times*, May 18, 1902; "Fear a Famine in Baltimore," *New York Times*, May 18, 1902; "Coal Market Tight," *New York Times*, May 19, 1902; "Hard Coal Famine Near," *New York Times*, May 30, 1900.

58. "Feared a Water Famine," *New York Times*, May 20, 1902.

59. "Hard-Coal Famine Faces Householders," *New York Times*, August 5, 1902; "Coal Famine Widespread," *New York Times*, August 15, 1902; "Fuel Famine in Pittsburg," *New York Times*, August 20, 1902; "Anthracite Coal Famine," *New York Times*, September 20, 1902; "No Hard Coal in Chicago," *New York Times*, September 12, 1902; "Washington's Coal Famine," *New York Times*, September 22, 1902; "Washington's Coal Famine," *New York Times*, September 23, 1902; "Connecticut Coal Famine," *New York Times*, September 28, 1902; "Chicago Hard Coal Famine," *New York Times*, August 22, 1902.

60. "Coal Price in Washington," *New York Times*, September 27, 1902; "Oil Used Instead of Coal: One Result of the Anthracite Famine in Washington," *New York Times*, September 21, 1902.

61. "Horse Chestnuts as Fuel," *New York Times*, September 28, 1902.

62. "Greenwich's Coal Famine," *New York Times*, September 30, 1902; "Coal Famine Closes Steel Mill," *New York Times*, October 6, 1902.

63. "Worn-Out Tenpins for Fuel," *New York Times*, November 17, 1902.

64. National Bureau of Economic Research, "Wholesale Price of Bituminous Coal, Georges Creek,"; National Bureau of Economic Research, "Wholesale Price of Anthracite Coal, Chestnut; Tidewater, New York Harbor for New York, NY (M04G4AUS35620M288NNBR)," Federal Reserve Bank of St. Louis, https://fred.stlouisfed.org/series/M04G4AUS35620M288NNBR; National Bureau of Economic Research, "Index of the General Price Level."

65. "Virginia's Coal Famine," *New York Times*, October 11, 1902.

66. "Coal Famine Closes Steel Mill"; "Coal Famine in Northwest," *New York Times*, October 12, 1902; "Coal Famine Closes Plants," *New York Times*, January 11, 1903; "Coal Famine Embarrasses Flour Mills," *New York Times*, January 10, 1903; "Works Shut Down

in Iowa," *New York Times*, January 10, 1903; "Coal Famine Stays Business," *New York Times*, October 15, 1902; "Connecticut's Coal Famine," *New York Times*, December 14, 1902.

67. "Harvard Students Shiver," *New York Times*, December 10, 1902.

68. "Car Shortage Hampers Mines," *New York Times*, August 11, 1903; "The Coal Situation," *New York Times*, February 11, 1903; National Bureau of Economic Research, "Anthracite Coal Shipments."

69. "Many Kinds of Fuel Briquettes," *New York Times*, February 1, 1903; "To Avoid Coal Famines," *New York Times*, November 13, 1903.

70. Willard Thorpe, "The Annals of the United States of America," in *Business Annals* (National Bureau of Economic Research, 1926), 139.

71. Thorpe, 171, 178.

72. National Bureau of Economic Research, "Coal Production for Great Britain."

73. Florence Peterson, *Strikes in the United States 1880–1936* (US Government Printing Office, August 1937), 21, https://fraser.stlouisfed.org/files/docs/publications/bls/bls_0651_1938.pdf.

74. National Bureau of Economic Research, "Bituminous Coal Production for United States (M01118USM448NNBR)," Federal Reserve Bank of St. Louis, https://fred.stlouisfed.org/series/M01118USM448NNBR.

75. National Bureau of Economic Research, "Wholesale Price of Bituminous Coal, Mines for United States (M0490AUSM294NNBR)," Federal Reserve Bank of St. Louis, https://fred.stlouisfed.org/series/M0490AUSM294NNBR; US Bureau of Labor Statistics, "Consumer Price Index for All Urban Consumers: All Items in U.S. City Average (CPIAUCNS)," Federal Reserve Bank of St. Louis, https://fred.stlouisfed.org/series/CPIAUCNS; National Bureau of Economic Research, "Retail Price of Bituminous Coal for United States (M04047USM238NNBR)," Federal Reserve Bank of St. Louis, https://fred.stlouisfed.org/series/M04047USM238NNBR; "Higher Oil Prices Result of Mexican Situation," *New York Times*, January 20, 1920; "South American Oil Needed Badly Now: Operators Look to Colombia, Peru and Venezuela to Avert Shortage," *New York Times*, March 16, 1920; Philip S. Gillette, "American Capital in the Contest for Soviet Oil, 1920–23," *Soviet Studies* 24, no. 4 (1973): 477–90; Robert Shiller, "Narrative Economics," *American Economic Review* 107, no. 4 (2017): 985; Alan L. Olmstead and Paul Rhode, "Rationing Without Government: The West Coast Gas Famine of 1920," *American Economic Review* 75, no. 5 (1985): 1044; Christina D. Romer, "World War I and the Postwar Depression: A Reinterpretation Based on Alternative Estimates of GNP," *Journal of Monetary Economics* 22, no. 1 (1988): 91–115, https://doi.org/10.1016/0304-3932(88)90171-7; J. R. Vernon, "The 1920–21 Deflation: The Role of Aggregate Supply," *Economic Inquiry* 29, no. 3 (1991): 572–80, https://doi.org/10.1111/j.1465-7295.1991.tb00847.x. Soft or bituminous coal was approximately 85 percent of US coal production by weight, and coal of all types was approximately 75 percent of US primary energy consumption. However, soft coal was approximately half as energy efficient as hard coal. Postwar disruptions to Mexican and Soviet oil supply simultaneously contributed to a crude oil shortage; oil prices spiked over 50 percent from mid-1919 through 1920, with the real price rising to its highest level until the 1979 Iranian Revolution. Meanwhile in the spring and summer of 1920, an acute "gas famine" effectively "crippled the entire West Coast, shutting down businesses and threatening vital services." Consistent with the sector-specific nature of the 1919–20 shocks, later analysis would find

that the decline in aggregate demand during the recession was both less than earlier estimates implied, and concentrated in heavy manufacturing, especially iron and steel—that is, in highly energy-intensive and strike-impacted sectors.

76. Peterson, *Strikes*, 21, 24–25.

77. Christina D. Romer and David H. Romer, "Does Monetary Policy Matter? A New Test in the Spirit of Friedman and Schwartz," in *NBER Macroeconomics Annual 1989*, vol. 4, ed. Olivier Jean Blanchard and Stanley Fischer (MIT Press, 1989), 126.

78. Romer, "World War I and the Postwar Depression"; Vernon, "The 1920–21 Deflation."

79. *Estimated Primary Energy Consumption.*

80. James D. Hamilton, "Historical Causes of Postwar Oil Shocks and Recessions," *Energy Journal* 6, no. 1 (1985): 97–116; James D. Hamilton, "Historical Oil Shocks," in *Routledge Handbook of Major Events in Economic History*, ed. Randall E. Parker and Robert Whaples (Routledge, 2013), 239–65.

81. Hamilton, "Historical Oil Shocks"; Hamilton, "Historical Causes," 110.

82. Takatoshi Ito and Andrew K. Rose, introduction to *Commodity Prices and Markets*, vol. 20, ed. Takatoshi Ito and Andrew K. Rose, National Bureau of Economic Research East Asia Seminar on Economics (University of Chicago Press, 2011), 2.

83. Federal Reserve Bank of St. Louis, "Spot Crude Oil Price: West Texas Intermediate (WTI) (WTISPLC)," Federal Reserve Bank of St. Louis, https://fred.stlouisfed.org/series /WTISPLC; Hamilton, "Historical Causes," 110.

84. *New York Times*, June 8, 1973, quoted in Hamilton, "Historical Oil Shocks."

85. Hamilton, "Historical Causes," 110.

86. Hamilton, "Historical Oil Shocks."

87. *Extension of Remarks* (Congressional Record, March 11, 1975); US Energy Information Administration, "U.S. Primary Energy Consumption by Major Sources, 1950–2022, Table 1.3," *Monthly Energy Review*, April 2023.

88. John A. Schnittker, "The 1972–73 Food Price Spiral," *Brookings Papers on Economic Activity*, no. 2 (1973): 498–507.

89. Hamilton, "Historical Oil Shocks."

90. H. E. III Frech and W. C. Lee, "The Welfare Cost of Rationing-by-Queuing Across Markets: Theory and Estimates from the U.S. Gasoline Crises," *Quarterly Journal of Economics* 102 (1987): 97–108, cited in Hamilton.

91. Quoted in Hamilton.

92. Hamilton.

93. Federal Reserve Bank of St. Louis, "Spot Crude Oil Price"; US Bureau of Labor Statistics, "Consumer Price Index for All Urban Consumers: All Items in U.S. City Average (CPIAUCSL)," Federal Reserve Bank of St. Louis, https://fred.stlouisfed.org/series /CPIAUCSL.

94. US Bureau of Labor Statistics, "Average Price: Gasoline, Leaded Regular (Cost per Gallon/3.8 Liters) in U.S. City Average (APU000074712)," Federal Reserve Bank of St. Louis, https://fred.stlouisfed.org/series/APU000074712; US Bureau of Labor Statistics, "Consumer Price Index for All Urban Consumers: All Items in U.S. City Average (CPIAUCSL)."

95. W. J. Usery Jr. and Julius Shiskin, *Analysis of Work Stoppages, 1974* (Bureau of Labor Statistics, 1976), 8.

96. Usery and Shiskin, 8; Ray Marshall and Julius Shiskin, *Analysis of Work Stoppages, 1975* (Bureau of Labor Statistics, 1977), 14.

97. Roger Fouquet, "A Historical Energy Data Set for the UK" (National Infrastructure Commission's collection of historical energy statistics, March 26, 2022); Energy Institute—Statistical Review of World Energy, "Energy Consumption by Source, United Kingdom," Our World in Data, 2024, https://ourworldindata.org/energy/country/united-kingdom#what-sources-does-the-country-get-its-energy-from.

98. Broadberry et al., "Dating Business Cycles," A60.

99. Hamilton, "Historical Oil Shocks."

100. John D. Turner, *Banking in Crisis: The Rise and Fall of British Banking Stability, 1800 to the Present*, Cambridge Studies in Economic History (Cambridge University Press, 2014), 88, 92.

101. Turner, 92; Margaret Reid, *Secondary Banking Crisis, 1973–75: Its Causes And Course* (Palgrave Macmillan, 1982), 3, 10. Turner reports the meetings as having endured for nineteen hours, while Reid reports seventeen. However, Reid also reports the meetings as having extended from 9:00 a.m. on Wednesday, December 19, until 3:00 a.m. the following morning, implying eighteen hours.

102. Reid, 11.

103. Turner, *Banking in Crisis*, 92–93.

104. Hamilton, "Historical Causes," 111.

105. Federal Reserve Bank of St. Louis, "Spot Crude Oil Price"; US Bureau of Labor Statistics, "Consumer Price Index for All Urban Consumers: All Items"; Hamilton, 111; "Oil Production Measured in Terawatt-Hours," Our World in Data, https://ourworldindata.org/grapher/oil-production-by-country?country=SAU~IRQ~USA~IRN~OWID_WRL.

106. "Oil Production Measured"; Hamilton, 111.

107. Federal Reserve Bank of St. Louis, "Spot Crude Oil Price"; US Bureau of Labor Statistics, "Consumer Price Index for All Urban Consumers: All Items"; US Bureau of Labor Statistics, "Average Price: Gasoline, Unleaded Regular (Cost per Gallon/3.785 Liters) in U.S. City Average (APU000074714)," Federal Reserve Bank of St. Louis, https://fred.stlouisfed.org/series/APU000074714; US Bureau of Labor Statistics, "Average Price: Gasoline, Leaded Regular (Cost per Gallon/3.8 Liters)."

108. Quoted in Hamilton, "Historical Oil Shocks."

109. Hamilton.

110. Hamilton.

111. US Energy Information Administration, "Henry Hub Natural Gas Spot Price (MHHNGSP)," Federal Reserve Bank of St. Louis, https://fred.stlouisfed.org/series/MHHNGSP; US Bureau of Labor Statistics, "Consumer Price Index for All Urban Consumers: All Items."

112. "Oil Production Measured."

113. US Bureau of Labor Statistics, "Average Price: Gasoline, Unleaded Regular (Cost per Gallon/3.785 Liters)"; US Bureau of Labor Statistics, "Consumer Price Index for All Urban Consumers: All Items."

114. Census Bureau, "Total Number of Households, Break-Adjusted (Thous) [POPHMJ@USECON]," Haver Analytics; Bureau of Economic Analysis, "PCE: Chain Price Index (SA, 2017 = 100) [JCBM@USECON]," Haver Analytics; Bureau of

Economic Analysis, "Personal Consumption Expenditures: Energy Goods and Services (DNRGRC1M027SBEA)," Federal Reserve Bank of St. Louis, https://fred.stlouisfed.org /series/DNRGRC1M027SBEA.

115. Census Bureau, "Total Number of Households"; Bureau of Economic Analysis, "PCE: Chain Price Index"; Bureau of Economic Analysis, "Mortgage Interest Paid: Owner/ Tenant-Occupied Nonfarm Housing (SAAR, Mil$) [FMOROT@USECON]," Haver Analytics.

116. Lauren Etter, "Lofty Prices for Fertilizer Put Farmers in a Squeeze," *Wall Street Journal*, May 27, 2008.

117. US Bureau of Labor Statistics, "Producer Price Index by Industry: Nitrogenous Fertilizer Manufacturing (PCU325311325311)," Federal Reserve Bank of St. Louis, https:// fred.stlouisfed.org/series/PCU325311325311. Fertilizer inflation was also a factor in the context of high energy prices in 1973–75; see: Victor K. McElheny, "Rising World Fertilizer Scarcity Threatens Famine for Millions: Twice as Large Yields Fertilizer Shortage Threatens a Famine Wide-Ranging Impact Dependence on Fertilizer Cut by 10 Million Tons Several Plants Planned Sulphur a Key to Phosphate Rise in Nutrient Use," *New York Times*, September 1, 1974.

118. Wen-yuan Huang, *Impact of Rising Natural Gas Prices on U.S. Ammonia Supply* (United States Department of Agriculture, August 2007).

119. US Bureau of Labor Statistics, "Consumer Price Index for All Urban Consumers: Food in U.S. City Average (CPIUFDNS)," Federal Reserve Bank of St. Louis, https://fred .stlouisfed.org/series/CPIUFDNS.

120. Anne Trafton, "Amid Food Price Spike, Nobel Laureate Eyes Fertilizer MIT Chemist Schrock Seeks to Streamline Production," *MIT News On Campus and Around the World* (blog), August 13, 2008, https://news.mit.edu/2008/fertilizer-0813.

121. Chakrabortty, "Secret Report: Biofuel Caused Food Crisis; Internal World Bank Study Delivers Blow to Plant Energy Drive," *The Guardian*, July 3, 2008; *Reflections on the Global Food Crisis: How Did It Happen? How Has It Hurt? And How Can We Prevent the Next One?* (International Food Policy Research Institute, 2010), https://doi.org/10.2499/97 80896291782RM165.

122. *Reflections on the Global Food Crisis*, xiii.

123. Chakrabortty, "Secret Report."

124. Chakrabortty; George W. Bush, "Press Conference by the President," press conference, Rose Garden, White House, April 29, 2008, https://georgewbush-whitehouse. archives.gov/news/releases/2008/04/20080429-1.html. Curiously, a journalist had confronted President Bush on the role of biofuels in the ongoing food inflation crisis during a press conference in the White House Rose Garden, noting that "the World Bank says about 85 percent of the increase in corn price since 2002 is due to . . . increased demand for biofuels." With both parties evidently confused, Bush responded that he "thought it was 85 percent of the world's food prices are caused by the weather, increased demand and energy prices . . . and that 15 percent has been caused by ethanol."

125. Kelsi Bracmort, *Renewable Fuel Standard (RFS): Overview and Issues* (Congressional Research Service, November 22, 2013), 1.

126. Congressional Budget Office, *Using Biofuel Tax Credits to Achieve Energy and Environmental Policy Goals*, July 2010, 2; Bracmort, 20.

127. MTBE itself had earlier replaced toxic tetraethyllead (lead) in gas.

128. Andrew Martin, "Food Report Criticizes Biofuel Policies," *New York Times*, May 30, 2008.

129. James D. Hamilton, "Causes and Consequences of the Oil Shock of 2007–08," *Brookings Papers on Economic Activity*, Spring 2009, 215–61; James D. Hamilton, "Oil Prices, Exhaustible Resources, and Economic Growth," in *Handbook of Energy and Climate Change*, ed. Roger Fouquet (Edward Elgar, 2013), 29–57.

130. Hamilton, "Oil Prices"; Valerie A. Ramey and Daniel J. Vine, "Oil, Automobiles, and the U.S. Economy: How Much Have Things Really Changed?," *NBER Macroeconomics Annual* 25, no. 1 (2011): 333–68, https://doi.org/10.1086/657541; Hamilton, "Causes and Consequences," 245. Illustrative of the energy-specific nature of the decline, spending on larger domestically manufactured vehicles with lower average fuel economy plummeted in 2008, sales of smaller, imported cars increased.

131. Hamilton, "Causes and Consequences," 245.

132. Christiane Baumeister and Gert Peersman, "Time-Varying Effects of Oil Supply Shocks on the US Economy," *American Economic Journal: Macroeconomics* 5, no. 4 (2013): 1–28, https://doi.org/10.1257/mac.5.4.1.

133. See for example: Mary G. Finn, "Perfect Competition and the Effects of Energy Price Increases on Economic Activity," *Journal of Money, Credit and Banking* 32, no. 3 (2000): 400, https://doi.org/10.2307/2601172; Julio J. Rotemberg and Michael Woodford, "Imperfect Competition and the Effects of Energy Price Increases on Economic Activity," *Journal of Money, Credit and Banking* 28, no. 4 (1996): 549, https://doi.org/10.2307/2078071; James D. Hamilton and Ana Maria Herrera, "Comment: Oil Shocks and Aggregate Macroeconomic Behavior: The Role of Monetary Policy," *Journal of Money, Credit and Banking* 36, no. 2 (2004): 265–86; James D. Hamilton, "Oil and the Macroeconomy Since World War II," *Journal of Political Economy* 91, no. 2 (1983): 228–48, https://doi.org/10.1086/261140; Hamilton, "Historical Causes"; Hamilton, "Historical Oil Shocks"; James D. Hamilton, "Oil and the Macroeconomy," in *The New Palgrave Dictionary of Economics* (Palgrave Macmillan UK, 2008), 1–7, https://doi.org/10.1057/978-1-349-95121-5_2119-1; Kristie M. Engemann, Kevin L. Kliesen, and Michael T. Owyang, "Do Oil Shocks Drive Business Cycles? Some U.S. and International Evidence," *Macroeconomic Dynamics* 15, no. S3 (2011): 498–517, https://doi.org/10.1017/S1365100511000216.

134. Lutz Kilian, "The Economic Effects of Energy Price Shocks," *Journal of Economic Literature* 46, no. 4 (2008): 881.

135. James A. Wilcox, "Why Real Interest Rates Were So Low in the 1970s," *American Economic Review* 73, no. 1 (1983): 44–53. Later models formalized the possibility that the capital stock may be able to adjust only gradually to changes in the cost of energy inputs. See: Andrew Atkeson and Patrick J. Kehoe, "Models of Energy Use: Putty-Putty Versus Putty-Clay," *American Economic Review* 89, no. 4 (1999): 1028–43.

136. Steven J. Davis and John Haltiwanger, "Sectoral Job Creation and Destruction Responses to Oil Price Changes," *Journal of Monetary Economics* 48, no. 3 (2001): 465–512, https://doi.org/10.1016/S0304-3932(01)00086-1. They further found an asymmetrical employment response to oil price spikes versus oil price declines; manufacturing employment declines more sharply in response to energy price increases than it rises in response to energy price decreases, consistent with firms facing higher costs to adjusting to higher energy prices than to lower energy prices.

137. Finn, "Perfect Competition."

138. Stout, *Autobiography*, 135.

139. Wataru Miyamoto, Thuy Lan Nguyen, and Dmitriy Sergeyev, "How Oil Shocks Propagate: Evidence on the Monetary Policy Channel," Working Paper Series 2024-07 (Federal Reserve Bank of San Francisco, December 10, 2023), https://doi.org/10.24148/wp2024-07.

140. W. Douglas Mcmillin and Randall E. Parker, "An Empirical Analysis of Oil Price Shocks in the Interwar Period," *Economic Inquiry* 32, no. 3 (1994): 486–97, https://doi.org/10.1111/j.1465-7295.1994.tb01345.x.

141. Joseph H. Davis, Christopher Hanes, and Paul Rhode, "Harvests and Business Cycles in Nineteenth-Century America," *Quarterly Journal of Economics* 124, no. 4 (2009): 1675–727.

142. John B. Long Jr. and Charles I. Plosser, "Real Business Cycles," *American Economic Review* 91, no. 1 (1983): 39–69; Daron Acemoglu et al., "The Network Origins of Aggregate Fluctuations," *Econometrica* 80, no. 5 (2012): 1977–2016, https://doi.org/10.3982/ECTA9623; Daron Acemoglu, Asuman Ozdaglar, and Alireza Tahbaz-Salehi, "Microeconomic Origins of Macroeconomic Tail Risks," *American Economic Review* 107, no. 1 (2017): 54–108, https://doi.org/10.1257/aer.20151086.

143. Enghin Atalay, "How Important Are Sectoral Shocks?," *American Economic Journal: Macroeconomics* 9, no. 4 (2017): 254, https://doi.org/10.1257/mac.20160353; Enghin Atalay, Thorsten Drautzburg, and Zhenting Wang, "Accounting for the Sources of Macroeconomic Tail Risks," *Economics Letters* 165 (2018): 65–69, https://doi.org/10.1016/j.econlet.2018.01.032.

144. Atalay, 254.

145. Atalay, 254–55.

146. Atalay, 276; Atalay, Drautzburg, and Wang, "Accounting for the Sources"; Andrew T. Foerster, Pierre-Daniel G. Sarte, and Mark W. Watson, "Sectoral Versus Aggregate Shocks: A Structural Factor Analysis of Industrial Production," *Journal of Political Economy* 119, no. 1 (2011): 1–38, https://doi.org/10.1086/659311; David Rezza Baqaee and Emmanuel Farhi, "The Macroeconomic Impact of Microeconomic Shocks: Beyond Hulten's Theorem," *Econometrica* 87, no. 4 (2019): 1155–203, https://doi.org/10.3982/ECTA15202; Acemoglu, Ozdaglar, and Tahbaz-Salehi, "Microeconomic Origins"; Acemoglu et al., "The Network Origins."

Chapter 6: A Great Deal of Ruin

1. "Wet Weather Aids Crops. Winter Wheat Condition Averages 89%—Spring Seeding Under Way," *New York Times*, April 5, 1931.

2. Jeffrey A. Lockwood, *Locust: The Devastating Rise and Mysterious Disappearance of the Insect That Shaped the American Frontier* (Basic Books, 2009); History.com Editors, "South Dakota Governor Begs for Federal Assistance over Grasshopper Plague," *This Day in History* (blog), November 13, 2009, https://history.com/this-day-in-history/grasshoppers-bring-ruin-to-midwest.

3. Associated Press, "Grasshoppers Clean Fields in 3 States: Iowa, Nebraska and South Dakota Farmers Fight and Pray Against Plague," *New York Times*, July 28, 1931.

4. History.com Editors, "South Dakota Governor."

5. Associated Press, "Grasshoppers Clean Fields"; "Middle West's Grasshopper Reminiscences Vie with Tallest Fish Stories Ever Told," *New York Times*, August 2, 1931; W. H.

Larrimer, "Grasshoppers Ravage Vast Farm Areas: Their Destructive Onslaught in the West Is Said to Be the Worst Since 1876," *New York Times*, August 9, 1931.

6. "Grasshopper War Ordered By Hoover," *New York Times*, August 1, 1931.

7. David E. Hamilton, "Herbert Hoover and the Great Drought of 1930," *Journal of American History* 68, no. 4 (1982): 850–51, 851n.

8. "Grasshopper Peril Added to a Drought," *New York Times*, July 30, 1931; "Grasshopper War Ordered"; "Enlist States' Aid on Grasshoppers," *New York Times*, August 2, 1931; Larrimer, "Grasshoppers Ravage."

9. "Breeze Cools City but Heat Still Grips West; Middle States Hardest Hit; Death Toll Rises," *New York Times*, June 30, 1931; Chuck Lyons, "1874: The Year of the Locust," HistoryNet, February 5, 2012, https://historynet.com/1874-the-year-of-the-locust/; Tammy Partsch, *It Happened in Nebraska: Stories of Events and People That Shaped Cornhusker State History*, 2nd ed., It Happened in . . . Series (Globe Pequot, 2019), 56.

10. Alan Boyle, "Locust Swarm of Biblical Proportions Strikes Egypt, Israel Before Passover," NBC News, March 4, 2013, https://nbcnews.com/science/cosmic-log/locust-swarm-biblical-proportions-strikes-egypt-israel-passover-flna1c8687357; Rachel Nuwer, "Swarm," *New York Times*, April 9, 2013.

11. History.com Editors, "South Dakota Governor Begs."

12. *Commercial West: The Weekly News Magazine of Finance and Industry*, August 1, 1931, 7, 16, https://fraser.stlouisfed.org/title/commercial-west-7196/august-1-1931-664616; *Commercial West: The Weekly News Magazine of Finance and Industry*, August 8, 1931, 6, 9, 18, 28, 32, https://fraser.stlouisfed.org/title/commercial-west-7196/august-8-1931-664617; *Commercial West: The Weekly News Magazine of Finance and Industry*, September 19, 1931, 10, https://fraser.stlouisfed.org/title/commercial-west-7196/september-19-1931-664623; *Commercial West: The Weekly News Magazine of Finance and Industry*, December 26, 1931, 11, https://fraser.stlouisfed.org/title/commercial-west-7196/december-26-1931-664637; *Monthly Review of Agricultural, Industrial, Trade and Financial Conditions in the Eighth Federal Reserve District*, August 31, 1931, https://fraser.stlouisfed.org/title/review-federal-reserve-bank-st-louis-820/august-31-1931-23975; *Monthly Review of Agricultural, Industrial, Trade and Financial Conditions in the Eighth Federal Reserve District*, October 30, 1931, https://fraser.stlouisfed.org/title/review-federal-reserve-bank-st-louis-820/october-30-1931-23976; *Commercial & Financial Chronicle*, August 15, 1931, 1033, 1036–38, 1050, https://fraser.stlouisfed.org/title/commercial-financial-chronicle-1339/august-15-1931-518523.

13. Federal Reserve Board, *Federal Reserve Bulletin* (US Government Printing Office, January 1932), https://fraser.stlouisfed.org/files/docs/publications/FRB/1930s/frb_011932.pdf?utm_source=direct_download; Federal Reserve Board, *Federal Reserve Bulletin* (US Government Printing Office, July 1931), https://fraser.stlouisfed.org/files/docs/publications/FRB/1930s/frb_011932.pdf?utm_source=direct_download.

14. Though Arkansas appears to have escaped the locust scourge, the state was devastated by the droughts of 1930–31, with failed banks explicitly attributing their suspension to "the failure of crops in the long dry spell." See: "Banks Fail in Drought," *New York Times*, August 9, 1930; "Arkansas' Drought Its Worst Disaster," *New York Times*, January 30, 1931; "Where Drought Sears Land and People," *New York Times*, February 15, 1931.

15. B. R. Stauber, *The Farm Real Estate Situation, 1931–32* (United States Department of Agriculture, January 1933), 3, 22, 41–42.

16. B. R. Stauber, *The Farm Real Estate Situation, 1932–33* (United States Department of Agriculture, December 1933), 26.

17. Stauber, *The Farm Real Estate Situation, 1931–32*, 10.

18. Stauber, *The Farm Real Estate Situation, 1932–33*, 36–37. See also: Lawrence A. Jones and David Durand, *Mortgage Lending Experience in Agriculture*, National Bureau of Research Financial Research Program: Studies in Agricultural Finance (Princeton University Press, 1954).

19. Raghuram Rajan and Rodney Ramcharan, "The Anatomy of a Credit Crisis: The Boom and Bust in Farm Land Prices in the United States in the 1920s," *American Economic Review* 105, no. 4 (2015): 1439–77, https://doi.org/10.1257/aer.20120525; Matthew Jaremski and David C. Wheelock, "Banking on the Boom, Tripped by the Bust: Banks and the World War I Agricultural Price Shock," *Journal of Money, Credit and Banking* 52, no. 7 (2020): 1719–54, https://doi.org/10.1111/jmcb.12725; Barry Eichengreen and Kris Mitchener, "The Great Depression as a Credit Boom Gone Wrong," BIS Working Papers (Bank of International Settlements, September 5, 2003).

20. Incidentally, four years after Roosevelt's first inaugural address, a locust plague again descended on the American West and Midwest, coinciding almost precisely with the onset of recession. On this occasion, however, the United States was better prepared for what was ultimately a less severe infestation than that of 1931, and it is unlikely that it was a primary contributor to the US-specific recession of 1937–38. With assistance from the US Bureau of Entomology and the National Guard, states that had endured the 1931 locust plague now effectively waged "war" on the hoppers, employing poisoned bran, poison dust, and even flamethrowers and explosives. Roland M. Jones, "Grasshopper Hordes in Corn Belt Will Get a Diet of Poisoned Bran. Federal Funds to Help," *New York Times*, April 4, 1937; Robert E. Miller, "Crickets in Nine States Will Be Treated to Sprays of Deadly Dust. Plague of 1848 Recalled," *New York Times*, April 4, 1937; "Grasshopper War Begins," *New York Times*, May 9, 1937; "Last Ditch Fight on in Grasshopper War," *New York Times*, July 8, 1937; Adam Morgan, "In 1937, Colorado Guard Used Flamethrowers and Explosives against Plague of Locusts," National Guard, June 9, 2014, https://nationalguard.mil/news/article-view/article/575751/in-1937-colorado-guard-used-flamethrowers-and-explosives-against-plague-of-locu/.

21. *The Correspondence of the Right Honourable Sir John Sinclair, Bart.*, vol. 1 (London, 1831), 390–91; Adam Smith, *The Glasgow Edition of the Works and Correspondence of Adam Smith. 1: An Inquiry into the Nature and Causes of the Wealth of Nations*, ed. R. H. Campbell (Liberty Fund, 2009), 262n.

22. "Historical U.S. Federal Individual Income Tax Rates & Brackets, 1862–2021," Tax Foundation, August 24, 2021, https://taxfoundation.org/data/all/federal/historical-income-tax-rates-brackets/.

23. "Historical U.S. Federal Corporate Income Tax Rates & Brackets, 1909–2020," Tax Foundation, August 24, 2021, https://taxfoundation.org/data/all/federal/historical-corporate-tax-rates-brackets/; Samuel Williamson, "Seven Ways to Compute the Relative Value of a U.S. Dollar Amount, 1790 to Present," Measuring Worth, 2025, https://measuringworth.com/calculators/uscompare/. I compute the 2024 value as the relative income value of a commodity, and alternatively as relative income or wealth.

24. William D. Lastrapes and George Selgin, "The Check Tax: Fiscal Folly and the Great Monetary Contraction," *Journal of Economic History* 57, no. 4 (1997): 859–78.

25. Elmus Wicker, "The Banking Crisis of 1930," in *The Banking Panics of the Great Depression*, Studies in Macroeconomic History (Cambridge University Press, 1996), 24–61.

26. Elmus Wicker, "Banking Crises of the Great Depression: A Reassessment," in *The Banking Panics of the Great Depression*, Studies in Macroeconomic History (Cambridge University Press, 1996), 152.

27. Elmus Wicker, "The Two Banking Crises of 1931," in *The Banking Panics of the Great Depression*, Studies in Macroeconomic History (Cambridge University Press, 1996), 152; Charles W. Calomiris and Joseph R. Mason, "Fundamentals, Panics, and Bank Distress During the Depression," *American Economic Review* 93, no. 5 (2003): 1617.

28. Wicker, "The Banking Crisis of 1930"; Wicker, "Banking Crises of the Great Depression."

29. Wicker, "The Two Banking Crises of 1931," 68.

30. Federal Reserve Board, *Federal Reserve Bulletin*, January 1932, 73; Federal Reserve Board, *Federal Reserve Bulletin*, July 1931, 414; Wicker, "Banking Crises of the Great Depression," 152–53; Wicker, "The Two Banking Crises of 1931," 69.

31. Wicker, "Banking Crises of the Great Depression," 161; Wicker, "The Two Banking Crises of 1931," 72.

32. Wicker, "The Two Banking Crises of 1931."

33. Wicker, 62; Wicker, "Banking Crises of the Great Depression," 161; Hugh Rockoff, "Deflation, Silent Runs, and Bank Holidays, in the Great Contraction," NBER Working Paper Series (National Bureau of Economic Research, February 2003), 21.

34. Wicker, "The Two Banking Crises of 1931," 62, 65; Wicker, "Banking Crises of the Great Depression," 161.

35. Stauber, *The Farm Real Estate Situation, 1932–33*, 10, 35.

36. E. A. Goldenweiser et al., *Bank Suspensions in the United States, 1892–1931* (Federal Reserve System Committee on Branch, Group, and Chain Banking, 1932); Jones and Durand, *Mortgage Lending Experience in Agriculture*; Calomiris and Mason, "Fundamentals, Panics"; David C. Wheelock and Paul W. Wilson, "Why Do Banks Disappear? The Determinants of U.S. Bank Failures and Acquisitions," *Review of Economics and Statistics* 82, no. 1 (2000): 127–38; Tyler Goodspeed, "Liability Insurance, Extended Liability, Branching, and Financial Stability," *Cato Journal* 37, no. 2 (2017): 329–60; Sergio Correia, Stephan Luck, and Emil Verner, *Failing Banks*, Staff Reports No. 1117 (Federal Reserve Bank of New York), https://doi.org/10.59576/sr.1117; Eugene N. White, "A Reinterpretation of the Banking Crisis of 1930," *Journal of Economic History* 44, no. 1 (1984): 119–38; Clifford Thies and Daniel Gerlowski, "Bank Capital and Bank Failure, 1921–1932: Testing the White Hypothesis," *Journal of Economic History* 53, no. 4 (1993): 908–14.

37. Calomiris and Mason, 1615; Correia, Luck, and Verner.

38. Kris James Mitchener and Gary Richardson, "Network Contagion and Interbank Amplification during the Great Depression," *Journal of Political Economy* 127, no. 2 (2019): 465–507, https://doi.org/10.1086/701034; Sanjiv R. Das, Kris James Mitchener, and Angela Vossmeyer, "Bank Regulation, Network Topology, and Systemic Risk: Evidence from the Great Depression," *Journal of Money, Credit and Banking* 54, no. 5 (2022): 1261–312, https://doi.org/10.1111/jmcb.12871; Haelim Anderson, Mark Paddrik, and Jessie Jiaxu Wang, "Bank Networks and Systemic Risk: Evidence from the National Banking Acts," *American Economic Review* 109, no. 9 (2019): 3125–61.

39. Mitchener and Richardson; Das, Mitchener, and Vossmeyer.

40. National Bureau of Economic Research, "Index of Total Crop Production for United States (A0105BUSA337NNBR)," Federal Reserve Bank of St. Louis, https://fred.stlouisfed.org/series/A0105BUSA337NNBR.

41. The only larger cumulative contraction in the money supply in US history was that following the Panic of 1837. Conventionally blamed on an alleged boom during the two-year recovery from 1835–36, or President Andrew Jackson's decision to allow the Second Bank of the United States' charter to expire in January 1836, or the Bank of England raising interest rates, or Jackson's July 1836 order that the federal government accept only gold and silver for the sale of public lands, the severe recession of 1837–38 likely had a more mundane cause. For while Jackson's Specie Circular may have "pricked the bubble" of western land speculation, bringing an end to the "'boom' of the West," an even blunter shock to the US economy during 1836 and 1837 was the widespread destruction of crops in Pennsylvania, Maryland, Virginia, and Delaware on account of the Hessian fly. Even Tennessee was ravaged by the native Asian species, alleged to have arrived in North America via the straw bedding of Hessian troops during the American Revolution. In the ensuing recession, more than six hundred banks failed, while starving mobs in New York and Philadelphia broke into warehouses in search of flour. John Bach McMaster, *A History of the People of the United States: From the Revolution to the Civil War*, vol. 6 (D. Appleton and Company, 1923), 390; David Saville Muzzey, *An American History* (Ginn and Company, 1911), 288; H. W. Somsen and K. L. Oppenlander, *Hessian Fly Biotype Distribution, Resistant Wheat Varieties and Control Practices In Hard Red Winter Wheat* (Agricultural Research Service, United States Department of Agriculture, December 1975), 1.

42. Stauber, *The Farm Real Estate Situation, 1932–33*, 21–22; Michael D. Bordo, "The Effects of Monetary Change on Relative Commodity Prices and the Role of Long-Term Contracts," *Journal of Political Economy* 88, no. 6 (1980): 1088–109.

43. Elmus Wicker, "The Banking Panic of 1933," in *The Banking Panics of the Great Depression*, Studies in Macroeconomic History (Cambridge University Press, 1996), 108.

44. Robert Jabaily, "Bank Holiday of 1933," *Federal Reserve History* (blog), November 22, 2013, https://federalreservehistory.org/essays/bank-holiday-of-1933.

45. Peter Temin and Barrie A. Wigmore, "The End of One Big Deflation," *Explorations in Economic History* 27, no. 4 (1990): 483–502, https://doi.org/10.1016/0014-4983(90)90026-U; Gauti B. Eggertsson, "Great Expectations and the End of the Depression," *American Economic Review* 98, no. 4 (2008): 1476–516, https://doi.org/10.1257/aer.98.4.1476; Andrew J. Jalil and Gisela Rua, "Inflation Expectations and Recovery in Spring 1933," *Explorations in Economic History* 62 (2016): 26–50, https://doi.org/10.1016/j.eeh.2016.07.001; Joshua K. Hausman, Paul W. Rhode, and Johannes F. Wieland, "Recovery from the Great Depression: The Farm Channel in Spring 1933," *American Economic Review* 109, no. 2 (2019): 427–72, https://doi.org/10.1257/aer.20170237; Christina D. Romer, "It Takes a Regime Shift: Recent Developments in Japanese Monetary Policy Through the Lens of the Great Depression," *NBER Macroeconomics Annual* 28, no. 1 (2014): 383–400.

46. Irving Fisher, "The Debt-Deflation Theory of Great Depressions," *Econometrica* 1, no. 4 (1933): 337–57.

47. Sylvanus Urban, "Historical Chronicle, January 1763," *The Gentleman's Magazine, and Historical Chronical*, 1763, 42; Stephen Broadberry et al., "Dating Business Cycles in the United Kingdom, 1700–2010," *Economic History Review*, January 27, 2023, A21, https://doi.org/10.1111/ehr.13238.

48. Urban, 42.

49. Urban, 613; Hubert H. Lamb, *Climate, History and the Modern World* (Methuen, 1982), 235.

50. Stephen Quinn and William Roberds, "Responding to a Shadow Banking Crisis: The Lessons of 1763," *Journal of Money, Credit and Banking* 47, no. 6 (2015): 1161–62; W. O. Henderson, "The Berlin Commercial Crisis of 1763," *Economic History Review* 15, no. 1 (1962): 96.

51. Quinn and Roberds, 1161–62; Henderson, 96; Tyler Beck Goodspeed, *Legislating Instability: Adam Smith, Free Banking, and the Financial Crisis of 1772* (Harvard University Press, 2016), 88; Isabel Schnabel and Hyun Song Shin, "Liquidity and Contagion: The Crisis of 1763," *Journal of the European Economic Association* 2, no. 6 (2004): 941–42.

52. Goodspeed, 88.

53. "Wheat Scarcities in Europe Bend Nations' Political Fate," *New York Times*, March 18, 1946; "Rationing of Bread Decreed in Britain," *New York Times*, June 28, 1946.

54. "English Deluge," *New York Times*, September 15, 1946; "Britain's Harvest Worst in Memory; Rains Go On," *New York Times*, September 8, 1946.

55. "Severe Winters," Met Office, https://metoffice.gov.uk/weather/learn-about/weather/case-studies/severe-winters.

56. Paul Simons, "Weather Disasters Explained," *The Times*, October 1, 2008.

57. "Great Britain: Panorama by Candlelight," *Time*, February 24, 1947, 32; Simons.

58. John Bew, *Clement Attlee: The Man Who Made Modern Britain* (Oxford University Press, 2017), 452; Simons; "Great Britain," 32.

59. "Great Britain," 32; Simons.

60. "Great Britain," 32.

61. "Great Britain," 32; Simons, "Weather Disasters Explained."

62. Simons.

63. *1947 U.K. River Floods: 60-Year Retrospective*, RMS Special Report (Risk Management Solutions, 2007).

64. "Miners Quit Pits as Strike Begins in Soft Coal Field," *New York Times*, April 1, 1927.

65. "Limit Coal Strike to Central Field," *New York Times*, February 24, 1927; "Miners Quit Pits"; "Bituminous Miners Consider Demands," *New York Times*, January 9, 1927; National Bureau of Economic Research, "Bituminous Coal Production for United States (M01118USM448NNBR)," Federal Reserve Bank of St. Louis, https://fred.stlouisfed.org/series/M01118USM448NNBR; "Soft Coal Supply Lower," *New York Times*, June 5, 1927; "Soft Coal Output in June," *New York Times*, July 5, 1927.

66. "Coal Strike Crisis Looms in Illinois," *New York Times*, July 10, 1927; "Bituminous Coal Dearer," *New York Times*, August 20, 1927; David J. McDonald and Edward A. Lynch, *Coal and Unionism: A History of the American Coal Miners' Unions* (Cornelius Printing Company, 1939), 177.

67. "Oil Now Competitor of Anthracite Coal," *New York Times*, August 29, 1927.

68. Christina D. Romer, "Remeasuring Business Cycles," *Journal of Economic History* 54, no. 3 (1994): 592; US Department of Labor Bureau of Labor Statistics, "Major Stoppages in the Bituminous Coal Mining Industry" (Department of Labor Bureau of Labor Statistics, 1949); National Bureau of Economic Research, "Wholesale Price of Bituminous Coal, Mines for United States (M0490AUSM294NNBR)," Federal Reserve Bank of St.

Louis, https://fred.stlouisfed.org/series/M0490AUSM294NNBR; National Bureau of Economic Research, "Wholesale Price of Anthracite Coal, Chestnut; Tidewater, New York Harbor for New York, NY (M04G4AUS35620M288NNBR)," Federal Reserve Bank of St. Louis, https://fred.stlouisfed.org/series/M04G4AUS35620M288NNBR. A puzzle with the 1927 recession and coincident coal strike is that while the effect of the strike on coal supply appears in statistics on coal quantity, there is only a modest impact on coal price. After surging nearly 20 percent in 1926 during the UK coal strike, the retail price of bituminous coal in the United States eased through the first half of 1927, before ticking up again by 5 percent in the second half of the year. Wholesale prices for both bituminous and anthracite coal in the United States follow a similar pattern: spiking in 1926 before moderating in the first half of 1927 and then ticking up again in the second half.

69. James C. Young, "Ford's New Car Keeps Motor World Guessing," *New York Times*, June 26, 1927; Gene Smiley, "The U.S. Economy in the 1920s," EH.Net Encyclopedia, ed. Robert Whaples, June 29, 2004, https://eh.net/encyclopedia/the-u-s-economy-in-the -1920s/#:~:text=The%201927%20recession%20was%20also,the%20new%20Model%20 A%20automobile.

70. National Bureau of Economic Research, "Automobile Production, Passenger Cars, Factory Production for United States (M0107AUSM543NNBR)," Federal Reserve Bank of St. Louis, https://fred.stlouisfed.org/series/M0107AUSM543NNBR; National Bureau of Economic Research, "New Passenger Car Registrations for United States (M01109USM543NNBR)," Federal Reserve Bank of St. Louis, https://fred.stlouisfed.org /series/M01109USM543NNBR.

71. R. W. Leiby, "Cotton Boll Weevil Damage During 1927," *Journal of Economic Entomology* 21, no. 1 (1928): 151, https://doi.org/10.1093/jee/21.1.151.

72. National Bureau of Economic Research, "Cotton Crop for United States (A01028US-A558NNBR)," Federal Reserve Bank of St. Louis, https://fred.stlouisfed.org/series /A01028USA558NNBR.

73. NASDAQ, "NASDAQ Composite Market Capitalization [SPNACAP@USECON]," Haver Analytics.

74. James M. Poterba, "Stock Market Wealth and Consumption," *Journal of Economic Perspectives* 14, no. 2 (2000): 99–118, https://doi.org/10.1257/jep.14.2.99; F. Thomas Juster et al., "The Decline in Household Saving and the Wealth Effect," *Review of Economics and Statistics* 88, no. 1 (2006): 20–27, https://doi.org/10.1162/rest.2006.88.1.20; Christopher D. Carroll, Misuzu Otsuka, and Jiri Slacalek, "How Large Are Housing and Financial Wealth Effects? A New Approach," *Journal of Money, Credit and Banking* 43, no. 1 (2011): 55–79, https://doi.org/10.1111/j.1538-4616.2010.00365.x; Gabriel Chodorow-Reich, Plamen T. Nenov, and Alp Simsek, "Stock Market Wealth and the Real Economy: A Local Labor Market Approach," *American Economic Review* 111, no. 5 (2021): 1613–57, https:// doi.org/10.1257/aer.20200208

75. World Bank, "Gross Domestic Product for China (MKTGDPCNA646NWDB)," Federal Reserve Bank of St. Louis, https://fred.stlouisfed.org/series/MKTGDPCNA646N WDB; US Bureau of Economic Analysis, "Gross Domestic Product: Implicit Price Deflator (GDPDEF)," Federal Reserve Bank of St. Louis, https://fred.stlouisfed.org/series/GDPDEF.

76. Justin R. Pierce and Peter K. Schott, "The Surprisingly Swift Decline of US Manufacturing Employment," *American Economic Review* 106, no. 7 (2016): 1633, https://doi .org/10.1257/aer.20131578

77. Kate Bronfenbrenner et al., "Impact of U.S.–China Trade Relations on Workers, Wages, and Employment," Pilot Study Report Submitted to the US–China Security Review Commission / US Trade Deficit Review Commission, June 30, 2001, 18–19, https://ecommons.cornell.edu/server/api/core/bitstreams/c557546b-f9bd-4b9d-b632-6a51301e8b5c/content.

78. "Job Openings and Labor Turnover Survey (JOLTS): Job Openings, Hires and Total Separations (Table A)," US Bureau of Labor Statistics.

79. David H. Autor, David Dorn, and Gordon H. Hanson, "The China Syndrome: Local Labor Market Effects of Import Competition in the United States," *American Economic Review* 103, no. 6 (2013): 2121–68, https://doi.org/10.1257/aer.103.6.2121; Daron Acemoglu et al., "Import Competition and the Great US Employment Sag of the 2000s," *Journal of Labor Economics* 34, no. S1 (2016): S141–98, https://doi.org/10.1086/682384; Pierce and Schott, "The Surprisingly Swift Decline"; David Autor, David Dorn, and Gordon Hanson, "On the Persistence of the China Shock," NBER Working Paper 29401 (National Bureau of Economic Research, October 2021), https://doi.org/10.3386/w29401.

80. Autor, Dorn, and Hanson, "The China Syndrome"; Autor, Dorn, and Hanson, "On the Persistence."

81. Pierce and Schott, "The Surprisingly Swift Decline."

82. James D. Hamilton, "Historical Oil Shocks," in *Routledge Handbook of Major Events in Economic History*, ed. Randall E. Parker and Robert Whaples (Routledge, 2013), 239–65.

83. Organization for Economic Co-operation and Development, "Consumer Price Indices (CPIs, HICPs), COICOP 1999: Consumer Price Index: Energy for United States (USACPIENGMINMEI)," Federal Reserve Bank of St. Louis, https://fred.stlouisfed.org/series/USACPIENGMINMEI.

84. Christopher Weare, *The California Electricity Crisis: Causes and Policy Options* (Public Policy Institute of California, 2003).

85. Neela Banerjee, "OPEC to Cut Production, Officials Say: Exporters Said to Plan 4% Decrease in Output," *New York Times*, March 17, 2001; Neela Banerjee, "OPEC Ratifies Oil Cutback; Iraq Remains a Puzzle: With Iraq the Imponderable, OPEC Ratifies Oil Cutback," *New York Times*, January 18, 2001; Neela Banerjee, "OPEC Reported in Agreement to Cut Oil Production by 5%," *New York Times*, January 17, 2001; "Hoping to Shore Up Prices, OPEC Agrees to Cut Output by 4%," *New York Times*, March 18, 2001.

86. Robert Hall et al., "Business Cycle Dating Committee Announcement November 26, 2001," NBER, November 26, 2001, https://nber.org/news/business-cycle-dating-committee-announcement-november-26-2001.

87. Dominik Collet, "Extreme Winters during the 18th Century," in *Extremereignis ›Kältewinter‹ im 18. Jahrhundert*, ed. Anna Axtner-Borsutzky and Joana van de Löcht (De Gruyter, 2025), 27–28.

88. Joseph Stiglitz, "Growth and Fluctuations: An Overview," NBER Working Paper 33218 (National Bureau of Economic Research, December 2024).

Chapter 7: Firefighters and Arsonists

1. Edward H. Bonekemper, *Ulysses S. Grant: A Victor, Not a Butcher: The Military Genius of the Man Who Won the Civil War* (Regnery, 2010).

2. Simon Adams, "Battle of Cold Harbor," in *Encyclopaedia Britannica*, November 20, 2023, https://britannica.com/event/battle-of-Cold-Harbor.

3. M. John Lubetkin, *Jay Cooke's Gamble: The Northern Pacific Railroad, the Sioux, and the Panic of 1873* (University of Oklahoma Press, 2006), 284.

4. "The Panic of 1873," *Banker's Magazine and Statistical Register*, November 1891, 394.

5. Richard H. Timberlake, "Ideological Factors in Specie Resumption and Treasury Policy," *Journal of Economic History* 24, no. 1 (1964): 31, https://doi.org/10.1017/S0022050700089877; E. G. Spaulding, *History of the Legal Tender Paper Money Issued During the Great Rebellion. Being a Loan without Interest and a National Currency* (Buffalo, 1869), 199–200; Eugene B. Patton, "Secretary Shaw and Precedents as to Treasury Control over the Money Market," *Journal of Political Economy* 15, no. 2 (1907): 68, https://doi.org/10.1086/251290. Technically, the wartime legal tender acts had authorized $450 million, but $50 million of that was authorized specifically for the redemption of temporary loans.

6. Timberlake, 31; Patton, 69–70.

7. Timberlake, 31–32; Patton, 70–72; Samuel Williamson, "Seven Ways to Compute the Relative Value of a U.S. Dollar Amount, 1790 to Present," Measuring Worth, 2025, https://measuringworth.com/calculators/uscompare/. I compute the 2024 value as the relative economic share of a commodity, and alternatively as relative output and economy cost.

8. Timberlake, 36–37; Patton, 73–74.

9. Timberlake, 37–38.

10. "At the Fifth Avenue Hotel," *New York Times*, September 22, 1873; "Condition of Affairs in Other Cities," *New York Times*, September 21, 1873.

11. "Condition of Affairs in Other Cities"; Patton, "Secretary Shaw and Precedents," 82.

12. "At the Fifth Avenue Hotel."

13. "At the Fifth Avenue Hotel"; "The Panic Subsiding: Condition of Affairs in the Street Yesterday," *New York Times*, September 23, 1873; "The Presidential Action: Reasons for the Course Pursued Set Forth Clearly by Gen. Grant Himself," *New York Times*, September 23, 1873.

14. "Condition of Affairs in Other Cities"; "The Panic Subsiding"; "The Presidential Action"; "The Financial Crisis: Attitude of the Government," *New York Times*, September 26, 1873.

15. "The Presidential Action"; Patton, "Secretary Shaw and Precedents," 83.

16. "The Financial Crisis"; Patton, 83; Timberlake, "Ideological Factors," 41.

17. "The Financial Crisis"; Patton, 83–84; Samuel Williamson, "Seven Ways to Compute the Relative Value of a U.S. Dollar Amount, 1790 to Present," Measuring Worth, 2025, https://measuringworth.com/calculators/uscompare/. I compute the 2024 value as the relative economic share of a commodity, and alternatively as relative output and economy cost.

18. Timberlake, "Ideological Factors," 34.

19. "The Panic and the General Government," *New York Times*, October 19, 1857; Williamson, "Seven Ways to Compute." I compute the 2024 value as the relative economic share of a commodity, and alternatively as relative output and economy cost. On a single day in early-mid October, the Treasury redeemed $165,000 worth of public stocks, with interest and premium bringing the sum to $181,000. See: "Latest Intelligence: By Telegraph to the New-York Times," *New York Times*, October 12, 1857.

20. Justin Fox, "Bob Lucas on the Comeback of Keynesianism," *Time*, October 28, 2008, https://business.time.com/2008/10/28/bob-lucas-on-the-comeback-of-keynesianism/.

21. Board of Governors of the Federal Reserve System, "Assets: Total Assets: Total Assets (Less Eliminations from Consolidation): Wednesday Level (WALCL)," Federal Reserve Bank of St. Louis, https://fred.stlouisfed.org/series/WALCL.

22. Robert E. Lucas, "The Death of Keynesian Economics," *Issues and Ideas* 2, Winter 1980: 18–19.

23. Arthur F. Burns, "Progress Towards Economic Stability," *American Economic Review* 50, no. 1 (1960): 3–4.

24. Burns, 4–5.

25. Burns, 1–2.

26. Martin Neil Baily, Edmund S. Phelps, and Benjamin M. Friedman, "Stabilization Policy and Private Economic Behavior," *Brookings Papers on Economic Activity* 1978, no. 1 (1978): 11, https://doi.org/10.2307/2534361.

27. J. Bradford De Long and Lawrence Summers, *The Changing Cyclical Variability of Economic Activity in the United States* (National Bureau of Economic Research, September 1984), https://doi.org/10.3386/w1450; J. Bradford DeLong and Lawrence H. Summers, "The Changing Cyclical Variability of Economic Activity in the United States," in *The American Business Cycle: Continuity and Change*, ed. Robert J. Gordon, Studies in Business Cycles 25 (University of Chicago Press, 1986).

28. Christina Romer, "Spurious Volatility in Historical Unemployment Data," *Journal of Political Economy* 94, no. 1 (1986): 1–37, https://doi.org/10.1086/261361; Christina Romer, "The Instability of the Prewar Economy Reconsidered: A Critical Examination of Historical Macroeconomic Data," *Journal of Economic History* 46, no. 2 (1986): 494–96, https://doi.org/10.1017/S0022050700046301; Christina Romer, "New Estimates of Prewar Gross National Product and Unemployment," *Journal of Economic History* 46, no. 2 (1986): 341–52; Christina D. Romer, "Changes in Business Cycles: Evidence and Explanations," *Journal of Economic Perspectives* 13, no. 2 (1999): 23–44; Christina D. Romer, "Is the Stabilization of the Postwar Economy a Figment of the Data?," *Journal of Economic History* 76, no. 3 (1986): 314–34.

29. Nathan Balke and Robert Gordon, "The Estimation of Prewar GNP Volatility, 1869–1938," NBER Working Paper 1999 (National Bureau of Economic Research, August 1986), https://doi.org/10.3386/w1999; Nathan S. Balke and Robert J. Gordon, "The Estimation of Prewar Gross National Product: Methodology and New Evidence," *Journal of Political Economy* 97, no. 1 (1989): 38–92, https://doi.org/10.1086/261593; David R. Weir, "The Reliability of Historical Macroeconomic Data for Comparing Cyclical Stability," *Journal of Economic History* 46, no. 2 (1986): 353–65, https://doi.org/10.1017/S0022050700046179; Francis X. Diebold and Glenn D. Rudebusch, "Have Postwar Economic Fluctuations Been Stabilized?," *American Economic Review* 82, no. 4 (1992): 993–1005.

30. Diebold and Rudebusch.

31. Scott Miller, "Ten Facts About the American Economy in the 18th Century," *George Washington—Colonial Life* (blog), https://mountvernon.org/george-washington/colonial-life-today/early-american-economics-facts/#:~:text=Between%201774%20and%201789%2C%20the,resulted%20in%20widespread%20economic%20collapse.

32. Patrick O'Brien and Nuno Palma, "Not an Ordinary Bank but a Great Engine of State: The Bank of England and the British Economy, 1694–1844," *Economic History Review* 76, no. 1 (February 2023): 305–29.

33. Gregory C. Chow, "Tests of Equality Between Sets of Coefficients in Two Linear Regressions," *Econometrica* 28, no. 3 (1960): 591, https://doi.org/10.2307/1910133; Jan Ditzen, Yiannis Karavias, and Joakim Westerlund, "Testing and Estimating Structural Breaks in Time Series and Panel Data in Stata," arXiv, October 27, 2021, https://doi.org/10.48550 /ARXIV.2110.14550.

34. Using the alternative Davis-Romer chronology, a sequential test for multiple breaks at unknown breakpoints does suggest 1940 as a possible breakpoint, but it also suggests 1751, 1787, 1857, and 1908 as possible breakpoints, so it seems that 1940 is hardly unique. Moreover, if we restrict the test to a maximum of two breakpoints, the estimated breakpoints are 1798 and 1885.

35. While the sixteen-year US expansion that ended in 1856, according to the Davis-Romer chronology, spanned the Mexican-American War, that conflict was comparatively short (just over 1.5 years), with modest mobilization, relatively light casualties for the United States, and waged on Mexican and disputed territory. Even so, according to the NBER series, the United States experienced recession in the first (1846) and final (1848) years of the war.

36. D. Hamberg, "The Recession of 1948–49 in the United States," *Economic Journal* 62, no. 245 (1952): 1, https://doi.org/10.2307/2227168.

37. Stacey L. Schreft, "Credit Controls: 1980," *Economic Review*, Federal Reserve Bank of Richmond, December 1990, 26; H. Walton Cloke, "New Curbs on Time-Buying Ordered in Effect Sept. 20," *New York Times*, August 20, 1948.

38. Raymond E. Owens and Stacey L. Schreft, "Identifying Credit Crunches," *Contemporary Economic Policy* 13 (1995): 67–68.

39. Schreft, "Credit Controls," 27.

40. Owens and Schreft, "Identifying Credit Crunches," 65, 67–68.

41. Ben S. Bernanke, "Irreversibility, Uncertainty, and Cyclical Investment," *Quarterly Journal of Economics* 98, no. 1 (1983): 85, https://doi.org/10.2307/1885568; "The Impact of Uncertainty Shocks," *Econometrica* 77, no. 3 (2009): 623–85, https://doi.org/10.3982 /ECTA6248; Scott R. Baker, Nicholas Bloom, and Steven J. Davis, "Measuring Economic Policy Uncertainty," *Quarterly Journal of Economics* 131, no. 4 (2016): 1593–636, https:// doi.org/10.1093/qje/qjw024; Nicholas Bloom et al., "Really Uncertain Business Cycles," *Econometrica* 86, no. 3 (2018): 1031–65, https://doi.org/10.3982/ECTA10927; Iván Alfaro, Nicholas Bloom, and Xiaoji Lin, "The Finance Uncertainty Multiplier," *Journal of Political Economy* 132, no. 2 (2024): 577–615, https://doi.org/10.1086/726230; Michael D. Bordo, John V. Duca, and Christoffer Koch, "Economic Policy Uncertainty and the Credit Channel: Aggregate and Bank Level U.S. Evidence over Several Decades," *Journal of Financial Stability* 26, October 2016: 90–106, https://doi.org/10.1016/j.jfs.2016.07.002; Scott R. Baker, Nicholas Bloom, and Stephen J. Terry, "Using Disasters to Estimate the Impact of Uncertainty," *Review of Economic Studies* 91, no. 2 (2024): 720–47, https://doi.org/10.1093 /restud/rdad036.

42. Schreft, "Credit Controls," 27.

43. Schreft, 28–32.

44. Clyde H. Farnsworth, "Kahn Calls Credit Curb Possible in New Plan," *New York Times*, February 15, 1980.

45. Peter L. Rousseau, "Jacksonian Monetary Policy, Specie Flows, and the Panic of 1837," *Journal of Economic History* 62, no. 2 (2002), https://doi.org/10.1017/S0022050702000566.

46. DeLong and Summers, "The Changing Cyclical Variability."

47. I assume that national income approximately equals national output and therefore use nominal gross domestic product as a proxy for national income. For more on evaluating money supply as weeks of income, see: Milton Friedman and Anna J. Schwartz, "Movements of Money, Income, and Prices," in *Monetary Trends in the United States and United Kingdom: Their Relation to Income, Prices, and Interest Rates, 1867–1975*, National Bureau of Economic Research Monograph (University of Chicago Press, 1982), 138–204; Milton Friedman and Anna J. Schwartz, "Velocity and the Demand for Money," in *Monetary Trends in the United States and United Kingdom: Their Relation to Income, Prices, and Interest Rates, 1867–1975*, National Bureau of Economic Research Monograph (University of Chicago Press, 1982), 205–304.

48. Charles Read, "Laissez-Faire, the Irish Famine, and British Financial Crisis," *Economic History Review* 69, no. 2 (2016): 417–22, https://doi.org/10.1111/ehr.12274.

49. Rudiger Dornbusch and Jacob A. Frenkel, "The Gold Standard and the Bank of England in the Crisis of 1847," in *A Retrospective on the Classical Gold Standard, 1821–1931*, ed. Michael D. Bordo and Anna J. Schwartz (University of Chicago Press, 1984), 250; Rudiger Dornbusch and Jacob A. Frenkel, "The Gold Standard Crisis of 1847," *Journal of International Economics* 16, nos. 1–2 (1984): 1–27, https://doi.org/10.1016/0022-1996(84)90040-0; Read, 420, 425.

50. Ivan Luzardo-Luna and Meredith Parker, "Economic Relief in Recession: Poverty and Unemployment Benefits During the Great Depression in Britain," Penn Institute for Economic Research Working Paper 24-027 (University of Pennsylvania, September 2024).

51. P. H. J. H. Gosden, *The Friendly Societies in England, 1815–1875* (Manchester University Press, 1961); Simon Cordery, *British Friendly Societies, 1750–1914* (Palgrave Macmillan, 2003).

52. "The Panic and the General Government."

53. "The Panic and the General Government."

54. "The Financial Crisis."

Chapter 8: The Patriotic Recession

1. Ben Bernanke, Timothy F. Geithner, and Henry M. Paulson, *Firefighting: The Financial Crisis and Its Lessons* (Penguin Books, 2019), 66–67.

2. David Wessel, *In Fed We Trust: Ben Bernanke's War on the Great Panic* (Three Rivers Press, 2010), 20; Andrew Ross Sorkin, *Too Big to Fail: The inside Story of How Wall Street and Washington Fought to Save the Financial System from Crisis—and Themselves* (Penguin Books, 2018), 345–48.

3. Bernanke, Geithner, and Paulson, *Firefighting*, 67.

4. Bernanke, Geithner, and Paulson, 67; Sorkin, *Too Big to Fail*, 351.

5. Sorkin; Henry M. Paulson, *On the Brink: Inside the Race to Stop the Collapse of the Global Financial System* (Business Plus, 2010).

6. Sorkin, 351.

7. PricewaterhouseCoopers LLP, *Lehman Brothers International (Europe)—In Administration: Joint Administrators' Proposals for Achieving the Purpose of Administration* (PricewaterhouseCoopers LLP, October 28, 2008), 4–5, https://pwc.co.uk/assets/pdf/lbie-proposals-28-oct-2008.pdf.

8. Jennifer Hughes, "Winding Up Lehman Brothers," *Financial Times*, November 7, 2008, https://ft.com/content/e4223c20-aad1-11dd-897c-000077b07658.

9. PricewaterhouseCoopers LLP, *Lehman Brothers International (Europe)*, 4–5.

10. Hughes, "Winding Up."

11. Hughes.

12. Hughes; DealBook, "Left in Limbo—or Worse—by Lehman," *New York Times*, October 1, 2008, https://archive.nytimes.com/dealbook.nytimes.com/2008/10/01/left-in-limbo-or-worse-by-lehman/.

13. PricewaterhouseCoopers LLP, *Lehman Brothers International (Europe)*.

14. James Mackintosh, "Lehman Collapse Puts Prime Broker Model in Question," *Financial Times*, September 24, 2008, https://ft.com/content/442f0b24-8a71-11dd-a76a-0000779fd18c; Emelia Sithole-Matarise and Jamie McGeever, "Interbank Dollar Lending Markets Remain Stressed," Reuters, September 17, 2008, https://reuters.com/article/us-markets-deposits/interbank-dollar-lending-markets-remain-stressed-idINLH44465720080917; Aaron Ross Sorkin et al., "As Credit Crisis Spiraled, Alarm Led to Action," *New York Times*, October 1, 2008, https://nytimes.com/2008/10/02/business/02crisis.html.

15. Reuters Staff, "HBOS Leads Bank Fall as Lehman Stokes Funding Worry," Reuters, September 15, 2008, https://reuters.com/article/uk-hbos-shares/hbos-leads-bank-fall-as-lehman-stokes-funding-worry-idUKWLA957520080915.

16. Wikipedia, "List of Oldest Banks in Continuous Operation," accessed July 18, 2023, https://en.wikipedia.org/w/index.php?title=List_of_oldest_banks_in_continuous_operation&oldid=1159275622.

17. Alistair Darling, *Back from the Brink: 1000 Days at Number 11* (Atlantic Books, 2012).

18. Graeme Wearden and Deborah Summers, "Gordon Brown Unveils £50bn Rescue Package for Britain's Banks," *The Guardian*, October 8, 2008, https://theguardian.com/business/2008/oct/08/banking.economy1.

19. Hyun Song Shin, "Reflections on Northern Rock: The Bank Run That Heralded the Global Financial Crisis," *Journal of Economic Perspectives* 23, no. 1 (2009): 102, https://doi.org/10.1257/jep.23.1.101; House of Commons Treasury Committee, *The Run on the Rock: Fifth Report of Session 2007–08* (House of Commons, January 26, 2008), 12–13, https://publications.parliament.uk/pa/cm200708/cmselect/cmtreasy/56/56i.pdf.

20. Shin, 102.

21. Gregory Zuckerman, James Hagerty, and David Gauthier-Villars, "Impact of Mortgage Crisis Spreads," *Wall Street Journal*, August 10, 2007, https://wsj.com/articles/SB118664884606092848?mod=article_inline; Colin Barr, "Aug. 9, 2007: The Day the Mortgage Crisis Went Global," *Wall Street Journal*, August 9, 2017, https://wsj.com/articles/aug-9-2007-the-day-the-mortgage-crisis-went-global-1502271004; House of Commons Treasury Committee, *The Run on the Rock*, 15.

22. House of Commons Treasury Committee, 15–16.

23. House of Commons Treasury Committee, 64–65.

24. House of Commons Treasury Committee, 65; "Northern Rock Gets Bank Bail Out," BBC News, September 13, 2007, http://news.bbc.co.uk/2/hi/business/6994099.stm.

25. "Northern Rock Gets Bank Bail Out."

26. House of Commons Treasury Committee, *The Run on the Rock*, 67–68.

27. "All Around the Horizon," *Christian Work and Evangelist*, November 23, 1907, 660.

28. Federal Open Market Committee, *Historical Minutes* (Federal Reserve System, February 7, 1961), 31, https://federalreserve.gov/monetarypolicy/files/fomchistmin19610307.pdf.

29. Norman Davies, *Europe: A History* (Oxford University Press, 1997), 762.

30. Edward N. Lorenz, *The Essence of Chaos*, Jessie and John Danz Lectures (University of Washington Press, 2008), 14–15.

31. Organisation for Economic Co-operation and Development, "Employed Population: Aged 15 and Over: All Persons for the United Kingdom (LFEMTTTTGBQ647S)," Federal Reserve Bank of St. Louis, June 23, 2023, https://fred.stlouisfed.org/series/LFEMTTTTG BQ647S; "Gross Domestic Product: Chained Volume Measures: Seasonally Adjusted £m, Office of National Statistics, https://ons.gov.uk/economy/grossdomesticproductgdp /timeseries/abmi/pn2.

32. Stephen Broadberry et al., "Dating Business Cycles in the United Kingdom, 1700–2010," *Economic History Review*, January 27, 2023, 13, https://doi.org/10.1111 /ehr.13238; "US Business Cycle Expansions and Contractions," National Bureau of Economic Research, https://nber.org/research/data/us-business-cycle-expansions-and-contractions.

33. "Real GDP per Capita, 1875 to 2020," Our World in Data, https://ourworldindata .org/grapher/uk-real-gdp-per-capita-in-2011-us-dollars.

34. US Bureau of Economic Analysis, "Real Gross Domestic Product per Capita (A939RX0Q048SBEA), Federal Reserve Bank of St. Louis, https://fred.stlouisfed.org /series/A939RX0Q048SBEA/.

35. Council of Economic Advisers, *Economic Report of the President: Together with the Annual Report of the Council of Economic Advisers* (US Government Printing Office, 2020), 137; "U.S. Electricity Generation by Major Energy Source, 1950–2023," US Energy Information Administration, https://eia.gov/energyexplained/electricity/electricity-in-the-us.php.

36. Department for Energy Security and Net Zero, "Electricity Since 1920," Gov.UK, https://gov.uk/government/statistical-data-sets/historical-electricity-data; Roger Fouquet, "A Historical Energy Data Set for the UK" (National Infrastructure Commission's collection of historical energy statistics, March 26, 2022); Department for Energy Security and Net Zero and Department for Business, Energy & Industrial Strategy, "Historical Coal Data: Coal Production, Availability and Consumption," Gov.UK, https://gov.uk/government /statistical-data-sets/historical-coal-data-coal-production-availability-and-consumption.

37. Department for Energy Security and Net Zero, "Electricity since 1920"; Bureau of Labor Statistics, "Producer Price Index by Commodity: Fuels and Related Products and Power: Electric Power (WPU054)," Federal Reserve Bank of St. Louis, https://fred.stlouis-fed.org/series/WPU054; Bureau of Labor Statistics, "Consumer Price Index for All Urban Consumers: Electricity in U.S. City Average (CUUR0000SEHF01)," Federal Reserve Bank of St. Louis, https://fred.stlouisfed.org/series/CUUR0000SEHF01.

38. Fouquet, "A Historical Energy Data Set."

39. Maurice J. Tobin and Ewan Clague, *Analysis of Work Stoppages During 1949* (US Government Printing Office, June 2, 1950); Ewan Clague and Martin P. Durkin, *Analysis of Work Stoppages During 1952* (United States Department of Labor, June 4, 1953); J. D. Hodgson and Geoffrey H. Moore, *Analysis of Work Stoppages, 1969* (United States Department of Labor, 1971); J. D. Hodgson and Geoffrey H. Moore, *Analysis of Work Stoppages, 1970*" (United States Department of Labor, 1972).

40. Fouquet, "A Historical Energy Data Set."

41. "Oil Production Measured in Terawatt-Hours," Our World in Data, https://ourworld-indata.org/grapher/oil-production-by-country?country=SAU~IRQ~USA~IRN~OWID _WRL; Organization for Economic Co-operation and Development, "Consumer Price Indices (CPIs, HICPs), COICOP 1999: Consumer Price Index: Energy for United States (USACPIENGMINMEI)," Federal Reserve Bank of St. Louis, https://fred.stlouisfed.org /series/USACPIENGMINMEI; Organization for Economic Co-operation and Development, "Consumer Price Indices (CPIs, HICPs), COICOP 1999: Consumer Price Index: Energy for United Kingdom (CPGREN01GBM659N)," Federal Reserve Bank of St. Louis, https://fred.stlouisfed.org/series/CPGREN01GBM659N.

42. Michael Brick, "Inflation Index Jumps, Thanks to Energy Costs: Inflation Index Jumps, Thanks to Energy Costs," *New York Times*, February 22, 2001; US Energy Information Administration, "Henry Hub Natural Gas Spot Price (MHHNGSP)," Federal Reserve Bank of St. Louis, https://fred.stlouisfed.org/series/MHHNGSP; Daniel Yergin and Tom Robinson, "The Other Energy Crisis," *New York Times*, January 18, 2001.

43. Willard Thorpe, "The Annals of England," in *Business Annals* (National Bureau of Economic Research, 1926), 171; Broadberry et al., "Dating Business Cycles," A50.

44. S. N. Broadberry et al., *British Economic Growth, 1270–1870* (Cambridge University Press, 2015); Susan B. Carter, ed., *Historical Statistics of the United States: Earliest Times to the Present*, Millennial ed., vol. 3 (Cambridge University Press, 2006); Jutta Bolt and Jan Luiten van Zanden, "Maddison Style Estimates of the Evolution of the World Economy. A New 2020 Update," University of Groningen, Maddison Project Database, October 2020, https:// rug.nl/ggdc/historicaldevelopment/maddison/releases/maddison-project-database-2020.

45. The correlation coefficient for annual working-age population growth in the United States and United Kingdom is 0.36 since 1978. Organisation for Economic Co-operation and Development, "Working Age Population: Aged 15–64: All Persons for the United Kingdom (LFWA64TTGBQ647S)," Federal Reserve Bank of St. Louis, https://fred.stlou-isfed.org/series/LFWA64TTGBQ647S; Organisation for Economic Co-operation and Development, "Working Age Population: Aged 15–64: All Persons for the United States (LFWA64TTUSM647S)," Federal Reserve Bank of St. Louis, https://fred.stlouisfed.org /series/LFWA64TTUSM647S.

46. Wesley C. Mitchell, *Business Cycles* (University of California Press, 1913), 371.

47. Board of Governors of the Federal Reserve System (US), Committee on Branch, Group, and Chain Banking, *Branch Banking in the United States: Material Prepared for the Information of the Federal Reserve System by the Federal Reserve Committee on Branch, Group, and Chain Banking*, 1932, 3.

48. Forrest Capie and Alan Webber, *A Monetary History of the United Kingdom, 1870–1982*, vol. 1 (Routledge, 2006), 576.

49. For extensive analysis of the risks and political economy of unit banking, see: Charles W. Calomiris and Stephen H. Haber, *Fragile by Design: The Political Origins of Banking Crises and Scarce Credit* (Princeton University Press, 2015); George A. Selgin, *The Theory of Free Banking: Money Supply under Competitive Note Issue* (Rowman & Littlefield, 1988).

50. Tyler Beck Goodspeed, *Legislating Instability: Adam Smith, Free Banking, and the Financial Crisis of 1772* (Harvard University Press, 2016), 26, 93, 119, 139.

51. David Maude and William Perraudin, *Pricing Deposit Insurance in the United Kingdom* (Monetary Analysis Division, Bank of England, 1995), https://bankofengland.co.uk/- /media/boe/files/working-paper/1995/pricing-deposit-insurance-in-the-uk.pdf; Federal

Deposit Insurance Corporation, *A Brief History of Deposit Insurance in the United States* (Federal Deposit Insurance Corporation, 1998).

52. Goodspeed, *Legislating Instability*, 93.

53. Broadberry et al., "Dating Business Cycles"; Seán Kenny, Jason Lennard, and John D. Turner, "The Macroeconomic Effects of Banking Crises: Evidence from the United Kingdom, 1750–1938," *Explorations in Economic History* 79 (2021): 101357, https://doi.org/10.1016/j.eeh.2020.101357.

54. Vincent Stuckey, "Thoughts on the Improvement of the System of Country Banking," *Edinburgh Review* 63 (1836): 419–41, quoted in John D. Turner, *Banking in Crisis: The Rise and Fall of British Banking Stability, 1800 to the Present*, Cambridge Studies in Economic History (Cambridge University Press, 2014).

55. John Ramsay McCulloch, "Thoughts on Banking," *Edinburgh Review* 86 (February 1826): 281; John Wilson, *Some Illustrations of Mr. McCulloch's Principles of Political Economy* (Edinburgh, 1826), 52.

56. McCulloch, 281. Though McCulloch's name is not listed in *The Edinburgh Review* article, he worked for the magazine and was identified as the author by Scottish literary critic and author John Wilson, writing under the pseudonym "Mordecai Mullion, private secretary to Christopher North," the latter being a common pseudonym of Wilson's.

57. *Parliamentary History and Review; Containing Reports of the Proceedings of the Two Houses of Parliament during the Session of 1826: 7 Geo. IV* (London, 1826).

58. Ian Bond, "The British Banking Population: 1790–1982," in *Complexity and Crisis in the Financial System: Critical Perspectives on the Evolution of American and British Banking*, ed. Matthew Hollow, Folarin Akinbami, and Ranald Michie (Edward Elgar, 2016), 100.

59. Capie and Webber, *A Monetary History*, 576.

60. Walter Bagehot, *Lombard Street: A Description of the Money Market* (London, 1873), 18.

61. Mrs. Russell Barrington, *Life of Walter Bagehot* (Longmans, Green and Co., 1914), 50–51.

62. Barrington, 55–58; James Grant, *Bagehot: The Life and Times of the Greatest Victorian* (W. W. Norton, 2019).

63. Barrington, 52, 56; "Stuckey's Banking Co Ltd," NatWest Group, accessed August 28, 2023, https://natwestgroup.com/heritage/companies/stuckeys-banking-co-ltd.html.

64. "Parr's Bank Ltd," NatWest Group, accessed August 29, 2023, https://natwestgroup.com/heritage/companies/parrs-bank-ltd.html; "London & Westminster Bank Ltd," NatWest Group, accessed August 29, 2023, https://natwestgroup.com/heritage/companies/london-and-westminster-bank-ltd.html; "Westminster Bank Ltd," NatWest Group, accessed August 29, 2023, https://natwestgroup.com/heritage/companies/westminster-bank-ltd.html; "Jones, Loyd & Co," NatWest Group, accessed August 29, 2023, https://natwestgroup.com/heritage/companies/jones-loyd-and-co.html.

65. "Westminster Bank Ltd"; "National Westminster Bank Plc," NatWest Group, accessed August 29, 2023, https://natwestgroup.com/heritage/companies/national-westminster-bank-plc.html.

66. Ranald Michie, *British Banking: Continuity and Change from 1694 to the Present* (Oxford University Press, 2016), 271–90; Bond, "The British Banking Population," 85–120; Federal Deposit Insurance Corporation, "Annual Historical Bank Data: Savings Institutions—Structure," BankFind Suite, https://banks.data.fdic.gov/bankfind-suite

/historical; Federal Deposit Insurance Corporation, "Annual Historical Bank Data: Commercial Banks—Structure," BankFind Suite, https://banks.data.fdic.gov/bankfind-suite /historical.

67. Bagehot, *Lombard Street*, 17, 108.

68. Bagehot; Paul Tucker, "The Repertoire of Official Sector Interventions in the Financial System—Last Resort Lending, Market-Making, and Capital" (Bank of Japan 2009 International Conference, Financial System and Monetary Policy: Implementation, Tokyo, May 27, 2009), 3, https://bis.org/review/r090608c.pdf.

69. Gary Richardson and William Troost, "Monetary Intervention Mitigated Banking Panics During the Great Depression: Quasi-Experimental Evidence from a Federal Reserve District Border, 1929–1933," *Journal of Political Economy* 117, no. 6 (2009): 1031–73, https://doi.org/10.1086/649603; Andrew J. Jalil, "Monetary Intervention Really Did Mitigate Banking Panics During the Great Depression: Evidence Along the Atlanta Federal Reserve District Border," *Journal of Economic History* 74, no. 1 (2014): 259–73, https://doi .org/10.1017/S0022050714000096.

70. George Nurisso and Edward Simpson Prescott, "The 1970s Origins of Too Big to Fail," Economic Commentary, October 18, 2017, 1–6, https://doi.org/10.26509 /frbc-ec-201717.

71. R. S. Kroszner and P. E. Strahan, "What Drives Deregulation? Economics and Politics of the Relaxation of Bank Branching Restrictions," *Quarterly Journal of Economics* 114, no. 4 (1999): 1441, https://doi.org/10.1162/003355399556223.

72. Board of Governors of the Federal Reserve System (US), Committee on Branch, Group, and Chain Banking, *Branch Banking in England: Material Prepared for the Information of the Federal Reserve System by the Federal Reserve Committee on Branch, Group, and Chain Banking*" 1932, 90.

73. Board of Governors of the Federal Reserve System (US), 70, 90, 93.

74. Mark Carlson and Kris James Mitchener, "Branch Banking as a Device for Discipline: Competition and Bank Survivorship during the Great Depression," *Journal of Political Economy* 117, no. 2 (2009): 165–210, https://doi.org/10.1086/599015; Mark Carlson and Kris James Mitchener, "Branch Banking, Bank Competition, and Financial Stability," *Journal of Money, Credit and Banking* 38, no. 5 (2006): 1293–1328.

75. Board of Governors of the Federal Reserve System (US), *Branch Banking in England*, 9–10.

76. Board of Governors of the Federal Reserve System, 8.

77. Michie, *British Banking*; Bond, "The British Banking Population"; Kenny, Lennard, and Turner, "The Macroeconomic Effects."

Chapter 9: Purge the Rottenness

1. According to Geoffrey Moore and Victor Zarnowitz's annual chronology, the 1816–21 recession following the eruption of Mount Tambora endured for six years. However, the improved Davis chronology reports just a one-year recession in 1816. See Richard Sutch, "Business Cycle Turning Dates and Duration—Annual: 1790–1855, Table Cb1–4," in *Historical Statistics of the United States, Earliest Times to the Present: Millennial Edition*, ed. Susan B. Carter et al. (Cambridge University Press, 2006); Joseph Davis, "An Improved Annual Chronology of U.S. Business Cycles Since the 1790s," *Journal of Economic History* 66, no. 1 (2006): 103–21.

2. David Cannadine, *Mellon: An American Life* (A.A. Knopf, 2006), 54–59, 63–64.

3. Thomas Mellon and Mary Louise Briscoe, *Thomas Mellon and His Times*, 2nd ed. (Pittsburgh: University of Pittsburgh Press, 1994), 263–64.

4. Cannadine, *Mellon*, 61.

5. Cannadine, 61; Mellon and Briscoe, *Thomas Mellon*, 271.

6. Cannadine, 22–24, 57.

7. Mellon and Briscoe, *Thomas Mellon*, 25.

8. Herbert Hoover, *The Memoirs of Herbert Hoover: The Great Depression, 1929–1941* (MacMillan Company, 1952), 30–31, https://hoover.archives.gov/sites/default/files/research /ebooks/b1v3_full.pdf.

9. Hoover, 30.

10. Joseph A. Schumpeter and Richard V. Clemence, *Essays: On Entrepreneurs, Innovations, Business Cycles, and the Evolution of Capitalism* (Transaction Publishers, 1989), 115, 117.

11. Joseph A. Schumpeter and Richard Swedberg, *Capitalism, Socialism and Democracy*, Transferred to digital print (Routledge, 2005), 82–84.

12. Schumpeter and Clemence, *Essays*, 113.

13. Schumpeter and Swedberg, *Capitalism, Socialism and Democracy*, 82–83.

14. Robert E. Hall, "Recessions as Reorganizations" (Prepared for the NBER Macro Annual Conference, March 8–9, 1991, February 18, 1991), https://web.stanford.edu /~rehall/Recessions%20as%20Reorganizations%201991.pdf; Robert E. Hall, "Labor Demand, Labor Supply, and Employment Volatility," *NBER Macroeconomics Annual* 6 (1991): 38, https://doi.org/10.1086/654155.

15. Olivier Jean Blanchard et al., "The Cyclical Behavior of the Gross Flows of U.S. Workers," *Brookings Papers on Economic Activity* 1990, no. 2 (1990): 146–47, https://doi .org/10.2307/2534505.

16. Hall, "Labor Demand"; Steven J. Davis and John Haltiwanger, "Gross Job Creation and Destruction: Microeconomic Evidence and Macroeconomic Implications," *NBER Macroeconomics Annual* 5 (1990): 123–68, https://doi.org/10.1086/654135.

17. Blanchard et al., "The Cyclical Behavior."

18. Blanchard et al., 87, 115; Andrei Shleifer, "Implementation Cycles," *Journal of Political Economy* 94, no. 6 (1986): 1163–90, https://doi.org/10.1086/261428. Though Blanchard and Diamond explicitly disavowed a "Schumpeterian" theory of economic fluctuations, theirs is a very narrow reading of Schumpeter. Blanchard and Diamond viewed Schumpeter's as a theory of booms as periods when clusters of new inventions yield high rates of job creation, which did not fit their observation of employment fluctuations driven by large fluctuations in job destruction rather than job creation.

19. Blanchard et al., 146.

20. Timothy F. Bresnahan and Daniel M. G. Raff, "Intra-Industry Heterogeneity and the Great Depression: The American Motor Vehicles Industry, 1929–1935," *Journal of Economic History* 51, no. 2 (1991): 317–31.

21. Brad Hershbein and Lisa B. Kahn, "Do Recessions Accelerate Routine-Biased Technological Change? Evidence from Vacancy Postings," *American Economic Review* 108, no. 7 (2018): 1737–72, https://doi.org/10.1257/aer.20161570.

22. Lucia Foster, Cheryl Grim, and John Haltiwanger, "Reallocation in the Great Recession: Cleansing or Not?," *Journal of Labor Economics* 34, no. S1 (2016): S293–331, 337,

https://doi.org/10.1086/682397. Also, see Table E6, page 23, of the online web appendix: https://journals.uchicago.edu/doi/suppl/10.1086/682397.

23. Martin Neil Baily, "[Labor Demand, Labor Supply, and Employment Volatility]: Comment," *NBER Macroeconomics Annual* 6, January 1991: 53, https://doi.org/10.1086/654156.

24. Lawrence H. Summers, "[Labor Demand, Labor Supply, and Employment Volatility]: Comment," *NBER Macroeconomics Annual* 6, January 1991: 54, 59 https://doi.org/10.1086/654157.

25. Blanchard et al., "The Cyclical Behavior," 152–53.

26. Robert J. Gordon and Martin Neil Baily, "The Jobless Recovery: Does It Signal a New Era of Productivity-Led Growth?," *Brookings Papers on Economic Activity*, no. 1, 1993: 271, https://doi.org/10.2307/2534606; George L. Perry et al., "Was This Recession Different? Are They All Different?," *Brookings Papers on Economic Activity*, no. 1, 1993: 145, https://doi.org/10.2307/2534604; Congressional Budget Office, *The Economic and Budget Outlook: An Update*, Report to the Senate and House Committees on the Budget as Required by Public Law 93-344 (Government Printing Office, September 1993), https://cbo.gov/sites/default/files/103rd-congress-1993-1994/reports/09-1993-outlookentirerpt_0.pdf.

27. US Bureau of Labor Statistics, "JOLTS: Hires Rate: Total (SA, %) [LJHTPA@USECON]," Haver Analytics; Bureau of Labor Statistics, "JOLTS: Layoffs and Discharges Rate: Total (SA, %) [LJLTPA@USECON]," Haver Analytics; US Bureau of Labor Statistics, "JOLTS: Hires: Total (SA, Thous) [LJHTLA@USECON]," Haver Analytics.

28. US Bureau of Labor Statistics, "Average Duration of Unemployment (SA, Weeks) [LUAD@USECON]," Haver Analytics; US Bureau of Labor Statistics, "Median Duration of Unemployment (SA, Weeks) [LUMD@USECON]," Haver Analytics.

29. National Bureau of Economic Research, "Labor Turnover, Quit Rate, Manufacturing for United States (M0851AUSM498NNBR)," Federal Reserve Bank of St. Louis, https://fred.stlouisfed.org/series/M0851AUSM498NNBR; National Bureau of Economic Research, "Labor Turnover, Layoff Rate, Manufacturing for United States (M0852AUSM497NNBR)," Federal Reserve Bank of St. Louis, https://fred.stlouisfed.org/series/M0852AUSM497NNBR; National Bureau of Economic Research, "Labor Turnover, Gross Accession Rate, Manufacturing for United States (M0855AUSM497NNBR)," Federal Reserve Bank of St. Louis, https://fred.stlouisfed.org/series/M0855AUSM497NNBR; National Bureau of Economic Research, "Labor Turnover, Discharge Rate, Manufacturing for United States (M0853AUSM498NNBR)," Federal Reserve Bank of St. Louis, https://fred.stlouisfed.org/series/M0853AUSM498NNBR.

30. Gadi Barlevy, "The Sullying Effect of Recessions," *Review of Economic Studies* 69, no. 1 (2002): 65–96, https://doi.org/10.1111/1467-937X.00198.

31. John Haltiwanger et al., "Cyclical Worker Flows: Cleansing vs. Sullying," NBER Working Paper 28802 (National Bureau of Economic Research, May 2021), https://doi.org/10.3386/w28802.

32. Giuseppe Moscarini and Fabien Postel-Vinay, "Did the Job Ladder Fail After the Great Recession?," *Journal of Labor Economics* 34, no. S1 (2016): S58, https://doi.org/10.1086/682366.

33. Audra Bowlus, "Job Match Quality over the Business Cycle," in *Panel Data and Labour Market Dynamics*, ed. H. Bunzel, Peter Jensen, and Niels Westergård-Nielsen

(Elsevier, 1993), 21–41; Steven J. Davis, John C. Haltiwanger, and Scott Schuh, *Job Creation and Destruction* (MIT, 1998); referenced in Barlevy, "The Sullying Effect," 66.

34. Steven Davis and Till Von Wachter, "Recessions and the Cost of Job Loss," NBER Working Paper 17638 (National Bureau of Economic Research, December 2011), https://doi.org/10.3386/w17638.

35. Christopher Huckfeldt, "Understanding the Scarring Effect of Recessions," *American Economic Review* 112, no. 4 (2022): 1273–310, https://doi.org/10.1257/aer.20160449.

36. Bowlus, "Job Match Quality"; referenced in Barlevy, "The Sullying Effect," 66; Davis and Von Wachter, "Recessions."

37. Min Ouyang, "The Scarring Effect of Recessions," *Journal of Monetary Economics* 56, no. 2 (2009): 184–99, https://doi.org/10.1016/j.jmoneco.2008.12.014.

38. Teresa C. Fort et al., "How Firms Respond to Business Cycles: The Role of Firm Age and Firm Size," *IMF Economic Review* 61, no. 3 (2013): 520–59, https://doi.org/10.1057/imfer.2013.15; Michael Siemer, "Employment Effects of Financial Constraints During the Great Recession," *Review of Economics and Statistics* 101, no. 1 (2019): 16–29, https://doi.org/10.1162/rest_a_00733.

39. C. W. F. Baden-Fuller, "Exit from Declining Industries and the Case of Steel Castings," *Economic Journal* 99, no. 398 (1989): 949, https://doi.org/10.2307/2234083.

40. José Mustre-Del-Río, "Job Duration over the Business Cycle," *Journal of Money, Credit and Banking* 51, no. 6 (2019): 1691–711, https://doi.org/10.1111/jmcb.12565; Ismail Baydur and Toshihiko Mukoyama, "Job Duration and Match Characteristics over the Business Cycle," *Review of Economic Dynamics* 37, July 2020: 33–53, https://doi.org/10.1016/j.red.2020.01.003; Lisa Kahn, "Job Durations, Match Quality and the Business Cycle: What We Can Learn from Firm Fixed Effects," Harvard University, May 8, 2008, https://citeseerx.ist.psu.edu/document?repid=rep1&type=pdf&doi=88bd5602f4386095375119e29a86189f4d061a2d.

41. Robert E. Hall and Marianna Kudlyak, "The Inexorable Recoveries of Unemployment," *Journal of Monetary Economics* 131, October 2022: 15–25, https://doi.org/10.1016/j.jmoneco.2022.06.003; Robert E. Hall and Marianna Kudlyak, "Why Has the US Economy Recovered So Consistently from Every Recession in the Past 70 Years?," *NBER Macroeconomics Annual* 36 (2022): 1–55, https://doi.org/10.1086/718588; Robert E. Hall and Marianna Kudlyak, "Churn and Stability: The Remarkable Heterogeneity of Flows among Employment, Job Search, and Non-Market Activities in the US Population," September 2022, https://dropbox.com/scl/fi/rqrzhgxjiyndh8mkzsio8/New_JFJL_Aug15_2022.pdf?rlkey=5t17r3u0e4ecqais2hrba5r24&e=1&dl=0.

42. To estimate the trend share of GDP by component, I use a Hodrick–Prescott filter with a high smoothing parameter (λ) of 32,000 to avoid mistaking cyclical movements for trend. Results are robust to estimating trend shares using a Hamilton filter. See Gebhard Flaig, "Why We Should Use High Values for the Smoothing Parameter of the Hodrick–Prescott Filter," *Jahrbücher Für Nationalökonomie Und Statistik* 235, no. 6 (2015): 518–38, https://doi.org/10.1515/jbnst-2015-0602; James D. Hamilton, "Why You Should Never Use the Hodrick–Prescott Filter," *Review of Economics and Statistics* 100, no. 5 (2018): 831–43, https://doi.org/10.1162/rest_a_00706.

43. The August 1981 Economic Recovery Tax Act of 1981 created the Accelerated Cost Recovery System (ACRS), which allowed companies to depreciate new investments

in structures over fifteen years instead of thirty-six. The combination of accelerated cost recovery with the deductibility of interest in the high-interest rate environment of the early 1980s meant that companies borrowing to invest in structures could deduct both the direct cost of the investment as well as interest payments on loans taken out to finance the investment, which could create negative tax rates and thus a large incentive to invest in structures. See Alex Muresianu, "1980s Tax Reform, Cost Recovery, and the Real Estate Industry: Lessons for Today," *Fiscal Fact*, Tax Foundation, July 2020, https://files.taxfoundation .org/20200721170847/1980s-Tax-Reform-Cost-Recovery-and-the-Real-Estate-Industry -Lessons-for-Today.pdf.

44. Employment shares are from Table B-1 of the Bureau of Labor Statistics' Establishment Survey, accessed via Haver Analytics.

45. Sectoral indices are from "A Millennium of Macroeconomic Data," Bank of England, https://bankofengland.co.uk/statistics/research-datasets.

46. Gadi Barlevy, "On the Cyclicality of Research and Development," *American Economic Review* 97, no. 4 (2007): 1131–64, https://doi.org/10.1257/aer.97.4.1131; Galo Nuño, "Optimal Research and Development and the Cost of Business Cycles," *Journal of Economic Growth* 16, no. 3 (2011): 257–83.

47. Bureau of Economic Analysis, "Private Fixed Investment: Research and Development (Mil. $) [FNPRY@USNA]," Haver Analytics; Bureau of Economic Analysis, "Gross Domestic Product (Mil. $) [GDPY@USNA]," Haver Analytics.

48. Ricardo J. Caballero and Mohamad L. Hammour, "The Cleansing Effect of Recessions," *American Economic Review* 84, no. 5 (1994): 1350–68; R. J. Caballero and M. L. Hammour, "On the Timing and Efficiency of Creative Destruction," *Quarterly Journal of Economics* 111, no. 3 (1996): 805–52, https://doi.org/10.2307/2946673; Ricardo J. Caballero and Mohamad L. Hammour, "The Cost of Recessions Revisited: A Reverse-Liquidationist View," *Review of Economic Studies* 72, no. 2 (2005): 313–41, https:// doi.org/10.1111/j.1467-937X.2005.00334.x; Ricardo J. Caballero, "Creative Destructions," in *The New Palgrave Dictionary of Economics*, ed. Steven N. Durlauf and Lawrence E. Blume, 2nd ed. (Palgrave Macmillan UK, 2008); Ricardo Caballero and Mohamad Hammour, "Institutions, Restructuring and Macroeconomic Performance," in *Advances in Macroeconomic Theory*, ed. Jacques Drèze (Palgrave Macmillan UK, 2001), 171–93, https://doi .org/10.1057/9780333992753_9.

49. Ricardo J. Caballero, "Creative Destruction," in *Economic Growth*, ed. Steven N. Durlauf and Lawrence E. Blume (Palgrave Macmillan UK, 2010), 24–29, https://doi .org/10.1057/9780230280823_5.

50. Caballero.

Chapter 10: An Object in Motion

1. US Bureau of Labor Statistics, "Days Idle as Percent of Estimated Working Time (Includes Agricultural & Government Employees but Excludes Household, Forestry & Fishery Employees) [WSTOPP@USECON]," Haver Analytics; James P. Mitchell and Ewan Clague, *Analysis of Work Stoppages, 1959* (Washington, DC: United States Department of Labor, September 1960), 22.

2. US Bureau of Labor Statistics, "All Employees, Manufacturing (MANEMP)," Federal Reserve Bank of St. Louis, https://fred.stlouisfed.org/series/MANEMP.

3. B. R. Stauber, *The Farm Real Estate Situation, 1931–32* (United States Department of Agriculture, January 1933), 22, 48; B. R. Stauber, *The Farm Real Estate Situation, 1932–33* (United States Department of Agriculture, December 1933), 62–63.

4. Franklin Delano Roosevelt, First Inaugural Address (Washington, DC, March 4, 1933).

5. "Business to Make Stabilization Study," *New York Times*, February 9, 1931.

6. Sylvanus Urban, "Historical Chronicle, January 1763," *Gentleman's Magazine, and Historical Chronical*, 1763, 42.

7. Angus Konstam, *The Pirate World: A History of the Most Notorious Sea Robbers* (Osprey Publishing, 2019), 177.

8. *The Annals of King George, Year the Fifth. Containing Not Only the Affairs of Great-Britain, But Also the Most Important Transactions of Europe, Both Civil and Ecclesiastical* London, 1720), 398.

9. Charles Johnson, *A General History of the Pyrates, from Their First Rise and Settlement in the Island of Providence, to the Present Time*, 2nd ed. (London, 1724), 73.

10. A. Boyer, *The Political State of Great Britain. Containing The Months of January, February, March, April, May, and June, MDCCXIX*, vol. 17 (London, 1719), 443; *The Annals of King George*, , 400; Konstam, *The Pirate World*, 163.

11. Johnson, *A General History of the Pyrates*, 145; Konstam, 175.

12. *The Annals of King George*, 398.

13. Konstam, *The Pirate World*, 159.

14. Johnson, *A General History of the Pyrates*, 80–85, 91–112.

15. Johnson, 158; Kris E. Lane, *Pillaging the Empire: Global Piracy on the High Seas, 1500–1750*, 2nd ed. (Routledge, 2016), 197–98; Konstam, *The Pirate World*, 165.

16. Johnson, 156; *The History and Lives of All the Most Notorious Pirates, and Their Crews* (London, 1725), 47–48, 55; *The Tryals of Captain John Rackham and Other Pirates, Viz.* (Jamaica, 1721).

17. Johnson, 165; Tony Bartelme, "A 22-Year-Old YouTuber May Have Solved Anne Bonny Pirate Mystery 300 Years after Trial," *Post and Courier*, November 28, 2020, https://postandcourier.com/news/a-22-year-old-youtuber-may-have-solved-anne-bonny-pirate-mystery-300-years-after/article_78fc0a2e-2914-11eb-a5f5-03b65f4d281a.html.

18. Johnson, 173.

19. Johnson, 173; "The Legend of Ann Bonny," YouTube video, 1:13:50, posted by Debunk File, November 20, 2020, https://youtube.com/watch?v=KOiUgXyk0Fs. Thereafter, there is no record of what happened to Bonny, though in November 2020—exactly three hundred years since Bonny and Read's trial—a twenty-two-year-old YouTube sleuth discovered in a ledger of deaths for St. Catherine's Parish in Spanish Town, Jamaica, one "Ann Bonny," buried December 29, 1733.

20. *The Tryals of Captain John Rackham*, 24, 37–40; Johnson, *A General History of the Pyrates*, 149.

21. Konstam, *The Pirate World*, 164.

22. Johnson, *A General History of the Pyrates*, 35, 117, 119, 240–41.

23. Johnson, 237–39; Lane, *Pillaging the Empire*, 201–2.

24. Lane, 202.

25. Council of Economic Advisers, *Economic Report of the President, Together with the Annual Report of the Council of Economic Advisers* (US Government Printing Office, January 1969), 73–74.

26. John B. Judis, "Bust Busting: The End of Economic History," *New Republic*, June 1997, 12.

27. Judis, 12–13.

28. *Economic Report of the President: Transmitted to the Congress, January 2001 Together with the Annual Report of the Council of Economic Advisers* (US Government Printing Office, 2001), 79.

29. Robert E. Lucas, "Macroeconomic Priorities," *American Economic Review* 93, no. 1 (2003): 1, 11, https://doi.org/10.1257/000282803321455133.

30. Ben S. Bernanke, "The Great Moderation" (Remarks by Governor Ben S. Bernanke At the meetings of the Eastern Economic Association, Washington, DC, February 20, 2004), https://federalreserve.gov/boarddocs/speeches/2004/20040220/.

31. *Pre-Budget Statement* (Hansard, November 25, 1997), https://hansard.parliament .uk/commons/1997-11-25/debates/e9c29db6-c1fb-4840-b5d5-1760462a5855/Pre -BudgetStatement.

32. Gordon Brown, "Economic Stability and the World Economy" (Council on Foreign Relations, New York, NY, September 16, 1999), https://ciaotest.cc.columbia.edu/conf/brg01/.

33. Milton Friedman and Anna J. Schwartz, *A Monetary History of the United States, 1867–1960* (Princeton University Press, 1963); Gary Richardson and William Troost, "Monetary Intervention Mitigated Banking Panics during the Great Depression: Quasi-Experimental Evidence from a Federal Reserve District Border, 1929–1933," *Journal of Political Economy* 117, no. 6 (2009): 1031–73, https://doi.org/10.1086/649603; Andrew J. Jalil, "Monetary Intervention Really Did Mitigate Banking Panics During the Great Depression: Evidence Along the Atlanta Federal Reserve District Border," *Journal of Economic History* 74, no. 1 (2014): 259–73, https://doi.org/10.1017/S0022050714000096; Charles Read, "Laissez-Faire, the Irish Famine, and British Financial Crisis," *Economic History Review* 69, no. 2 (2016): 411–34, https://doi.org/10.1111/ehr.12274; Charles Read, *The Great Famine in Ireland and Britain's Financial Crisis* (Boydell and Brewer, 2022), https:// doi.org/10.1017/9781800106277.

34. Wilhelm Röpke, "Socialism, Planning, and the Business Cycle," *Journal of Political Economy* 44, no. 3 (1936): 318–38; Gottfried Haberler et al., "Business Cycles in a Planned Economy," in *Conference on Business Cycles*, Special Conference Series (National Bureau of Economic Research, 1951), 375–404.

35. Haberler et al., 387.

36. Haberler et al., 387–88. The Columbia colleague was Abram Bergson.

37. Haberler et al., 399.

38. David McCord Wright, *The Economics of Disturbance* (Macmillan Co., 1947); David McCord Wright, "How Much Can Planning Do?," *Journal of Political Economy* 56, no. 4 (1948): 337–41.

39. Lawrence R. Klein, "Review of the Economics of Disturbance by David McCord Wright," *Journal of Political Economy* 55, no. 6 (1947): 576.

40. Sergey Smirnov, "Economic Fluctuations in Russia (from the Late 1920s to 2015)," *Russian Journal of Economics* 1, no. 2 (2015): 144, https://doi.org/10.1016/j.ruje.2015.11.002;

Andrei Markevich, Natalya Naumenko, and Nancy Qian, "The Causes of Ukrainian Famine Mortality, 1932–33," NBER Working Paper 29089, forthcoming in *Review of Economic Studies*, February 22, 2024.

41. Smirnov, 144.

42. Jutta Bolt and Jan Luiten van Zanden, "Gross Domestic Product (GDP), 1820 to 2022," Our World in Data, https://ourworldindata.org/grapher/gdp-maddison-project -database?tab=chart&country=.

43. Haberler et al., "Business Cycles," 398.

44. Wayne M. Morrison, *China's Economic Rise: History, Trends, Challenges, and Implications for the United States* (Congressional Research Service, June 25, 2019), 2–3, https:// crsreports.congress.gov/product/pdf/RL/RL33534.

45. Morrison, 3; Bolt and van Zanden, "Gross Domestic Product (GDP)"; Jutta Bolt and Jan Luiten van Zanden, "GDP per Capita, 1000 to 2022," Our World in Data, https:// ourworldindata.org/grapher/gdp-per-capita-maddison?tab=chart&country=.

46. Bolt and van Zanden, "Gross Domestic Product (GDP)"; Bolt and van Zanden, "GDP per Capita."

47. Robert Shiller, "Narrative Economics," *American Economic Review* 107, no. 4 (2017): 990.

48. Shiller, 991, 993.

49. Julio J. Rotemberg, "Penitence after Accusations of Error: 100 Years of Monetary Policy at the U.S. Federal Reserve," in *The First 100 Years of the Federal Reserve: The Policy Record, Lessons Learned, and Prospects for the Future* (National Bureau of Economic Research, 2013), 2, https://users.nber.org/~confer/2013/SI2013/FED/Rotemberg.pdf.

50. Rotemberg, 3–5.

51. Friedman and Schwartz, *A Monetary History*; Allan H. Meltzer, *A History of the Federal Reserve. 1: 1913–1951* (University of Chicago Press, 2003); Ben S. Bernanke, "Remarks by Governor Ben S. Bernanke" (Conference to Honor Milton Friedman, University of Chicago, Chicago, Illinois, November 8, 2002), https://federalreserve.gov/boarddocs /Speeches/2002/20021108/default.htm.

52. Michael D. Bordo and John V. Duca, "The Impact of the Dodd-Frank Act on Small Business," NBER Working Paper 24501 (National Bureau of Economic Research, April 2018), https://nber.org/system/files/working_papers/w24501/w24501.pdf.

53. "The Real Reason UK Growth Collapsed After 2008 with Tyler Goodspeed | IEA Live", YouTube video, 1:12:59, posted by Institute of Economic Affairs, January 2, 2025, https://youtube.com/watch?v=nmBe8NAMmbY.

54. Bank for International Settlements, "Total Credit to Private Non-Financial Sector, Adjusted for Breaks, for United Kingdom (CRDQGBAPABIS)," Federal Reserve Bank of St. Louis, https://fred.stlouisfed.org/series/CRDQGBAPABIS; Bank for International Settlements, "Total Credit to Private Non-Financial Sector, Adjusted for Breaks, for United States (QUSPAMUSDA)," Federal Reserve Bank of St. Louis, https://fred.stlouisfed.org /series/QUSPAMUSDA. I deflate both series using the implicit GDP deflator for each economy.

55. Stephen Broadberry and John Joseph Wallis, "Growing, Shrinking, and Long Run Economic Performance: Historical Perspectives on Economic Development," NBER Working Paper 23343 (National Bureau of Economic Research, April 2017), https://nber.org /system/files/working_papers/w23343/w23343.pdf.

1. Data Appendix

Stephen Broadberry et al., "Dating Business Cycles in the United Kingdom, 1700–2010," *Economic History Review*, January 27, 2023, ehr.13238, https://doi.org/10.1111/ehr.13238.

2. "A Millennium of Macroeconomic Data," Bank of England, https://bankofengland .co.uk/statistics/research-datasets.

3. "A Millennium."

4. Willard Thorpe, "The Annals of England," in *Business Annals* (National Bureau of Economic Research, 1926), 146–79.

5. Christina D. Romer, "Remeasuring Business Cycles," *Journal of Economic History* 54, no. 3 (1994): 573–609.

6. Geoffrey H. Moore and Victor Zarnowitz, "Appendix A: The Development and Role of the National Bureau of Economic Research's Business Cycle Chronologies," in *The American Business Cycle: Continuity and Change*, ed. Robert J. Gordon (University of Chicago Press, 1986), 735–80; Richard Sutch, "Business Cycle Turning Dates and Duration— Annual: 1790–1855, Table Cb1–4," in *Historical Statistics of the United States, Earliest Times to the Present: Millennial Edition*, ed. Susan B. Carter et al. (Cambridge University Press, 2006).

7. John J. McCusker, "Value of Imports into and Exports from Scotland, by Colony or Locality: 1740–1791, Table Eg443–460," in *Historical Statistics of the United States, Earliest Times to the Present: Millennial Edition*, ed. Susan B. Carter et al. (Cambridge University Press, 2006).

8. John J. McCusker, "Paper Money in Circulation, by Colony: 1703–1775 [Local Colonial Currencies], Table Eg302–314," in *Historical Statistics of the United States, Earliest Times to the Present: Millennial Edition*, ed. Susan B. Carter et al. (Cambridge University Press, 2006); John J. McCusker, "Commodity Price Index: 1665–1790, Table Eg247," in *Historical Statistics of the United States, Earliest Times to the Present: Millennial Edition*, ed. Susan B. Carter et al. (Cambridge University Press, 2006); John J. McCusker, "Rates of Exchange on London, by Colony or State: 1649–1790 [Local Colonial Currencies], Table Eg315–324," in *Historical Statistics of the United States, Earliest Times to the Present: Millennial Edition*, ed. Susan B. Carter et al. (Cambridge University Press, 2006).

9. John J. McCusker, "Vessels Clearing Boston—Number and Tonnage, by Origin or Destination: 1714–1772, Table Eg474–513," in *Historical Statistics of the United States, Earliest Times to the Present: Millennial Edition*, ed. Susan B. Carter et al. (Cambridge University Press, 2006); John J. McCusker, "Vessels Clearing Charleston—Number and Tonnage, by Origin or Destination: 1717–1772, Table Eg634–673," in *Historical Statistics of the United States, Earliest Times to the Present: Millennial Edition*, ed. Susan B. Carter et al. (Cambridge University Press, 2006); John J. McCusker, "Vessels Clearing James River, Lower Part—Number and Tonnage, by Origin or Destination: 1727–1772, Table Eg594–633," in *Historical Statistics of the United States, Earliest Times to the Present: Millennial Edition*, ed. Susan B. Carter et al. (Cambridge University Press, 2006); John J. McCusker, "Vessels Clearing New York—Number and Tonnage, by Origin or Destination: 1715–1772, Table Eg514–553," in *Historical Statistics of the United States, Earliest Times to the Present: Millennial Edition*, ed. Susan B. Carter et al. (Cambridge University Press, 2006); John J. McCusker, "Vessels Clearing Philadelphia—Number and Tonnage, by Origin or Destination: 1719–1772, Table Eg554–593," in *Historical Statistics of the United States, Earliest Times to the Present: Millennial Edition*, ed. Susan B. Carter et al. (Cambridge University Press, 2006).

10. John J. McCusker, "Pig Iron Exported, by Colony and Destination: 1768–1772, Table Eg816–850," in *Historical Statistics of the United States, Earliest Times to the Present: Millennial Edition*, ed. Susan B. Carter et al. (Cambridge University Press, 2006); John J. McCusker, "Pig Iron Imported Coastwise, by Importing Colony: 1768–1772, Table Eg851–860," in *Historical Statistics of the United States, Earliest Times to the Present: Millennial Edition*, ed. Susan B. Carter et al. (Cambridge University Press, 2006); John J. McCusker, "Pig Iron Imported into England from British North America, by Colony: 1723–1776, Table Eg811–815," in *Historical Statistics of the United States, Earliest Times to the Present: Millennial Edition*, ed. Susan B. Carter et al. (Cambridge University Press, 2006); John J. McCusker, "Bar Iron Exported from England, by Importing Colony: 1711–1750, Table Eg861–866," in *Historical Statistics of the United States, Earliest Times to the Present: Millennial Edition*, ed. Susan B. Carter et al. (Cambridge University Press, 2006); John J. McCusker, "Bar Iron Exported, by Colony and Destination: 1768–1772, Table Eg887–936," in *Historical Statistics of the United States, Earliest Times to the Present: Millennial Edition*, ed. Susan B. Carter et al. (Cambridge University Press, 2006); John J. McCusker, "Bar Iron Imported Coastwise, by Importing Colony: 1768–1772, Table Eg873–886," in *Historical Statistics of the United States, Earliest Times to the Present: Millennial Edition*, ed. Susan B. Carter et al. (Cambridge University Press, 2006); John J. McCusker, "Bar Iron Imported into England from British North America, by Colony: 1718–1776, Table Eg867–872," in *Historical Statistics of the United States, Earliest Times to the Present: Millennial Edition*, ed. Susan B. Carter et al. (Cambridge University Press, 2006); John J. McCusker, "Cast Iron Ware Imported and Exported, by Colony and by Origin or Destination: 1768–1772, Table Eg937–992," in *Historical Statistics of the United States, Earliest Times to the Present: Millennial Edition*, ed. Susan B. Carter et al. (Cambridge University Press, 2006); John J. McCusker, "Wrought Iron Ware Exported from England, by Importing Colony: 1711–1773, Table Eg993–1000," in *Historical Statistics of the United States, Earliest Times to the Present: Millennial Edition*, ed. Susan B. Carter et al. (Cambridge University Press, 2006); John J. McCusker, "Imports and Exports of Selected Iron and Steel Products, by Origin or Destination: 1768–1772, Table Eg1001–1012," in *Historical Statistics of the United States, Earliest Times to the Present: Millennial Edition*, ed. Susan B. Carter et al. (Cambridge University Press, 2006).

11. John J. McCusker, "Pitch, Tar, and Turpentine Exported from Charleston: 1712–1787, Table Eg1171–1173," in *Historical Statistics of the United States, Earliest Times to the Present: Millennial Edition*, ed. Susan B. Carter et al. (Cambridge University Press, 2006); John J. McCusker, "Timber and Timber Products Exported from Charleston and Savannah: 1717–1787, Table Eg1174–1179," in *Historical Statistics of the United States, Earliest Times to the Present: Millennial Edition*, ed. Susan B. Carter et al. (Cambridge University Press, 2006).

12. McCusker, "Timber and Timber Products Exported."

13. John J. McCusker, "Indigo and Silk Exported from South Carolina and Georgia: 1747–1788, Table Eg1027–1032," in *Historical Statistics of the United States, Earliest Times to the Present: Millennial Edition*, ed. Susan B. Carter et al. (Cambridge University Press, 2006); John J. McCusker, "Trade of Raw Silk and Silk Goods between England and the Carolinas: 1731–1755, Table Eg1033–1037," in *Historical Statistics of the United States, Earliest Times to the Present: Millennial Edition*, ed. Susan B. Carter et al. (Cambridge University Press, 2006).

14. John J. McCusker, "Tobacco Exported from Virginia, by Port: 1745–1773, Table Eg1135–1141," in *Historical Statistics of the United States, Earliest Times to the Present: Millennial Edition*, ed. Susan B. Carter et al. (Cambridge University Press, 2006); John J. McCusker, "Tobacco Imported into and Reexported from Great Britain: 1697–1791, Table Eg1046–1053," in *Historical Statistics of the United States, Earliest Times to the Present: Millennial Edition*, ed. Susan B. Carter et al. (Cambridge University Press, 2006); John J. McCusker, "Tobacco Imported into England, by Origin: 1697–1775, Table Eg1038–1045," in *Historical Statistics of the United States, Earliest Times to the Present: Millennial Edition*, ed. Susan B. Carter et al. (Cambridge University Press, 2006).

15. John J. McCusker, "Coal Imported, by Origin and Port of Entry: 1768–1772, Table Eg766–810," in *Historical Statistics of the United States, Earliest Times to the Present: Millennial Edition*, ed. Susan B. Carter et al. (Cambridge University Press, 2006); John J. McCusker, "Coal Exported from James River, Virginia, by Destination: 1758–1765, Table Eg755–765," in *Historical Statistics of the United States, Earliest Times to the Present: Millennial Edition*, ed. Susan B. Carter et al. (Cambridge University Press, 2006).

16. Bureau of Economic Analysis, "Gross Domestic Product [GDPA@USECON]," Haver Analytics.

17. Richard Sutch, "Table Ca9–19—Gross Domestic Product: 1790–2002 [Continuous Annual Series]," in *Historical Statistics of the United States, Earliest Times to the Present: Millennial Edition*, ed. Susan B. Carter et al. (Cambridge University Press, 2006).

18. Bureau of Economic Analysis, "Real Gross Domestic Product [GDPHA@USECON]," Haver Analytics.

19. Sutch, "Table Ca9–19—Gross Domestic Product."

20. Bureau of Economic Analysis, "Real Private Fixed Investment [FHA@USECON]," Haver Analytics; Bureau of Economic Analysis, "Real State and Local Government Gross Investment (GSIHA@USECON)," Haver Analytics; Bureau of Economic Analysis, "Real Federal Nondefense Gross Investment (GFNIHA@USECON)," Haver Analytics; Bureau of Economic Analysis, "Real National Defense Gross Investment (GFDIHA@USECON)," Haver Analytics.

21. Bureau of Economic Analysis, "Investment in Total Fixed Assets, Real Cost [ZTOH@CAPSTOCK]," Haver Analytics; Bureau of Economic Analysis, "Real Private Fixed Investment [FHA@USECON]"; Bureau of Economic Analysis, "Real National Defense Gross Investment (GFDIHA@USECON)"; Bureau of Economic Analysis, "Real Federal Nondefense Gross Investment (GFNIHA@USECON)"; Bureau of Economic Analysis, "Real State and Local Government Gross Investment (GSIHA@USECON)."

22. Bureau of Economic Analysis, "Real Private Fixed Investment [FHA@USECON]."

23. Bureau of Economic Analysis, "Investment in Total Private Fixed Assets, Real Cost [ZPH@CAPSTOCK]," Haver Analytics.

24. Bureau of Economic Analysis, "Investment in Total Private Fixed Assets, Chained Quantity Index [ZPQ@CAPSTOCK]," Haver Analytics.

25. Bureau of Economic Analysis, "Real Private Nonresidential Fixed Investment [FNHA@USECON]," Haver Analytics.

26. Bureau of Economic Analysis, "Investment in Total Private Nonresidential Fixed Assets, Real Cost [ZPNH@CAPSTOCK]," Haver Analytics.

27. Bureau of Economic Analysis, "Real Private Residential Fixed Investment [FRHA@USECON]," Haver Analytics.

28. Bureau of Economic Analysis, "Investment in Total Private Residential Fixed Assets, Real Cost [ZPRH@CAPSTOCK]," Haver Analytics.

29. Bureau of Labor Statistics, "Civilians Employed: 16 Years and over [LEN@USECON]," Haver Analytics.

30. US Department of Commerce, Bureau of the Census, "Civilian Employment: 14 Years+ [LEA2@USECON]," Haver Analytics.

31. Susan B. Carter, "Labor Force, Employment, and Unemployment: 1890–1990 [Weir], Table Ba470–477," in *Historical Statistics of the United States, Earliest Times to the Present: Millennial Edition*, ed. Susan B. Carter et al. (Cambridge University Press, 2006).

32. US Department of Commerce, Bureau of the Census, "Resident Population: Total (All Ages) [POP@USECON]," Haver Analytics.

33. Sutch, "Table Ca9–19—Gross Domestic Product."

34. John J. McCusker, "Population, by Race and by Colony or Locality: 1610–1780, Table Eg1–59," in *Historical Statistics of the United States, Earliest Times to the Present: Millennial Edition*, ed. Susan B. Carter et al. (Cambridge University Press, 2006).

35. Bureau of Labor Statistics, "Unemployment Rate: 16 Years+ [LRN@USECON]," Haver Analytics.

36. US Department of Commerce, Bureau of the Census, "Unemployment Rate: 14 Years+ [LRA@USECON]," Haver Analytics.

37. Carter, "Labor Force, Employment, and Unemployment."

38. Bureau of Labor Statistics, "Total Unemployed: 16 Yr+ [LTUN@USECON]," Haver Analytics.

39. US Department of Commerce, Bureau of the Census, "Unemployed, 14 Years+ [LTUA@USECON]," Haver Analytics.

40. Carter, "Labor Force, Employment, and Unemployment."

41. Bureau of Labor Statistics, "Civilian Labor Force: 16 Yr+ [LFN@USECON]," Haver Analytics.

42. US Department of Commerce, Bureau of the Census, "Civilian Labor Force: 14 Yr+ [LFA@USECON]," Haver Analytics.

43. Carter, "Labor Force, Employment, and Unemployment."

44. Bureau of Labor Statistics, "Average Hourly Earnings of Production and Nonsupervisory Employees, Total Private (CEU0500000008)," Federal Reserve Bank of St. Louis, https://fred.stlouisfed.org/series/CEU0500000008.

45. Robert A. Margo, "Index of Money Wages for Unskilled Labor: 1774–1974, Table Ba4218," in *Historical Statistics of the United States, Earliest Times to the Present: Millennial Edition*, ed. Susan B. Carter et al. (Cambridge University Press, 2006).

46. US Department of Commerce, Bureau of the Census, "Probable Hourly Rates: Unskilled Labor [LEUNLAHA@USECON]," Haver Analytics.

47. Margo, "Index of Money Wages."

48. Bureau of Labor Statistics, "Consumer Price Index, All Urban Consumers: All Items (CPI-U) [PCUN@USECON]," Haver Analytics.

49. Peter H. Lindert and Richard Sutch, "Consumer Price Indexes, for All Items: 1774–2003, Table Cc1–2," in *Historical Statistics of the United States, Earliest Times to the Present: Millennial Edition*, ed. Susan B. Carter et al. (Cambridge University Press, 2006).

50. McCusker, "Commodity Price Index."

51. Bureau of Economic Analysis, "Real Personal Consumption Expenditures [CHA@ USECON]," Haver Analytics.

52. Lee A. Craig, "Consumption Expenditures, by Type: 1900–1929 [1987 Dollars], Table Cd78–152," in *Historical Statistics of the United States, Earliest Times to the Present: Millennial Edition*, ed. Susan B. Carter et al. (Cambridge University Press, 2006).

53. Robert E. Gallman and Paul W. Rhode, "Gallman's Annual Product Series, 1834–1909," in *Capital in the Nineteenth Century*, ed. Robert E. Gallman and Paul W. Rhode, NBER Long-Term Factors in Economic Development (University of Chicago Press, 2020), 102–31.

54. Board of Governors of the Federal Reserve System (US), "Industrial Production: Total Index (IPB50001N)," Federal Reserve Bank of St. Louis, https://fred.stlouisfed.org /series/IPB50001N.

55. National Bureau of Economic Research, "Index of Industrial Production and Trade for United States (M1204BUSM363SNBR)," Federal Reserve Bank of St. Louis, https:// fred.stlouisfed.org/series/M1204BUSM363SNBR.

56. Sutch, "Table Ca9–19—Gross Domestic Product."

57. US Department of the Treasury, "Federal Outlays [FTO@USECON]," Haver Analytics.

58. National Bureau of Economic Research, "Federal Budget Expenditures, Total for United States (M1505AUSM144NNBR), Federal Reserve Bank of St. Louis https://fred .stlouisfed.org/series/M1505AUSM144NNBR; National Bureau of Economic Research, "Federal Budget Expenditures, Total for United States (M1505BUSM144NNBR), Federal Reserve Bank of St. Louis, https://fred.stlouisfed.org/series/M1505BUSM144NNBR; National Bureau of Economic Research, "Federal Budget Expenditures, Total for United States (M1505CUSM144NNBR)," Federal Reserve Bank of St. Louis, https://fred.stlouis-fed.org/series/M1505CUSM144NNBR; National Bureau of Economic Research, "Federal Budget Expenditures, Total for United States (M1505DUSM144NNBR)," Federal Reserve Bank of St. Louis, https://fred.stlouisfed.org/series/M1505DUSM144NNBR; National Bureau of Economic Research, "Federal Budget Expenditures, Total for United States (M1505EUSM144NNBR)," Federal Reserve Bank of St. Louis, https://fred.stlouisfed.org /series/M1505EUSM144NNBR; National Bureau of Economic Research, "Federal Budget Expenditures, Total for United States (M1505FUSM144NNBR)," Federal Reserve Bank of St. Louis, https://fred.stlouisfed.org/series/M1505FUSM144NNBR.

59. John Joseph Wallis, "Federal Government Finances—Revenue, Expenditure, and Debt: 1789–1939, Table Ea584–587," in *Historical Statistics of the United States, Earliest Times to the Present: Millennial Edition*, ed. Susan B. Carter et al. (Cambridge University Press, 2006).

60. US Department of the Treasury, "Federal Receipts [FTR@USECON]," Haver Analytics.

61. National Bureau of Economic Research, "Federal Budget Receipts, Total for United States (M1504AUSM144NNBR)," Federal Reserve Bank of St. Louis, https://fred .stlouisfed.org/series/M1504AUSM144NNBR; National Bureau of Economic Research, "Federal Budget Receipts, Total for United States (M1504BUSM144NNBR)," Federal Reserve Bank of St. Louis, https://fred.stlouisfed.org/series/M1504BUSM144NNBR; National Bureau of Economic Research, "Federal Budget Receipts, Total for United States

(M1504CUSM144NNBR)," Federal Reserve Bank of St. Louis, https://fred.stlouisfed.org /series/M1504CUSM144NNBR.

62. Wallis, "Federal Government Finances."

63. US Department of the Treasury, "Total Public Debt Outstanding [PDO@ USECON]," Haver Analytics.

64. Council of Economic Advisers (US), "Gross Federal Debt (FYGFD)," Federal Reserve Bank of St. Louis, https://fred.stlouisfed.org/series/FYGFD.

65. US Department of the Treasury, "Total Public Debt Held by the Public [PDOU@ USECON]," Haver Analytics.

66. Council of Economic Advisers (US), "Gross Federal Debt Held by the Public (FYGF-DPUB)," Federal Reserve Bank of St. Louis, https://fred.stlouisfed.org/series/FYGFDPUB.

67. Wallis, "Federal Government Finances."

68. Bureau of Economic Analysis, "State and Local Government Total Expenditures (W079RCQ027SBEA)," Federal Reserve Bank of St. Louis, https://fred.stlouisfed.org /series/W079RCQ027SBEA.

69. Bureau of Economic Analysis, "State and Local Government Total Receipts (W077RC1Q027SBEA)," Federal Reserve Bank of St. Louis, https://fred.stlouisfed.org /series/W077RC1Q027SBEA.

70. Board of Governors of the Federal Reserve System (US), "State and Local Governments; Debt Securities and Loans; Liability, Level (BOGZ1FL214104005A)," Federal Reserve Bank of St. Louis, https://fred.stlouisfed.org/series/BOGZ1FL214104005A.

71. Standard & Poor's, "S&P Global Fixed Income Research: Industrials BBB Bond Yields: 10 Yr [FSBBB10@USECON]," Haver Analytics.

72. Standard & Poor's, "S&P Industrials BBB Bond Yield [FSHBBB@USECON]," Haver Analytics.

73. Nathan Balke and Robert J. Gordon, "Appendix B: Historical Data," in *The American Business Cycle: Continuity and Change*, vol. 25, ed. Robert Gordon, National Bureau of Economic Research Studies in Business Cycles (University of Chicago Press, 1986), 781–850, https://nber.org/research/data/tables-american-business-cycle.

74. Federal Reserve Board, "3-Month Nonfinancial Commercial Paper [FCP3@ USECON]," Haver Analytics.

75. Balke and Gordon, "Appendix B."

76. John A. James and Richard Sylla, "Money Market Rates: 1831–1997, Table Cj1223–1237," in *Historical Statistics of the United States, Earliest Times to the Present: Millennial Edition*, ed. Susan B. Carter et al. (Cambridge University Press, 2006).

77. Standard & Poor's, "Standard & Poor's 500 Composite Stock Price Index [SP500@ USECON]," Haver Analytics.

78. Balke and Gordon, "Appendix B."

79. National Bureau of Economic Research, "Index of All Common Stock Prices, Cowles Commission and Standard and Poor's Corporation for United States (M1125AUSM343N-NBR)," Federal Reserve Bank of St. Louis, https://fred.stlouisfed.org/series /M1125AUSM343NNBR.

80. Peter L. Rousseau, "Common Stock Prices: 1802–1999, Table Cj797–807," in *Historical Statistics of the United States, Earliest Times to the Present: Millennial Edition*, ed. Susan B. Carter et al. (Cambridge University Press, 2006).

81. Rousseau.

82. Federal Reserve Board, "10-Year Treasury Note Yield at Constant Maturity [FCM10@USECON]," Haver Analytics; Federal Reserve Board, "20-Year Treasury Note Yield at Constant Maturity [FCM20@USECON]," Haver Analytics; Federal Reserve Board, "30-Year Treasury Note Yield at Constant Maturity [FCM30@USECON]," Haver Analytics.

83. John A. James and Richard Sylla, "Yields of Government Bonds, by Term to Maturity: 1950–1998, Table Cj1243–1249," in *Historical Statistics of the United States, Earliest Times to the Present: Millennial Edition*, ed. Susan B. Carter et al. (Cambridge University Press, 2006).

84. John A. James and Richard Sylla, "Long-Term Bond Yields: 1798–1997, Table Cj1192–1197," in *Historical Statistics of the United States, Earliest Times to the Present: Millennial Edition*, ed. Susan B. Carter et al. (Cambridge University Press, 2006).

85. Federal Reserve Board, "10-Year Treasury Note Yield."

86. James and Sylla, "Yields of Government Bonds."

87. Federal Reserve Board, "20-Year Treasury Note Yield."

88. James and Sylla, "Yields of Government Bonds."

89. Federal Reserve Board, "30-Year Treasury Note Yield."

90. James and Sylla, "Yields of Government Bonds."

91. Federal Deposit Insurance Corporation, "FDIC-Insured Commercial Banks: Number of Institutions Reporting [CBANKQ@USECON]," Haver Analytics.

92. Howard Bodenhorn, "Commercial Banks—Number and Assets: 1834–1980, Table Cj251–264," in *Historical Statistics of the United States, Earliest Times to the Present: Millennial Edition*, ed. Susan B. Carter et al. (Cambridge University Press, 2006).

93. Federal Deposit Insurance Corporation, "Failures of All Institutions for the United States and Other Areas (BKFTTLA641N)," Federal Reserve Bank of St. Louis, https://fred.stlouisfed.org/series/BKFTTLA641N.

94. "Series X 741–755, Bank Suspensions—Number and Deposits of Suspended Banks: 1864–1970," in *Historical Statistics of the United States: Colonial Times to 1970*, vol. 2, Bicentennial Edition (US Department of Commerce, Bureau of the Census, 1975), 1038.

95. Federal Reserve Board, "Total Assets: All Commercial Banks [FAN@USECON]," Haver Analytics.

96. Bodenhorn, "Commercial Banks—Number and Assets."

97. Federal Reserve Board, "Total Liabilities: All Commercial Banks [FBLN@USECON]," Haver Analytics.

98. Howard Bodenhorn, "Commercial Banks—Liabilities: 1834–1980, Table Cj265–272," in *Historical Statistics of the United States, Earliest Times to the Present: Millennial Edition*, ed. Susan B. Carter et al. (Cambridge University Press, 2006).

99. Federal Reserve Board, "Loans and Leases in Bank Credit: All Commercial Banks [FABWN@USECON]," Haver Analytics.

100. Bodenhorn, "Commercial Banks—Number and Assets."

101. Federal Reserve Board, "Real Estate Loans in Bank Credit: All Commercial Banks [FABWRN@USECON]," Haver Analytics.

102. Bodenhorn, "Commercial Banks—Number and Assets."

103. Federal Reserve Board, "Securities in Bank Credit: All Commercial Banks [FABYN@USECON]," Haver Analytics.

104. Bodenhorn, "Commercial Banks—Number and Assets."

105. Federal Reserve Board, "Cash Assets: All Commercial Banks [FAVN@USECON]," Haver Analytics.

106. Bodenhorn, "Commercial Banks—Number and Assets."

107. Federal Reserve Board, "Deposits: All Commercial Banks [FBDN@USECON]," Haver Analytics.

108. Bodenhorn, "Commercial Banks—Liabilities."

109. Federal Reserve Board, "Monetary Base [FARMB@USECON]," Haver Analytics; Federal Reserve Board, "Monetary Base: Currency in Circulation [FARMCN@ USECON]," Haver Analytics.

110. Balke and Gordon, "Appendix B."

111. Richard G. Anderson, "Stock of Money and Its Components: 1867–1947 [Friedman and Schwartz], Table Cj42–48," in *Historical Statistics of the United States, Earliest Times to the Present: Millennial Edition*, ed. Susan B. Carter et al. (Cambridge University Press, 2006).

112. Hugh Rockoff, "Stock of Money and Its Components: 1859–1866 [Friedman, Schwartz, and Mitchell], Table Cj26–41," in *Historical Statistics of the United States, Earliest Times to the Present: Millennial Edition*, ed. Susan B. Carter et al. (Cambridge University Press, 2006).

113. Federal Reserve Board, "Money Stock: M1 [FM1N@USECON]," Haver Analytics.

114. Balke and Gordon, "Appendix B."

115. Federal Reserve Board, "Money Stock: M2 [FM2N@USECON]," Haver Analytics.

116. Balke and Gordon, "Appendix B."

117. Anderson, "Stock of Money."

118. Rockoff, "Stock of Money."

119. GB Office for National Statistics, "Gross Domestic Product for United Kingdom (UKNGDP)," Federal Reserve Bank of St. Louis, https://fred.stlouisfed.org/series /UKNGDP.

120. Bank of England, "Nominal Gross Domestic Product at Market Prices in the United Kingdom (NGDPMPUKA)," Federal Reserve Bank of St. Louis, https://fred.stlouisfed.org/series/NGDPMPUKA.

121. International Monetary Fund, "Real Gross Domestic Product for Great Britain (NGDPRSAXDCGBQ)," Federal Reserve Bank of St. Louis, https://fred.stlouisfed.org /series/NGDPRSAXDCGBQ.

122. Bank of England, "Real Gross Domestic Product at Market Prices in the United Kingdom (RGDPMPUKA)," Federal Reserve Bank of St. Louis, https://fred.stlouisfed.org /series/RGDPMPUKA.

123. Organisation for Economic Co-operation and Development, "Private Final Consumption Expenditure in the United Kingdom (GBRPFCEQDSNAQ)," Federal Reserve Bank of St. Louis, https://fred.stlouisfed.org/series/GBRPFCEQDSNAQ.

124. Bank of England, "Real Consumption Expenditures in the United Kingdom (RLCMEXUKA)," Federal Reserve Bank of St. Louis, https://fred.stlouisfed.org/series /RLCMEXUKA.

125. Organisation for Economic Co-operation and Development, "Real Gross Capital Formation for Great Britain (NIRNSAXDCGBQ)," Federal Reserve Bank of St. Louis, https://fred.stlouisfed.org/series/NIRNSAXDCGBQ.

126. Bank of England, "Real Investment Expenditures in the United Kingdom (RIVEXUKA)," Federal Reserve Bank of St. Louis, https://fred.stlouisfed.org/series /RIVEXUKA.

127. Organisation for Economic Co-operation and Development, "Production: Industry: Total Industry Excluding Construction for United Kingdom (PRINTO01G-BQ657S)," Federal Reserve Bank of St. Louis, https://fred.stlouisfed.org/series/PRINTO01 GBQ657S.

128. Bank of England, "Industrial Production Index in the United Kingdom (IPI-UKM)," Federal Reserve Bank of St. Louis, https://fred.stlouisfed.org/series/IPIUKM.

129. Bank of England, National Bureau of Economic Research, "Index of Physical Volume of Industrial Production for Great Britain (A01181GBA324NNBR)," Federal Reserve Bank of St. Louis, https://fred.stlouisfed.org/series/A01181GBA324NNBR.

130. Organisation for Economic Co-operation and Development, "Infra-Annual Labor Statistics: Monthly Unemployment Rate Total: 15 Years or over for United Kingdom (LRHUTTTTGBM156S)," Federal Reserve Bank of St. Louis, https://fred.stlouisfed.org /series/LRHUTTTTGBM156S.

131. Bank of England, "Unemployment Rate in the United Kingdom (UNRTUKA)," Federal Reserve Bank of St. Louis, https://fred.stlouisfed.org/series/UNRTUKA.

132. Organisation for Economic Co-operation and Development, "Infra-Annual Labor Statistics: Employment Total: 15 Years or over for United Kingdom (LFEMTTTTG-BQ647S)," Federal Reserve Bank of St. Louis, https://fred.stlouisfed.org/series /LFEMTTTTGBQ647S.

133. Bank of England, "Employment in the United Kingdom (EMPUKA)," Federal Reserve Bank of St. Louis, https://fred.stlouisfed.org/series/EMPUKA.

134. Organisation for Economic Co-operation and Development, "Infra-Annual Labor Statistics: Labor Force Total: 15 Years or over for United Kingdom (LFACTTTTG-BA647N)," Federal Reserve Bank of St. Louis, https://fred.stlouisfed.org/series LFACTTTTGBA647N.

135. University of Groningen and University of California, Davis, "Number of Persons Engaged for United Kingdom (EMPENGGBA148NRUG)," Federal Reserve Bank of St. Louis, https://fred.stlouisfed.org/series/EMPENGGBA148NRUG.

136. Organisation for Economic Co-operation and Development, "Labor Compensation: Earnings: All Activities: Weekly for United Kingdom (LCEATT02GBA661N)," FRED, Federal Reserve Bank of St. Louis, https://fred.stlouisfed.org/series/LCEATT02GBA661N.

137. Bank of England, "Average Weekly Earnings Per Person in the United Kingdom (AWEPPUKA)," Federal Reserve Bank of St. Louis, https://fred.stlouisfed.org/series /AWEPPUKA.

138. Bank of England, "Aggregate Bank and Building Society Credit in the United Kingdom (ABBSCUKA)," Federal Reserve Bank of St. Louis, https://fred.stlouisfed.org /series/ABBSCUKA.

139. "Monthly 12 Month Growth Rate of UK Resident Monetary Financial Institutions' (Excl. Central Bank) Sterling Net Lending to Private Sector Excluding Intermediate OFCs (in Percent) Seasonally Adjusted (RPMB62Q)," Bank of England, https://bankofengland.co.uk /boeapps/database/fromshowcolumns.asp?Travel=NIxSUx&FromSeries=1&ToSeries=50& DAT=RNG&FD=1&FM=Jan&FY=2014&TD=13&TM=Oct&TY=2024&F NY=&CSVF=TT&html.x=152&html.y=32&C=MEB&C=ME8&Filter=N.

140. Bank of England, "Secured Bank and Building Society Credit in the United Kingdom (SBBSCUKA)," Federal Reserve Bank of St. Louis, https://fred.stlouisfed.org/series /SBBSCUKA.

141. "Monthly Average Amount Outstanding of Total Sterling Notes and Coin in Circulation, Excluding Backing Assets for Commercial Banknote Issue in Scotland and Northern Ireland Adjusted for Specific Non-Seasonal Events Total (in Sterling Millions) Seasonally Adjusted (LPMB8H4)," Bank of England, https:// bankofengland.co.uk/boeapps/database/fromshowcolumns.asp?Travel=NIx STxTAxSUx&FromSeries=1&ToSeries=50&DAT=RNG&FD=1&FM=Jan& FY=2016&TD=31&TM=Dec&TY=2025&FNY=&CSVF=TT&html.x=110&html y=45&C=IQ5&C=IRR&Filter=N; "Monthly Average of Amounts Outstanding (on Wednesdays) of Bank of England Banking Department Sterling Reserves Balance Liabilities (in Sterling Millions) Not Seasonally Adjusted (LPMBL22)," Bank of England, https:// bankofengland.co.uk/boeapps/database/fromshowcolumns.asp?Travel=NIxSTxTAxSUx &FromSeries=1&ToSeries=50&DAT=RNG&FD=1&FM=Jan&FY=2016&T D=31&TM=Dec&TY=2025&FNY=&CSVF=TT&html.x=110&html.y=45&C=IQ5&C=IRR &Filter=N.

142. Bank of England, "M0 Money Stock in the United Kingdom (MBM0UKQ)," Federal Reserve Bank of St. Louis, https://fred.stlouisfed.org/series/MBM0UKQ.

143. "Quarterly Break Adjusted Level of UK Resident Monetary Financial Institutions' Sterling M4 Liabilities to Private Sector Excluding Intermediate OFCs (in Sterling Millions) Seasonally Adjusted (RPQB8FP)," Bank of England, https://bankofengland.co.uk/boeapps /database/fromshowcolumns.asp?Travel=NIxSTxTAxSUx&FromSeries=1&ToSeries=50& DAT=RNG&FD=1&FM=Jan&FY=2016&TD=31&TM=Dec&TY=2025& FNY=&CSVF=TT&html.x=156&html.y=63&C=ML8&Filter=N.

144. Bank of England, "Broad Money (Break Adjusted) in the United Kingdom (BMBAUKQ)," Federal Reserve Bank of St. Louis, https://fred.stlouisfed.org/series /BMBAUKQ.

145. International Monetary Fund, "Geographical Outreach: Number of Commercial Banks for United Kingdom (GBRFCIODCNUM)," Federal Reserve Bank of St. Louis, https://fred.stlouisfed.org/series/GBRFCIODCNUM.

146. Seán Kenny, Jason Lennard, and John D. Turner, "The Macroeconomic Effects of Banking Crises: Evidence from the United Kingdom, 1750–1938," *Explorations in Economic History* 79 (2021): 101357, https://doi.org/10.1016/j.eeh.2020.101357.

147. Ranald Michie, "Appendix 1: Number of British Banks, 1700–2008," in *British Banking: Continuity and Change from 1694 to the Present* (Oxford University Press, 2016), 271–77; Ranald Michie, "Appendix 2: Number of Registered Building Societies, 1876–2010," in *British Banking: Continuity and Change from 1694 to the Present* (Oxford University Press, 2016), 278–80; Ranald Michie, "Appendix 3: Number of Trustee Savings Banks, 1829–1967," in *British Banking: Continuity and Change from 1694 to the Present* (Oxford University Press, 2016), 281–83.

148. Kenny, Lennard, and Turner, "The Macroeconomic Effects."

149. Kenny, Lennard, and Turner.

150. Organisation for Economic Co-operation and Development, "Financial Market: Share Prices for United Kingdom (SPASTT01GBQ661N)," Federal Reserve Bank of St. Louis, https://fred.stlouisfed.org/series/SPASTT01GBQ661N.

151. Bank of England, "Share Prices in the United Kingdom (SPPUKA)," Federal Reserve Bank of St. Louis, https://fred.stlouisfed.org/series/SPPUKA.

152. Organization for Economic Co-operation and Development, "Consumer Price Indices (CPIs, HICPs), COICOP 1999: Consumer Price Index: Total for United Kingdom (GBRCPIALLMINMEI)," Federal Reserve Bank of St. Louis, https://fred.stlouisfed.org /series/GBRCPIALLMINMEI.

153. Bank of England, "Consumer Price Index in the United Kingdom (CPIUKA)," Federal Reserve Bank of St. Louis, https://fred.stlouisfed.org/series/CPIUKA.

154. Bank of England, "Discount Rate on Short-Term Commercial Paper in the United Kingdom (DRSTCPUKQ)," Federal Reserve Bank of St. Louis, https://fred.stlouisfed.org /series/DRSTCPUKQ.

155. Bank of England, "Corporate Borrowing Rate from Banks in the United Kingdom (CBRBUKA)," Federal Reserve Bank of St. Louis, https://fred.stlouisfed.org/series /CBRBUKA.

156. World Bank, "Population, Total for United Kingdom (POPTOTG-BA647NWDB)," Federal Reserve Bank of St. Louis, https://fred.stlouisfed.org/series /POPTOTGBA647NWDB.

157. Bank of England, "Population in the United Kingdom (POPUKA)," Federal Reserve Bank of St. Louis, https://fred.stlouisfed.org/series/POPUKA.

158. Bank for International Settlements, "Nominal Total Credit to General Government, Adjusted for Breaks, for United Kingdom (QGBGANXDCA)," Federal Reserve Bank of St. Louis, https://fred.stlouisfed.org/series/QGBGANXDCA.

159. Bank of England, "Public Sector Debt Outstanding in the United Kingdom (PSDOUKA)," Federal Reserve Bank of St. Louis, https://fred.stlouisfed.org/series /PSDOUKA.

160. Bank of England, "Public Sector Total Managed Expenditure in the United Kingdom (PSTMEUKA)," Federal Reserve Bank of St. Louis, https://fred.stlouisfed.org/series /PSTMEUKA.

161. Bank of England, "Public Sector Total Receipts in the United Kingdom (PSTRUKA)," Federal Reserve Bank of St. Louis, https://fred.stlouisfed.org/series/PSTRUKA.

162. Bank of England, "Consol (Long-Term Bond) Yields in the United Kingdom (LTCYUKA)," Federal Reserve Bank of St. Louis, https://fred.stlouisfed.org/series /LTCYUKA.

163. Organisation for Economic Co-operation and Development, "Interest Rates: Long-Term Government Bond Yields: 10-Year: Main (Including Benchmark) for United Kingdom (IRLTLT01GBM156N)," Federal Reserve Bank of St. Louis, https://fred.stlouis fed.org/series/IRLTLT01GBM156N.

164. Bank of England, "10 Year (Medium-Term) Government Bond Yields in the United Kingdom (GBMT10UKA)," Federal Reserve Bank of St. Louis, https://fred.stlouisfed.org /series/GBMT10UKA.

165. Board of Governors of the Federal Reserve System (US), "U.S. Dollars to U.K. Pound Sterling Spot Exchange Rate (EXUSUK)," Federal Reserve Bank of St. Louis, https://fred.stlouisfed.org/series/EXUSUK.

166. Bank of England, "U.S. / U.K. Foreign Exchange Rate in the United Kingdom (USUKFXUKA)," Federal Reserve Bank of St. Louis, https://fred.stlouisfed.org/series /USUKFXUKA.

167. Bank of England, "Real U.S. / U.K. Foreign Exchange Index in the United Kingdom (RUSUKFXUKA)," Federal Reserve Bank of St. Louis, https://fred.stlouisfed.org/series/RUSUKFXUKA.

168. Bureau of Economic Analysis, "Gross Domestic Product [GDP@USECON]," Haver Analytics.

169. Balke and Gordon, "Appendix B"; Sutch, "Table Ca9–19."

170. Bureau of Economic Analysis, "Real Gross Domestic Product [GDPH@USECON]," Haver Analytics.

171. Balke and Gordon, "Appendix B"; Sutch, "Table Ca9–19."

172. Bureau of Labor Statistics, "Consumer Price Index, All Urban Consumers: All Items."

173. Bureau of Labor Statistics, "All Employees: Total Nonfarm [LANAGRA@USECON]," Haver Analytics.

174. Bureau of Labor Statistics, "Civilian Employment: Sixteen Years and Over [LE@USECON]," Haver Analytics.

175. Bureau of Labor Statistics, "Civilian Unemployment Rate: 16 Yr + [LR@USECON]," Haver Analytics.

176. Board of Governors of the Federal Reserve System (US), "Industrial Production: Total Index (INDPRO)," Federal Reserve Bank of St. Louis, https://fred.stlouisfed.org/series/INDPRO.

177. National Bureau of Economic Research, "Index of Industrial Production."

178. National Bureau of Economic Research, "American Telephone and Telegraph Company Index of Industrial Activity for United States (M12001USM317SNBR)," Federal Reserve Bank of St. Louis, https://fred.stlouisfed.org/series/M12001USM317SNBR.

179. Federal Reserve Board, "3-Month Nonfinancial Commercial Paper."

180. National Bureau of Economic Research, "Commercial Paper Rates for New York, NY (M13002US35620M156NNBR)," Federal Reserve Bank of St. Louis, https://fred.stlouisfed.org/series/M13002US35620M156NNBR.

181. Standard & Poor's, "S&P Global Fixed Income Research."

182. Balke and Gordon, "Appendix B."

183. Balke and Gordon.

184. National Bureau of Economic Research, "Index of All Common Stock Prices."

185. Federal Reserve Board, "10-Year Treasury Note Yield"; Federal Reserve Board, "20-Year Treasury Note Yield"; Federal Reserve Board, "30-Year Treasury Note Yield."

186. National Bureau of Economic Research, "Yield on Long-Term United States Bonds for United States (M1333AUSM156NNBR)," Federal Reserve Bank of St. Louis, https://fred.stlouisfed.org/series/M1333AUSM156NNBR.

187. Federal Reserve Board, "10-Year Treasury Note Yield."

188. Federal Reserve Board, "Monetary Base [FARMB@USECON]."

189. Balke and Gordon, "Appendix B."

190. Federal Reserve Board, "Money Stock: M1."

191. Balke and Gordon, "Appendix B."

192. Federal Reserve Board, "Money Stock: M2."

193. Balke and Gordon, "Appendix B."

194. US Department of the Treasury, "Federal Receipts."

195. National Bureau of Economic Research, "Federal Budget Receipts, Total for United States (M1504CUSM144NNBR)."

196. National Bureau of Economic Research, "Federal Budget Receipts, Total for United States (M1504BUSM144NNBR)."

197. National Bureau of Economic Research, "Federal Budget Receipts, Total for United States (M1504AUSM144NNBR)."

198. US Department of the Treasury, "Federal Outlays."

199. National Bureau of Economic Research, "Federal Budget Expenditures, Total for United States (M1505FUSM144NNBR)."

200. National Bureau of Economic Research, "Federal Budget Expenditures, Total for United States (M1505EUSM144NNBR)."

201. National Bureau of Economic Research, "Federal Budget Expenditures, Total for United States (M1505DUSM144NNBR)."

202. National Bureau of Economic Research, "Federal Budget Expenditures, Total for United States (M1505CUSM144NNBR)."

203. National Bureau of Economic Research, "Federal Budget Expenditures, Total for United States (M1505BUSM144NNBR)."

204. National Bureau of Economic Research, "Federal Budget Expenditures, Total for United States (M1505AUSM144NNBR)."

205. Bureau of Economic Analysis, "State and Local Government Total Receipts (W077RC1Q027SBEA)."

206. Bureau of Economic Analysis, "State and Local Government Total Expenditures (W079RCQ027SBEA)."

207. Organization for Economic Co-operation and Development, "Consumer Price Indices (CPIs, HICPs), COICOP 1999: Consumer Price Index: Total for United Kingdom."

208. Bank of England, "Consumer Price Index in the United Kingdom (CPIUKQ)," Federal Reserve Bank of St. Louis, https://fred.stlouisfed.org/series/CPIUKQ.

209. GB Office for National Statistics, "Gross Domestic Product."

210. International Monetary Fund, "Real Gross Domestic Product."

211. Broadberry et al., "Dating Business Cycles."

212. Bank of England, "Real Gross Domestic Product at Market Prices in the United Kingdom (RGDPMRPUKM)," Federal Reserve Bank of St. Louis, https://fred.stlouisfed.org/series/RGDPMRPUKM.

213. Organisation for Economic Co-operation and Development, "Infra-Annual Labor Statistics: Monthly Unemployment Rate Total."

214. Bank of England, "Unemployment Rate in the United Kingdom (AURUKM)," Federal Reserve Bank of St. Louis, https://fred.stlouisfed.org/series/AURUKM.

215. Organisation for Economic Co-operation and Development, "Infra-Annual Labor Statistics: Employment Total."

216. Bank of England, "Employment in the United Kingdom (EMPUKQ)," Federal Reserve Bank of St. Louis, https://fred.stlouisfed.org/series/EMPUKQ.

217. Organisation for Economic Co-operation and Development, "Financial Market: Share Prices."

218. Bank of England, "Share Prices in the United Kingdom (SPPUKQ)," Federal Reserve Bank of St. Louis, https://fred.stlouisfed.org/series/SPPUKQ.

219. Organisation for Economic Co-operation and Development, "Production: Industry."

220. Bank of England, "Industrial Production Index."

221. Bank of England.

222. Bank of England, "Discount Rate on Short-Term Commercial Paper."

223. Bank of England, "Corporate Borrowing Rate on Loans from Banks in the United Kingdom (CBRLBUKQ)," Federal Reserve Bank of St. Louis, https://fred.stlouisfed.org /series/CBRLBUKQ.

224. Bank of England, "Consol (Long-Term Bond) Yields in the United Kingdom (LTCYUK)," Federal Reserve Bank of St. Louis, https://fred.stlouisfed.org/series/LTCYUK.

225. Organisation for Economic Co-operation and Development, "Interest Rates: Long-Term Government Bond Yields."

226. Bank of England, "10 Year (Medium-Term) Government Bond Yields."

227. "Monthly Average Amount Outstanding of Total Sterling Notes"; "Monthly Average of Amounts Outstanding (on Wednesdays)."

228. "M0 Money Stock."

229. "Quarterly Break Adjusted Level of UK."

230. "Broad Money (Break Adjusted)."

Tyler Goodspeed is the chief economist of ExxonMobil. Previously, he chaired the White House Council of Economic Advisers. With PhDs in economics and history from Cambridge and Harvard, he has held faculty appointments at Stanford and Oxford. The author of three previous books on economics, he lives in Spring, Texas.